CULTURE & POWER

CULTURE

THE SOCIOLOGY OF PIERRE BOURDIEU

DAVID SWARTZ

POWER

&

The
University
of Chicago
Press
Chicago
& London

The University of Chicago Press, Chicago 60637
The University of Chicago Press, Ltd., London
© 1997 by The University of Chicago
All rights reserved. Published 1997
Printed in the United States of America
17 16 15 14 13 12 11   6 7 8 9

ISBN-13: 978-0-226-78595-0 (paper)
ISBN-10: 0-226-78595-5 (paper)

Library of Congress Cataloging-in-Publication Data

Swartz, David, 1945–
    Culture and power : the sociology of Pierre Bourdieu /
David Swartz.
        p.   cm.
    Includes bibliographical references.
    ISBN 0-226-78594-7. — ISBN 0-226-78595-5 (pbk.)
        1. Bourdieu, Pierre. 2. Sociology—France—History.
    3. Sociology—Methodology. I. Title.
    HM22.F8B773   1997
    301'.0944—dc21   97-7479
                                          CIP

CONTENTS

ACKNOWLEDGMENTS

This book grows out of a largely solitary undertaking: reading and re-flecting on a rich and complex body of theoretically framed, empirically informed, and politically oriented sociology. Yet, it has benefited from sev-eral friends and colleagues whose help and support I wish to acknowledge.

In France, Jean Bazin first introduced me to the work of Pierre Bour-dieu and provided valuable insights on the French intellectual world. Phi-lippe Besnard, Mohamed Cherkaoui, Maud Espéro, Monique de Saint Martin, and Michel Pialoux, each in their own way, helped and encouraged me on numerous occasions. I also want to thank Pierre Bourdieu whose rigorous attention to sociological method rescued me from the temptation of intellectual dilettantism during my student years at the Sorbonne. His sociology has inspired my subsequent teaching and research, and he kindly met with me to discuss aspects of his work. No doubt he would like to see some of my arguments stated differently, or not at all. I have tried to be an understanding reader of his work, but not a disciple. Hopefully this book will both clarify and invite further exploration of the rich complexity of Bourdieu's sociological imagination.

In the United States, a very special thanks to Jerry Karabel who "re-cruited" me in Paris and has supported my work in countless ways through the bad times as well as the good. He introduced me to a wonderful group of sociologists who logged in countless "lebaraks" while researching strati-fication in American higher education and who formed a lively study group at what was then called the Huron Institute. Steve Brint, Paul DiMaggio,

Kevin Dougherty, David Karen, Katherine McClelland, and Mike Useem have, at various times and in a variety of ways—beginning with the famous "BouBou" paper—offered helpful advice and support throughout this intellectual journey. Special thanks to Peter Kilby and Bob Wood, who extended a hand of solidarity in a difficult period. Vera Zolberg helped keep me *au courant* of the French intellectual world.

I also want to thank Doug Mitchell at the University of Chicago Press for his gracious support through the ups and downs of this book project. My thanks to Claudia Rex who edited the manuscript with precision and insight. I am grateful to the American Council of Learned Societies for a fellowship that made possible a research trip to France. Finally, and most importantly, I am deeply indebted to the sustaining support of my family throughout this endeavor, and dedicate this book to my wife, Lisa, and our two children, Elena and Daniel.

1 INTRODUCING PIERRE BOURDIEU

Culture provides the very grounds for human communication and interaction; it is also a source of domination. The arts, science, religion, indeed all symbolic systems—including language itself—not only shape our understanding of reality and form the basis for human communication; they also help establish and maintain social hierarchies. Culture includes beliefs, traditions, values, and language; it also mediates practices by connecting individuals and groups to institutionalized hierarchies. Whether in the form of dispositions, objects, systems, or institutions, culture embodies power relations. Further, many cultural practices in the advanced societies constitute relatively autonomous arenas of struggle for distinction. Intellectuals—the specialized producers and transmitters of culture—play key roles in shaping those arenas and their institutionalized hierarchies. So argues Pierre Bourdieu, today's leading French social scientist.

With his election in 1981 to the chair of sociology at the prestigious Collège de France, Pierre Bourdieu joined the distinguished ranks of the most revered postwar French social scientists, Raymond Aron and Claude Lévi-Strauss. A prolific writer and extraordinarily productive researcher, Bourdieu has published more than 30 books and 340 articles over the period 1958 to 1995. Many of these works are collaborative, as Bourdieu is also founder and director of his own research center, the Centre de Sociologie

Européenne.[1] He directs his own sociological journal, *Actes de la Recherche en Sciences Sociales*, and his own collection (under the imprint, *Le sens commun*) of more than sixty books with the French publishing house, Editions de Minuit.[2] Indeed, it is no exaggeration to say that Bourdieu's efforts have culminated in the development of a veritable new school of French sociology on a scale comparable to that produced earlier this century by one of his principal sources of inspiration: Emile Durkheim.

Prompted in part by increased accessibility due to numerous recent English-language translations of his work, interest in Bourdieu is rapidly growing in Britain and the United States. By the late 1980s Bourdieu had already become one of the French social scientists most frequently cited in the United States—surpassing Lévi-Strauss.[3] Bourdieu is perhaps most widely known among sociologists for his early work with Jean-Claude Passeron on French higher education, particularly for their most frequently cited book, *Reproduction: In Education, Society and Culture* (1977).[4] But he is also recognized, particularly among anthropologists, for his work on colonial Algeria, which appears in *The Algerians* (1962a), *Outline of a Theory of Practice* (1977c), and *The Logic of Practice* (1990h). In addition, his contributions to the study of relations between culture and social class (*Distinction: A Social Critique of the Judgement of Taste* [1984a]), the sociology of language (*Language and Symbolic Power* [1991c]), and the sociology of culture (*The Field of Cultural Production* [1993b]) are rapidly gaining recognition. Many of his works are becoming standard references in current growth sectors like the sociology of culture. His work spans a broad range of subjects from ethnography among peasants in Algeria, to sociological analysis of nineteenth-century artists and writers, education, language, consumer and cultural tastes, religion, and science in modern French society. Bourdieu is a major social theorist who also does empirical research.

1. Since entering the Collège de France, Bourdieu has shifted much of his work to those facilities, leaving the administration of his center to former collaborators, including Monique de Saint Martin and Jean-Claude Combessie.

2. In 1993 Bourdieu left Editions de Minuit to publish with Editions du Seuil.

3. The *Social Science Citation Index* ranking from high to low in 1989 for leading French intellectuals was the following: Foucault, Bourdieu, Lévi-Strauss, Derrida, Althusser, Sartre, Poulantzas, Touraine, Lacan, Baudrillard, Boudon, and Aron.

The intellectual notoriety of Bourdieu has not always been so extensive, particularly in professional sociology. An examination of the number of articles or reviews devoted to his work in the core publications of the American Sociological Association (plus *The American Journal of Sociology* and *Social Forces*) shows that over the period 1971 to 1985, Raymond Boudon and Alain Touraine in particular as well as Michel Crozier received considerably more attention (*Cumulative Index of Sociology Journals, 1971–1985*).

4. Indeed, *Reproduction* has become something of a citation classic, particularly in the sociology of education. His more recent work on French higher education is assembled in *Homo Academicus* (1988b) and *La Noblesse d'Etat* (1989c).

At the same time, acquaintance with his work has been fragmentary in Anglo-Saxon countries. An early problem of lack of translations of key works has now been rectified. Some of his work stressing the social reproduction effects of French education (Bourdieu 1973a; Bourdieu and Passeron 1977) was translated before some of his earlier reflection on a theory of practices (Bourdieu 1972). His conceptual development was thus read out of sequence and he became narrowly classified as a social reproduction theorist rather than appreciated for the broad range of conceptual concerns animating his thinking. By 1994, however, all of Bourdieu's major books had been translated into English.

A second problem has been that early interest in Bourdieu emerged along sectorial lines of academic specialization, which tended to limit knowledge of his oeuvre to the special concerns of selected fields, such as anthropology or the sociology of education. His early international reputation and much of the initial critical evaluation in sociology were based on his work on French education—notably *Reproduction*—rather than his earlier studies of Algerian peasants. Sociologists of education missed the anthropological concerns, garnered from his early research experience in Algeria, that animate his sociology of modern France. Thus, his overall conceptual framework has not received the kind of attention it deserves. Some of his most significant contributions to social theory have gone relatively unnoticed. Moreover, some of the criticisms leveled at Bourdieu appear to be based on a partial understanding of his overall approach to the study of social life.[5] Yet, as I explain in chapters 3 and 4, Bourdieu's sociology emerges from a broad interdisciplinary background that reflects the particular organization of intellectual discourse that characterized France in the 1950s and '60s.

And third, the reception of Bourdieu's work has been frequently polarized between uncritical acclaim by disciples and disdainful dismissal by certain critics.[6] Even in France Bourdieu's work has received strikingly little sympathetic critical review.[7] This is no doubt due in part to the sharply

5. See Wacquant 1993a for a lucid examination of the uneven reception of Bourdieu's work in the United States. The reception of Bourdieu's work has been uneven in France as well, as can be seen in Accardo 1983, Caillé 1992, Collectif "Révoltes logiques" 1984, and Ferry and Renault 1990. The collaborative presentation of Bourdieu's work in *An Invitation to Reflexive Sociology* (Bourdieu and Wacquant 1992) helps rectify the fragmented acquaintance with Bourdieu's overall sociological project.

6. A few exceptions must be noted. "Rethinking Classical Theory: The Sociological Vision of Pierre Bourdieu," by Rogers Brubaker (1985), and "Review Essay: On Pierre Bourdieu," by Paul DiMaggio (1979), are both sympathetic but critical examinations of key dimensions of Bourdieu's work. The collection of analytical essays *Bourdieu: Critical Perspectives* (Calhoun, LiPuma, and Postone 1993) represents an important step in this direction.

7. Illustrative of the two extremes would be the sympathetic but uncritical popularization of Bourdieu's work by Alain Accardo (Accardo 1983; Accardo and Corcuff 1986), and the

critical stance Bourdieu takes toward most established approaches in the social sciences. His critical style tends to recruit disciples or establish enemies.

It is time for a more comprehensive presentation and critical assessment of Bourdieu's mode of sociological inquiry. This book joins the important efforts by Bourdieu and Wacquant (1992), Harker, Mahar, and Wilkes (1990), Jenkins (1992), Robbins (1991), and Thompson (1991), to accomplish that task. It will elucidate and critically evaluate Bourdieu's overall conceptual framework and situate it within the French intellectual context. While it attempts to give an overall grasp of Bourdieu's sociological project, it does not aim to be an exhaustive examination of Bourdieu's oeuvre. It offers a sympathetic but critical examination of selected themes and concepts central to Bourdieu's sociological project, some of which have thus far received relatively little attention in the Anglo-Saxon literature on Bourdieu. While considerable attention has been given to his concepts of cultural capital and habitus, relatively little attention has been given to the concept of field. Yet the concept of field is crucial to a fuller understanding of his theory of practices and the way he conceptualizes relations between culture and social structure. His analysis of intellectuals, their key role as specialists of cultural production and creators of symbolic power, their position in the social class structure, and their relation to politics have been noted but not sufficiently explored. Yet, as I will show in chapters 9 and 10, a theory of intellectuals stands at the heart of Bourdieu's sociological project. Moreover, his normative vision for the scientific intellectual and the critical practice of sociology have received almost no attention. These all represent essential components in Bourdieu's work and thus far have not received appropriate recognition or critical assessment. The objective of this book is to help address these lacunae in the Anglo-American literature on Bourdieu's work.

*   *   *

The rich complexity of Bourdieu's conceptual world resists easy summary.[8] Few bodies of work are as comprehensive, complex, and innovative. Few approach Bourdieu's sophistication in scrutinizing the mundane operations of empirical research in terms of their epistemological and philosophical

contemptuous dismissal of Bourdieu's sociology by arch-rival Raymond Boudon, in his *L'Ideologie: Ou l'origin des idées reçues* (1986:227–28).

8. Miller and Branson (1987:214) doubt that the complexity and range of Bourdieu's framework can be succinctly summarized within a few pages. Calhoun, LiPuma, and Postone (1993:12) note that "Bourdieu's work resists a simple ordering of the priority of concepts or themes." See, however, Wacquant 1992 for an insightful effort by a close collaborator to identify a systematic unity throughout Bourdieu's work.

presuppositions. And few employ the kind of practical and strategic—indeed political—orientation to their sociological work that renders a strictly "theoretical reading" of its products potentially misleading.[9] Bourdieu forges his concepts as correctives to opposing viewpoints. His work can be read as an ongoing polemic against positivism, empiricism, structuralism, existentialism, phenomenology, economism, Marxism, methodological individualism, and grand theory.[10] He frames his rejection of these opposing views, however, by criticizing the subjectivist and objectivist forms of knowledge and the substantialist view of reality that he believes pervade them.

Thus, Bourdieu's primary concern is not one of conceptual genealogy, or faithful adherence to any given theoretical tradition. Bourdieu is a theorist but hardly a systems theorist in the tradition of Talcott Parsons. He in fact sharply criticizes "theoretical theory" for emphasizing abstract conceptualization independent of objects of empirical investigation. Bourdieu's concepts are not designed to respond in the first instance to the formal canons of internal consistency, generalizability, etc. Rather, they are pragmatically forged out of empirical research and confrontation with opposing intellectual viewpoints. His concepts shift in emphasis and scope depending on the opposing viewpoints they address. Nonetheless, they reveal a fairly consistent set of underlying metasociological principles that guide all of his investigations.

Bourdieu is a conceptual strategist whose choice of conceptual language is explicitly designed to establish distance from opposing viewpoints, particularly from those subjectivist and objectivist forms of knowledge that he believes hinder the development of a unified theory of practices. For this reason, I devote considerable attention, particularly in chapter 2, to the intellectual context and research experiences out of which Bourdieu develops his sociology. Chapter 3 presents Bourdieu's critique of subjectivist and objectivist forms of knowledge and chapter 11 outlines his alternative general theory of practices including a reflexive practice of sociology.

9. Brubaker (1993:217) argues that Bourdieu's work "is particularly ill-suited to a conceptualist, theoretical logocentric reading, one that treats it as the bearer of a set of logically interconnected propositions framed in terms of precise, unambiguous concepts." Rather than indicators of specific empirical phenomena, or building blocks of systematic theory, his concepts are better understood as heuristic devices for communicating a general approach to the study of the social world. I would stress that Bourdieu's texts are fundamentally political as well as scientific: they both reflect the intellectual issues of specific substantive fields and are strategically oriented toward producing a symbolic effect in those fields.

10. Bourdieu in fact borrows from each of these theoretical enemies—from structuralism in particular. He considers that each offers important, if partial, insights into the social world. It is Bourdieu's ambition to discard their respective weaknesses and build their respective strengths into a general science of practices.

Chapter 10 outlines the political project that undergirds his sociological program.

Finally, Bourdieu has developed distinct theories relative to action, culture, power, stratification, and sociological knowledge. Yet they intersect and interweave in complex ways that make it difficult to abstract one from the other even for expository purposes. This book attempts to highlight the principal conceptual interweavings so as to provide a richer understanding of Bourdieu's sociology. Chapters 3 through 6 explore the central arguments and concepts. Chapters 7 through 9 bring to the conceptual discussion substantive areas of investigation (social class structure, education, and intellectuals) that are particularly crucial to Bourdieu's sociological agenda.

Culture, Power, and Reproduction

Bourdieu proposes a sociology of symbolic power that addresses the important topic of relations between culture, social structure, and action. Whether he is studying Algerian peasants, university professors and students, writers and artists, or the church, a central underlying preoccupation emerges: the question of how stratified social systems of hierarchy and domination persist and reproduce intergenerationally without powerful resistance and without the conscious recognition of their members.[11] The answer to this question, Bourdieu argues, can be found by exploring how cultural resources, processes, and institutions hold individuals and groups in competitive and self-perpetuating hierarchies of domination. He advances the bold claim that *all* cultural symbols and practices, from artistic tastes, style in dress, and eating habits to religion, science and philosophy—even language itself—embody interests and function to enhance social distinctions. The struggle for social distinction, whatever its symbolic form, is for Bourdieu a fundamental dimension of all social life. The larger issue, then, is one of power relations among individuals, groups, and institutions (particularly the educational system). Indeed, for Bourdieu power is not a separate domain of study but stands at the heart of all social life.[12] And the successful exercise of power requires legitimation. The focus of his work, therefore, is on how cultural socialization places individuals and groups within competitive status hierarchies, how relatively autonomous fields of conflict interlock individuals and groups in struggle over valued resources,

11. This is a variant on Durkheim's fundamental concern for what produces social solidarity, though for Bourdieu the social order is a stratified order with hierarchical and inegalitarian arrangements among individuals and groups (see DiMaggio 1979; Sulkunen 1982:105).

12. For Bourdieu, no expression of sociability or its symbolic representations can be detached from its constitutive power relations.

how these social struggles are refracted through symbolic classifications, how actors struggle and pursue strategies to achieve their interests within such fields, and how in doing so actors unwittingly reproduce the social stratification order. Culture, then, is not devoid of political content but rather is an expression of it.[13]

The exercise and reproduction of class-based power and privilege is a core substantive and unifying concern in Bourdieu's work. It is his ambition to create a science, applicable to all types of societies, of the social and cultural reproduction of power relations among individuals and groups. In an early statement (Bourdieu 1973a), he calls for a "science of the reproduction of structures" that would be

a study of the laws whereby structures tend to reproduce themselves by producing agents invested with the system of dispositions which is able to engender practices adapted to these structures and thus contribute to their reproduction.

In a more recent statement, Bourdieu (1987b:92) describes his work as offering a *genetic theory of groups*. Such a theory would explain how groups, especially families, create and maintain unity and thereby perpetuate or improve their position in the social order. He charges the sociologist to ask "the question with which all sociology ought to begin, that of the existence and the mode of existence of collectives" (1985e:741). Bourdieu focuses on the role culture plays in social reproduction. How groups pursue strategies to produce and reproduce the conditions of their collective existence and how culture is constitutive of this reproductive process is for him a unifying problem in both sociology and anthropology and a substantive theme throughout his work (see Bourdieu 1985e:741).

At the core of Bourdieu's intellectual project for over thirty years stands the central issue in Western social thought since Marx: the debate between cultural idealism and historical materialism. Bourdieu's sociology represents a bold attempt to find a middle road that transcends the classic idealism/materialism bipolarity by proposing a materialist yet nonreductive account of cultural life.[14] His thinking begins with Marx but draws more substantively from Durkheim and Weber.

13. And for Bourdieu (1987b:36), a critical theory of culture "leads very naturally to a theory of politics."

14. Bourdieu claims that he began devoting attention to culture because it was a *neglected* dimension, not because it holds some theoretical priority for understanding the social world. In a 1983 interview he (1987b:61) recalls that at the time of his work on Algerian peasants in the late 1950s he found the substantive area of culture to be largely neglected. According to him, the prevailing conceptions of culture at that time were split between Marxists who assigned it the status of superstructure, and therefore secondary to the economy, and those non-Marxists who idealized it. Bourdieu sees his approach as an effort to transcend these two radically opposed views of culture.

In his approach to culture, Bourdieu develops a political economy of practices and symbolic power that includes a theory of symbolic interests, a theory of capital, and a theory of symbolic violence and symbolic capital. His theory of symbolic interests reconceptualizes the relations between the symbolic and material aspects of social life by extending the idea of economic interest to the realm of culture. There are symbolic interests just as there are material interests. He conceptualizes culture as a form of capital with specific laws of accumulation, exchange, and exercise. The exercise of power, he argues, requires legitimation, so he also proposes a theory of symbolic violence and capital that stresses the active role that symbolic forms play as resources that both constitute and maintain power structures. These are not tidy, well-delimited theoretical arguments but orienting themes that overlap and interpenetrate. They draw from a wide variety of intellectual influences including Marxism, structuralism, phenomonology, the philosophy of science, and the classical sociological tradition, and they will be explored in chapters 3 and 4.

The Agency/Structure Problem

Another general area of concern is the relationship between individual action and social structure. What motivates human action? Do individuals act in response to external causes as much mainstream academic sociology tends to assume? Is individual action determined by "culture," "social structure," or "mode of production"? Or do actors act for their own identifiable reasons as the phenomenological, interpretative, and rational-actor schools in the social sciences maintain? Relatedly, what in fact is to be the epistemological status of actor conceptions in social scientific accounts of their behavior? Are they, as in the Durkheimian tradition, to be dismissed as epistemologically unreliable? Or are they to become the essential building blocks of scientific accounts, as the hermeneutical tradition would have it? These questions point to what Giddens (1979) identifies as one of the central problems in contemporary social theory, namely, the relation of agency and structure.

Bourdieu is among the first of the post–World War II generation of sociologists to make the agency/structure issue central to his sociology. He proposes connecting agency and structure in a "dialectical relationship." He argues against conceptualizing human action as a direct, unmediated response to external factors, whether they be identified as micro-structures of interactions or macro-level cultural, social, or economic factors. Nor does Bourdieu see action as the simple outgrowth from internal factors, such as conscious intentions and calculation, as posited by voluntarist and rational-actor models of human action. For Bourdieu, explanations that highlight either the macro or the micro dimension to the exclusion of the other simply perpetuate the classic subjective/objective antinomy. Bourdieu wants to transcend this dichotomy by conceptualizing action so that micro and macro, voluntarist and determinist dimensions of human activity are integrated into a single conceptual movement rather than isolated as mutually exclusive forms of explanation. He thus proposes a structural theory of practice that connects action to culture, structure, and power. This theory undergirds his key concept, *habitus*, which, along with cultural capital, has become one of his conceptual trademarks. We examine this theoretical concern and his concept of habitus in chapter 5.

Fields of Power

Practices occur in structured arenas of conflict called *fields*. This central concept in Bourdieu's sociology connects the action of habitus to the stratifying structures of power in modern society. Bourdieu conceptualizes modern society as an array of relatively autonomous but structurally homologous fields of production, circulation, and consumption of various forms of cultural and material resources. Fields mediate the relationship between social structure and cultural practice. Developed later than his more familiar concepts of cultural capital and habitus, Bourdieu's concept of field is less well known. But it has become a central pillar of his conceptual edifice, and I explore its key dimensions in chapter 6.

I conclude chapter 6 with a recapitulation of the full conceptual model of Bourdieu's general theory of practices. In chapters 7, 8, and 9, I will demonstrate how Bourdieu combines his concepts of habitus and cultural and symbolic capital in a field analytic perspective to analyze the social class structure, the education system, and intellectuals in modern France.[15]

Sociology as Socioanalysis

Since, according to Bourdieu, actors by and large "mis-recognize" how cultural resources, processes, and institutions lock individuals and groups into

15. One important substantive area in Bourdieu's work that I do not examine is his analysis of language. Language is a central vehicle of habitus as the generator of practices, which include linguistic practices; it also functions as a form of cultural and symbolic capital and is susceptible to Bourdieu's field analytic perspective. See Bourdieu 1991c for key papers by Bourdieu on the social uses of language and an insightful introduction by John B. Thompson. Also see the informative papers relating Bourdieu's analysis of language to education (Collins 1993) and to semantics (Hanks 1993).

reproducing patterns of domination, the task of sociology is to unveil this hidden dimension of power relations. Bourdieu thinks of the practice of sociology as *socioanalysis* where the sociologist is to the "social unconscious" of society as the psychoanalyst is to the patient's unconscious.[16] The social unconscious consists of those unacknowledged interests that actors follow as they participate in an unegalitarian social order. Since, according to Bourdieu, it is the misrecognition of those embedded interests that is the necessary condition for the exercise of power, he believes that their public exposure will destroy their legitimacy and open up the possibility for altering existing social arrangements. By exposing those underlying interests that bind individuals and groups into unequal power relations, sociology becomes an instrument of struggle capable of offering a measure of freedom from the constraints of domination. Here Bourdieu's sociology intersects with critical theory.

Bourdieu believes that one indicator of how well the socioanalysis is carried out can be seen by the degree to which it elicits resistance. To the extent that sociological analysis touches the vital unacknowledged interests of actors, it will often elicit resistance. And Bourdieu (1987b:7–10) admits that he self-consciously orients his sociological criticism to what he thinks are the vital but unacknowledged interests of particular groups.[17]

For a Reflexive Practice of Social Science

The possibility of revealing the underlying interests of practical social life is, however, for Bourdieu no simple matter. Since according to his theory *all* symbolic forms function to generate social distinctions, the practice of social science itself is not exempt from processes of social differentiation. Thus, Bourdieu rejects scientific positivism and its ideal of value-neutral objectivity. How, therefore, is it possible to practice a social science—itself an institution of cultural symbols and practices—that might expose the underlying nexus between action, culture, stratification, and power without simultaneously creating the same effects of social distinction observed in everyday social life? Since social scientists cannot themselves escape the

---

16. Bourdieu's conception of sociology as a sort of "social psychoanalysis" is perhaps most evident in *Distinction* (1984a:11), where he writes that "sociology is rarely more akin to social psychoanalysis than when it confronts an object like taste, one of the most vital stakes in the struggles fought in the field of the dominant class and the field of cultural production."

17. There is also a disconcerting tendency by Bourdieu to see criticism of his work in socioanalytic terms; that is, to view it as a form of resistance to the exposure of the vital interests as defined by his own analysis. While in many instances this may be correct, it also runs the danger of reducing appropriate criticism to forms of alleged self-interest.

social logic of symbolic distinctions, their socioanalysis is itself not exempt from underlying interests. What form of objective scientific knowledge is therefore possible?

Faced with this dilemma, Bourdieu insists that socioanalysis simultaneously requires *reflexivity*, that is, a systematic and rigorous self-critical practice of social science. Chapter 2 describes how Bourdieu draws from the French philosopher of science, Gaston Bachelard, whose nonpositivist epistemology calls for a reflexive monitoring of the cognitive and social conditions that make scientific work possible. Following Bachelard, Bourdieu demands that the standards of critical inquiry be applied to observing social scientists as well as to their subjects of observation. This does not mean that Bourdieu rejects all possibility of scientific objectivity in favor of a thoroughly interpretative and relativist approach to understanding the social world. Rather, he argues that it is *only* through a reflexive practice of social inquiry that one can hope to achieve a desirable degree of objectivity on the social world.

Further, Bourdieu (1971c:181) equates the practice of reflexivity with the practice of science itself when he writes, "the scientific project and the very progress of science presuppose a reflective return to the foundations of science and the making explicit of the hypotheses and operations which make it possible." He sees a sociology of sociology as a *necessary* means for freeing the social scientist from the constraints of symbolic struggle in the field of science. Thus, he most certainly disagrees with Skocpol (1986:11–12) who warns sociologists "from wandering into the dead end of metatheory." Bourdieu explicitly engages a series of metatheoretical issues that he believes will establish a firm epistemological base for sociology (see chapters 3 and 10). At the same time, Bourdieu does not share Ritzer's (1988) vision of establishing sociological metatheory as a legitimate subfield within the discipline of sociology. For Bourdieu, the sociology of sociology must be made an essential component of *all* sociological inquiry. "It is the necessary prerequisite of any rigorous sociological practice" (Bourdieu 1989b:385). For Bourdieu, the practice of a genuine social science *requires* a "reflexive return" upon itself.

This call for a reflexive return on the practice of social science charts for Bourdieu both a distinctive mode of inquiry and a substantive orientation. Indeed, Bourdieu views this dimension of his approach to social inquiry as what most distinguishes it from all others:

I believe that if the sociology I propose differs in any significant way from the other sociologies of the past and of the present, it is above all in that it *continually turns back onto itself the scientific weapons it produces.* (Wacquant 1989:55)

In fact, a critical reflection on the use of social scientific categories has characterized Bourdieu's work from the very start. Bourdieu (1990h:15) describes the critical examination of the relations between the researcher and the object of research as "the most significant product of my whole undertaking." It also justifies his research in the substantive arenas of education and intellectuals. For Bourdieu, these substantive and metatheoretical questions are inseparably linked, and much of his work simultaneously reflects on both. This approach enriches and increases the complexity of his thought as he investigates both the role of culture in social class reproduction and the epistemological conditions that make it possible to study culture reflexively and objectively. His claim that a properly constructed reflexive sociology holds promise for emancipating individuals and groups from the constraints of social determination and domination represents a unique contribution to critical social theory and research.[18]

Sociology as Politics

Thus, Bourdieu's work is not to be thought of as strictly academic social science; it also represents a mode of *political intervention*. Bourdieu thinks of his practice of sociology as a means to provide a corrective to prevailing forms of mis-recognition; as I explain in chapter 10, it is a form of political practice conducted in the name of science. Much of this political intervention is aimed against the self-image and self-esteem of the intelligentsia as the carriers of universal cultural values freed from economic and political determinants. Since fellow intellectuals bear the brunt of Bourdieu's critical socioanalysis and represent a recurring key topic in his work, I devote chapter 9 to Bourdieu's treatment of intellectuals. Chapter 10, then, examines Bourdieu's vision for a critical role of the social scientist in the modern world.

Career

Little published biographical information on Bourdieu currently exists, and Bourdieu resists public self-disclosure. Yet, the social and intellectual context in which he developed his sociology is important for understanding the origins of the sharply critical posture Bourdieu has taken toward French education, sociology, and intellectual life more generally. Bourdieu's soci-

18. Though Bourdieu does not identify with the Frankfurt School, he is nonetheless a critical theorist and does share with Horkheimer and Adorno three core features: criticism of accepted categories, criticism of the practice of theory itself, and criticism of everyday life (Calhoun, LiPuma, and Postone 1993).

ology emerges from an unusual experience of upward social mobility and from a broader range of intellectual influences and career experiences than usually is found among sociologists. He is a cultural and social "outsider" to the French intellectual elite, who trained in philosophy, began his career as an anthropologist, and draws on Anglo-American and German as well as French intellectual traditions.

Writing Style

Finally, it is perhaps appropriate to say something about Bourdieu's writing style, since many find it to be a formidable obstacle to hurdle (Jenkins 1992). Bourdieu is both a superb stylist and the author of some impenetrable prose. He writes long, complex sentences with many phrases embedded in one another. Commas and semicolons proliferate. His prose is charged with polemic, paradox, negation, and an occasional pun that make his work difficult for those readers who are not familiar with the French intellectual context in which he is writing. Bourdieu can never be read casually.

Nonetheless, three observations might enhance understanding of Bourdieu's writing style. First, Bourdieu consciously employs rhetorical techniques for gaining distance from the taken-for-granted world. Since, according to Bourdieu, it is the experience of familiarity that stands as one of the principal obstacles to a scientific understanding of the social world, he self-consciously selects terminology and cultivates a writing style that establishes distance from everyday language use. Second, his style is a calculated challenge to the stylistic conventions of orthodox academic discourse in France. France is a country where clarity of exposition (la clarté) is elevated to a national virtue, where it is seen as truly a mark of natural talent and intelligence. Bourdieu's prose style can be seen as a reaction against this particular academic orthodoxy, a critical reaction that is designed to shatter the notion of excellence as a sort of natural ability. And third, though unacknowledged, Bourdieu's writing style undoubtedly represents an intellectual strategy to demarcate his distinctive product on the French intellectual market just as Barthes, Foucault, and Lacan have invented their respective writing styles.[19]

---

19. See Wacquant (1993a) for suggestive reasons why many Anglo-American social scientists single out Bourdieu's prose for criticism. Wacquant discusses the issue, however, solely from the standpoint of the field of intellectual consumption. My observations situate Bourdieu within his field of intellectual production. They indicate the degree of commitment Bourdieu has made to a distinctive professionalized sociological discourse. And they leave him open to C. Wright Mills's (1959:219) familiar admonition: "To overcome the academic prose you have first to overcome the academic pose."

These observations point to a fundamental paradox in Bourdieu's rhetorical strategy. If his sociology is indeed to be an instrument of struggle against all forms of symbolic domination and this project is to have some collective as well as personal benefit, then the problem of diffusion beyond the specialized circles of academia must be addressed. Bourdieu appears to have recognized this problem by using in a number of his more recent works a more readily accessible style of the interview (see in particular Bourdieu and Wacquant 1992).

2 CAREER AND FORMATIVE INTELLECTUAL INFLUENCES

For a fuller appreciation of Bourdieu's general approach to sociological inquiry, this chapter examines key features of his career and intellectual heritage. I do not attempt a biography of Bourdieu; that task awaits another. I focus only on selected factors that seem most decisive in shaping his intellectual agenda.

Little published biographical information on Bourdieu currently exists. Bourdieu, himself, says very little about his own life. In contrast to many other leading French intellectuals who have published personal memoirs, for example Raymond Aron (1983a; 1983b), Alain Touraine, or Emmanuel Le Roy Ladurie (1982), Bourdieu resists public self-disclosure. He deplores personal and anecdotal observations by intellectuals, considering "biographical writing" to be a form of narcissism that wallows in the celebration of individual subjectivity and is devoid of genuine sociological insight (see Bourdieu 1987a). In the few places where he does offer information on his career and intellectual development, observations are cast as being sociological rather than personal. The biographical information presented below is extrapolated from Bourdieu's published work,[1] from personal observation during the period 1970 to 1976 when I was a student in Paris and attended

---

1. The few pieces where he does offer insight into the formative influences on his sociology include Bourdieu 1990c:3–33, 1990h:1–29; Bourdieu and Passeron 1967; and Honneth, Kocyba, and Schwibs 1986.

Bourdieu's seminars, from many conversations since 1976 with observers both in France and the United States, and from a few conversations with Bourdieu.

This chapter includes relatively more information on Bourdieu's early years than on the period subsequent to his 1981 election to the Collège de France. I believe this is justified in light of the degree to which the formative intellectual years establish the intellectual dispositions that one tends to carry throughout life. It is rare indeed for someone to "undo" their early education—a point stressed in Bourdieu's own theory of habitus and supported by his analysis of the enduring effects of education on French intellectuals. This view is supported by the findings of Derek Robbins, in his chronological study of Bourdieu's works. Robbins (1991:178, 181) concludes that Bourdieu acquires his intellectual framework early in his career and does not substantially alter it subsequently. Bourdieu of course tests, reexamines, elaborates, and in some ways renders more supple his framework in response to social, cultural, political, and intellectual changes. I will note those shifts in emphasis where appropriate. But I, like Robbins, am struck by the consistency and recurring intellectual patterns displayed throughout Bourdieu's work.

This work emerges from quite diverse intellectual sources and professional experiences; indeed, it is not easy to situate Bourdieu on the contemporary map of currents in Western intellectual thought. There are, nonetheless, a few general sources of influence that decisively shape his work: his philosophical training while a student at the Ecole Normale Supérieure, his reading of three of the classic figures in sociological theory (Marx, Durkheim, and Weber), the general intellectual climate of postwar France—particularly the influence of structuralism—and his ethnographic fieldwork in Algeria.

Bourdieu's Professional Career

Pierre Bourdieu's professional career follows an extraordinary trajectory of upward mobility. He climbs from marginal cultural and social origins to the apex of the French intellectual pyramid, the Collège de France. He was born in 1930 into a lower-middle-class family (his father was a village postman) in Deguin, a small town in Southwestern France. He spent his early years in this remote rural region of Béarn and spoke the regional dialect. A particularly gifted and industrious student, he first entered the Lycée de Pau, then the prestigious and academically selective Parisian Lycée Louis-le-Grand (1949–51). In 1951, he entered the academically elite Ecole Normale Supérieure (rue d'Ulm) in Paris where he prepared the *agrégation* in philosophy. He also took courses at the Faculty of Letters in Paris.

One of the most famous French *grandes écoles*, the Ecole Normale Supérieure (ENS), was originally set up to prepare academically gifted students as teachers for the French *lycées*. It became France's highest expression of the academic meritocracy by selecting secondary-school students through rigorous competitive examinations and providing them with the best preparatory training for passing the national competitive examinations for teaching positions. Successful candidates enter the prestigious and academically powerful alumni network of *normaliens* who exercise considerable influence over curriculum, examinations, and teaching appointments in French education.

ENS also became the premier preparatory school for French intellectuals. Among ENS alumni one finds such notables as Louis Althusser, Henri Bergson, Georges Canguilhem, Régis Debray, Michel Foucault, Jean Jaurès, Claude Lévi-Strauss, Maurice Merleau-Ponty, Paul Nizan, and Jean-Paul Sartre. One also finds several of France's leading French sociologists, including the founder of French sociology, Emile Durkheim. ENS was in fact the "breeding ground of young Durkheimians at the turn of the century" and the shared educational experience for leading postwar French sociologists including Raymond Aron, George Friedmann, and Jean Stoetzel (Karady 1981:37). Alain Touraine preceded Bourdieu at the ENS in 1945 and Raymond Boudon followed in 1954. Jacques Derrida and Emmanuel Le Roy Ladurie were among Bourdieu's peers at the Ecole.

It is not surprising to find an extraordinarily successful student of modest social background like Bourdieu pass through the doors of ENS. ENS is undoubtedly the most academically oriented of all the French *grandes écoles* and relatively less influenced by family background in its recruitment. Sirinelli (1988) documents that historically there have been just enough upwardly mobile recruits to give plausibility to its meritocratic image.[2] Yet, as research by Bourdieu (1989c) and others show, the meritocratic image of the *grandes écoles*, including ENS, represents an ideology that deflects attention from the very large number of recruits from privileged backgrounds.[3] Being from the extreme southwest provinces, Bourdieu shared

2. Among the more striking examples is the late Georges Pompidou, whose grandparents were peasants, whose parents were elementary school teachers, and who excelled academically, attended ENS, and eventually became President of the French Republic.

3. Christain Baudelot, director of Social Sciences at ENS, reported that ENS has never been a major source of upward social mobility from the lowest reaches of French society (presentation at the Center For European Studies, Harvard University, 23 March 1995). According to Baudelot, only about 5 percent of ENS students today represent the popular classes.

in neither the cultural nor social advantages of the majority of his ENS classmates.

Bourdieu, of course, was not unique in being viewed by his Parisian peers as a young "provincial"—there were many others. Foucault too was a provincial outsider to the Parisian intellectual heirs (Eribon 1991:15). Indeed, as Bourdieu (1988b) remarks, the anti-institutional disposition of all three—Bourdieu, Derrida, and Foucault—may stem in part from their respective backgrounds as outsiders to a milieu dominated socially and culturally by Paris.

ENS is known for cultivating an abundance of *esprit critique*, and in this Bourdieu excelled. Little escaped his critical flair: peers, professors, the school itself. The reputation that would characterize his later sociological work—that of being a sharp and relentless critic of the French educational establishment—is already in evidence at ENS. What is striking is Bourdieu's self-perception of being an outsider within the academic establishment and his sharply critical attitude toward the very institution that helped make his phenomenal rise to intellectual renown possible. Bourdieu experienced ENS not only as a miraculous survivor of strenuous academic selection, but also as a cultural and social outsider. One of Bourdieu's ENS peers recalls Bourdieu having an "extraordinary desire for revenge" against the Parisian intellectual world that dominated the Ecole (Dufay and Dufort 1993:196). This would find an echo later in *The Inheritors*, Bourdieu's analysis of French university culture as hostile toward the popular classes and as privileging individualized stylistic distinction rather than genuine intellectual inquiry.

It is sometimes said that behind every cynic lies a disappointed idealist. This can perhaps be said of Bourdieu, who likens his relation to French schooling to that of a frustrated "oblate" (1988b:xxvi). Bourdieu borrows this religious term to refer to the intense institutional loyalty felt by those teachers of humble origins who owe their cultural, social, and professional success to the educational system.[4] Bourdieu, however, refuses to give allegiance to the institution that makes his success possible. He is frustrated by the gap between the lofty ideals of universalism promulgated by French education and the actual practices of academic power regulating relations among faculty and students. He is incensed by the French academic mandarins who impose curriculum orthodoxy, who themselves do little or no empirical research, and who exercise tight control over the careers of aspiring

---

4. The religious term refers to the boy who shows intense institutional loyalty to the Church since it selected him from very humble social origins for training for the priesthood (Bourdieu 1988b:31, 291).

future academics.[5] He is offended by the thinly veiled prejudice against the lower classes he perceives in French academic culture.[6] He rails against the traditional curriculum, pedagogy, and evaluation that foster academic routinization rather than artistic and scientific exploration. This personal experience of alienation within French academe motivates him to submit French schooling to critical examination in his later work.[7] But it also informs his approach to all institutions. Indeed, one finds Bourdieu normalizing this critical disposition as a desirable—if not necessary—ingredient for the successful pursuit of sociology itself.[8]

One might have expected Bourdieu's revolt to take him into the French Communist Party. In the late '40s and early '50s, ENS, like much of France, had became highly politicized. French intellectual life was sharply divided between adherents to the French Communist Party, those sympathetic to Marxist class analysis but critical of the Party, and existentialists who were more concerned with personal freedom and meaningful individual involvement (Poster 1975). At that time, the French Communist Party and its associated labor organizations enjoyed the most clout on the political left. Moreover, the Communists enjoyed considerable legitimacy for having played an important role in the French resistance during the war. Even Sartre, who dominated French intellectual life in the early '50s, produced in *Les Temps Modernes* his ardent debates with Merleau-Ponty, Claude Lefort, and Albert Camus over allegiance to the Soviet Union and the Party.

ENS did not escape this heated political debate. Everyone was called upon to "choose sides" either for the workers or for the political right (Eribon 1991:33). Le Roy Ladurie (1982:79), who entered ENS in 1949 and became head of the ENS communist cell, recalls that about 20 percent of

5. He cites as prime examples Georges Davy and George Gurvitch (Honneth, Kocyba, and Schwibs 1986:37). The disdain by Gurvitch for Lévi-Strauss, who did not follow the elite academic track before entering the Collège de France—he did not write a doctoral thesis—is legendary. The story is told of Gurvitch summarily flunking a student who simply mentioned Lévi-Strauss during an oral examination.

6. Later, he will judge professorial evaluations of student work to be in fact social judgments of their class origins (Bourdieu 1988b:194–210).

7. In a rare moment of personal disclosure Bourdieu writes, "the special place held in my work by a somewhat singular sociology of the university institution is no doubt explained by the peculiar force with which I felt the need to gain rational control over the disappointment felt by an 'oblate' faced with the annihilation of the truths and values to which he was destined and dedicated, rather than take refuge in feelings of self-destructive resentment" (1988b:xxvi).

8. Bourdieu suggests that students most likely to be receptive to the kind of critical sociology he advocates are those who not only are strong in science but also have "a certain revolt against, or distance from, that culture (most often rooted in an estranged experience of the academic universe) that pushes them not to 'buy it' at its face value or, quite simply, a form of resistance to the asepticized and derealized representation of the social world offered by the socially dominant discourse in sociology" (Bourdieu and Wacquant 1992:249).

the students became members, though not all attended meetings regularly. In addition to peer pressure, some highly respected ENS faculty were party members and actively recruited students. For example, Jean-Toussaint Desanti, specialist of Marxism and phenomenology, a "fervent Communist" and a "brilliant professor . . . exerted enormous influence on the ENS students and helped make membership in the Communist party attractive" (Eribon 1991:31–32). Louis Althusser exerted considerable influence over a significant number of ENS students as their adviser. Michel Foucault joined the party in 1950 largely through Althusser's influence and remained member until 1953, though not active in the ENS cell. Foucault formed his own small band of Marxist followers who were tolerated but considered insufficiently orthodox by party standards (Eribon 1991:50–51). Bourdieu's eventual collaborator, Jean-Claude Passeron, was an active member of Foucault's group.

Yet unlike many of his *normalien* peers of the period, Bourdieu did not join the party. Indeed, Bourdieu (1990c:3) recalls having created with several other ENS students, including Jacques Derrida, during the Stalinist era, a committee for the defense of liberties that was denounced by Le Roy Ladurie before the school cell.[9] Though Bourdieu attended Althusser's seminar, he never became a convert.[10] When Althusserian Marxism came to dominate much of French intellectual life, Bourdieu became a sharp critic of its followers.[11] Nonetheless, Bourdieu's encounter with Althusserian Marxism during those early years clearly shaped his work. That influence can be seen in some of the intellectual issues that Bourdieu addressed. The idea of the relative autonomy of culture is one example (Bourdieu 1990c:7). Moreover, some of Bourdieu's conceptual language can be understood as a reaction to Althusserian rhetoric. And finally, Le Roy Ladurie (1982:79) recalls that among all of his *normalien* peers who went into the social sciences, it was above all Bourdieu who was able to develop and estab-

9. More than thirty years later the facts of Bourdieu's relationship to the ENS communists are disputed and remain a sensitive issue. In a 1988 interview in the French newspaper *Liberation*, Pierre Juquin, one of Bourdieu's ENS peers who later became a political bureau member of the Party, alleged that Bourdieu had belonged to the ENS communist cell. Bourdieu responded with a sharply worded denial in the next issue. Juquin in turn maintained that "if Bourdieu wasn't a member, he in any case attended cell reunions" (recounted in Dufay and Dufort 1993:197).

10. Though not one of Althusser's circle of ENS students, Bourdieu has refrained from publicly judging him. In an interview with the author (Paris, 19 November 1987) Bourdieu maintained that one of the contributions of Althusser was that he encouraged ENS students to read Marx beyond the usual platitudes and slogans dictated by the Party.

11. See his particularly pointed attack in *Actes de la recherche en sciences sociales* (Bourdieu 1975a). According to Bourdieu, Althusserianism exercised an oppressive role on social-scientific inquiry (Public communication at the Conference on the Social Theory of Pierre Bourdieu, March 31–April 2, 1989 at the Center for Psychosocial Studies, Chicago, Ill.).

lish in the contemporary French intellectual world a central idea shaped by the Marxist climate of the Ecole during those years; namely that the French school system and the culture it transmitted fundamentally served the dominant classes.

FRENCH SOCIOLOGY IN THE FIFTIES AND SIXTIES

When Bourdieu entered ENS, French sociology had a very weak institutional base. The French intellectual world in the early 1950s was dominated by existentialism and Marxism. Both the antipositivism of existentialism and the official scientific Marxism of French communists discouraged the development of an independent base of social theory and empirical research. The rich heritage of Durkheim had fallen into decline even before World War II, because of the premature deaths of its most promising heirs and because of its marginal position in the French academic establishment (Karady 1981). Newcomers to the few teaching positions in sociology after 1945 had to find their intellectual inspiration abroad. They imported to France some specialized orientation for their work, as Jean Stoetzel did in social psychology (Karady 1981:42).

Sociology was not taught in the *lycées*. No sociology degree was offered in the university. In 1949 only eighteen researchers in the Centre Nationale de Recherche Scientifique covered the area of sociodemography and in 1950 only four chairs of sociology existed in all of France (Amiot 1984: 281–82). What little structure to the academic discipline existed in the early '50s was firmly in the hands of George Gurvitch and Georges Davy, who held chairs at the Sorbonne.[12] They were veritable university mandarins rather than practicing social scientists, more social philosophers than professional research sociologists. Moreover, the empirical work of Jean Stoetzel and George Friedmann did not have legitimate intellectual status in the eyes of young *normaliens* with a taste for philosophy (Bourdieu 1987b:15). These researchers had not "followed the royal road—Ecole normale and *agrégation*"; rather than as sociologists, they were perceived as failed philosophers (Bourdieu 1990c:5–6).

Yet, if French sociology of the 1950s offered little professional status appeal to young *normaliens* like Bourdieu, its relative lack of institutionalization and professionalization nonetheless offered him an intellectual market opportunity that was not already overcrowded as was academic philosophy. But he would not realize that opportunity before first doing field research as an ethnologist in Algeria and without the help of a powerful sponsor, Raymond Aron.

---

12. Raymond Aron would replace Davy at the Sorbonne in 1955.

After finishing the *agrégation* in 1955, Bourdieu, like so many *agrégés* in philosophy before him, went to the provinces to teach philosophy at the secondary level. He began teaching at the Lycée Moulins just outside of Paris. But the war with Algeria intervened, and he was called into military service.

Colonial Algeria was important to Bourdieu's career, for it was there that he actually began his social scientific work as a "self-taught" ethnologist (Honneth, Kocyba, and Schwibs 1986:39). His first book, published in 1958, was *Sociologie de l'Algerie*.[13] In that same year, Bourdieu became a teaching assistant at the Faculty of Letters in Algiers, and it was from there that he initiated two large-scale studies on the transformation of Algerian social structure under colonialism and the war. This research resulted in two co-authored books *Travail et travailleurs en Algerie* (Bourdieu, Darbel, et al. 1963), *Le Déracinement* (Bourdieu and Sayad 1964), and numerous articles. It also forms the basis for three subsequent and widely acknowledged books: *Esquisse d'une théorie de la pratique* (1972); its revised and updated translation, *Outline of a Theory of Practice* (1977c); and *The Logic of Practice* (1990h).

Like many French intellectuals, Bourdieu opposed the French war effort, and for this reason was eventually obliged to leave Algiers and return to Paris. There he assumed an appointment as one of Raymond Aron's teaching assistants at the Sorbonne. He taught at the Sorbonne from 1961 to 1962 and then at the Faculty of Letters at the University of Lille through 1964. In 1964 he became one of the directors of studies at the Ecole des Hautes Etudes en Sciences Sociales (EHESS) in Paris.[14] He did not, however, go on to complete the state doctorate degree, which is the standard requirement for those seeking chairs in the French universities.[15]

13. This work was translated into English as *The Algerians* (1962).

14. Raymond Aron and Alain Touraine had become directors of studies in 1960. In 1964 the nomination was actually to the "sixth section" of the Ecole Pratique des Hautes Etudes. The Ecole was created in 1868 under the second Empire outside of the university structure for the purpose of linking research and teaching. In 1947 two historians, Fernand Braudel and Lucien Febvre, founders of the famed *Annales* school in historical research, created within the Ecole the sixth section, oriented toward the economic and social sciences. The sixth section rapidly became a key center for social scientific research and teaching in France. In 1975 the name was changed to the Ecole des Hautes Etudes en Sciences Sociales and the institution was given a degree granting status analogous to the university. Today it has an autonomy analogous to a *grande école*. The appointment gave Bourdieu a key institutional base to develop his own research outside of the traditional teaching and career structures of the university. The nomination was made possible by the combined support of Aron, Braudel, and Lévi-Strauss.

15. As a consequence, Bourdieu cannot preside over dissertation defense committees for doctoral degrees in the French university. This is another illustration of his "outsider as insider" status within French academe. In this respect, Foucault, who did his state doctorate,

Raymond Aron was a key sponsor for Bourdieu in those early years as he was to many of today's leading French sociologists.[16] Jean-Claude Raynaud, Eric de Dampierre, and Claude Lefort were also early members of Aron's entourage. As professor at the Sorbonne, Aron was a member of the doctoral dissertation committee of many of today's leading French sociologists, among them, Michel Crozier and Alain Touraine. In 1961, with monies from the Ford Foundation, Aron founded his European Center for Historical Sociology. Aron saw in Bourdieu a promising and particularly industrious scholar who combined a keen interest in classical social theory (particularly Max Weber) with empirical research. Bourdieu was also a *normalien* and *agrégé* in philosophy, as was Aron. He called upon Bourdieu in 1964 to assume administrative responsibilities of the center. It was while co-directing Aron's center that Bourdieu recruited the core of his early research team: Luc Boltanski, Yvette Delsaut, Claude Grignon, Jean-Claude Passeron, and Monique de Saint Martin.

In politics and temperament Bourdieu and Aron were quite different,[17] but initially there was mutual respect.[18] Sharp differences emerged after the

was the more *universitaire* of the two. Bourdieu would follow the pattern of Lévi-Strauss, who also did not complete this academic requirement.

16. It is noteworthy that in the few biographical statements Bourdieu makes regarding his intellectual background, no mention is made of Aron. Yet Aron made available crucial institutional resources to Bourdieu in the early 1960s.

Aron was a central figure in the development of academic sociology in France during the years following World War II. Postwar sociological research in France developed initially outside of the university under the leadership of pioneers like Georges Friedmann in empirical research institutes as the Centre d'Etudes Sociologiques. When Aron was elected Professor of Sociology at the Sorbonne in 1955, he joined Georges Gurvitch, a social philosopher, and Jean Stoetzel, a social psychologist, the two other chaired professors of sociology, to teach a body of knowledge that was taught only at four universities in France—Paris, Bordeaux, Strasbourg and Toulouse—and led to no formal degree. Up until then, sociology was taken only as partial credit for completing degrees in philosophy or in a non-teaching degree (*licence libre*). In 1958, Aron introduced a *licence* degree in sociology. Starting with only one teaching assistant in 1955, he ended his career at the Sorbonne in 1968 with ten. With such a key figure as Aron giving direction to a renewed academic sociology, it is not surprising that Bourdieu's career would intersect with Aron's.

17. Aron and Bourdieu were both *normaliens* and shared a common interest in classical social theory, particularly Max Weber. But politically they were different: Bourdieu was on the left and Aron on the center right of the French political spectrum. Moreover, Aron was a public intellectual who wrote regularly as a journalist on current political affairs as well as carrying out his academic activities. Bourdieu concentrated his attention on scholarly and research activities and has always been highly critical of the type of public intellectual role that Aron symbolized.

18. Aron's initial respect for Bourdieu is captured in the preface he wrote to *The Algerians* (1962): "This book by my friend Pierre Bourdieu" and goes on to claim that the book concerns itself with Algeria, not with the war in Algeria. Bourdieu, a sociologist and philosopher, has lived in that country for many years. He has the ability to observe with detachment and to understand with

1964 publication of *The Inheritors*, in which Bourdieu, along with his co-author Jean-Claude Passeron, advanced stinging criticism of the class-based character of the French university population and of student culture.[19] A sharp break finally occurred in the spring of 1968 when, in response to the student revolt, Aron publicly advocated limiting student participation in the life of the university and designated his center as a rallying point for like minds (Colquhoun 1986:339–40).[20] Bourdieu exited, taking his closest collaborators with him, and founded his own Center for European Sociology.[21]

Years after the break, Aron's influence was, however, still to be felt and on occasions solicited. Aron's support aided Bourdieu's election to the Collège de France in 1981. Moreover, Bourdieu's efforts to sponsor his own candidates for positions at the Ecole des Hautes Etudes en Sciences Sociales and at the Centre National de Recherche Scientifique were often successful only with Aron's support.[22]

---

sympathy, to reconstruct the outlook and system of values of different communities at the same time that he perceives the growing unity of those communities as they ranged themselves against the colonial condition.

Despite what Aron claims, Bourdieu's analysis of Algerian peasant communities is inseparable from an analysis of the French Colonialism in Algeria and the war. Indeed, he concludes the work with a last chapter "The Revolution within the Revolution" focusing on the war.

Bourdieu reciprocated by dedicating the 1965 publication of *Un art moyen* to Aron.

19. It is important to recall the symbolic importance of the role of secular public education in France at the time when Bourdieu and Passeron offered their criticism. The secular and tuition-free public education system was a crowning achievement of the Third Republic in its conflict with the Church, the monarchy, and conservatism. In the eyes of many French, the school was a symbol of egalitarianism against elitism; of democracy against the monarchy; and of liberty against the control of the Church and the dominant classes.

Aron himself had been critical of French university education. As early as 1959 — only four years after his election to the chair of sociology at the Sorbonne—Aron wrote for *Le Figaro* an article, "The Great Misery of the Sorbonne," in which he complained of overcrowding. In 1960 he followed with four major articles on "The University in Crisis" in which he denounced the tendency in French higher education to emphasize "rhetorical qualities" and the learning of a "general culture" rather than preparing teachers and students in research skills. These were criticisms also voiced by Bourdieu and Passeron. But the class-based indictment by Bourdieu and Passeron of university culture and the teaching profession was too unsettling for Aron.

20. That the break between the two left a sense of deep disappointment and frustrated expectations, there can be no doubt. In his memoirs, Aron echoes his side of that deception: "At the time, he promised everything that he has fulfilled, one of the 'greats' of his generation; but he gave no indication of what he has become—the leader of a sect, self-confident and domineering, skilled in university intrigue and merciless towards any who might cause him offense. In human terms, I expected differently of him" (quoted in Colquhoun 1986:10). Bourdieu has never written his version of the affair.

21. Bourdieu was not alone in his sharp disagreement with Aron over May 1968. Aron and Touraine as well broke off communication over Touraine's enthusiastic embrace of the events of May (Colquhoun 1986:340).

22. An account of the relations between Aron and Bourdieu that is favorable to Aron can be found in Baverez 1993.

If Bourdieu broke with Aron over May 68, this was not because of Bourdieu's enthusiastic embrace of the student revolt as was the case of Touraine (1968). Bourdieu's relationship to the student movement was in fact ambivalent. Like other leading French thinkers, Bourdieu did not anticipate the May 1968 revolt. *The Inheritors* had contributed to the growing critical consciousness among some student leaders of class inequalities in French higher education (Lindenberg 1975:31). Yet, his theory and research on French higher education at that time emphasized the reproduction of French social structure, not its possibility for change. Indeed, the book was criticized in *Les temps moderns* for suggesting that French university students did not form a social class and were hence incapable of class-based mobilization (Bourdieu and Hahn 1970:19–20). In 1970 he and Passeron would publish *Reproduction: In Education, Society and Culture*, where the theme of the social reproduction of educational institutions receives its strongest emphasis. Moreover, in 1968, Bourdieu, Chamboredon, and Passeron published *The Craft of Sociology*, in which the central concern was one of defining the necessary conditions for an epistemologically informed practice of sociology rather than advocating political practice.[23]

Bourdieu's early silence regarding the events of 1968 is conspicuous, for the French student movement received special attention from all the other leading French sociologists at the time.[24] Only when secure in the highest and most prestigious academic position in French academe at the Collège de France did Bourdieu publish, in *Homo Academicus*, his interpretation of May 1968.[25] This critical study, which will be examined in chapter 7, emphasizes the role of the professional interests within the university teaching profession in contributing to the crisis. Though himself a critic of the status quo, Bourdieu remains skeptical of the real significance of the French May 1968 experience. Even today, he describes it as only a "symbolic revolution" or "collective trauma" that, while contributing to the reemergence of cultural conservatism in the academy, has been "without political consequences" or any genuine social transformation (Bourdieu and Haacke 1994:72).

PROFESSIONALIZING AND DEVELOPING A CENTER

It became something of an initiation rite for the post–World War II generation of French sociologists to make their pilgrimage to the Mecca of soci-

23. As one of Aron's teaching assistants at the Sorbonne in the sixties when Aron was preparing *Main Currents in Sociological Thought* (1965), Bourdieu taught Durkheim and other sociological classics rather than social movements or action-oriented sociology.

24. Aron (1968), Crozier (1969), Boudon (1969, 1970, 1971) and Touraine (1968), for example, all offered analyses of the events.

25. In a 1971 article "la defense du corps" (Bourdieu, Boltanski, and Maldidier 1971) Bourdieu did indicate some of the main ideas that would be developed in *Homo Academicus*.

ology, the United States. Several made their name in France for the intellectual products they imported from the United States. Stoetzel brought social psychology and opinion polling, Bourricaud brought Parsonian functionalism, and Boudon brought methods from the Lazsarsfeld tradition. Bourdieu, too, went to the United States in the 1960s for brief visits to the Institute for Advanced Study in Princeton and the University of Pennsylvania. At Penn he met Erving Goffman, whose work Bourdieu helped introduce in France through translation. Bourdieu claims Goffman influenced him considerably, though he seldom cites him. While it would be incorrect to say that Bourdieu founded a Goffman current in French sociology, he employs some of Goffman's concepts, such as the "total institution," in his own work (Bourdieu 1989c:112). More importantly, Bourdieu finds in Goffman's strong sense of agency a strategic corrective to French structuralism.

Bourdieu's efforts during the 1960s and early '70s focused on developing a professional sociology as distinct from the academic sociology taught in the universities and the media-oriented sociology that flourished in French intellectual circles. Early pieces critical of Touraine's sociology of action (Bourdieu 1974b) and Morin's focus on the mass media (Bourdieu 1963) would help demarcate a distinct niche in French sociology. Bourdieu's sociology would be critical though not prophetic, theoretical though empirically researchable, and scientific though not positivist. In the Durkheimian tradition he worked to found a school that would legitimize and institutionalize his vision for sociological inquiry. He did all of his teaching in graduate research seminars at the Ecole des Hautes Etudes en Sciences Sociales and the Ecole Normale. Rarely did he make public political declarations in the tradition of Parisian intellectuals. Initially active in the publication and professional life of French sociology, he redirected his efforts to develop his own research center and successfully attracted a number of able collaborators.[26] Most of Bourdieu's published work has been generated out of his research center, and bears the imprint of these collaborative efforts. Failing to secure the commanding voice he sought in the principal French sociological journal, the *Revue Française de Sociologie* (and also with *Theory and Society*, where there is a brief collaborative effort with Alvin Gouldner), he founded in 1975 his own journal, *Actes de la Recherche en Sciences Sociales*. This made him the only contemporary French sociologist

26. Bourdieu's Center for European Sociology is situated in that institutional arena of semipublic research centers outside of the university where most sociology in postwar France was in fact produced. Though he did receive funding from Kodak for the study of photography (Bourdieu, Boltanski et al. 1965), his center did not depend on private funding nor has it thrived on government contract research. Bourdieu built up his center largely through public resources from the EHESS (see Drouard 1982).

with his own professional review. Many of his books since 1975 are in fact elaborations of articles first published in *Actes*.[27]

An extensive survey of French consumer practices, cultural tastes and lifestyles and further analysis of his Algerian data in the 1970s culminated in two major books, *Distinction: A Social Critique of the Judgement of Taste* [1979] and *The Logic of Practice* [1980] that helped him gain entry into the Collège de France in 1981.[28] *Distinction* was a commercial success and brought Bourdieu considerable media attention. The new public notoriety, however, did not diminish his productivity. The 1980s brought to fruition his long-standing efforts of critical study of the French university and the system of the *grandes écoles*. His study of the university faculties and professorate culminated in the 1984 publication of *Homo Academicus*. The research project on the *grandes écoles*, begun in the early '70s, finally was published in *La noblesse d'Etat* in 1989. In 1992 he would publish *Les règles de l'art*, which assembles his work on Flaubert—a sort of sociological response to Sartre—and the rise of artistic and literary fields in France.

Near the end of the decade he began a new research project on public housing policy in France (Bourdieu 1990b; Bourdieu, Bouhedja, and Givry 1990; Bourdieu, Bouhedja et al. 1990). This was followed in the early nineties by a massive interviewing project of lower-middle-class individuals on the theme of "social suffering." This research lead to the publication of *La Misère du monde* (1993), which was also a commercial success.

In 1993 he received the CNRS Gold Metal for outstanding contribution to scientific research. This prestigious award is seldom given to someone in the social sciences, and therefore represents special recognition by the French scientific community of sociology as a social science and of Bourdieu as its most recognized spokesperson.[29]

Despite continuing a rigorous research agenda, Bourdieu made a shift in the style of his published work. An increasing number of his publications in the 1980s and '90s consisted of collections of interviews, lectures, and conferences (Bourdieu 1990c, 1993d, 1994; Bourdieu and Haacke 1994; Bourdieu and Wacquant 1992). More and more, he adopted the interview format rather than the highly formalized writing characterizing most of his previous work.

27. After the creation of *Actes*, Bourdieu stopped publishing in the *Revue Française de Sociologie*—a further indication of his firm intention to found his own school of sociology.

28. Founded in 1549 by François I, the Collège is an academically prestigious institute for advanced study whose small tenured faculty (slightly over 50 chairs) are selected by voting members as the most accomplished representatives of their disciplines. Bourdieu's election to the Collège pitted him against his principal competitor at the EHESS, Alain Touraine. The influential voices of Aron, Lévi-Strauss, and Braudel made Bourdieu's victory possible.

29. Lévi-Strauss had received it in 1968.

After 1981, Bourdieu also shifted his time and interests from his Center for European Studies and the EHSS to the Collège. Having solidified his position in French sociology and the French intellectual world, he is now able to devote increased attention to international intellectual markets. There has been increased travel to other European countries, United States, and Japan.

He launched in 1989 *Liber: Revue Européenne des Livres*, which is designed to provide an independent forum for intellectual exchange that struggles against all forms of national, regional, and professional provincialism that divide intellectuals. Because of financial limitations, it has since become an annex of *Actes*. In the late '80s and early '90s one saw increased political activism with high profile media attention.

The Significance of Philosophical Thought on Bourdieu

Next I examine several pivotal intellectual influences that have shaped Bourdieu's approach to sociological inquiry. I have been selective, as Bourdieu draws from an unusually wide range of sources. I focus on Bachelard, Sartre, Lévi-Strauss, Marx, Weber, and Durkheim, and on his early ethno-graphic field experience in Algeria. Bourdieu also draws inspiration from Austin, Cassirer, Heidegger, Husserl, Merleau-Ponty, and Wittgenstein in developing his logic of practice and particularly the role of language. I note but do not examine systematically these influences. Their impact on Bourdieu's treatment of language, which is not examined in this book, can be observed in the edited collection of Bourdieu's papers on language and the helpful introduction by John B. Thompson (Bourdieu 1991c).

In approaching the Bourdieu's work it is helpful—particularly for British and American social scientists—to keep in mind that he originally studied philosophy and approaches his social scientific work through distinctly philosophical concerns.[30] Bourdieu (1987b:40) himself explains that

philosophers are much more present in my work than I can say. . . . Sociological research as I conceptualize it is also a good terrain for doing what Austin called "fieldwork in philosophy."

30. Philosophy has played a much more central role in the formation of French sociologists of Bourdieu's generation than it has in British and particularly in North American sociology. Several of Bourdieu's contemporaries, such as Raymond Boudon and Alain Touraine, were also trained in philosophy, and it is possible to see traces of that formative period on their subsequent work. Boudon (1980), for example, has written on the epistemology of social science. But none has used as self-consciously and systematically as has Bourdieu social science to explore key philosophical questions relative to knowledge, perception, action, choice, and determinism.

It is indeed appropriate to think of Bourdieu's sociology as "fieldwork in philosophy." Some of his work quite explicitly seeks to translate philosophical issues and concepts into social scientific research.[31] Moreover, a polemical thrust emerges in this effort, namely, to dethrone the idealist tradition of philosophy—particularly strong in the French academy—by taking the noble concepts, such as Kant's theory of aesthetics, and finding their embodiment not in the life of the mind or movement of reason, but in the mundane, practical activities of everyday life, such as eating, dressing, and exercising.[32] For Bourdieu, philosophy is an ideal-typical form of symbolic violence that lays claim to universal forms of knowledge totally independent of their social location. He is sharply critical of all forms of intellectual practice—particularly philosophical—that resist being situated socially (see Bourdieu 1983b).

But it is also Bourdieu's clear aim to set sociological inquiry on a firm epistemological foundation.[33] To do this, Bourdieu draws from several different philosophical currents that have shaped French intellectual thought since the 1930s. One of the most distinctive features of his sociology is his effort to integrate into his sociology elements from these philosophical schools.

Foucault (1978b) observes that French philosophy since 1930 has been divided by two broad traditions: the phenomenological/existential and the history and philosophy of science. The former focuses on experience, perception, and subjectivity as it tackles the problem of relations between knowledge and the knowing subject. Both Merleau-Ponty's phenomenology and Sartre's existentialism flow from this tradition. The latter focuses on knowledge itself and queries the development and structure of scientific reason independent of the knowing subject. Lévi-Strauss's structuralism comes out of this tradition. Bourdieu's intellectual lineage clearly owes much more to the second camp; yet his intellectual project represents a critical dialogue with both.

As a student in the 1950s, Bourdieu studied the key phenomenological

31. In *Distinction*, for example, he frames his study of French patterns of lifestyle and taste with a critique of Kant's thought on aesthetic judgment.

32. The sheer idea that sociology could address philosophical issues shows how Bourdieu takes aim at the core of the elite intellectual tradition in postwar France. As Jean d'Ormesson observed, "immediately after the war, and for several years thereafter, philosophy carried incomparable prestige. I don't know if I can describe, now, at this distance, what it represented for us. The nineteenth century was, perhaps, the century of history; the mid twentieth century seemed dedicated to philosophy . . . literature, painting, historical studies, politics, theater, and film were all in philosophy's hands" (quoted in Eribon 1991:17).

33. This project finds formal expression in *The Craft of Sociology* in which Bourdieu, along with Chambordeon and Passeron, define a program for an epistemologically informed practice of sociology.

writings of Heidegger, Husserl, Schutz, Merleau-Ponty, and Sartre. His student generation clearly felt the towering influence of Sartre, though by the 1950s a shift away from existentialism was already apparent. Reflecting upon his student experience, Bourdieu (1987b:15) says he "never participated in the existentialist *mood*"—an intellectual orientation that provided more appeal to students of bourgeois origins than to those of lower-middle-class background from the provinces, such as himself. Despite his training in philosophy and the influence of existentialism on postwar French thought, Bourdieu developed an early preference for the sciences, and in fact at one point considered majoring in biology. The popularity of existentialist thought, he contends, worked to impede the development of the social sciences in France. Sartre, in particular, held the social sciences in low esteem, making them unattractive options for aspiring young French intellectuals. Hence the importance Bourdieu attributes to the phenomenologist Merleau-Ponty, who played for young Bourdieu a key role by taking seriously into account the social sciences in his philosophical work. It was in fact Merleau-Ponty and philosophers of science, such as Gaston Bachelard, Georges Canguilhem, and Jules Vuillemin, whom Bourdieu (1987b:14) recalls as the most formative philosophical influences upon his early intellectual life.

The influence of phenomenology and existentialism is nonetheless both substantively and conceptually present in Bourdieu's work. Substantively, he carried out later in his career a study situating Heidegger in his political and intellectual milieu (Bourdieu 1991f). Moreover, it was clearly Sartre who motivated Bourdieu's (1988a) study of Flaubert. Conceptually, his interest in reintroducing agency into structural analysis reflects the early influence of existentialism. And from phenomenology Bourdieu (1967) takes the idea that even the most mundane activities of human life may be subjected to philosophical inquiry.[34]

Nevertheless, the more important formative influence is to be found in the history and philosophy of science of postwar France. Pointing to this intellectual tradition Foucault (1978b:ix) remarks that if "you take away Canguilhem . . . you will no longer understand much about Althusser, Althusserism and a whole series of discussions which have taken place among French Marxists." Speaking of his own work, Bourdieu says, "I tried to transpose into the field of the social sciences a whole epistemological tra-

---

34. Bourdieu would have us see his attention to lifestyles and their relevance for understanding contemporary stratification in France in critical contrast to the more august topics among French leftist social scientists of working-class culture and organization, political mobilization, contemporary capitalism and the state.

dition represented by Bachelard, Canguilhem, [and] Koyré" (Bourdieu, Chamboredon, and Passeron 1991:248). This is a French philosophy-of-science tradition not widely familiar to English-speaking social scientists. It predates yet overlaps with many of the widely acknowledged tenets of Thomas Kuhn's (1962) seminal work on scientific paradigms.[35] As a student, both Bachelard and Canguilhem were for Bourdieu "exemplary prophets in Weber's sense" (Honneth, Kocyba, and Schwibs 1986:36). Their epistemological legacy in Bourdieu's work continues to this day. Indeed, many of Bourdieu's central theoretical concerns remain somewhat elusive to much British and American sociology unless they are understood in light of this philosophical tradition. I turn therefore to a brief discussion of key ideas from Bachelard—the more central thinker for Bourdieu—that animate Bourdieu's conception of the social scientific method.[36]

As a philosopher of science, Bachelard argues that philosophy must come to grips with early-twentieth-century revolutionary changes in physics.[37] For Bachelard, relativity theory and quantum mechanics completely revolutionized the philosophical task as well as the nature of philosophy itself. These changes, he concluded, undermined the existing philosophical traditions of both idealism and empiricism. Philosophy could no longer find grounding in *a priori* categories of reason (Kant), language structures, or in a transcendental subject (Hegel). Reason is historical since modern physics demonstrates that there is historical development within the rational structures and standards of science itself. This historical development unfolds from the confrontation between theory and the empirical world, thereby discrediting both idealist and empiricist views of reality. Scientific knowledge is "constructed" and "dialectical" knowledge, one that does not arrive at final truths but proceeds as an ongoing project of correction and rectification of past errors. Thus, the logic of scientific discovery, Bachelard argues, points to a new kind of philosophical task that must be carried on without the traditional foundations. The philosopher must adopt the "dialectical reason" of science, which does not need to be grounded in the *a priori* reasoning capacities of a knowing subject or in an independent empirical world. Bachelard therefore proposes a reflexive epistemology, one that

35. Bourdieu's generation of *normalien* philosophy students were familiar with the Bachelard, Canguilhem, and Koyré epistemological tradition prior to the publication of Kuhn's work.

36. The influence of Bachelard can be readily seen in *The Craft of Sociology*.

37. This short summary of Bachelard represents a reading of Bachelard with an eye toward explicating Bourdieu rather than providing a coherent introduction to Bachelard's intellectual project. I have drawn from Bachelard's *La formation de l'esprit scientifique* (1980), the selected Bachelard texts appearing in Bourdieu's methodological textbook, *The Craft of Sociology* (1991), and the fine works on Bachelard by Chiari (1975) and Tiles (1984, 1987).

is historical, discontinuous, dialectical, and no longer centered in some continuous, unchanging, or ever-renewing *cogito*.

Bachelard's understanding of dialectical reasoning is not to be confused with Hegelian or Marxist dialectics (Tiles 1987:146). For Bachelard, the dialectical mode of reasoning in science does not replace one theory by another that contradicts the first. Rather, the movement of thought proceeds from a limited conceptual framework, which is closed to some important aspect of experience, to the development of a broader framework that includes the previously excluded aspect. In this way, for example, Euclidean geometry was not replaced but rather superseded and regionally situated within a broader non-Euclidean, space-time conceptual space. Dialectical reason situates the previous theory in a broader conceptual space that highlights both its strengths and limitations. This mode of dialectical thought can include several different theories, which at a given level of logic contradict each other by virtue of their limits, but, when situated within a broader framework, stand in complementary relationships. Former knowledge is not rejected but changed by a sort of realignment in which new fields of knowledge are opened up, forcing a reevaluation of what was previously taken for granted. Such a shift in thought constitutes what Bachelard calls an "epistemological break" with the previous theories.[38]

The logic of scientific discovery thus proceeds by epistemological breaks or paradigmatic shifts. These are cognitive discontinuities or ruptures in logical relations in which previous conceptualizations are superseded by broader, more encompassing frameworks. This means that science is not a cumulative knowledge that progressively broadens its base and builds over time a higher and higher edifice of findings. Rather, Bachelard insists on the discontinuous character of scientific achievement. Scientific progress is marked by abrupt shifts in outlook, not by cumulative knowledge. Earlier conceptualizations and constructs are displaced and replaced by new, more encompassing understandings.[39]

Full awareness of epistemological breaks develops, however, only after they occur. The limitations of existing theories are not immediately apparent. Indeed, Bachelard argues that previous theories can actually operate as "epistemological obstacles" to the progress of science. They be-

---

38. The term is more commonly associated with Althusser. It is in fact Althusser's extrapolation from Bachelard's thought more than Bachelard himself that gives this term currency in French intellectual thought. Althusser (1970:257) claims that the term is rarely found in Bachelard's work and that Canguilhem did not "use this concept *systematically* as I have tried to do." Nonetheless, as Althusser admits, the idea is clearly present in Bachelard's writings.

39. This idea is of course captured in Kuhn's (1962) concept of paradigm.

come obstacles when they assume a necessary, taken-for-granted status in ordering scientific work. In the history of science, Bachelard argues, both rationalism and empiricism were important constructions in the early phases of the history of science. But as they became part of the everyday reasoning of practicing scientists they became epistemological obstacles to further progress and therefore needed to be rejected in favor of new constructions.

If scientific progress is marked by fundamental shifts in conceptualization of reality, how can such shifts be facilitated, particularly since the obstacles to progress in scientific thought never become visible until after the fact? Bachelard's answer is that the dialectical reason of science operates by negation; it operates as an ongoing polemic against existing, established procedures and theories. By refusing to grant existing theories a kind of universal status, dialectical reason offers the dynamic potential for transformation. Further, relevant knowledge for seeking out and overcoming epistemological obstacles goes beyond the conceptual, cognitive foundations of an intellectual discipline to include all the social, cultural, and psychological factors that shape our perception of particular theoretical issues and our theorizing about them. Here Bachelard opens the door to sociological factors as conditions that can shape the processes of reason and scientific discovery. He sees a unique role for epistemology as a necessary reflexive monitoring instrument for increasing awareness of both the cognitive and social conditions that shape and limit existing scientific work. Epistemological reflection on previous theories makes it possible to investigate precisely what they assume and to enhance the chances for an epistemological break.

Bachelard therefore sees his philosophy of science as "open," since scientific reason is historical, discontinuous, dialectical, and reflexive. New scientific knowledge obtains through an ongoing process of negations and new syntheses. Since this dynamic process is continually modifying and bringing into perspective new angles on the past through elimination and rectification of past errors, the task of scientific construction is never fully completed once and for all. The scientist continually confronts epistemological obstacles that must be overcome in order to achieve new scientific knowledge. For Bachelard, error continually reasserts itself as existing theories assume the status of a necessary truth.

Finally, for Bachelard, scientific knowledge must be constructed in opposition to everyday practical knowledge, by struggling against such spontaneous proclivities of the human mind as taking events and experiences at face value or becoming easily captivated by particularly vivid impressions.

Bachelard argues that these natural inclinations of human thought are the working matter for art and poetry. But science is a constructed knowledge that can be developed only through an epistemological break, or rupture, with everyday reasoning.[40]

Bourdieu draws inspiration from these aspects of Bachelard's thought in developing his sociological method. Like Bachelard, Bourdieu is sharply critical of empiricism and positivism. He presents his early programmatic statement on the sociological method in *The Craft of Sociology*—where his indebtedness to Bachelard is most explicit—as a means of correcting for the positivist climate in French sociology of the 1950s and '60s. In that work, Bourdieu charges that empiricism and positivism focus on the logic of verification while leaving unattended the sources of scientific discovery. Bourdieu wants to remove the process of theory construction from the realm of individual intuition or genius to discover its underlying logic (Bourdieu, Chamboredon, and Passeron 1991:vi–vii). He is interested in calling attention to the *research process* itself and stresses that the sociologist's relationship to his or her practice is usually mediated by values, attitudes and their representations that are frequently quite remote from the formal standards of verification. Thus one can see his interest in and influence by Bachelard, who calls attention to the "constructed" nature of scientific knowledge and who calls for reflexive monitoring of the assumptions that enter into the scientific construction process. Bourdieu adopts this reflexive method as the trademark of his sociology.

Bourdieu extrapolates from Bachelard's dialectical reason three epistemological checkpoints for sociological research (ibid., 11). He builds from "Bachelard's premise that the *scientific fact is won, constructed, and confirmed*." First, and foremost, is the idea that scientific knowledge must break with received views of the social world, whether they be everyday lay constructions or taken-for-granted theoretical perspectives. Scientific knowledge is a constructed knowledge, one that is built *against* previous conceptualizations. Second, the scientific method involves the construction of formalized models; and, third, these models must receive empirical verification. Each of the three epistemological acts can be associated with a particular research technique:

40. The idea that the most important scientific discoveries oppose everyday, common-sense assumptions is an argument made not only by Bachelard but by many other philosophers of science, including the eminent British scientist, Lewis Wolpert. One of Wolpert's (1993) main theses is precisely that the most significant discoveries of the sciences violate the precepts of common sense. He argues that the styles of thought employed in the fundamental principles of science are radically different from those employed by humans in everyday reasoning.

the break with the distancing power of ethnological vocabulary, construction with the specific effect of formalism, or verification with the most standardized forms of the questionnaire. (57)[41]

Bourdieu proposes these three epistemological acts in a *logical* rather than a chronological order. Rather than a series of discrete steps, each is simultaneously present in all phases of the research process. Theory formulation, data collection, concept measurement, and analytical techniques are for Bourdieu all intimately related. Theory calls forth and is rooted in data; data and their organization and verification embody theory.

Bourdieu sees this epistemological monitoring as a necessary corrective to positivism where the logic of verification (considered the substance of the scientific method) is detached from the logic of hypothesis formation and theory generation. Bourdieu, like Bachelard before him, emphasizes the importance of theory formation and the development of a kind of mental orientation (what Bourdieu calls a "scientific habitus") that implements an "epistemological vigilance" over *all* aspects of the research process. Just as Bachelard's epistemology rejects both idealism and empiricism, Bourdieu too rejects the distinction between theory and research in sociology. His method emphasizes integrating the two at every stage of sociological inquiry.

Finally, one can observe Bourdieu adopting Bachelard's "applied rationalism" to argue for a social science situated between two epistemological extremes: idealism and realism (221). Bourdieu adopts a similar cognitive strategy to Bachelard's in an effort to construct an epistemological consciousness for the social sciences that transcends but incorporates within a broader framework the partial views of what he calls "subjectivism" and "objectivism." By *subjectivism*, Bourdieu means all those forms of knowledge that focus on individual or intersubjective consciousness and interactions. By *objectivism* he means all those forms of knowledge that focus on the statistical regularities of human conduct. Both his key concepts, *habitus* and *field* display a similar movement of thought. Habitus calls for moving to a conception of action and structure that breaks with and transcends the traditional dichotomies of subjectivism and objectivism. Field follows a similar movement by situating individuals, groups, and institutions within a broader matrix of structuring relations. Chapters 3 and 4 will explore these conceptual strategies in more detail.

---

41. But Bourdieu resists reducing the epistemological requirements to the use of particular research instruments.

Sartre and Lévi-Strauss

Two towering intellectual figures, Jean-Paul Sartre and Claude Lévi-Strauss, have been imposing references for all contemporary French thinkers in the period following World War II. For Bourdieu, the confrontation between these two intellectual models clearly shaped his intellectual and professional orientation. They represent, for Bourdieu, opposite types of knowledge and vocation for intellectuals: Sartre the subjectivist and engaged humanist and Lévi-Strauss the objectivist and detached scientist.[42] Both models are important for understanding the kind of synthesis that Bourdieu develops in his own work and career.

In terms of models for the political vocation of an intellectual in postwar France, Sartre had come to incarnate the prophetic image of the "total" intellectual, fully committed to political engagement, and the carrier of a world view that could be applied to every issue of the day. Sartre zealously pursued this intellectual and political agenda. Quoting Sartre's familiar imperative from the manifesto in the first issue of *Les Temps Modernes*, "We must miss nothing of our time," Bourdieu observed that in fact Sartre rarely did (Bourdieu and Passeron 1967:175). From pronouncements on the Algerian War, reasons for adhering or not adhering to the French Communist Party, criticism of colonialism and the Vietnam War, to commentary on art and theater, Sartre and his fellow travelers of *Les Temps Modernes* were "perfect illustrations of this policy of being present at all the outposts of the intellectual front and participating in all the avant-garde movements" (157). They were "always . . . chasing after the latest 'alienation'" motivated "by the desire to 'miss nothing'" (176). Bourdieu, however, has from the beginning followed a quite different intellectual role, one that is much closer to the model of a professional sociologist than of a public intellectual.

In sharp contrast to the Sartrean model of the total intellectual, Lévi-Strauss emerged to offer for the young Bourdieu a more compelling intellectual vocation. Bourdieu describes in the preface of *The Logic of Practice* (1990h:1–2) how Lévi-Strauss appeared for Bourdieu in the postwar period as an antithetical model for the intellectual vocation.

It is not easy to communicate the social effects that the work of Claude Lévi-Strauss produced in the French intellectual field, or the concrete mediations through which a whole generation was led to adopt a new way of conceiving intellectual activity that was opposed in a thoroughly dialectical fashion to the figure of the politically committed "total" intellectual represented by Jean-Paul Sartre.

---

42. Poster (1975:323–34) provides a good summary of the spirited exchange between Lévi-Strauss and Sartre in the early sixties.

It is Lévi-Strauss who offers to Bourdieu a "new way of conceptualizing intellectual activity" that in contrast to Sartre made it possible to "reconcile theoretical and practical aims, scientific and ethical or political vocations . . . through a more humble and responsible manner of fulfilling their task as researchers" (8). "Equally removed from pure science as from exemplary prophecy" Bourdieu's intellectual vocation, which will be explored further in chapter 10, is to use science to demystify relations of power. It is to be fundamentally a political project, but one that finds its method in the practice of science rather than in the public practice of political position-taking à la Sartre.

This is not to say that Bourdieu does not share many of Sartre's political sentiments or that he has been totally absent from the French political scene. Bourdieu has been consistently on the French political left since his student days at the Ecole Normale Supérieure. He published five articles in *Les Temps Modernes* during the 1960s and has regularly been associated with the CFDT, the Socialist trade union. But his "political practice" has been markedly different from that of Sartre or the common image one has of the Parisian Left Bank intellectual. Bourdieu rarely signs public petitions, participates in public demonstrations, or writes about strategies for political engagement.

Bourdieu sees his intellectual vocation as one of providing conceptual tools and research findings that can be employed by political activists in various struggles against domination. It is his "wish to approach burning political issues in a scientifically disciplined way" (Honneth, Kocyba, and Schwibs 1986:43). His response to the Algerian War was characteristic. Rather than participate in public demonstrations in Paris against the war, Bourdieu researched peasant attitudes and behavior toward their changing economic situation and wrote scholarly publications on the topic. He admits in retrospect that this effort had no impact on the course of the war or French policy toward Algeria (39).

A piece of research that did have an important public impact and that first gave Bourdieu public visibility in France was *The Inheritors*. Although it was used by French student activists in 1968 and probably influenced some of their analysis of the class bias of the French university, the book was written primarily as a scholarly work that critically examined patterns of class-based educational opportunity and cultural ideals in the student population.

But Sartre and Lévi-Strauss also represented for Bourdieu two radically different approaches for understanding social life. Sartre emphasized the role of the freely choosing, creative, undetermined consciousness of the individual subject whereas Lévi-Strauss focused on the causal power of structures that operate beyond the consciousness of individuals to shape their choices. Bourdieu sees in this paradigmatic opposition the roots of a broader, and more fundamental, opposition that structures all intellectual thought and stands as a veritable obstacle to the development of a genuine social science of practices (Bourdieu 1990h:43). Two modes of knowledge, the subjectivist epitomized by Sartre and the objectivist represented by Lévi-Strauss, stand in sharp opposition and find expression in a variety of forms in the social sciences.

Bourdieu sees his work as an effort to identify the social and epistemological conditions that make possible these two forms of knowledge. Indeed, his work can be read as an effort to "move beyond the antagonism between these modes of knowledge, while preserving the gains from each of them" (Bourdieu 1990h:25). The influence of Bachelard's dialectical method is obvious. Chapter 3 examines how Bourdieu attempts to construct a general social theory that addresses this dilemma.

Classical Sociological Theory

Though Bourdieu actively eschews association with any one of the three classical sociologists—Marx, Durkheim, and Weber—he in fact draws significantly and selectively from each, synthesizing their works in two respects. First, he suggests that whereas Durkheim, Marx, and Weber hold sharply contrasting theories of the social world, they in fact share the same "epistemological and logical principles of social knowledge" (Bourdieu 1968:682). Their theories of sociological knowledge actually converge in what Bourdieu calls the "principle of non-consciousness" (Bourdieu, Chamboredon, and Passeron 1991:15–18), which posits that the scientific explanation of social life does not reduce to common everyday perceptions or individual ideas or intentions. Here Bourdieu joins the classical sociological tradition with Bachelard.

Second, Bourdieu pursues a sort of "dialectical eclecticism" in which he critically juxtaposes Marx, Weber, and Durkheim by highlighting what he views as their respective contributions and limitations to the study of symbolic power (Bourdieu 1977d, 1991b, 1993d; Bourdieu and Passeron 1977:4–5). Chapter 4 will examine this synthesis. Here we will identify the central themes he adopts from each.[43]

MARX

While some early British and American interpretations of Bourdieu's work wrongly identify him as a Marxist (notably Inglis 1979), more recent critical

---

43. My presentation of Bourdieu's connection to the classic sociological tradition draws in part from the important article by Brubaker (1985).

reviews rightfully recognize the relatively stronger influence of Durkheim and especially Weber (see Brubaker 1985; DiMaggio 1979).[44] Marxist critics point out in particular the Durkheimian lineage. These critics notwithstanding, Bourdieu clearly appropriates for his work a number of key themes from Marx. At the same time he reserves some of his harshest criticism for Marxist theorizing.

From Marx, Bourdieu draws his general program to write a sociology of reproduction. He accepts from historical materialism the primacy of class conflict and material interests as fundamental pillars of social inequality in modern societies. Yet, he is sharply critical of class reductionist accounts of cultural life. Chapter 7 will show that Bourdieu does not restrict the concept of class to position in the social relations of production; he thinks of class in more general terms of conditions of existence that can include education, gender, age, and status as well as property.

Bourdieu is a materialist in the sense that he roots human consciousness in practical social life. He is also concerned with forms of false consciousness or, in his terms, *misrecognition* of power relations. He accepts the Marxian idea that symbolic systems fulfill social functions of domination and reproduction of class inequality. Yet he is critical of the view of ideology that focuses largely on the social functions of symbolic goods and practices without showing how they are necessary features for the enactment of social practices. While Bourdieu accepts the Marxist claim that cultural practices function to legitimate and perpetuate class inequality, he resists focusing on the symbolic dimension of social life as separate and derivative of the more fundamental material components of social life. He in fact rejects the Marxist infrastructure/superstructure conceptual distinction, which he believes to be rooted in the classic idealism/materialism dichotomy that must be transcended. Here Bourdieu parts company with the structuralist Marxism of Althusser (1970).[45] In his revisionist approach to the Marxist distinction between infrastructure and superstructure, Althusser theorizes that in certain historical situations superstructural instances, such as culture, ideology,

44. Honneth (1986:55) and Garnham and Williams (1980:129) see a significant Marxist lineage in Bourdieu's emphasis on the role of class struggle in shaping contemporary culture. But, as we shall see in chapter 7, Bourdieu's concept of class is hardly Marxist, and his emphasis on struggle stems more from an anthropological premise that the search for distinction constitutes a fundamental dynamic of social identity than it does from dynamics specific to capitalism. The erroneous classification of Bourdieu as fundamentally Marxist is not confined to British and American observers, however. Some French critics (e.g., Ferry and Renault 1990) also situate Bourdieu broadly within a Marxist intellectual framework.

45. Bourdieu sharply criticizes Althusserian Marxism for three reasons: it treats actors as simple adjuncts to structures, it relegates culture to a highly formalized subsystem of superstructure, and it discourages actual empirical investigation.

religion, and politics, can obtain relative autonomy from infrastructure and play a dominant role in shaping class relations; in the last instance, however, the economy is always determinative. Bourdieu shares the basic materialist outlook of Althusser and his emphasis on the relative autonomy of religion and culture from politics and economics.[46] Still, Bourdieu's position is not fundamentally Althusserian. Inspired by Marx's first thesis on Feuerbach, which emphasizes the underlying unity of all social life as practical activity,[47] Bourdieu (1984a:467) rejects the idea that social existence can be segmented and hierarchically organized into distinct spheres, such as the social, the cultural, and the economic. Rather than explore the various forms of articulation of the superstructure and infrastructure as Althusserians do, Bourdieu argues that the two realms are not to be separated in the first place. Instead of distinguishing superstructure from infrastructure, Bourdieu conceptualizes the social world as a series of relatively autonomous but structurally homologous fields of production, circulation, and consumption of various forms of cultural as well as material resources. Bourdieu's concept of field functions as a mediation area between the infrastructure and superstructure where cultural producers and their institutionalized arena of production reunite the two instances that Marxist theory separates. Bourdieu seeks to write a general science of practices that combines both material and symbolic dimensions and thereby emphasizes the fundamental *unity* of social life. Nonetheless, Bourdieu's central concern with the problem of relations between the symbolic and material aspects of social life and between structure and agency stem in part from his early confrontations with this particular Marxist tradition. And his idea of the relative autonomy of fields bears the imprint of Althusser's thought.

Finally, like Marx, Bourdieu employs a critical method in constructing his social science. Nevertheless, the significance of Bourdieu's relationship to Marx lies less in an attempt to appropriate particular concepts and to give them a specific Marxist application in his work than in an effort to elaborate upon certain themes inherited from Marx by drawing more directly from the work of Durkheim and especially Weber (Brubaker 1985).

46. Indeed, at times Bourdieu echoes the Althusserian position when, for example, he posits that actor dispositions are "engendered . . . in the last analysis, by the economic bases of the social formation in question" (Bourdieu 1977c:83).

47. The epigraph to *Outline of a Theory of Practice* (1977c) is from Marx's first thesis on Feuerbach: "The chief defect of all hitherto existing materialism—that of Feuerbach included—is that the thing, reality, sensuousness, is conceived only in the form of the object or of *contemplation*, but not as *human sensuous activity*, *practice*, not subjectively. Hence it happened that the *active* side, in contradistinction to materialism, was developed by idealism— but only abstractly, since, of course, idealism does not know real, sensuous activity as such" (quoted from Tucker 1978:143).

WEBER

From Marx, Bourdieu turns to Max Weber for the conceptual tools to elaborate a theory of symbolic goods and practices that would transcend both class reductionism and idealism. Bourdieu (1990h:17) remarks that it is Weber "who, far from opposing Marx, as is generally thought, with a spiritualist theory of history, in fact carries the materialist mode of thought into areas which Marxist materialism effectively abandons to spiritualism." Bourdieu (1990c:36) sees Weber offering a "political economy of religion" that brings out "the full potential of the materialist analysis of religion without destroying the properly symbolic character of the phenomenon." One central objective of Bourdieu's sociology is to elaborate Weber's model for a political economy of religion to *all* cultural and social life. Indeed, Bourdieu (107) sees his sociology of culture to be of the same character as that of Weber who used "the economic model to extend materialist critique into the realm of religion." It is to be a "generalized" or "radical" materialism, but one that avoids the class reductionism that Bourdieu believes characterizes Marxism (1990c:17; 1993d:12). Bourdieu believes he has found in this generalized materialism a way to transcend the classic idealism/materialism dichotomy in the social sciences.

Bourdieu's work represents an important elaboration of Weber's notion of ideal goods and interests.[48] The idea of "religious interest" comes from Weber's emphasis on the "this-worldly" character of behavior motivated by religious belief. Weber (1978:399) writes that "the most elementary forms of behavior motivated by religious or magical factors are oriented to *this* world." He goes on to stress that "religious or magical behavior or thinking must not be set apart from the range of everyday purposive conduct, particularly since even the ends of the religious and magical actions are predominantly economic." Bourdieu (1990h:4) argues that by insisting on the "this-worldly" character of behavior motivated by religious factors Weber provides a "way of linking the contents of mythical discourse (and even its syntax) to the religious interests of those who produce it, diffuse it, and receive it." Thus, Weber provides a means for connecting religious beliefs and practices to the interests of those who produce and administer them.

Bourdieu (1987d:122), however, considers Weber's notion of "religious interest" to be "only weakly elaborated" since it limits the scope of interest to be "determined by the agents' conditions of existence." In contrast, Bourdieu stresses that religious interests—and symbolic interests

---

48. Recall Weber's famous declaration that "not ideas, but material and ideal interests, directly govern men's conduct" (Gerth and Mills 1970:280).

more generally—"are also determined in their form and their conditions of expression by the supply of religion and the action of the religious professionals." Nonetheless, Weber's thinking permits one to construct a

system of religious beliefs and practices as the more or less transfigured expression of the strategies of different categories of specialists competing for monopoly over the administration of the goods of salvation and of the different classes interested in their services. (Bourdieu 1991b:4)

Bourdieu extends the idea of interest to include nonmaterial goods by arguing that *all* practices are fundamentally "interested" whether directed toward material or symbolic items. He wants to construct a "science of practices" that will analyze "all practices" as "oriented towards the maximization of material or symbolic profit" (Bourdieu 1990h:209). The research program he proposes would unite what has traditionally been thought of as economic (interested and material) and noneconomic (disinterested and symbolic) forms of action and objects. Thus, symbolic interest and material interest are viewed as two equally objective forms of interest. Actors pursue symbolic as well as material interests and exchange one for the other under specified conditions.

While extending the idea of interest from material to ideal goods, Weber nonetheless retains analytical distinctions for different types of behavior. Weber (1978:24–25, 339) analytically distinguishes the following types of action: "instrumentally rational," "value-rational," "affectional," and "traditional." Weber does not consider every action as economic. To be economic, action must satisfy a need that depends upon relatively scarce resources and a limited number of actions. Such distinctions disappear altogether in Bourdieu's work. Moreover, the idea that action is interest-oriented is for Bourdieu a fundamental presupposition not a hypothesis for testing. And he does not consider whether some practices might be more self-interested than others.

 The extension of Weber's idea of religious interest permits Bourdieu to develop concepts such as *religious capital* and *cultural capital* as irreducible forms of power though interchangeable with economic capital. With the concept of cultural capital, Bourdieu expands Weber's idea of social closure to include more subtle, informal kinds of exclusionary practices.[49] Bourdieu

---

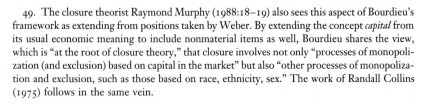

49. The closure theorist Raymond Murphy (1988:18–19) also sees this aspect of Bourdieu's framework as extending from positions taken by Weber. By extending the concept *capital* from its usual economic meaning to include nonmaterial items as well, Bourdieu shares the view, which is "at the root of closure theory," that closure involves not only "processes of monopolization (and exclusion) based on capital in the market" but also "other processes of monopolization and exclusion, such as those based on race, ethnicity, sex." The work of Randall Collins (1975) follows in the same vein.

(1989c:375) conceptualizes resources as capital when they function as a "social relation of *power*" by becoming objects of struggle as valued resources. Bourdieu's (1991b:9) concept of religious capital is close to Weber's idea of religious "qualification." It represents "accumulated symbolic labor" and is connected to the "constitution of a religious field" where a group of religious specialists is able to monopolize the administration of religious goods and services. Religious capital is a power resource, since it implies a form of "objective dispossession" by the constitution of a "laity" who by definition are those without, yet in need of the valued resources controlled by specialists. Bourdieu's concept of cultural capital covers a wide variety of resources, such as verbal facility, general cultural awareness, aesthetic preferences, scientific knowledge, and educational credentials. His point is to suggest that culture (in the broadest sense of the term) can become a power resource.

Bourdieu draws from Weber's notions of charisma and legitimacy to develop a theory of *symbolic power*. This theory stresses the active role played by taken-for-granted assumptions in the constitution and maintenance of power relations. Like Weber, Bourdieu contends that the exercise of power requires legitimation. Bourdieu argues that the logic of self-interest underlying all practices—particularly those in the cultural domain—goes "misrecognized" as a logic of "disinterest." Misrecognition is a key concept for Bourdieu; akin to the idea of "false consciousness" in the Marxist tradition, misrecognition denotes "denial" of the economic and political interests present in a set of practices. Symbolic practices, Bourdieu thus argues, deflect attention from the interested character of practices and thereby contribute to their enactment as disinterested pursuits. Activities and resources gain in symbolic power, or legitimacy, to the extent that they become separated from underlying material interests and hence go misrecognized as representing disinterested forms of activities and resources. Individuals and groups who are able to benefit from the transformation of self-interest into disinterest obtain what Bourdieu calls a *symbolic capital*. Symbolic capital is "denied capital"; it disguises the underlying "interested" relations to which it is related giving them legitimation. Symbolic capital is a form of power that is not perceived as power but as legitimate demands for recognition, deference, obedience, or the services of others.[50] Symbolic capital is a reformulation of Weber's idea of charismatic authority that legitimates power relations by accentuating selected personal qualities of elites as supposedly superior and natural. Bourdieu, however, does not think of the concept as

50. See Bourdieu 1972:227–43, 1977c:171–83, 1990h:112–21, and 1991c:163–70 for key formulations of this concept.

an ideal type or restrict it to leadership but extends the idea as a dimension of all legitimation.[51]

For Bourdieu, the focus by Weber on religious leadership provides the key for understanding how relations of interest become transformed into disinterested relations to create symbolic capital. It is the "symbolic labor" by specialists that transforms relations of power into forms of disinterested honorability (Bourdieu 1977c:171). Bourdieu (1987d:122–24; 1991b:5–13) highlights as particularly insightful Weber's (1978:1177–81) analysis of the "ethicalization" and "systematization" of religious needs of the rising urban bourgeoisie as the product of religious labor by specialists. Religious labor by specialists creates religious understandings of the particular social conditions of existence of specific groups. Symbolic labor produces symbolic power by transforming relations of interest into disinterested meanings. Symbolic labor points to the central role that Bourdieu assigns to intellectuals (symbolic producers) in his analysis of social stratification.

Also from Weber's sociology of religion, Bourdieu derives in part his concept of field to designate competitive arenas where other forms of capital (e.g., symbolic, cultural, social) as well as economic capital are invested, exchanged, and accumulated.[52] The concept is inspired by Weber's discussion of the relations between priest, prophet, and sorcerer (Bourdieu 1991b: 49).[53] Weber identifies the specific and opposing interests of the principal types of religious leadership and the structures of the "competition which opposes them to one another" (Bourdieu 1990c:107). Bourdieu (1987d; 1992:260) proposes a structuralist reinterpretation of Weber's analysis by stressing more than Weber how the interactions between the types of religious leadership are structured by their opposing interests and how these interests are in turn related to broader power structures. Bourdieu (1987d: 121) believes that Weber restricts his analysis to an "interactionist" perspective by focusing on the interpersonal or intersubjective relations among actors. A field perspective, however, introduces a broader grasp of structural conditions that shape the interactions of actors without their being aware of them. Weber's discussion of the specific and opposing interests of the principal types of religious leadership permits Bourdieu to show how particular fields of cultural life emerge through the development of specialized

51. Whereas Weber tended to associate charismatic authority with precapitalist societies, Bourdieu finds it in the form of the ideology of the gifted individual even in modern societies where the rationalized, bureaucratic type of authority predominates.

52. In developing the concept, Bourdieu (1987d) draws primarily from chapter 6 of *Economy and Society* and chapter 15 devoted to domination. He also takes into account the sections of chapter 1 entitled "The Concept of Conflict" and "Hierocratic Organization."

53. It also parallels Weber's idea of "life-orders," which inspires Gerth and Mills's (1964) conceptualization of "institutional orders."

corps of cultural producers. Chapter 6 is devoted to a detailed examination of this key concept.

From Weber's concepts of social classes and status groups, Bourdieu reconceptualizes the relations between class and status by proposing a theory that systematically relates the distinctive marks of lifestyle patterns and attributions of prestige and honor to their material conditions of existence.[54] Whereas Weber thought of class and status as distinct ideal types that can be used to compare and contrast historically specific societies, Bourdieu posits a fundamental principle linking class and status. Status culture is a sort of veneer that legitimates class interest by presenting it under the guise of disinterestedness. Status groups and status distinctions are classes and class distinctions in disguise. Bourdieu thus emphasizes the complementary rather than oppositional nature of relations between class and status. This dimension of Bourdieu's thought is explored further in Chapter 7.

Finally, Bourdieu borrows from Weber's methodology a fundamental distinction for his class analysis. Weber held that "classes" are aggregates of common life chances but not real social groups. Bourdieu adopts this distinction to argue for a "relational" as opposed to a realist approach to social classes. For Bourdieu, social classes are probabilistic constructs that should not be conflated with reality. Modifying the classic Marxist distinction, Bourdieu argues that "classes-on-paper" can become "classes-in-reality" only if there is symbolic and political work to give them actual identity and mobilization. Like Weber, Bourdieu wants to stress that one should not assume that class consciousness and action necessarily flow from objective class conditions. Bourdieu emphasizes the symbolic dimension of class analysis.

DURKHEIM

The influence of Durkheim in Bourdieu's work is beginning to be acknowledged (see Miller and Banson 1987; Wacquant 1992) but seldom given the emphasis that it deserves.[55] Virtually ignored by the immediate postwar generation, Durkheim found renewed interest in the 1960s with the second generation of postwar French sociologists, including Bourdieu. This is the period when several French sociologists sought to find an alternative to

---

54. This is most extensively developed in *Distinction* (Bourdieu 1984a:xi–xii) where in the preface to the English edition Bourdieu writes: "The model of the relationships between the universe of economic and social conditions and the universe of life-styles which is put forward here [is] based on an endeavor to rethink Max Weber's opposition between class and *Stand*."

55. Durkheim is the most frequently referenced thinker in Bourdieu's 1968 methodological textbook *The Craft of Sociology*.

the academic tradition of French sociology, epitomized by Georges Gurvitch at the Sorbonne, and the immediate postwar empiricism imported from the United States (Besnard 1987:209–10). A return to the classics, especially Durkheim and Weber, was a way for Bourdieu's generation of French sociologists to distinguish themselves from their empiricist predecessors.[56]

In this light, it is significant that Aron lectured at the Sorbonne from 1959 to 1962 on the classical writers Montesquieu, Comte, Marx, Tocqueville, Durkheim, Pareto, and Weber, and that these lectures became the material for his two volumes of *Main Currents in Sociological Thought* (Colquhoun 1986:7). As Aron's teaching assistant, Bourdieu also taught Durkheim. For Bourdieu, it was Durkheim as well as Saussure who represented the significant intellectual precursors of the scientific method that became fashionable under structuralism.

Bourdieu adopted as a cardinal principle of method Durkheim's position that science must break with everyday understandings and representations of social life in order to establish a genuinely scientific explanation.[57] Indeed, Bourdieu has energetically pursued with all the ambition and passion of Durkheim the project of establishing sociology as science rather than as social philosophy. Bourdieu, of course, went on to distance himself from Durkheimian objectivism by integrating actor representations into his structural account. But like Durkheim, he began sociological investigation with the "methodological decision to 'treat social facts as things'" (Bourdieu, Boltanski et al. 1990:2).[58]

Bourdieu shares with Durkheim the impulse to reveal the social in the apparently most individual forms of behavior. Following Durkheim's methodological design in *Suicide* (1951), Bourdieu selects objects of study, such as photography and tastes, that appear most readily understandable in terms of individual choice or motivation to illustrate the power of sociological explanation. To discover the social at the very heart of the most subjective experience is a central aim of Bourdieu, just as it was for Durkheim (Bour-

56. Mannheim's (1956) idea of "intellectual generations" seems appropriate here.

57. In *The Rules of Sociological Method* Durkheim (1966:32) insists that the social scientist "must emancipate himself from the fallacious ideas that dominate the mind of the layman; he must throw off, once and for all, the yoke of these empirical categories, which from long continued habit have become tyrannical."

58. This does not conflict with Bourdieu's criticism of Durkheimian objectivism in another passage where he observes that "social science cannot 'treat social realities as things,' in accordance with Durkheim's famous precept, without neglecting all that these realities owed to the fact that they are objects of cognition (albeit a misrecognition) within the very objectivity of social existence" (Bourdieu 1990h:135). As we will see in chapter 3, Bourdieu makes both claims as representing two distinct but necessary steps in the research process.

dieu 1990c). Indeed, his early study of photography frames the research issue in quintessential Durkheimian terms of a sociological (e.g., degree of group integration) rather than a psychological explanation of picturing taking (see Bourdieu, Boltanski et al. 1990).

Durkheim's fundamental theme of the increasing division of labor is evident in the distinction Bourdieu draws between undifferentiated and differentiated societies. Like Durkheim, Bourdieu (1989c:376) works with the idea of a historical transition from fairly unified and undifferentiated societies to modern societies where various cultural modes of expression become differentiated and constituted as relatively autonomous fields. Indeed Bourdieu's general view of society as a web of interweaving fields of struggle over various kinds of valued resources is consistent with the Durkheimian idea of an ongoing process of differentiation.

Bourdieu extends Durkheims's sacred/profane opposition to an analysis of contemporary cultural forms. In his sociology of education, Bourdieu (1989c:164) sees French schooling as a "religious instance" in the Durkheimian sense for it produces social and mental boundaries that are analogous to the sacred/profane distinction. The elite tracks and institutions in French education function analogously to religious orders, as they set apart as superior and separate a secular elite with quasi-religious properties of public legitimation or symbolic power. The significance of this analogy to the sacred—indeed its polemical character—can be more fully appreciated if one recalls that France is a country with a strong anticlerical tradition and where secular public education has been embraced as one of the enduring legacies of the French Revolution.

More generally, Bourdieu believes that the religious sacred is but a particular case of the more general idea that social distinctions, whether applied to individuals, groups, or institutions, assume a taken-for-granted quality that elicits acceptance and respect. Symbolic power is a power to "consecrate," to render sacred. He thus associates the concept of the sacred with legitimation, particularly in high culture and art where boundaries delimiting the legitimate from the illegimate are particularly strong.[59] In this sense, he can declare that his sociology of culture is in reality a "science of the sacred" (Bourdieu 1992:210, 260–61).

Bourdieu revives Durkheim's project to develop a sociological theory of knowledge and social perception to explain the "social origins of schemes of thought, perception, appreciation and action." Durkheim argues in *The*

59. Bourdieu (1993d:161) suggests that religion, which Durkheim "defined by the setting-up of a frontier between the sacred and the profane, is simply a particular case of all the acts of instituting *frontiers* through which differences of *nature* are set up between realities that in 'reality' are separated by infinitesimal, sometimes imperceptible differences."

Elementary Forms of Religious Life that symbolic classifications correspond to social classifications. Bourdieu (1991b:5) follows closely this idea when he writes that

> if one takes seriously both the Durkheimian hypothesis of the social origins of schemes of thought, perception, appreciation, and action and the fact of class divisions, one is necessarily driven to the hypothesis that a correspondence exists between social structures (strictly speaking, power structures) and mental structures. This correspondence obtains through the structure of symbolic systems, language, religious, art, and so forth.

In *Distinction*, where Bourdieu (1984a:468) systematically relates social class to lifestyles and cultural consumption patterns, he defines his research objective as identifying "the cognitive structures which social agents implement in their practical knowledge of the world [and which] are internalized, 'embodied' social structures." Like Durkheim, Bourdieu sees symbolic systems as classification systems that provide both *logical and social integration.* He emphasizes the social as well as cognitive functions of "collective representations" and "primitive classifications." But if for Durkheim this integrative force operates to produce a desired consensual unity for the social order, for Bourdieu it produces domination. Thus, Bourdieu is concerned with the function of differentiation as well as with that of integration. The pressing question for Bourdieu is not, as it was primarily for Durkheim, how solidarity is reinforced, but rather how solidarity is constructed and maintained in a social order characterized by hierarchy, conflict, and struggle.[60] Bourdieu's theoretical effort to combine the issue of social reproduction with that of social classification amounts to a "revisionist approach to the Durkheimian problem of order" (DiMaggio 1979).[61] Bourdieu (1980c: 52–53) sees this effort as an attempt to mate Durkheim and Marx, anthropology and sociology.

The Significance of Ethnographic Fieldwork in Algeria

While trained in philosophy, Bourdieu began his social-scientific career as an ethnologist, doing his first fieldwork in the late 1950s among the Berber

60. See Cherkaoui 1981, Giddens 1982, and Wacquant 1993c for views that Durkheim was more concerned with conflict than is generally credited and that his concern for the problem of order was not formulated in response to the Hobbesian problem as Parsons (1968) suggests.

61. Durkheim is also concerned with the social basis of disorder. His concept of "anomie" reflects his concern for forces that deregulate as well as those that integrate the social body. In Bourdieu, however, we find little attention devoted to deviancy though there are notable exceptions, such as Bourdieu 1989c: 259–64, and Bourdieu, Boltanski et al. 1990:39–46.

peasants in Algeria. Out of this first research experience of crossing disciplinary boundaries between anthropology and sociology, Bourdieu sees himself joining

a new generation of sociologists, who started out in philosophy and were schooled in ethnology, [and who brought about] a reunification of the ethnological and sociological interests that had been completely dissociated by neo-positivism. (Bourdieu and Passeron 1967:198)

He believes that at the heart of the Durkheimian tradition there is no substantive distinction between sociology and anthropology.

This early research experience inaugurates specific motifs and points of method that become recurring themes in Bourdieu's later work. Four fundamental conceptual issues in particular emerge: the problem of relations between individual dispositions and external structures, the problem of agency in structuralist analysis, the problem of relating cognitive structures to social structures, and more generally the problem of relations between material and symbolic aspects of social life. The Algerian research also demonstrates the kind of political activism that Bourdieu would pursue as a professional social scientist.

The first problem emerged from the particular situation he encountered in colonial Algeria during the Algerian War. He says retrospectively (in Honneth 1986:40) that his personal way of dealing with the war was to carry out a study that would combine theoretical and political aims. As an opponent of the war, Bourdieu was interested in identifying those social forces in Algeria most likely to overthrow French colonial power and inaugurate a new democratic order. He therefore turned his attention to the differences between the Algerian proletariat and sub-proletariat and their different forms of "revolutionary consciousness."

The war accelerated the intrusion of the market economy by French colonialism into the traditional peasant social world. The French army's policy of forced resettlement (regroupement) destroyed, uprooted, and relocated peasant villages and thereby rapidly introduced traditional peasants to the modern exigencies of the market economy. Bourdieu explored how tradition and forced modernization intersected.[62] The newly imported and imposed money economy required of the peasants new attitudes toward time and new "modes of action based on rational anticipation" (Honneth, Kocyba, and Schwibs 1986:40). Yet, Bourdieu observed that peasants ini-

---

62. His two books Le Déracinement: La crise de l'agriculture traditionnelle en Algérie (Bourdieu and Sayad 1964) and Travail et Travailleurs en Algérie (Bourdieu, Darbel, et al. 1963) explore the patterns of adaptation to this new situation.

tially responded to the new economic conditions through the dispositions originally produced and shaped by their traditional economic order. Rather than consider this Kabyle peasant response as essentially irrational by modern economic standards, Bourdieu draws on the Durkheimian tradition to identify a deeper social rationality. The new structural demands were filtered through traditional dispositions, since peasant dispositions "do not change in the same rhythm as economic structures." Peasant behavior changed only as individual actors strategically adapted their dispositions to the new constraints and opportunities imposed by the new economy.

From this initial research experience Bourdieu developed a more formalized conceptual reflection on the relations between internalized dispositions and objective structures. For him, a proper account of practices will require a conceptual language that calls attention to the complex interaction between internalized dispositions and objective structures. Action will be theorized as a culturally mediated response to structural constraints and change. This problem became formalized in his key concept, habitus.

The second conceptual theme emerged from Bourdieu's efforts to apply Lévi-Strauss's structuralist analysis of myth, kinship, and ritual to Algerian Berber societies. In doing a statistical compilation of marriages, Bourdieu found that the parallel-cousin marriage rule posited by Lévi-Strauss actually occurred in less than 5 percent of cases. Similarly, by careful study of ritual, he found that the kinds of systemic oppositions posited by Lévi-Strauss for a structuralist analysis of ritual simply left out a number of significant practices (Bourdieu 1990c, 1990h). These field observations pointed up two glaring weaknesses in structuralism, namely, the absence of an adequate theory of agency and the limited capacity of formal models to account for action.

Like all ethnographic researchers, Bourdieu experienced the practical problems of data collection and analysis. In particular, he confronted the problem of the relations between the social scientist as the outside observer and the subjects of observation. The problem resided, for Bourdieu, in the gap between the practical logic and necessity of everyday activities carried out by actors, which the social scientist is interested in observing, understanding, and explaining, and the formalized accounts that the social scientist constructs. This research dilemma is familiar to all social scientists with fieldwork experience. Bourdieu stresses that theoretical knowledge constructed by the social scientist is fundamentally different from the practical knowledge employed by actors; yet it is this practical knowledge that guides actions and therefore should be the object of study by the social scientist. Rather than dismissing this difficulty as one of the necessary constraints of ethnographic observation, Bourdieu transforms it into a fundamental problem for all social science. A central question that permeates his work asks how one can write a science of the practical logic of practices that itself takes into account this fundamental difference.

A third conceptual problem points directly to Bourdieu's conceptual heritage stemming from Durkheim, Mauss, and Lévi-Strauss. Among the Algerian peasants, he confronted a world where ritual and myth intersect fully with the social and physical organization of everyday life. He would later publish his structuralist analysis of the Berber house demonstrating how ritual and symbolic classifications are embedded within with the spacial organization of the house (Bourdieu 1970). He then would generalize this problem of relations between cognitive structures and social structures to French schooling, where he saw contemporary French mentalities embedded in the social organization of French higher education (Bourdieu 1989c: 98). Thus, the theme of relations between symbolic classifications and social structures stems from both his Algerian fieldwork experience and the Durkheimian heritage.

The fourth problem stems from his observation in Kabylia that ritual and ceremony, feasts, and key symbolic observances were no less important to the maintenance and reproduction of group life than were its economic foundations. Indeed, Bourdieu concluded that in this traditional society it is impossible to distinguish the material or economic from the symbolic, and he reconceptualized the symbolic as a form of power, a kind of capital, that can be used to generate social advantages as well as exercise social control. This conceptual shift figured significantly in his criticism of economic reductionism by French Marxists, and led to a materialist but, what he believes to be, a nonreductive account of the symbolic practices of social life.

Finally, this first research project illustrates the style of political engagement that Bourdieu employs. Bourdieu advocates a leftist political role for the social scientist as one who should intervene in the public arena against all forms of domination, but in the name of science. Bourdieu's research projects are forms of political intervention presented primarily as works of science.

3 BOURDIEU'S METATHEORY OF SOCIOLOGICAL KNOWLEDGE

In attempting to write a critical sociology that will expose the power relationships produced and reproduced through cultural resources, processes, and institutions, Bourdieu encountered a number of methodological and theoretical enemies. This chapter first discusses his objections to "subjectivist" and "objectivist" modes of knowledge and shows how he proposes integrating them into a more general knowledge framework, which he calls a "general science of practices." It then takes up the problem of substantialism and examines his alternative "relational" method of analysis.

The Subjective/Objective Antinomy

A recurring theme throughout Bourdieu's work warns against the partial and fractured views of social reality generated by the subjectivism/objectivism antinomy.[1] The principal challenge, as he sees it, lies in writing a theory of symbolic power and an economy of practices—including intellectual practices—that will transcend this particularly troublesome and persistent dualism. Reflecting back over more than thirty years of work, he

---

1. As was noted in chapter 2, Bourdieu's central concern to transcend the subject/object dichotomy rooted in positivism finds inspiration in his philosophical training. Canguilhem's history and philosophy of science and Bachelard's historical epistemology posit a complex interaction relation between the subject and object of knowledge that displaces the traditional subject/object opposition. It also stems from criticism of Althusserian Marxism by positing a fundamental unity of practices that cannot be captured by the infrastructure/superstructure distinction.

observed that overcoming this antinomy has been "the most steadfast (and, in my eyes, the most important) intention guiding my work" (Bourdieu 1989d:15).[2]

Bourdieu sees the subjective/objective dichotomy manifested in several different forms throughout the social sciences. Table 1 displays a selection of issues, approaches, labels, and theorists that he associates with this underlying polarity.[3] As table 1 suggests, Bourdieu uses the dichotomy to group a broad variety of theoretical and research traditions, theorists, and opposing methods. Surface inspection might lead one to conclude that the classification is fairly arbitrary. Is there not, for example, a "subjectivist" dimension to Weber's *Verstehen* sociology, or is not an important current of ethnomethodology concerned with empirical observation? At times, the dichotomy means the opposition between interpretive and positivist approaches to social reality; at other times the opposition contrasts micro and macro levels of analysis; at still other times the opposition between the participant and the outside observer is indicated. One also finds the opposition referencing debates over relations between theory and method. Moreover, the various specifications of this abstract dichotomy are frequently conflated. One finds both interpretative and positivist variants of micro-level analysis lumped together and labeled "subjectivist." Such distinctions in micro-level work are lost in Bourdieu's generalized use of the term subjectivist.[4] Further, the dichotomy also expresses for Bourdieu the underlying structure of the Marxist/non-Marxist debate over relations between economic and noneconomic goods, between ideal and material interests, and between subjective and objective measures of class.

2. This theme goes back to some of his earliest work. It appears already in *Travail et travailleurs en Algérie* (Bourdieu, Darbel et al. 1963:3) where he argues that the transition from precapitalist to capitalist economies is not propelled primarily by either cultural or material factors but by their "dialectical relation." Drawing from Sombart, Bourdieu considers that the formation of the entrepreneurial spirit and the development of a capitalist economy were concurrent processes. In *Un art moyen* (Bourdieu, Boltanski et al. 1965:18–20), he proposes a "total anthropology" that would integrate and transcend subjective and objective forms of knowledge.

3. The table was assembled from several of Bourdieu's texts where he evokes the various dimensions of the subjective/objective dichotomy. See in particular Bourdieu 1977d, table 7.1, where he classifies several subjectivist and objectivist components in his theory of symbolic power.

4. An example is Bourdieu's tendency to classify interactionist sociology as subjectivist, whereas much treatment of the micro world of interactions tends to be highly empirical. In contemporary religious research, for example, one finds that it is religious belief that is treated as an attribute of the subject, whereas interpersonal networks become the objective infrastructure on which belief is erected (Wuthnow 1981:28). Ritzer (1988) argues that micro-macro and subjective-objective are *not* coterminous empirically or theoretically and need to be clearly distinguished.

TABLE I. The Subjective/Objective Dichotomy

Objectivism	Subjectivism
Lévi-Strauss	Sartre
Hegel	Kant
Saussure	Cassirer
Durkheim	Sapir
Marx	Whorf
Weber	?
Structuralism	Existentialism
Theoreticism	Phenomenology
Functionalism	Ethnomethodology
Marxism	Idealism
Empiricism	
Positivism	
Materialism	
Left Sociologist	Conservative Sociologist
Economic	Noneconomic
Matter	Ideas
Classes-in-themselves	Classes-for-themselves

Thus, Bourdieu employs the subjective/objective antinomy to reference a wide range of issues and intellectual traditions. But rather than effectively transcend this opposition, Bourdieu's work seems paradoxically plagued by it. Too frequently, it seems to become a technique for setting up opposing straw positions that can then be easily knocked down with Bourdieu's own preferred alternative. This "intellectual triangulation" technique may be a useful thinking tool if applied heuristically; it is a useful reminder that sociology must grasp the dual character of social life, both its subjective and objective aspects. But, as Brubaker (1993:227–28) insightfully points out, the technique can lead to an excessively polarized reading of social theory giving reductionist and misleading portrayals of other theorists.

Clearly Bourdieu employs the subjective/objective distinction in a variety of ways to reference different theoretical and methodological issues. Broadly speaking, subjectivist approaches include those emphasizing micro interactions, voluntarism, and methodological individualism. These include symbolic interactionism, ethnomethodology, phenomenology, and rational actor theory. Objectivism, on the other hand, seems to take two general forms for Bourdieu (1977c:27): (1) the uncritical recording and statistical analysis of empirical regularities of human behavior, and (2) forms of conceptual abstraction that tend to impute the properties of formal models to social realities. Objectivist approaches include Marxism, status attainment research, functionalism, French structuralism, and forms of empirical work that focus exclusively on macro-level concerns. Bourdieu believes that each side of the opposition offers important insights into social life but remains skewed if considered separately. Applying Bachelard's dialectical reason, Bourdieu argues that these various oppositions must be transcended and integrated into a broader knowledge framework.

When stated at a very general level, the subjective/objective dichotomy is recognized by most social scientists as one of the enduring metatheoretical dilemmas in the social sciences; few would disagree with Bourdieu's claim that it represents an obstacle to the construction of a total picture of social reality.[5] Most would accept the claim that the logic of structures must connect at some point with the beliefs and practices of individual actors. On the other hand, this very general dichotomy groups specific methodological and epistemological issues that divide social scientists and on which Bourdieu takes specific positions. In contemporary sociology, this antinomy and the various oppositions associated with it tend to revolve around three predominant divisions of intellectual labor: theory and empirical research, approaches focusing on symbolic forms versus those focusing on the material objects of social life, and micro versus macro levels of analysis. What is unique in Bourdieu is his contention that these divisions "have a social foundation but they have no scientific foundation" (1990c:34). He charges that the problem they pose is not simply epistemological, but also social, and in the final analysis political. The variations of the subjective/objective dualism stem from underlying struggles among social scientists for power and recognition (Bourdieu and Hahn 1970:14). They also stem from broader underlying social divisions among classes and status groups in the social order.[6]

5. Brubaker (1985:750) notes that such a program "might well have been endorsed by theorists as distant from one another as Parsons and Marx. (Parsons indeed explicitly constructs his theory with reference to the problem of the relation between objective conditions and subjective norms and values.)" Brubaker goes on to suggest that at this very general and abstract level, the subjective/objective polarity in fact remains a pseudo problem unless specific meanings are assigned to the opposing terms. Brubaker in fact identifies eight different specifications that can be subsumed under this very broad conceptual dichotomy.

6. Bourdieu also sees the subjective/objective opposition as a permanent feature of everyday struggles for distinction and power. Consider, for example, the strategy of presenting one's view as objective and that of one's adversary as too subjective.

For transcending the subjective/objective dichotomy, Bourdieu proposes a two-step model of epistemological reflection that integrates subjectivist and objectivist forms of knowledge into a more comprehensive, third form of knowledge which he calls a "general science of practices."[7] The first calls for breaking with subjectivist knowledge of social practices and the second for breaking with objectivist explanation.

BREAKING WITH SUBJECTIVISM

Since, for Bourdieu, the fundamental task of sociology is to disclose the means by which systems of domination impose themselves without conscious recognition by society's members, then recourse to the subjective perceptions of participants can only reinforce the very system of domination to be exposed. Sociology cannot, therefore, take everyday classifications and representations by actors at face value. The first task of the social scientist must be to initiate an epistemological break with commonsense, everyday representations by constructing the statistical regularities of practice. Scientific knowledge begins with an objectivist moment, since objective knowledge establishes the conditions in which interaction occurs and subjective knowledge is produced.

Bourdieu hence endorses Durkheim's epistemological objectivism as well as Bachelard's dialectical reasoning by arguing that the first step in the construction of social-scientific knowledge must break decisively with agents' self-understandings. This epistemological stance is necessitated by the very nature of insider accounts of their own practices. Insider representations reflect the practical logic of getting along in their social world, and hence are to be understood as instruments of struggle for practical accomplishments rather than attempts to draw a coherent and objective picture of actor behavior.[8] While scientific representations are constructed out of the representations of everyday practices, the latter cannot be substituted for the former (Bourdieu 1990h:14, 94–95).

7. The two steps are outlined in Bourdieu 1972:162–74, 1973b, 1977c:1–4, 1990h:25–29; Bourdieu, Chamboredon, and Passeron 1991. Bourdieu's terminology for his third type of theoretical knowledge has changed. In Bourdieu 1972, he calls it "praxeological" knowledge. Praxeological also appears in Bourdieu 1973b, which is the English translation of the section of Bourdieu 1972, where the three types of theoretical knowledge are presented. In Bourdieu 1977c, the third type of knowledge is labeled the "theory of theory and the theory of practice" or a "science of practices." Judging from an interview statement, Bourdieu likely dropped the term praxeological to differentiate his position from use of the term *praxis* current in Marxist thought (Honneth, Kocyba, and Schwibs 1986).

8. Bourdieu accepts the objectivist moment in sociological analysis, not because he considers, as does Durkheim, that actor accounts are unreliable or irrational. Rather, Bourdieu objects because they are guided by practical interests which differ from the theoretical interests that direct the attention of the social scientist.

The break with subjectivism calls for critical examination of "informant" accounts of peer behavior as well (Bourdieu 1977c:16–22). Informant reports likely assume too much and are too general for the kinds of details needed by researchers to uncover the underlying principles of practices. More importantly, however, informant accounts are likely to be oriented with an eye for the unusual rather than the mundane, to impress the researcher. And they tend to employ normative constructs rather than provide the descriptive detail needed to reconstruct the sequence of practices. Hence Bourdieu, like Bachelard, draws a sharp distinction between everyday practical knowledge and scientific knowledge.

Bourdieu identifies three forms of subjectivist knowledge that must be epistemologically corrected by recourse to structural indicators. One form of subjectivism Bourdieu singles out for criticism is Sartre's voluntarism. Bourdieu dismisses Sartre's existential notion of free will as an approach to the problem of practice, since it abstracts actor decisions from their social context.

A second form of the subjectivist perspective includes the broad range of micro approaches to the study of human interaction, such as ethnomethodology, symbolic interactionism, and phenomenology. Bourdieu takes issue with these approaches, which hold the epistemological position that scientific conceptions must be built up from actor accounts (Winch 1958). Such approaches, he charges, fail to link patterns of face-to-face interaction and socially constructed meaning systems to larger patterns of hierarchy and domination in social arrangements. Micro approaches, which build on actor accounts, forget that agents classify and construct their understanding of the social world from particular positions in a hierarchically structured social space. Since there is an unequal distribution of resources for reality construction, not all actors are equally situated to understand and act upon the world in similar terms.

Finally, a third approach to the problem of action that emphasizes the individual as the unit of analysis is rational actor theory, which Bourdieu also dismisses as an undersocialized view of action.

The first epistemological break with subjective knowledge forms, therefore, stresses that all human action is situated within determining structures that are not readily available to everyday consciousness but must be constructed by the social scientist.

BREAKING WITH OBJECTIVISM

If objective knowledge is needed to correct the limitations of subjective knowledge, a second epistemological break becomes necessary to correct for the limitations of objective knowledge. This second epistemological break moves in two directions. The first calls for critical reflection on the generative as well as situated character of practices. Bourdieu argues that *practices are constitutive of structures* as well as determined by them. He emphasizes that structures are themselves socially constructed through everyday practices of agents. This leads Bourdieu to explore the practical character of agency and develop his concept of habitus, which integrates actor-symbolic representations with structural factors.

Second, the break with objectivism also calls for critical reflection on the specific character of *theoretical* practices. Here Bourdieu introduces a reflexive perspective on sociological practice itself as a necessary moment in developing a general theory of practices. Indeed, a critical reflection on the cognitive and social basis of theoretical practices is a precondition for providing an adequate understanding of ordinary practices. Without this reflexive vigilance, the social scientist risks projecting his or her cognitive and social interests onto the nontheoretical work of practical action. Hence, Bourdieu calls for a theoretical language that reminds the social scientist of the gap between theoretical knowledge and practical knowledge. He thus focuses attention not only on the object of inquiry but also and simultaneously on the relationship of the researcher to the object of inquiry. He calls for "participant objectivation"—a critical reflection and empirical inquiry on the social and epistemological conditions that make possible a sociological view of the social world (Bourdieu and Wacquant 1992:68; Wacquant 1989:33). Bourdieu sees this as a distinctive feature of his approach to sociology, and we will examine it in more detail in chapter 11.

Bourdieu discusses the necessity of this second epistemological break with respect to three principal forms of objective knowledge: positivism, structuralism, and intellectualism.

Positivist social science gives priority to macro structures, often in the form of statistical regularities, which are rarely visible to the engaged actors and which must be constructed by the social scientist. Yet, it is the action of individuals that construct, sustain, and eventually change those statistical regularities. Moreover, actors act in terms of their practical knowledge of the social world, not with the insight of scientific knowledge. Since the "social reality" the social scientist identifies in the "objectivist" moment of research is "also an object of perception," actor perceptions must be incorporated into a comprehensive explanatory framework of practices (Bourdieu 1990c:130). The researcher also needs to reject the "objectivism" of statistical patterns and reappropriate and incorporate the representations of agents into the analysis in order to construct an "adequate science of practices" (Bourdieu 1977c). This means that social-scientific investigations must include both qualitative indicators as well as quantitative data. Bourdieu argues that an adequate scientific account requires conceptual mediation of the relationship between actor perceptions and formally constructed structures. As we will see in chapter 5, his concept of habitus serves this function.

Bourdieu criticizes strict structuralist approaches, especially those of Lévi-Strauss and Althusser, for reducing action to the mere execution of a theoretical, atemporal, and logical model. Bourdieu contends that, while objective structures exist, the social activity of individuals both originates and develops in the *practical mastery* of those structures, whether they be kinship rules or the mode of capitalist production. External structures are not apprehended for the most part through formalized rational assessment. Actors act through time without the benefit of the totalizing view available to the outside observer. Moreover, they organize their activities *practically* rather than seek to satisfy formal standards of logical coherence. Actors draw upon cultural and social resources, not for logical purposes, but for the practical purposes of getting on in everyday life activities. Objectivist science, however, tends to abstract from consideration this practical orientation of action.

In other words, an objectivist account of structures cannot explain the genesis of structures, which, according to Bourdieu, should be the principal objective of a theory of action. Actors act to accomplish practical purposes which involve social and economic interests and power and their symbolic representations. Practices are therefore constitutive of objective structures, which strictly objective accounts of social life fail to show.

"Intellectualism," or "theoreticism," represents a third type of objectivist knowledge against which a genuine science of practices must be constructed. Theoreticism, Bourdieu maintains, abstracts from consideration not only the practical knowledge of actors but also the theoretical practices of the researcher. He charges that the researcher commits the "intellectualist fallacy," or becomes blinded by the "intellectualist illusion," when theoretical explanation is substituted for the *practical mastery* or *practical intelligibility* that actors employ in their actions. Objectivist science conflates "the model of reality [with] the reality of the model" by forgetting that objectivist models merely describe practical action *as if* it were the case (Bourdieu 1977c). Uncritical applications of formal models, he charges, end up projecting the formal properties of theory onto the informal world of everyday practices. They thus become yet another form of symbolic domination. According to Bourdieu, social scientists are particularly prone to produce objectivist ideology—hence become producers of symbolic violence—by failing to recognize within their idealization of the social world the social and historical conditions that determine their own intellectual practices as well as those of the subjects of their investigation. They need to develop a reflexive practice of sociology—a key dimension of Bourdieu's sociology, which we will examine more fully in chapter 11.

His sharpest criticisms along this line are directed at the notion of rule in Lévi-Strauss's analysis of kinship exchange, at the Marxist theorization of social class, and at rational actor theory. What Bourdieu rejects in Lévi-Strauss is the tendency to assimilate the empirical reality of kinship groups to the theoretical model constructed by the social theorist. Kinship choice flows, Bourdieu argues, from actor strategies to maintain or enhance their positions within the social order rather than from abstract rules or norms.

Bourdieu criticizes Marxism for treating theoretical models and empirical displays of classes, or, in his words, "classes on paper" (Bourdieu 1987b: 153), as if they were real mobilized classes. Marxist class perspectives tend to presume from an observation of homogeneity among objective indicators of social class the existence of real culturally and socially unified social classes (Bourdieu 1987b:153). In short, there is a tendency to take "class-in-itself" for "class-for-itself."[9]

Finally, Bourdieu believes the "intellectualist fallacy" is particularly visible in rational actor theory where he charges that attributes of conscious, rational calculation to act are but a projection of the cognitive posture of the theorist.

Thus, Bourdieu (1977c:18) calls attention to the "distance between learned reconstruction of the native world and the native experience of that world," which social scientists "so often forget." Failure to take into account this fundamental gap between the theoretical knowledge and interests of the researcher and the practical knowledge and interests of the subjects of observation leads to nonreflexive concepts that are confounded with practical reality. Such concepts become reified with a kind of symbolic power they do not deserve. Bourdieu (ibid., 38, 202) rejects all approaches that would attempt to establish a direct, unmediated identity between theoretical concepts and practical reality. An adequate social science must construct concepts that *mediate* the relationship between the fundamentally different, theoretical and practical types of knowledge.

---

9. This is a blanket criticism leveled against Marxism. Bourdieu does not acknowledge that a number of researchers using Marxist class categories (e.g., Przeworski 1977) fully recognize the problem and have been careful to avoid the very tendency Bourdieu denounces. I discuss this further in chapter 7.

The Relational Method

Relational thinking also is central to Bourdieu's vision of sociology as a science. Bourdieu criticizes incessantly what he calls "substantialism," "realism," or the "spontaneous" theory of knowledge as a key obstacle to developing genuine scientific knowledge of the social world. For Bourdieu (1987f:3), the substantialist vision of social reality designates an epistemology that "recognizes no other reality than that which is directly given to the intuition of ordinary experience." It focuses on the "realities of ordinary sense-experience, and by individuals in particular." Substantialist thinking "privileges substances" over relationships, for "it treats the properties attached to agents—occupation, age, sex, qualifications—as *forces* independent of the relationship within which they 'act'" (Bourdieu 1984a:22). Bourdieu sees substantialist thinking in positivism, phenomenology, and the humanist/existentialist "philosophy of the subject." All three tend to reify attributes of individuals and groups by detaching them from their social and historical contexts.

As an alternative, Bourdieu advocates a "relational" or "structuralist" mode of thinking, which he identifies as fundamental to *all* scientific thought. This approach to the study of social life "identifies the real not with substances but with relationships" (ibid.). These are "invisible relationships" to the uninitiated eye, "because they are obscured by the realities of ordinary sense-experience." They must be constructed by science as "a space of positions external to one another and defined by their relative distance to one another."

The relational method is a cardinal principal of structural linguistics that locates meanings of signs not in themselves but in their contrastive relations. Bourdieu (1968) sees the relational method to be the "major contribution" of structuralism to the social sciences, and in fact considers relational thinking to be a foundational principle of *all* scientific knowledge as demonstrated in its highest formalized expressions: mathematics and physics.[10] Bourdieu maintains that the social sciences should deal with cultural and social relations just as modern geometry treats its subject matter. Just

---

10. Bourdieu identifies Ernst Cassirer's *Substance and Function: Einstein's Theory of Relativity* [1923] as his principal source of inspiration for relational thinking (Bourdieu and Wacquant 1992:97). He also notes that both the social psychologist Kurt Lewin and the sociologist Norbert Elias (1978) draw inspiration from Cassirer for a relational approach.

Relational thinking is a key methodological underpinning of the structuralist movement in linguistics (Sapir and Jakobson), anthropology (Lévi-Strauss), and history (Dumézil), all of which have been influential to Bourdieu's thinking. Moreover, Wacquant observes that the relational mode of analysis in the sociological tradition can be traced back to Durkheim and, particularly, Marx (Bourdieu and Wacquant 1992:16).

as points and lines in geometrical figures derive their significance from the relations that link them rather than from the intrinsic features of individual elements, so also models of social life must be constructed.[11] Individual facts are to be assembled into models of broader sets of relations so that the individual elements appear as, in the words of Bachelard, a "a particular case of the possible." In science, "the real is the relational" (Bourdieu and Wacquant 1992:97).

Thus for Bourdieu the relational method stands opposed to positivism and methodological individualism. In contemporary sociology, it has greater affinity with the growing use of network analysis than with regression techniques employed in status attainment research.

Bourdieu sees the relational method as the basic tool for imposing the necessary epistemological breaks with both subjectivist and objectivist forms of knowledge. Relational thinking extracts an object of inquiry from the context of everyday assumptions and perceptions, which reflect the practical interests of social life, and transforms it into an object of scientific knowledge (Bourdieu, Chamboredon, and Passeron 1991:253). For Bourdieu, however, this means more than the common practice in sociology of transforming attributes of individuals and groups into variables. Relational thinking emphasizes building variables into "systems of relations" that are differentially and hierarchically ordered. One simple technique he recommends for doing this is cross-tabular comparison of sets of agents across a wide variety of properties (Bourdieu and Wacquant 1992:230). Columns of properties that differentiate the greatest number of agents are selected to identify the system of variations among agents.

Bourdieu's preference for a relational approach to the study of social life leads him to reject linear modeling techniques in favor of correspondance analysis, which is a structural statistical procedure that is a graphical variant of discriminant analysis and multidimensional scaling. Developed by what some call the "French Data Analysis" school (Benzécri 1973; Lebard, Morineau, and Warwick 1984),[12] correspondance analysis is a technique for displaying the association between rows and columns of a data matrix as points in multidimensional space such that similarities and dispersions of clusters of points are emphasized and readily visible. For Bourdieu, it is

a relational technique of data analysis whose philosophy corresponds exactly to what, in my view, the reality of the social world is. It is a technique which "thinks"

---

11. See Bourdieu 1968 for an early statement indicating that the relational mode of reasoning is to be borrowed from the natural sciences and applied to the social sciences.

12. See Greenacre 1984 for a good introduction with illustrations.

in terms of relation, as I try to do precisely with the notion of field. (Bourdieu and Wacquant 1992:96)

The relational method provides the basis for substantive positions that Bourdieu takes on issues such as culture, lifestyles, class analysis, and popular culture. As a point of method, Bourdieu analyses cultural practices as structured relationally around binary oppositions such as high/low, distinguished/vulgar, pure/impure, and aesthetic/useful. The value of each element of a system is defined in relation to the other elements of the same system. Certain cultural practices obtain legitimacy in opposition to other practices. Cultural legitimation and domination are not thought of in terms of particular styles or ideas but in terms of contrastive practices, as when elements of one subculture are subordinated to those of the other.

We see, for example, this method put to work in his analysis of class-based lifestyles in France. We learn that the French working-class subculture is "virtue of necessity," whereas the French upper-class subculture is "freedom from necessity," and these translate into characteristic lifestyles and consumer preferences. But in Bourdieu's mind—and for him this is a fundamental point of method—these lifestyle characteristics are *not* intrinsic features of each class. Rather, they obtain analytical significance *only* in relation to and by way of contrast with each other. Thus, a dominated culture like a dominated social class is always defined in relation to a dominant culture and a dominant class, and vice versa. Bourdieu uses this point of method to criticize popular-culture theories for claiming a degree of autonomy from dominant culture that Bourdieu feels is unwarranted.

Though it has seldom been noted by his critics, Bourdieu's relational method intersects with core assumptions that he makes about the fundamental character of social life. The relations he constructs are invariably competitive rather than cooperative, unconscious rather than conscious, and hierarchical rather than egalitarian. The recurring image of social life one finds in Bourdieu's work is one of competitive distinction, domination, and misperception. Thus, when Bourdieu admonishes his fellow social scientists to "think relationally" (Bourdieu and Wacquant 1992:228), he is also inviting them to share his conflict view of the social world.

Bourdieu sees the relational method as key to his vision of the political mission of sociology. He charges that substantialist thinking provides the methodological basis for discriminatory practices by attributing individual and collective differences to intrinsic properties or essences (Bourdieu 1994:18). By stressing that individual and collective properties are specific to relative competitive positions in particular social and historical contexts, relational thinking relativizes and hence delegitmates such universalizing claims.

Bourdieu's relational method, however, seems to presuppose a tightly coupled social order where contrastive practices are continuously operative and always hierarchical. It tends to downplay processes of imitation or co-operation that can also be formative of social identity as are processes of distinction. Bourdieu uses this method with considerable success in analyzing the French intellectual world and the system of honor in Kabylia. But it needs testing across a broader range of social worlds where competition and centralization may not be the predominant features but where there is considerable variety and autonomy among class subcultures (Lamont and Lareau 1988:158).[13]

13. Even in France, the work of Grignon and Passeron (1984), two former collaborators of Bourdieu, suggests that the tightly relational model proposed by Bourdieu underestimates the degree of autonomy of French working-class cultural practices from those of dominant groups in that country.

4 BOURDIEU'S POLITICAL ECONOMY OF SYMBOLIC POWER

Beyond Structuralist Marxism

One way that Bourdieu attempts to transcend the subjective/objective antinomy in his general and unified science of practices is by reconceptualizing relations between the symbolic and material dimensions of social life. Here he enters into critical dialogue with Marxism, particularly the French structuralist Marxism of Louis Althusser. Out of this confrontation with structuralist Marxism, Bourdieu develops a political economy of symbolic power that includes a theory of symbolic interests, a theory of power as capital, and a theory of symbolic violence and capital.[1] These are not tidy, well-delimited theoretical arguments, but orienting themes that overlap and interpenetrate. They draw from a wide variety of intellectual influences, particularly Durkheim, French structuralism, and Weber's sociology of religion. But the starting point is the Althusserian Marxism that Bourdieu encountered during the 1960s and '70s.

As was noted in chapter 2, Althusser (1970) argues that cultural practices and institutions can assume a relative autonomy from the economy even though "in the final analysis" the latter always will be determinative. Bourdieu also affirms the relative autonomy of culture from the economy and politics, though he shuns the Marxist language of infrastructure and

---

1. This analytical division of Bourdieu's thinking follows in certain respects distinctions proposed by Brubaker (1985).

superstructure. Bourdieu's choice early in his career to focus on the symbolic dimension of social relations was made in the context of a debate with the Althusserians over just what the relative autonomy of the cultural instance might look like. More importantly, Bourdieu goes beyond Althusser by looking into the black box of cultural processes and institutions rather than relegating them to the abstract conceptualization of superstructure. Bourdieu's argument amounts to a revisionist approach to the problem of relations between infrastructure and superstructure in that he proposes a mediational view of the relative autonomy of superstructure from infrastructure.[2]

In this chapter I examine the three general theoretical arguments that Bourdieu develops in his critical dialogue with Marxism. In each he both draws inspiration and marks critical distance from Marxism.

A Sociology of Symbolic Interests

The first way Bourdieu distances himself from Marxism is by extending the notion of economic interest to ostensibly noneconomic goods and services. In stressing the centrality of economic structures in social life, Marxism, Bourdieu argues, reproduces the classic subjectivism/objectivism dualism by restricting the notion of interest to the material aspects of social life, whereas the symbolic and political dimensions are considered to lack their own proper interests. This same dualism undergirds the Marxist distinction between infrastructure and superstructure, which Bourdieu rejects by broadening the idea of economic interest to include symbolic or nonmaterial pursuits as well as material ones.

As I observed in chapter 2, Bourdieu draws from Weber's sociology of religion to posit that *all action* is *interested*, including symbolic pursuits. He extends the logic of economic calculation to "*all* goods, material as symbolic, without distinction, that present themselves as *rare* and worthy of being sought after in a particular social formation" (Bourdieu 1977c:178). Bourdieu (1980a:209) wants to construct a "science of practices" that will analyze "all practices" as "oriented towards the maximization of material or symbolic profit." His research program would unite what has traditionally been thought of as economic (i.e., interested and material) and noneconomic (i.e., disinterested and symbolic) forms of action and objects. He writes that "the theory of strictly economic practice is simply a particular

2. In this respect, Bourdieu's intellectual project is similar to that of Raymond Williams (1963, 1965), even though Williams works explicitly within the Marxist tradition whereas Bourdieu does not.

case of a general theory of the economics of practice" (1977c:177), Thus, symbolic interest and material interest are viewed as two equally objective forms of interest.[3]

Relatedly, Bourdieu speaks of action as strategy to emphasize the interest-orientation of human conduct. Strategy is associated with the "maximizing of material and symbolic profit" (Bourdieu 1990h:16). Action as strategy conveys the idea that individual practices are fundamentally interested, that actors attempt to derive advantages from situations. In discussing marriage patterns in precapitalist societies, Bourdieu (1977c:36) writes that kinship relations are the "product of strategies (conscious or unconscious) oriented towards the satisfaction of material and symbolic interests and organized by reference to a determinate set of economic and social conditions." Yet, for Bourdieu, *strategy* does not refer to the purposive and calculated pursuit of goals as it does for rational actor theorists (e.g., Coleman 1990). Rejecting the rational actor model of conduct, Bourdieu instead thinks of action as patterned and interest-oriented at a tacit, prereflective level of awareness that occurs through time.

One particularly forceful application of this interest perspective of action is Bourdieu's attack on the self-image of intellectuals as representatives of objectivity, disinterestedness, purity, and creativity. Bourdieu sees intellectual practices as all fundamentally interested pursuits despite their symbolic character.

Bourdieu has also critically applied this perspective to highbrow culture (Bourdieu 1992) and science (Bourdieu 1975b), both of which derive their legitimation precisely from the belief that they represent higher and more worthy forms in the inventory of human endeavor than material pursuits. The great merit of Bourdieu's work lies in the demonstration that there is a political economy of culture, that all cultural production—including science—is reward-oriented, and that stylistic preferences are selected and rejected in ways that are analogous to the general notions of investment and search for profits in the economy.

Bourdieu's application of the language of economic interest and strategy to all areas of cultural and social life has drawn sharp criticism. Several critics (Gartman 1991, Honneth 1986, Jenkins 1992, Joppke 1986, Miller and Banson 1987) have charged that Bourdieu's theory reduces to a form of

3. Bourdieu's effort to generalize a formal economic logic to all social relations goes counter to what much of the sociological tradition has held, namely, that not all of social life reduces to the logic of market relations (Caillé 1981; Nisbet 1966). Yet in another sense this conceptual move embraces a familiar sociological claim: that forms of conduct which appear as "irrational" by standards of economic maximization can in fact be seen to obey a deeper social rationality. The apparent affinity between Bourdieu's economy of practices and the resurgence of rational actor theory in recent years will be discussed later in the chapter.

economic determinism. Alain Caillé has offered perhaps the most sustained critique of Bourdieu's economy of practices as fundamentally one of economic determinism in the last instance. Caillé (1992:109–11) argues that all of Bourdieu's work is oriented by a single unitary argument in which "the ensemble of social practices reduce to a more or less mediated and more or less hidden game of material interests." His criticisms of Bourdieu summarize in three points. First, Bourdieu makes no attempt to delineate what part of social actions can be explained by conscious calculation and what part cannot. All action for Bourdieu reduces to underlying interest, whether conscious or unconscious. Second, material interest is the most fundamental of interests. Though Bourdieu criticizes economic reductionism, he is in fact himself a closet "economic determination in the last instance" theorist.[4] And third, while Bourdieu sharply criticizes humanism and rejects any ahistorial, universal view of human nature, he in fact implicitly formulates an anthropology that posits a fundamental human propensity to pursue interests and accumulate power.

I will evaluate this criticism and Bourdieu's response at various points in this and the next chapter. My own view is that many of Bourdieu's critics do not sufficiently appreciate the complexity of his thinking. I nonetheless find a problematic, utilitarian orientation in his work, but in ways not emphasized by his critics or acknowledged by Bourdieu. I will first examine his concept of interest before going on to present his theory of cultural capital.

The claim by Caillé and other critics that Bourdieu works from a fundamentally utilitarian framework is striking, for Bourdieu always has been a sharp critic of economism. His early work on peasant communities in North Africa rejected strictly economic explanations of underdevelopment and change in precapitalist colonized societies. In that research on Kabyle peasants he confronts the problem of how to account for a fundamental "discrepancy" he found between precapitalist peasant attitudes and comportment toward time, money, property, credit, and production, and those demanded by the encroaching capitalist economy (Bourdieu 1979:vii). From the outset, his theory of action is sharply critical of economistic views of human action.[5] His key concept, *habitus*, which we will examine in the next chapter, is used consistently to argue against forms of economic deter-

---

4. However, Caillé correctly notes that Bourdieu cannot be situated within an Althusserian framework. Ansart (1990) and Wacquant (1992) defend Bourdieu against the "last instance" determinism charge.

5. Bourdieu (ibid.) maintains that both neoclassical economics and structuralist Marxism share a fundamentally reductive view of human action as something essentially reflective of economic structures. Both vantage points, in Bourdieu's view, are "objectivist" and lack an adequate sense of agency.

minism. In *Distinction*, for example, habitus explains why tastes in food are not direct "functions of income but of inherited life-style" (Bourdieu 1984a: 130).

Two general views emerge from this research experience that have consistently guided Bourdieu's thinking about action. First, action is not a mechanical response to external determining structures, whether they be economic, political, social, or even cultural. Habits, traditions, customs, beliefs—the cultural and social legacy of the past—filter and shape individual and collective responses to the present and future. They *mediate* the effects of external structures to produce action.[6] Second, he explicitly rejects a "homo economicus" view of action.[7] The Algerian peasants he studied did not display the kind of future orientation that would have permitted a means-ends calculation in response to the challenges of the encroaching capitalist economy. They responded in terms of their traditional dispositions toward time.

In more recent writings, Bourdieu (1990c:106–19) vigorously defends his work against the utilitarian criticism. He defends his intellectual strategy as being the same as Weber's, who used "the economic model to extend materialist critique into the realm of religion and to uncover the specific interests of the great protagonists of the religious game" (107). Bourdieu's economy of practices can indeed be considered an important elaboration and extension of Weber's notion of ideal interests. But while Weber limits economic action to cases where there is means-ends calculation, Bourdieu sees interested pursuit in *all* types of action. He makes no attempt to weigh the evidence for or against the claim that all action is fundamentally self-interested.

One should ask critically whether different types of conduct vary in their degrees of interestedness. Might some forms of behavior be more interested than others; that is, might some forms of behavior respond more directly to survival needs than others? Moreover, the proposition that all action is interested stands in an uneasy relationship with Bourdieu's self-proclaimed materialism. Since Bourdieu appears willing to grant material conditions of existence some priority in the hierarchy of human values, he would likely accept the idea that not all types of activities are equally fruitful in providing for creature comforts. By dismissing all distinctions between

6. This conceptualization of action clearly sets Bourdieu against all forms of behaviorism. His concept of habitus challenges the theory that action is a response to the operant conditioning of a stimulus-response equation.

7. Raymond Boudon (1979, 1980) is the other leading contemporary French sociologist who represents this opposing view. He advocates a rational choice model of action that permits actors a measure of free, but interested choice within systems of structural constraints.

forms of interested and disinterested behavior, Bourdieu is no longer able to preserve the kind of priority he seems willing to accord material life. One of the theoretical consequences of the expanded use of the idea of interest to cover all forms of behavior is that we lose analytical power in distinguishing types of behavior that would seem to follow from the fundamental materialistic assumption Bourdieu wishes to make.[8]

Bourdieu's interest-oriented action does not assume conscious, rational calculation. Strategies are tacit and prereflective rather than conscious plans. There is, however, ambiguity in Bourdieu's work on this point. At times he admits conscious strategizing while at other times he insists on the unconscious character of interest calculation. Bourdieu makes no consistent distinction between conscious and unconscious forms of interest calculation. He clearly rejects a rational actor model of action and goes to great effort to explain that the type of action he focuses on escapes the realm of conscious manipulation. He generally stresses the unwitting complicity of actors in pursuing their own vested interests. Moreover, he claims that interested action gains in legitimation and efficacy the less visible its interested dimension is to actors:

The most profitable strategies are usually those produced, on the hither side of all calculation and in the illusion of the most "authentic" sincerity, by a habitus objectively fitted to the objective structures. (Bourdieu 1977c:214)

But this suggests that Bourdieu is willing to recognize degrees of awareness of the interested character of some forms of action; moreover, these presumably have some bearing on the success or failure of those pursuits. At other times he recognizes the fully conscious character that strategic calculation can have. He thus appears to be more attentive to the empirical variation that one finds in the social world than his conceptual formulations suggest. Bourdieu, however, does not spell out a clear position on this issue.

Bourdieu assumes, like Durkheim, that one cannot really talk about individual motivations in sociological analysis. The idea that all forms of action are interest oriented is what Alvin W. Gouldner (1970) calls a "domain assumption." By using an ostensibly economic model of human action, Bourdieu makes the "as if" assumption that individuals and groups

8. One exit from this dilemma, and one which Bourdieu occasionally uses, is to speak of certain types of action that are "more interested" than others. In the scientific field, for example, he observes that there can be "most brutally interested and egoistic confrontations" that can lead to the "forgery of scientific results" in order to gain in the competition (Bourdieu 1990c:111). Such examples appear to designate actions where conscious calculation of means-ends relationships occurs. This solution points toward a more nuanced enumeration of types of action, but it does so with a loss of analytical power.

do try to optimize—even at an unconscious level—and do so for status as well as for economic reasons. On this basis, he can make general predictions of how certain classes will behave in certain situations. This economic model seems useful, for example, in thinking about the post-1950s educational choices made by upper-middle-class American families for their children. The push for the "Ivys," private secondary schools, and even special preschool enrichment programs involves highly conscious calculation of how best to invest family resources in the future generation. At the same time, Bourdieu does not offer sufficiently convincing empirical evidence that individuals do indeed attempt to optimize their behavior in most situations. Moreover, are there not forms of behavior that go against the objective interests of actors? Bourdieu's domain assumption renders his theory of action inadequate for handling such possibilities. Though Bourdieu uses the language of "maximization," it seems likely that in many instances "satisficing" or "self-benefiting" seems closer to what he has in mind. But he does not provide the conceptual tools for identifying practices that are less self-benefiting than others.

Critics misinterpret Bourdieu's concept of interest by reading it as an independent principle of action in his conceptual framework. Bourdieu sees individual interests as defined by an actor's position within the social hierarchy. But he thinks of those interests as embodied dispositions of actors that operate at a tacit, taken-for-granted level. He does not think of interest as "goal orientation." Interested action is not a means-ends mode of organizing action. Rather, interest is "practical" and "dispositional" and does not have the goal orientation commonly associated with a utilitarian framework.

Bourdieu (1980c:33–35, 1990c:106, 109) talks about *interests* rather than some single underlying natural or universal interest. In an interview he declares:

Far from being an anthropological invariant, interest is a *historical arbitrary*, a historical construction that can be known only through historical analysis, *ex post*, through empirical observation, and not deduced *a priori* from some fictitious—and so naively Eurocentric—conception of "Man." (Wacquant 1989:41–42)

For Bourdieu, there can be as many interests as there are institutionalized arenas of conflict over valued resources. Moreover, interest is defined practically as whatever motivates or drives action toward consequences that matter (Bourdieu 1987b:107). Interest in this sense becomes associated with whatever does not leave one indifferent; it is what "interests" one and "motivates" one to act in some fashion. This is tantamount to saying that every action has its raison d'être (Bourdieu 1990h:290). But if there is a plurality of interests, then how does one identify the more important?

In another place Bourdieu defends his use of the term by associating it with "function" and "scientific explanation":

> . . . when I say that there is a form of interest or function that lies behind every institution or practice, I am simply asserting the *principle of sufficient reason* which is implied in the very project of "explaining" . . . and which is intrinsic to the notion of science. (1980c:18–19)

Here the idea of interested action appears to reduce to the more mundane claim that all behavior can be understood sociologically, that all human conduct has its reasons, its own proper rationality. If this is the case, then one might ask, why even use the term "interest," whose semantic field over-reaches considerably this more mundane point? The answer lies in Bourdieu's rhetorical strategy vis-à-vis Marxism and intellectuals.

Bourdieu explains his use of the economic language of interest as a conceptual strategy designed to correct for Marxist objectivism and econo-mism. In relegating culture to superstructure, Bourdieu contends, Marxists leave the door open to idealistic (i.e., disinterested) interpretations of culture. By identifying cultural as well as economic interests, Bourdieu hopes to eradicate this lingering idealism unwittingly sustained by Marxism itself.

If Bourdieu sees his own work in the same light as Weber's, as bringing a fully materialist perspective to the study of culture, is not his claim to transcend the materialism/idealism form of the subjective/objective dichotomy somewhat misleading? Should his work not be more accurately characterized as a thoroughly materialistic account that attempts to ex-punge all implicit as well as explicit vestiges of idealism from the study of cultural and social life? There is therefore a certain irony in Bourdieu's economy of practices: though sharply critical of reductionist forms of Marxism for not according sufficient importance to the symbolic dimen-sions of social life, Bourdieu's own view of action offers a more thoroughly materialistic account than the forms of reductionist Marxism it so sharply criticizes.

This conceptual strategy is also designed to attack the professional ide-ology of intellectuals as representatives of disinterested objectivity and cul-tural excellence. Bourdieu sees intellectual practices as all fundamentally interested pursuits despite their symbolic character. He acknowledges that his work is shaped to some extent by the very influences he tries to escape as he "twists the stick in the other direction" and places emphasis on the "interested" character of cultural production in a "somewhat provocative manner against the professional ideology of intellectuals" (Bourdieu 1990c: 106).[9] He sees the concept of interest as "an instrument of rupture" or means of gaining critical distance from the intellectual world where utilitarian interest is denied. In recent years he has increasingly employed the terms *illusio* and *libido* in place of interest (Bourdieu and Wacquant 1992: 115–16). This change in conceptual terminology likely represents an effort to distance himself from critics' utilitarian characterization of his work. Nevertheless, by using such terms as *interest* and *strategy*, Bourdieu (1987b: 63) calls attention to the subtle advantages that can be accumulated from ostensibly noneconomic activities. It is a conceptual strategy designed to expose what Bourdieu perceives to be one of the most vital but unacknowledged interests of intellectuals: their "interest in disinterestedness."

While insightful, these responses to criticisms do not remove all doubt from the fundamental orientation proposed. The problem is not entirely that critics "misread" Bourdieu by tacitly imposing economistic assumptions on his work, as Bourdieu and Wacquant (1992:24) assert. At a minimum, the terminology of *interest, strategy, investment,* and *profit* suggests some utilitarian orientation. Take for example the idea of "self-interest." Though Bourdieu rejects the criticism that he works with a universal conception of interest, he does talk about the "law of self-interest" in gift exchange (Bourdieu 1990h:112). While interest may take as many forms as there are instituted understandings of what and when gifts are appropriate to exchange, the idea that no conduct can escape the misrecognition of vested interest suggests something like a universalizing assumption. Moreover, it is confusing to find the language of self-interest in a sociological account that wishes to break with all vestiges of subjectivism for a fully socialized conception of human action.

Power as Capital

A second way that Bourdieu distances himself from Marxism is by extending the idea of capital to all forms of power, whether they be material, cultural, social, or symbolic. Individuals and groups draw upon a variety of cultural, social, and symbolic resources in order to maintain and enhance their positions in the social order. Bourdieu (1989c:375) conceptualizes such resources as capital when they function as a "social relation of *power*," that

---

9. In one interview he explains his view of action as a "deliberate and provisional reductionism," suggesting that it might be less a fundamental stance than a conceptual strategy designed to attack the professional ideology of "disinterestedness" among intellectuals, writers and artists (Wacquant 1989:41).

is, when they become objects of struggle as valued resources.[10] In undifferentiated traditional societies, the family patrimony depends not only on its land, animals, and instruments of production but also on its kinship relations and networks of alliances that represent

a heritage of commitments and debts of honour, a capital of rights and duties built up in the course of successive generations and providing an additional source of strength which can be called upon when extraordinary situations break in upon the daily routine. (Bourdieu 1977c:178)

In modern differentiated societies, access to sources of income in the labor market depends upon cultural capital in the form of educational credentials and social capital in the form of networks. These forms of power, and their unequal distribution among individuals and groups explain for Bourdieu why random and perfect competition models are inadequate for understanding social life. They also illustrate for Bourdieu why a Marxist focus on economic capital is based on a restricted concept of power.

Bourdieu's notion of capital approaches that of Marx when he writes that "capital is accumulated labor," or that "the universal equivalent, the measure of all equivalences" among various types of capital "is nothing other than labor-time (in the widest sense)" (Bourdieu 1986a:241, 253). Indeed, Bourdieu's concept of capital appears rooted in a kind of labor theory of value. Capital represents power "over the accumulated product of past labour . . . and thereby over the mechanisms which tend to ensure the production of a particular category of goods and thus over a set of revenues and profits" (Bourdieu 1991c:230). Labor can be embodied in a wide variety of forms though Bourdieu (1986a:243) generally speaks of four generic types of capital: economic capital (money and property), cultural capital (cultural goods and services including educational credentials), social capital (acquaintances and networks), and symbolic capital (legitimation). His concept of capital, unlike that of Marx, does not distinguish types of work specific to capitalism. Bourdieu treats capital as power relations founded on quantitative differences in amount of labor they embody. His

10. Bourdieu is of course not the first to apply the economic metaphor of capital to nonmaterial sources of power that shape the direction of a social collective. One finds this conceptual strategy employed by others in a wide variety of contexts and intentions. In "The Wesleyan Story: The Importance of Moral Capital," Burton Clark (1973) emphasizes the significance of normative bonds that carried a small elite college through a period of financial and social crisis. Bourdieu's use of the term differs, however, from most other uses in that he emphasizes the power dimension and he makes the economic metaphor a central part of his overall conceptualization for sociological analysis.

concept cannot therefore distinguish capitalist from noncapitalist forms of labor.[11]

Though Bourdieu is centrally concerned with power and domination, his concept of capital is not linked to a theory of exploitation in the sense of extracting surplus value or a dynamic of primitive accumulation, which is the Marxian understanding. But a key contribution of Bourdieu beyond Marx is to see a much broader range of types of labor (social, cultural, political, religious, familial, to name but a few) that constitute power resources, and that under certain conditions and at certain rates can be converted one into another. Indeed, it is the study of how and under what conditions individuals and groups employ strategies of capital accumulating, investing, and converting various kinds of capital in order to maintain or enhance their positions in the social order that constitutes a central focus of Bourdieu's sociology.

CULTURAL CAPITAL

A form of power as capital in the differentiated societies that Bourdieu conceptualizes by extending the logic of economic analysis to ostensibly noneconomic goods and services is *cultural capital*. His concept of cultural capital covers a wide variety of resources including such things as verbal facility, general cultural awareness, aesthetic preferences, information about the school system, and educational credentials.[12] His point is to suggest that culture (in the broadest sense of the term) can become a power resource.[13] This occurs when cultural markets emerge where investors exchange currencies, strive for profits, and, in the case of educational credentials in recent years, suffer from inflation.

Bourdieu's concept of cultural capital emerged initially from his research to explain unequal scholastic achievement of children originating from families with different educational though similar social origins (Bourdieu 1986a:243; Bourdieu and Wacquant 1992:160). He sees the concept as breaking with the received wisdom that attributes academic success or failure to natural aptitudes, such as intelligence or giftedness. School success, Bourdieu finds, is better explained by the amount and type of cul-

11. Calhoun (1993:67–69) makes a similar observation.

12. Lamont and Lareau (1988:155–56) document the variety of uses Bourdieu grants to his concept. These include informal academic standards, social class attributes, indicators of social class position, mechanisms for social selection, and types of expertise.

13. More recently, Bourdieu indicates that what he has called cultural capital should in fact be called *informational capital* (Bourdieu and Wacquant 1992:19). This shift in terminology distances the concept from the high-culture connotations that critics (Lamont and Lareau 1988) have noted in its earlier uses.

tural capital inherited from the family milieu than by measures of individual talent or achievement.

Cultural capital is analyzed by Bourdieu (1986a) as existing in three different states. First, it refers to the ensemble of cultivated dispositions that are internalized by the individual through socialization and that constitute schemes of appreciation and understanding. Cultural goods, Bourdieu notes, differ from material goods in that one can appropriate or "consume" them only by apprehending their meaning. This holds for music, works of art, and scientific formulas, as well as works of popular culture. Thus, cultural capital exists in an *embodied* state.

The accumulation of cultural capital in its embodied form begins in early childhood. It requires "pedagogical action": the investment of time by parents, other family members, or hired professionals to sensitize the child to cultural distinctions. The acquisition of cultivated dispositions presupposes "distance from economic necessity" and therefore translates original class-based inequalities into cultural differences. The investment of inherited cultural capital returns dividends in school, rewarding those with large amounts of incorporated cultural capital and penalizing those without. Some of Bourdieu's most insightful ethnographic observations about French schooling consist of showing how French schoolteachers reward good language style, especially in essay and oral examinations, a practice that tends to favor those students with considerable cultural capital who in general are from privileged family origins (Bourdieu 1989c:48–81).

But Bourdieu does not confine his analysis of cultural capital to explaining differential school attainment. He sees it operating much more broadly, ranging from hiring practices in firms to choice of spouse. Both tend to produce a high degree of class endogamy, whether in management or marriage (Bourdieu 1984a:214–43).

Second, cultural capital exists in the *objectified* form referring to objects, such as books, works of art, and scientific instruments, that require specialized cultural abilities to use.

Third, cultural capital exists in an *institutionalized* form, by which Bourdieu means the educational credential system. Bourdieu places great importance upon the growth of the higher education system and the role it has come to play in the allocation of status in the advanced societies. Expanded higher education has created massive credential markets that are today decisive in reproducing the social class structure. Since educational credentials increasingly have become necessary for gaining access to desirable positions in the job market, it becomes essential for parents to invest in a good education for their children so they can reap the "profit" on the job market. This process of investment involves the conversion of economic capital into cultural capital, which is a strategy more readily available to the affluent.

Bourdieu argues that it is the tremendous growth of the objectified and institutionalized forms of cultural capital into relatively autonomous markets that has been perhaps the single most important development to shape the stratification structure and the role of cultural producers in the advanced societies. He sees a historical trend of cultural capital becoming more and more the new basis of social stratification (Bourdieu and Boltanski 1977:33).[14] The unequal distribution of objectified and institutionalized cultural capital across social classes is for Bourdieu one of the key dimensions of social inequality in modern societies. And he sees the rise of cultural and credential markets as providing intellectuals a new autonomy from the traditional forms of domination through patronage (Bourdieu 1985d).[15] Key to the growth in autonomy of culture from economic and political power is the institutionalization and expansion of education. Educational institutions secure partial autonomy from political intervention and economic constraints by establishing their own criteria for legitimation and by recruiting and training their own personnel—that is, by securing control over their own reproduction.

Bourdieu's concept of cultural capital needs to be distinguished from Gary Becker's (1964, 1976) concept of "human capital." Unlike human-capital theorists, Bourdieu focuses on class-based variation in both the

14. Bourdieu finds even among traditional French capitalist families an increasing tendency to rely on educational credentials for controlling access to leadership positions in their firms (Bourdieu and de Saint Martin 1978). Bourdieu is of course not alone in making this claim. Daniel Bell (1973, 1988) argues that knowledge has become a new factor of production and replaced private property as the most significant source of stratification in the modern postindustrial society. Galbraith (1971) sees power and control of the large corporation increasingly associated with expertise rather than with actual ownership. More generally, New Class theorists have emphasized the knowledge base of the alleged New Class (Gouldner 1979; Szelenyi and Martin 1988/89). While emphasizing the growing importance of cultural capital in the distribution of power and privilege in the modern societies, Bourdieu sees it as a competitive principle of stratification but one that nonetheless remains subordinate to that of private property in capitalist societies.

15. Bourdieu (1987b:172) specifies that it is not a personal form of domination characteristic of earlier artist–patron relations, but a "form of structural domination exercised through very general mechanisms such as the market." In early formulations of this argument, Bourdieu (1971c, 1971d) draws on the works of L. L. Schücking (1966) and Raymond Williams (1963, 1965) for his understanding of the historical development of cultural markets for artists and writers in Western societies. Today Bourdieu cites the emergence of new forms of patronage, in the form of corporate and state funding of artists and writers, as threatening the autonomy of cultural life (Bourdieu and Haacke 1994).

meanings and uses of various types of capital. He redirects the focus of analysis from individual or global societal returns in productivity to the impact of cultural investments on the perpetuation of the social-class structure (Bourdieu 1986a:243–44). He gives more attention to the subtle dimensions of cultural socialization and transmission that cannot be easily quantified in monetary terms. Moreover, Bourdieu's theory of human action does not share the anthropological assumptions of a rational actor perspective. Bourdieu's actors pursue strategies, but not as conscious maximizers of limited means to achieve desired ends. Their choices are more tacit, practical, and dispositional, reflecting the encounter between the accumulated capital and corresponding dispositions from past experience and the present opportunities and constraints of fields where they act.

Bourdieu does share with human capital theorists—and rational actor theory more generally—the fundamental assumption that all action is interest oriented. While he would emphasize that the content of action will likely vary by social group, society, and historical period, he nonetheless does posit this invariant of human conduct. Moreover, though the types of interests can vary considerably, conduct always appears to be oriented toward accruing power and wealth, as Caillé correctly points out. In this sense Bourdieu's economy of practices indeed shares with human capital theory a key utilitarian dimension despite his disclaimers.[16]

CULTURE AS CAPITAL

Bourdieu therefore proposes a general science of the various forms of capital and the laws of their interconvertibility. How he conceptualizes the relationships between forms of capital is, however, fairly complex. Part of that complexity stems from how he thinks of capital. In *The Logic of Practice* (1990h:122), he remarks that capital is a kind of "energy of social physics" that can exist in a variety of forms and under certain conditions and exchange rates can interconvert from one into another. This image of capital suggests a conceptualization of power where no one form is given theoretical priority over the other. Indeed he offers a quote from Bertrand Russell to suggest that power is analogous to energy in that it occurs in many forms and no one form is more fundamental than the others or can be treated independently of the others (300). This suggests an empirical and historical orientation, which can certainly be found in Bourdieu's work, where only research can determine the key forms of capital and their interrelationships in a specific social order. One consequence of this orientation is that capitals

16. Bourdieu contends that, beyond some shared vocabulary, he actually has little in common with human capital theorists (Bourdieu and Wacquant 1992:118).

tend to proliferate, and there is accordingly a devaluation of his conceptual currency. Thus we find not only economic, cultural, social, and symbolic capital, but also family, religious, political, moral, and state capital, to mention but a few. However, with the increasingly refined identification of forms of power as capital, there emerges a tendency to see power everywhere and, in a sense therefore, nowhere—an extreme diffusion of power that Bourdieu himself rejects.[17]

Yet, in numerous other places in his work Bourdieu also gives conceptual priority to economic capital. He sees a "historical" opposition in Western capitalist societies between cultural capital and economic capital. As we will see in chapter 6, this opposition serves as the fundamental determinant of power relations in these societies. While cultural markets have emerged as formidable challengers to economic markets, cultural capital is always considered a "subordinate" or "dominated" form of capital.[18] Cultural markets and institutions remain only *relatively* autonomous from economic markets and institutions.[19] The development of important cultural markets has not, according to Bourdieu, switched the balance of power from the large corporation or the state to the university. In his analysis of class relations in contemporary France, Bourdieu notes that

the dominant fractions are what they are if and only if the economic principle of stratification asserts its real dominance, which it does, in the long run, even in the relatively autonomous field of cultural production, where the divergence between specific value and market value tends to disappear in the course of time. (1984a:583)

In spite of its autonomy, the realm of culture remains subordinate to the economy. Bourdieu (1986a:252) considers that "economic capital is at the

17. Indeed, he distinguishes his work from that of Foucault on precisely this point; he sees power more concentrated in particular institutional settings than does Foucault (Wacquant 1993b).

18. While willing to see cultural resources as forms of power, closure theorists are divided on the issue of how to compare cultural and economic resources. Murphy (1988:79) sides with Bourdieu when he sees in educational credentials a *derivative* rather than a primary form of exclusion. Parkin (1971, 1979), however, places credentials virtually on par with economic capital.

19. The relative autonomy of cultural capital represents for Martin and Szelenyi (1987) a welcomed "move away from economic reductionism and toward a *general theory of symbolic domination*," but does not go far enough. They contend that Bourdieu's analysis of class societies still does not accord the symbolic system sufficient autonomy to account for his own critical theory. Though inspired by Bourdieu's work, Martin and Szelenyi reject his capital metaphor for culture. They propose "symbolic mastery" as a more appropriate way of labeling those cultural practices that differentiate the "holders of principles" from the "mere practitioner," and thereby designate a new type of domination that may not always be subordinated to the power of financial capital.

root of all the other types of capital," such as cultural capital, social capital, and symbolic capital, and that these are in fact "transformed, disguised forms of economic capital." It is after all economic capital that makes possible the investment in cultural capital by making possible the investment of time needed to accumulate cultural capital. Economic structures shape decisively cultural arenas though Bourdieu (1991c:230) seldom sees that causal connection as direct.

Bourdieu (1986a:254, 1987b:131) also admits that cultural capital is not as stable or as universal a currency as is economic capital. Cultural capital is more unstable in that its accumulation can be undermined by criticism and suspicion. It encounters higher risks than economic capital in its inter-generational transmission for families and individuals. Moreover, unlike stocks and bonds, its institutionalized value (in the form of educational credentials) is not negotiable. Economic capital, then, is easier to manage rationally, easier to conserve, transmit, and calculate. Though Bourdieu criticizes Marxists for reducing culture to economics and resists any suggestion of economic determinism in his own work, he nonetheless makes claims that are suggestive of some degree of reduction in this direction, just as Caillé charges.[20]

How the various capitals interconvert also poses a problem. One contribution by Bourdieu to the sociological study of power relations is the forceful demonstration that cultural capital, social capital, and economic capital can be interchangeable. Yet the interchange is not equally possible in all directions. Social capital and cultural capital are more closely related to each other than to economic capital. In general, economic capital appears to convert more easily into cultural capital and social capital than vice versa. Bourdieu acknowledges that some goods and services can be obtained directly and immediately through economic capital. But other goods and services are accessible only through social capital and cultural capital—a point Bourdieu's (1986a:252) work stresses. Thus, while culture and social networks are forms of capital, they are not exactly on equal footing with money and property.

The idea of culture as capital insightfully calls attention to the power dimension of cultural dispositions and resources in market societies. It also poses problems for comparative work. As noted earlier, Bourdieu's concept of capital does not permit him to distinguish capitalist from noncapitalist social relations. That his concept of cultural capital may be more applicable

---

20. In recent statements, Bourdieu (Bourdieu and Wacquant 1992) qualifies earlier claims (Bourdieu 1977c) that in the last instance the economy is determinative. Today he is more willing to say that the relationship between different fields is fully historically contingent even though at present the economic field carries the most weight.

to market societies than to precapitalist social formations is suggested by how he actually employs the concept in the latter. In precapitalist societies, cultural capital appears only in its "incorporated" rather than in its "objectivified" or "institutionalized" form. But this shift to "form" in applying the concept indicates not only Bourdieu's flexible and strategic attitude toward the application of concepts but also an inherent weakness in this concept when exported to noncapitalist societies.

There may be limits to its application in highly differentiated societies as well. Since Bourdieu developed his concept within a distinct national high culture tradition, it appears tied to a strong assumption of high cultural hegemony. Some of its rhetorical power is lost when exported to other national contexts where there is more cultural pluralism. To the extent that cultural capital implies a broad consensus on valued cultural forms, its capacity to function as common currency may be limited in very large and highly differentiated societies, such as the United States, where high culture has not played quite the dominant role that it has in France (DiMaggio 1979; Lamont and Lareau 1988).

Further, the rate of interconvertibility between capitals might be particularly high in those advanced capitalist societies where market relations have penetrated more extensively in arenas of social relations, such as the family, formerly governed by tradition and status. There may be less interconvertibility in market societies with strong state welfare systems. If so, this would call for a more comprehensive explanatory framework than that of capital interconversion patterns and rates. Bourdieu's concept of capital lacks an analytical grip on the specificity of capitalist societies and important structural variations among them.

The use of a cultural market metaphor also gives mixed results in comparisons between capitalist and former state-socialist societies where private property did not have official recognition. Labeling stratification resources as forms of capital does not generalize well to state-socialist societies where the primary exclusion rule was party membership rather than private property (Murphy 1988). A more general conceptual language of forms of social closure might be more appropriate for such intersocietal comparisons.

Bourdieu's conceptual language of cultural capital, albeit distinct from human capital, does not entirely escape the penetrating critical observation that Karabel and Halsey (1977:13) offer of the theory of human capital: namely, that it has

direct appeal to pro-capitalist ideological sentiment that resides in its insistence that the worker is a *holder of capital* (as embodied in his skills and knowledge) and that he has the *capacity to invest* (in himself). Thus in a single bold conceptual stroke the *wage-earner*, who holds no property and controls neither the process nor the product of his labor, is transformed into a *capitalist*.[21]

In Bourdieu's world, all are capital holders and investors seeking profits.

The image of the cultural capitalist is perhaps fitting for certain professions in the media, the arts, and academe, where individuals with valued cultural resources are able to convert them into economic rewards. The image also would seem to apply to middle-class families who seek out valued types of education for their children. But the capital metaphor works less well for groups who have little or no capital to invest. As we will see in chapter 7, Bourdieu's framework seems much less useful for study of the working class or of the underclass. He employs the concept insightfully to identify sources of intraclass differentiation within the dominant and middle classes, yet stratification within the working class receives much less attention.

A Theory of Symbolic Violence and Capital

A third way that Bourdieu distances himself from Marxism is by emphasizing the role of symbolic forms and processes in the reproduction of social inequality. For Bourdieu, the traditional Marxist emphasis on economic and class structures underestimates the importance of the symbolic dimension of power relations in both the undifferentiated precapitalist and highly differentiated postindustrial societies. Indeed, Bourdieu (1989c:555, 1990h:122–34) believes that even in the advanced societies the principal mode of domination has shifted from overt coercion and the threat of physical violence to forms of symbolic manipulation. This belief justifies his focus on the role that cultural processes, producers, and institutions play in maintaining inequality in contemporary societies. There is symbolic power as well as economic power.

How Bourdieu thinks of symbolic power relates to how he conceptualizes *all* symbolic systems, whether they be art, religion, science, or language itself. In a sweeping synthesis of several different theoretical traditions, Bourdieu (1977d) argues that symbolic systems simultaneously perform

---

21. One might speculate why the idea of cultural capital has caught on so rapidly in American sociology, particularly in the field of education. One likely factor is the tremendous expansion of American education and the general idea of education as an investment. A related idea is the considerable extent to which utilitarian values permeate much of professional sociology (Caillé 1993; Gouldner 1970:61–87).

three interrelated but distinct functions: cognition, communication, and social differentiation.[22]

Drawing from the Sapir–Whorf tradition on language, the Kant–Humboldt–Cassirer philosophical tradition, and Durkheim's sociology of knowledge, Bourdieu sees symbolic systems as "structuring structures": as a means for ordering and understanding the social world. In this sense, different modes of knowledge, such as language, myth, art, religion, and science, represent different ways of apprehending the world. They therefore exercise a cognitive function.

Second, symbolic systems are also "structured structures" whose internal logic can be grasped by structural analysis as developed by Saussure for language and Lévi-Strauss for myth. Symbolic systems are "codes" that channel deep structural meanings shared by all members of a culture. Conceptual systems, therefore, function simultaneously as *instruments of communication* and as *instruments of knowledge* (Bourdieu 1971b:295). As instruments of both knowledge and communication, symbolic systems provide, as Durkheim (1965) argues, "logical" integration, which is a necessary condition of "moral" integration. Symbolic systems exercise therefore a communication and social integration function.

Third, and what Bourdieu emphasizes most, symbolic systems not only provide cognitive and integrative functions but also serve as *instruments of domination*. Dominant symbolic systems provide integration for dominant groups, distinctions and hierarchies for ranking groups, and legitimation of social ranking by encouraging the dominated to accept the existing hierarchies of social distinction (Bourdieu 1977d:114–15). They therefore fulfill a political function.

Bourdieu thus combines constructionist and structuralist perspectives to offer a theory of symbolic power that tightly couples the cognitive, communicative and political dimensions of all symbolic systems. This theory of symbolic power emerges from his concern with the problem of the relationship between symbolic representations and social structures—a problem that was at the forefront of debates among French Marxists and structuralists during the 1960s. This theory also illustrates Bourdieu's central concern with dominant culture. Nowhere in his work do we find a commensurate interest in subordinate cultural systems except in his claim that

---

22. This synthesis is most concisely set forth in the essay, "Symbolic Power" (Bourdieu 1977d), but the argument is more detailed in "Genesis and Structure of the Religious Field" (1991b) and in *Reproduction in Education, Society and Culture* (Bourdieu and Passeron 1977): 4–68.

they reflect the patterns of the dominant system (see Bourdieu and Passeron 1977:23).

In arriving at these three functions of symbolic systems, Bourdieu develops a sociology of symbolic forms and a theory of symbolic violence and capital that overlap and interpenetrate yet stand as relatively distinct analytical developments. We will first take up his sociology of symbolic forms and then examine his theory of symbolic violence and capital.

A SOCIOLOGY OF SYMBOLIC FORMS

Bourdieu borrows substantially from French structuralism and its linguistic model in formulating his sociology of symbolic forms. First, drawing from Saussure's model of language, Bourdieu posits that the fundamental logic of symbolic processes and systems, beginning with language itself, is one of establishing differences and distinctions in the form of binary oppositions. It is the "logic of difference, of differential deviation" (Bourdieu 1991c:237).[23] Symbolic systems, from this perspective, are classification systems built upon the fundamental logic of inclusion and exclusion. *All* symbolic systems follow this fundamental classification logic of dividing and grouping items into opposing classes and hence generating meanings through the binary logic of inclusion and exclusion. This logic of symbolic systems builds an ordered set of fundamental dichotomous distinctions, such as rare/common, good/bad, high/low, inside/outside, male/female, distinguished/vulgar, that operate as "primitive classifications"[24] undergirding all of our mental activities. As Bourdieu (1984a:468) puts it:

All agents in a given social formation share a set of basic perceptual schemes, which receive the beginnings of objectification in the pairs of antagonistic adjectives commonly used to classify and qualify persons or objects in the most varied areas of practice. The network of oppositions between high (sublime, elevated, pure) and low (vulgar, low, modest), spiritual and material, fine (refined, elegant) and coarse (heavy, fat, crude, brutal), light (subtle, lively, sharp, adroit) and heavy (slow, thick, blunt, laborious, clumsy), free and forced, broad and narrow, or, in another dimension, between unique (rare, different, distinguished, exclusive, singular, novel) and

23. The imprint of Jakobson's (1956) claim of the binary logic of phonology is obvious here. It is also the fundamental operating pattern that Lévi-Strauss (1966) attributes to the human brain.

24. The term comes from Durkheim and Mauss (1963). Bourdieu sees his theory of symbolic forms as an elaboration of the Durkheim–Mauss project of identifying the fundamental cognitive structures of social life. As we will see in chapter 7, he combines Durkheim and Mauss with Marx by considering "classification struggles" as expressions of "class struggles."

common (ordinary, banal, commonplace, trivial, routine), brilliant (intelligent) and dull (obscure, grey, mediocre), is the matrix of all the commonplaces which find such ready acceptance because behind them lies the whole social order.

Such paired oppositions are shared by all, are social in origin, and are used to enhance power relations in social life. They are the building blocks of the everyday classifications of social life. This array of "semi-codified oppositions contained in ordinary language" ultimately connects, however, to a more fundamental bipolarity: the dominant/dominated paired opposition. This is the ultimate source of all paired oppositions.

Bourdieu's structuralist method aims to reveal this "deep structure" of domination and subordination in social life. He wants to demonstrate that various permutations of this fundamental bipolarity can be found in a great diversity of areas. Take, for example, the paired opposition "light/heavy" as one permutation of the fundamental dominant/dominated opposition. In French schooling, he finds this bipolarity structuring evaluations of academic styles: light distinguishes positively valued bourgeois academic performance from the heavy and labored middle- and lower-class academic style.[25] In theater, the light/heavy opposition distinguishes positively the light, leisurely bourgeois theater from the heavy, "labored" and "tortured," more intellectual pieces. Sometimes the values can be inverted, as among intellectuals for whom light is associated with the less serious and probing forms of intellectual exercise and heavy with the more honorable, substantial, scholarly forms (Bourdieu 1984a:469). This, and similar paired oppositions, can take on quite different meanings in different social universes. They nonetheless all function as logical homologies from one domain to the next, and all point, if only tacitly, to the most fundamental "invariant opposition" between dominant and dominated.

Structuralist linguistics and semiology focus on the analogical transformations and permutations through which fundamental cultural polarities find expression across various symbolic systems. This type of analysis draws attention to the *internal* organization of conceptual systems but leaves unattended the issue of the source of sign systems. However, following Durkheim, Bourdieu stresses the connection between social and cognitive structures. He writes that "the cognitive structures which social agents implement in their practical knowledge of the social world are internalized, 'embodied' social structures" (468). Social structures become internalized

---

25. In chapter 8 we will examine some of Bourdieu's (1989c:19–47) empirical findings that show the paired opposition "brilliant/serious" structuring French academic evaluations.

into the cognitive structures of individuals and groups who then unwittingly reproduce the social order by classifying the social world with the same categories with which it classifies them.[26]

Unlike Durkheim, Bourdieu does not argue that symbolic systems simply mirror social reality; he does not attempt to establish a one-to-one correspondence between selected signs and symbols and given social realities as, for example, between particular values and social classes. Rather, Bourdieu embraces the antipositivist position held by structuralists that binary distinctions established through cognitive processes are fundamentally arbitrary in that they do not reflect directly social reality; instead, meanings obtain through the contrastive features between signs, though the connection between any particular symbol or sign and a given social phenomenon is arbitrary. Meanings obtain not from the intrinsic features of signs themselves but from their contrastive relations. This provides the cognitive basis for Bourdieu's claim that the dominant cultural standards of any social order are fundamentally arbitrary. Bourdieu refers to such standards of any society as the "cultural arbitrary," to signal that all cultural systems are fundamentally human constructions that are historical, that stem from the activities and interests of particular groups, and that legitimate unequal power relations among groups (Bourdieu and Passeron 1977, book 1: Foundation of a Theory of Symbolic Violence). Bourdieu rejects all claims to universal knowledge, values, and beliefs that would stand beyond any social influence.[27]

But if symbolic systems are essentially arbitrary in that they do not directly reflect social realities, for Bourdieu, they are not at all arbitrary in their social consequences. Rather, this fundamental logic of symbolic distinction operates socially and politically as well as culturally; it functions to differentiate and legitimate inegalitarian and hierarchial arrangements among individuals and groups. By arguing that the structuralist logic of contrastive relations applies not only to symbolic systems, such as language (à la Saussure), myth (à la Lévi-Strauss), or discourse (à la Foucault), but "also to the *social relations* of which these symbolic systems are a more or less transformed expression," Bourdieu (1983a:314) distinguishes his approach from that of other leading French structuralists. Bourdieu's theory of sym-

---

26. Bourdieu calls this internalized set of dispositions the *habitus*, which we will examine in chapter 5.

27. However, Bourdieu (1990c:181) also claims to reject radical cultural relativism, for he argues that social groups and their corresponding cultural activities are not commensurate but are hierarchically ordered in terms of their capacities to exercise power. Nevertheless, the principal thrust of his work is to "relativize" the claims to cultural legitimacy by dominant groups.

bolic forms is in fact a theory of the *social and political uses* of symbolic systems.

For Bourdieu, the problem with both structuralist semiology and Durkheim's concept of "collective representations" is that they carry an implicit theory of consensus. While he acknowledges, as the quotation above illustrates, that "all the agents in a given social formation share a set of basic perceptual schemes" (1984a:468), Bourdieu stresses the differentiating role of the logic of polarity in symbolic systems. His fundamental point is that this binary logic of symbolic distinction also determines our mode of apprehending the social world; it predisposes us to organize the social world according to the same logic of polarity and thus to produce social as well as cognitive distinctions. These cognitive distinctions are predisposed to simultaneously generate *social* as well as logical classifications by making dichotomous social as well as logical groupings, by creating forms of social inclusion and exclusion as well as at the level of symbols. Such distinctions become classification lenses through which we perceive the social world and give it meaningful order. Just as the double meaning of "distinction" indicates, this fundamental logic identifies the precise character of symbolic power: the simultaneous act of making conceptual and social discriminations.

This social function of the classification logic of symbolic representations generates, therefore, a *political* effect to the extent that the social groupings identified are hierarchically differentiated and therefore legitimated. Binary symbolic distinctions correlate with social distinctions turning symbolic classifications into expressions of social hierarchy. The relationship between mental structures and social structures obtains through the binary logic that imprints upon our cognitive and communicative capabilities and simultaneously provides a sort of map of social distinctions to be established between ingroups and outgroups. One dimension correlates with the other: social distinctions are internalized and structured by the polarity logic of cognitive processes. Symbolic systems can be thought of as forms of "vertical classification" where connections between the cognitive logic of polarity and the social logic in exclusion and inclusion are established (Schwartz 1981).[28] The binary logic of symbolic classifications

28. One application of this theme that Bourdieu has emphasized in recent work is the role of symbolic power in the formation of groups. He argues that group identity, indeed group existence as a collective body, is dependent on the exercise of symbolic power. He writes, "symbolic power, whose form *par excellence* is the power to make groups and to consecrate or institute them (in particular through rites of institution, the paradigm here being marriage), consists of the power to make something exist in the objectified, public, formal state which only previously existed in an implicit state" (Bourdieu 1987f:14).

insightfully suggests that ingroup/outgroup relations can be grounded in a cognitive dimension. They are overlapping social and cognitive distinctions.[29] According to Bourdieu, this is a fundamental property of all symbolic systems, not just those in primitive mythology or religion; it is operative in science and philosophy where the contemporary secular mind would least suspect its presence.[30]

Bourdieu accepts the "deep structure" of binary differentiation of social life as posited in structuralism. It is not clear, however, that binary codes are the fundamental building blocks of culture, since everyday practices are not always marked by such clear distinctions. One frequently finds, for example, a "shading off" of one category of meaning into the next (Geertz 1974). Moreover, the gender symbolism represented by the male/female binary opposition, which Bourdieu posits as a universal of social life, is *both* rigidly enforced and yet contested in actual practices. It is the multiplicity of gendered practices that renders gender itself a contested identity that Bourdieu's structuralist perspective does not take into account (McCall 1992).

If Bourdieu draws from a structuralist theory of signs and symbols to develop his theory of symbolic power, he nonetheless identifies the source of that power in the relationship of symbolic systems to social structure rather than within the symbolic systems themselves. Power is not in words or symbols per se but in the "belief in the legitimacy of the words and of him who utters them"; for Bourdieu, symbolic power resides not in the force of ideas but in their relation to social structure. Symbolic power "is defined in and by a determinate relationship between those who exercise this power and those who undergo it—that is to say, in the very structure of the field in which belief is produced and reproduced" (Bourdieu 1977d: 117).

SYMBOLIC VIOLENCE AND CAPITAL

The third way that Bourdieu distinguishes himself from Marxism is by stressing the specific contribution that "representations of legitimacy make to the exercise and perpetuation of power" (Bourdieu and Passeron 1977: 5). He emphasizes that in almost all instances the exercise of power requires some form of justification (9–10). It is the power of domination through legitimation that primarily concerns Bourdieu, who maintains that it is the

29. The cognitive dimension of inclusionary and exclusionary processes suggests a potentially useful but as yet unexplored avenue for social closure theory. See Murphy 1988.

30. Bourdieu (1984a:468–69, 596) remarks that the "opposition between the unique and the multiple" which "lies at the heart of the dominant philosophy of history" represents in "transfigured form" the "elite/masses" opposition in politics.

cement of class relations. This is of course the role that Marx assigns to ideology, and Bourdieu affirms this political function of symbolic systems. But Bourdieu stresses the active role played by taken-for-granted assumptions and practices in the constitution and maintenance of power relations. If his theory of practices extends the idea of interest to culture, then his theory of symbolic power extends culture to the realm of interest with the claim that all forms of power require legitimation.

Bourdieu understands ideology, or "symbolic violence," as the capacity to impose the means for comprehending and adapting to the social world by representing economic and political power in disguised, taken-for-granted forms. Symbolic systems exercise symbolic power "only through the complicity of those who do not want to know that they are subject to it or even that they themselves exercise it" (Bourdieu 1991c:164). In using the term "symbolic violence" Bourdieu stresses how the dominated accept as legitimate their own condition of domination (Bourdieu and Wacquant 1992: 167). But symbolic power is a legitimating power that elicits the consent of *both* the dominant and the dominated.

Bourdieu (1987f:13) thinks of symbolic power as *"worldmaking* power," for it involves the capacity to impose the "legitimate vision of the social world and of its divisions." Because symbolic power legitimizes existing economic and political relations, it contributes to the intergenerational reproduction of inegalitarian social arrangements. In a key passage Bourdieu offers the following definition:

Every power to exert symbolic violence, i.e. every power which manages to impose meanings and to impose them as legitimate by concealing the power relations which are the basis of its force, adds its own specifically symbolic force to those power relations. (Bourdieu and Passeron 1977:4)

Thus, for Bourdieu, symbolic power legitimizes economic and political power but does not reduce to them. This marks the difference between Bourdieu's view of culture and the orthodox Marxist view of superstructure.

The exercise of power in almost all cases requires some justification or legitimation that creates "misrecognition" of its fundamentally arbitrary character (Bourdieu 1989c:377). "Misrecognition" is a key concept for Bourdieu; akin to the idea of "false consciousness" in the Marxist tradition, misrecognition denotes "denial" of the economic and political interests present in a set of practices.[31] Misrecognition is tied to Bourdieu's strong

---

31. Bourdieu (1986a:107, 298; 1990h:242–43) sees misrecognition as tantamount to "denial" in the sense of the Freudian term *Verneinung*, though for Bourdieu denial comes through "symbolic labor" rather than through a psychic process, as described by Freud.

claim that all actions are interested. The logic of self-interest underlying all practices—particularly those in the cultural domain—is misrecognized as a logic of "disinterest." Symbolic practices deflect attention from the interested character of practices and thereby contribute to their enactment as disinterested pursuits. This misperception legitimizes these practices and thereby contributes to the reproduction of the social order in which they are embedded. Activities and resources gain in symbolic power, or legitimacy, to the extent that they become separated from underlying material interests and hence go misrecognized as representing disinterested forms of activities and resources. This is almost always the case in undifferentiated precapitalist societies, where material life, as Polanyi observes (Dalton 1968, 1944), is embedded in a complex matrix of social and cultural arrangements. Bourdieu (1990h:118) observes from his fieldwork in Kabylia that "even 'economic' capital cannot act unless it succeeds in being recognized through a conversion that can render unrecognizable the true principle of its efficacy." The purely economic cannot express itself autonomously but must be converted into symbolic form. There is, therefore, "symbolic power" as well as material or economic power. Individuals and groups who are able to benefit from the transformation of self-interest into disinterest obtain what Bourdieu calls "symbolic capital." Symbolic capital is "denied capital" (ibid.); it disguises the underlying interested relations as disinterested pursuits.[32]

Bourdieu initially developed the concept of symbolic capital in his early studies of Kabyle peasant society. There, in what Bourdieu (1990h:114) calls the "good-faith economy," the predominant form of circulation of goods occurs through the exchange of gifts, both material and symbolic, rather than through explicit market exchange. The significance of symbolic capital lies in its apparent negation of economic capital. Symbolic capital is a form of power that is not perceived as power but as legitimate demands for recognition, deference, obedience, or the services of others.[33]

Bourdieu takes his argument to a more general level by arguing that not only is all action interested but that much action can be carried out successfully *only if* its interested character goes misrecognized. He argues that a great many practices could not be performed if they were recognized as emanating from the pursuit of self-interest (Bourdieu 1986a:242–43).

---

32. Bourdieu (1977c:183) writes: "Symbolic capital, a transformed and thereby disguised form of physical 'economic' capital, produces its proper effect inasmuch, and only inasmuch, as it conceals the fact that it originates in 'material' forms of capital which are also, in the last analysis, the source of its effects."

33. See Bourdieu 1972:227–43, 1977c:171–83, 1989c, and 1990h:112–21 for key formulations of this concept.

"The operation of gift exchange," for example, "presupposes (individual and collective) misrecognition *(meconnaissance)* of the reality of the objective 'mechanism' of the exchange" (Bourdieu 1977c:5–6). Action occurs *as if* actors pursue their self-interests for this is the way it appears to the "outsider" sociologist who is able to calculate the statistical regularities of behavior. It is as if actors conspired to conceal from their own eyes the self-interested character of their actions. Bourdieu (1977c:6) writes that

everything takes place as if agents' practice, and in particular their manipulation of *time*, were organized exclusively with a view to concealing from themselves and from others the truth of their practice, which the anthropologist and his models bring to light simply by substituting the timeless model for a scheme which works itself out only in and through time.

Since action occurs through time, and largely at a tacit, taken-for-granted level, actors misperceive the objective consequences of their actions, which are nonetheless available to the social scientist.

Bourdieu applies the concept of symbolic capital to highly differentiated contemporary societies as well. Though the economy is differentiated from other aspects of social life in advanced industrialized societies, it nonetheless requires legitimation. The matter-of-fact realism that "business is business" rarely operates without recourse to some honorific justification. Indeed, Bourdieu sees the transition from the early phases of predatory capitalism to the advanced industrial and postindustrial societies as being accompanied by increased reliance on symbolic power and capital. Both the practice of philanthropy by early "robber baron" entrepreneurs and the increased investment in prestigious forms of higher education by capitalist families testify to the efforts to accumulate symbolic as well as economic capital. In response to changes in taxation and inheritance laws, capitalist families today invest more in higher education in order to legitimate the transfer of wealth to the new generation (Bourdieu and de Saint Martin 1978). Furthermore, charitable giving by private economic interests, for example, the funding of public broadcasting in the United States, further illustrates the importance accorded by monied interests to their symbolic legitimation. Because personal gain is generally associated in capitalist societies with material forms of accumulation, symbolic pursuits in philanthropy, science, religion, and the arts tend to be thought of as lacking vested interest. Indeed, philanthropy and the nonprofit sector functions to legitimate particular economic interests by converting them into forms of symbolic recognition for the collective good. Bourdieu (1990h:133) sees the expansion of the nonprofit sector as stemming from the "conversion of economic capital into symbolic capital" whereby dominant groups secure esteem in public opinion for their activities.

Symbolic capital thus represents for Bourdieu a way of talking about the legitimation of power relations through symbolic forms. It is a form of "legitimate accumulation, through which the dominant groups secure a capital of 'credit' which seems to owe nothing to the logic of exploitation" (Bourdieu 1977c:197). Tied to his stratification analysis of relations between dominant and dominated groups, Bourdieu understands symbolic capital as "a sort of advance," extended by the dominated to the dominant as long as the dominated find it is within their interest to accord recognition and legitimacy to the dominant. It is a "collective belief," a "capital of trust" that stems from social esteem as well as material wealth.

Symbolic capital, like material capital, can be accumulated, and under certain conditions and at certain rates be exchanged for material capital. Reflecting on his early ethnographic work in Algeria, Bourdieu (1980c:61) says "I wanted . . . to do an economy of symbolic phenomena and study the specific logic of the production and circulation of cultural goods." This component of his overall framework rests on the core claim that symbolic capital and economic capital are distinct, though under certain conditions and at certain rates interconvertible, forms of power that follow their own particular dynamics. His research program consists, therefore, of studying the production and consumption of symbolic goods, the pursuit of symbolic profit, the accumulation of symbolic capital, and the modes of conversion between symbolic and other forms of capital or power.

The problem of the relationship between the various forms of capital, which was discussed earlier in the chapter, is further complicated by the concept of symbolic capital. Symbolic capital obtains from the successful use of other capitals (Bourdieu 1990h:122). It suggests a state of legitimation of other forms of capital, as if other capitals obtain a special symbolic effect when they gain a symbolic recognition that masks their material and interested basis. This would suggest that different kinds of capital, such as economic capital and cultural capital, could have their own specific types of symbolic capital in different societies. If the case, this would point to overlapping power dimensions that are not sufficiently conceptualized with the appellation capital. In one place Bourdieu admits that social and symbolic capital overlap so extensively that it becomes virtually impossible to distinguish them.[34] To what extent, therefore, is it really appropriate to

---

34. In discussing social capital in the case of groups delegating authority to leadership and group representation, Bourdieu (1986a:257) adds in a footnote that "It goes without saying that social capital is so totally governed by the logic of knowledge and acknowledgment that it always functions as symbolic capital."

think of legitimation as another form of power that, like economic and cultural power, merits the appellation "capital"?

Critics such as Caillé see in Bourdieu's statements that symbolic capital is "denied capital" proof that in the final analysis symbolic capital is nothing more than a form of economic capital in disguise. This conclusion, however, does violence to the complexity of Bourdieu's thinking. We have also seen that Bourdieu argues that brute force or material possession are seldom sufficient for the effective exercise of power. Legitimation plays a necessary role in the exercise of material and political power. There would be, therefore, little point in stressing the absolute importance of material resources and physical strength if their effective deployment required legitimation. Thus, while Bourdieu does work with a hierarchy of capitals with material being the most fundamental, he also stresses the necessity of symbolic power for the effective exercise of political and economic power. Both aspects of his work need to be stressed.

SYMBOLIC LABOR

How does the interested dimension of human action become transformed into disinterested ideology? I observed in chapter 2 that Bourdieu answers this question by drawing from Weber's sociology of religious leadership. "Religious labor" by specialists creates religious understandings of the particular social conditions of existence of specific groups. More generally, Bourdieu (1977c:171, 1980a:191) answers this question by pointing to the role of *symbolic labor*, especially by specialized symbolic producers (i.e., intellectuals), that transforms interested social relations, such as kinship, neighborhood, and work, into elective relations, or transforms relations of exploitation into legitimate relations. Symbolic labor produces symbolic power by transforming relations of interest into disinterested meanings and by legitimating arbitrary relations of power as the natural order of things (Bourdieu 1990h:112). Bourdieu considers symbolic labor to be as important as economic labor in the reproduction of social life. The task for sociology, therefore, is to describe

the laws of transformation which govern the transmutation of the different kinds of capital into symbolic capital, and in particular the labour of dissimulation and transfiguration (in a word, of *euphemization*) which secures a real transubstantiation of the relations of power by rendering recognizable and misrecognizable the violence they objectively contain and thus by transforming them into symbolic power, capable of producing real effects without any apparent expenditure of energy. (Bourdieu 1991c:170)

Bourdieu assigns a key role to cultural producers (e.g., artists, writers, teachers, and journalists) in legitimating the social order by producing symbolic capital through symbolic labor. Bourdieu (1971d, 1985d) contends that *both* materialist and idealist views of culture neglect the relatively independent role that corps of specialists historically have come to play in producing symbolic systems. Cultural producers mediate the relationship between culture and class, between infrastructure and superstructure, by constituting cultural markets, or fields, that are vested with their own particular interests.

Bourdieu thus challenges *both* the Marxist theory of superstructure and idealist views of cultural life by proposing a theory of intellectuals that emphasizes the specific symbolic interests that shape cultural production. Bourdieu assigns a particularly important—though not exclusive—role to the arenas of symbolic specialization and their representatives in developing the material out of which the symbolic dimension of class struggle is carved. He conceptualizes these arenas as social-cultural markets or fields of force in which specialists struggle over definitions of what is to be considered as legitimate modes of expression.

In summary, Bourdieu's general science of the economy of practices attempts to reappropriate from the idealist/materialist bifurcation of human life the totality of practices as fundamentally interested but misrecognized forms of power or capital. Indeed, Bourdieu's sociological project is a study of the political economy of the various forms of symbolic capital. He focuses much of his work on the symbolic producers who specialize in creating symbolic power, but, as we will see in chapter 11, Bourdieu also thinks of his sociology as an instrument of struggle against the various forms of symbolic violence.

5 HABITUS: A CULTURAL THEORY OF ACTION

A central issue sets the agenda for Bourdieu's theory of practice. How is action regulated; how does action follow regular statistical patterns without being the product of obedience to rules, norms or conscious intention?[1] How do regular patterns of conduct occur over time without being the product either of some abstract external structure or of subjective intention? How can one take into account *both* the observed regularities of social action, which most frequently are visible only to the social scientist who takes the time and effort to calculate them, and the experiential reality of free, purposeful, reasoning human actors who carry out their everyday actions practically, without full awareness of or conscious reflection on structures? Moreover, how does one scientifically model practice without projecting the formal characteristics of the model onto the informal and dispositional dynamics of most everyday practices? Bourdieu tries to find a scientific language that does justice to these conceptual dilemmas. Two key concepts permit Bourdieu to do this: *habitus* and *field*. This chapter takes up his concept of habitus and explores its various dimensions; chapter 6 will discuss his concept of field. A summary statement of his theory of practice that incorporates these two concepts will be found at the end of chapter 6.

1. Bourdieu (1990c:65) declares: "I can say that all of my thinking started from this point: how can behaviour be regulated without being the product of obedience to rules?"

Bourdieu's concept of habitus is familiar to many sociologists and anthropologists though far from well understood. Even among those knowledgeable about Bourdieu's work, considerable disagreement exists on just what Bourdieu's concept represents.[2] Part of the problem is that the concept bears so much theoretical weight, leading one sympathetic critic (DiMaggio 1979:1464) to describe it as "a kind of theoretical deus ex machina by means of which Bourdieu relates objective structure and individual activity." Part of the problem is also, as Bourdieu and Wacquant (1992) charge, that critics have systematically misread Bourdieu's theoretical intent by unwittingly projecting variations of the subjective/objective dichotomy onto the very concept that Bourdieu employs to transcend that antinomy. This chapter clarifies the central dimensions of the action/structure relationship that the concept of habitus addresses. It surveys briefly several intellectual influences that have shaped the development of the concept, and illustrates the variety of uses Bourdieu has made of the concept. It also notes a number of tensions, difficulties, and contradictions generated by the concept.

The Individual/Society Dualism

Bourdieu's theory of practice may be seen as a probing reflection on one of the oldest problems in the Western intellectual tradition, namely, the relationship between the individual and society. He sees his approach, however, as transcending this classic dualism. He draws on the basic insight of the classical sociological tradition that maintains that social reality exists *both* inside and outside of individuals, both in our minds and in things. Bourdieu stresses that this dual character of social reality must be preserved in sociological inquiry, and his relentless attacks on various forms of subjectivism and objectivism are efforts to preserve that fundamental insight. Indeed, the purpose of his key concept of habitus is to suggest that "the socialized body (which one calls the individual or person) does not stand in opposition to society; it is one of its forms of existence" (Bourdieu 1980c: 29). Bourdieu's conceptual formulation does not oppose individual and society as two separate sorts of being—one external to the other—but constructs them "relationally" as if they are two dimensions of the same social reality.

Habitus emphasizes the mutually penetrating realities of individual subjectivity and societal objectivity after the fashion of social construction-

2. This observation stems not only from the variety of explanations and criticisms now available in the secondary literature but also from observing several "Bourdieu experts" discuss the concept at a conference on Bourdieu's work (Center for Psychosocial Studies in Chicago, March 31–April 2, 1989).

ist theorists such as Berger and Luckmann (1966).[3] Like Berger's and Luckmann's, Bourdieu's approach to understanding the relationship between actors and structures builds on one key idea: that objective structures have subjective consequences is not incompatible with the view that the social world is constructed by individual actors.

Bourdieu is sharply critical of the institutionalized form that the classical individual/society dualism has taken in contemporary Western academia, half appropriated by psychology, which tends to monopolize the study of the individual, and half appropriated by economics, political science, and sociology, which tend to be concerned with structures beyond individuals. In sociology, since the 1960s, a renewed and vibrant interest in the study of micro structures and processes has nonetheless emerged. Herbert Blumer (1969), Aaron V. Cicourel (1973), Harold Garfinkel (1967), Erving Goffman (1967, 1969, 1971, 1974, 1981) and their followers have produced bodies of work identified broadly as symbolic interactionism and ethnomethodology. In recent years renewed interest in a rational-actor model has also emerged among such prominent sociologists as Raymond Boudon (1979), James S. Coleman (1990), and Jon Elster (1979, 1985). Yet, within the professional discipline of sociology these micro approaches, which focus on various dimensions of individual decision making and interaction, tend to be isolated from the more prominent macro approaches.[4]

For Bourdieu, the problem goes beyond one of fragmenting the unity of human experience through the artificially constructed boundaries of academic knowledge; it is also a political problem. Bourdieu sees the individual/society dualism as a carrier of political effects that contaminate the scientific enterprise. This antinomy opposes "defenders of individualism ('methodological individualism') on the one side, and those defending 'society' on the other who are then denounced as 'totalitarian' " (Honneth, Kocyba, and Schwibs 1986:48). In other words, Bourdieu believes that this dualism translates into ostensibly scientific language fundamental political oppositions that pit those favorable to market-oriented public policies

3. Berger and Luckmann connect individuals to the social world through an ongoing dialectical process composed of three simultaneously occurring moments: internalization, externalization, and objectivation. While Bourdieu does not distinguish all three moments conceptually, he does write of his theory of practice as an "experimental science of the *dialectic of the internalization of externality and the externalization of internality*" (Bourdieu 1977c:72). In *Reproduction*, he describes habitus as the "product of structures, producer of practices, and reproducer of structures."

4. This bifurcation of the discipline has generated professional as well as intellectual concerns. Professionally, the so-called micro-macro problem was designated as the unifying theme of the 1989 annual meeting of the American Sociological Association. Intellectually, the topic has generated numerous articles in the professional literature. See, for example, Alexander et al. 1987 and Collins 1981b.

against advocates of the welfare state. This view reflects Bourdieu's desire to protect the autonomy of social science from all extrascientific influences. But it also points to ambiguity in Bourdieu's own position. In France, one can see this dualism employed by Boudon, who advocates "methodological individualism," and who situates Bourdieu's style of sociology and his support for leftist politics on the "society" side of the dichotomy. Thus Bourdieu finds himself embedded in the very antinomy he hopes to transcend.

Action as Strategy

Bourdieu developed his theory of practices not only in reaction to Althusserian Marxism, as we observed in the previous chapter, but also to the French structuralism of Lévi-Strauss. In the structuralist anthropology of Lévi-Strauss, the social scientist develops formal models of deep structural rules that supposedly regulate kinship, social rituals, and mythology.[5] Bourdieu adopts the language of "strategy" to distance himself from strict structuralist forms of determination by stressing the importance of agency within a structuralist framework.

He first employs this conceptual language in confronting a field experience familiar to anthropologists. In studying Algerian peasants, Bourdieu encountered a social order in which social solidarity is based on sentiment and honor rather than on codified rules and regulations. He explains that in Kabyle society "social regulations are not comprehended as an inaccessible ideal or as a restraining imperative, but are rather present in the consciousness of each individual." Differences and disputes are not adjudicated in a court of law but by "the sentiment either of honour or justice, which, according to each case, dictates both judgement and punishment, and not a rational and formal justice" (Bourdieu 1965:22).

Though lacking evidence of a formalized code for regulating behavior, many anthropologists nonetheless tend to conceptualize the behavior and statements of their informants *as if* they were indeed rule or norm governed. Bourdieu approaches the problem quite differently. He argues that models of action must include *time* as an essential component. "To restore to practice its practical truth," he argues, "we must therefore reintroduce time into the theoretical representation of a practice which, being temporally structured, is intrinsically defined by its *tempo*" (Bourdieu 1977c:8).

In a critical reexamination of the classic analyses of gift exchange by Mauss (1967) and Lévi-Strauss (1969, 1973), Bourdieu argues that a proper

---

5. In the American structural-functionalist tradition, models prescribe sets of roles to be played in response to specified norms.

conceptualization of gift exchange must go beyond the idea that gift giving and receiving are governed by the formal principle of reciprocity in which gifts automatically call forth countergifts. Rather, the giving and receiving of gifts involve the manipulation of the *tempo* of gift-giving so that the returned gift is not only different but also *deferred*. Thus, actors participate in the social interaction of gift exchange, not as conscious or even unwitting conformists to the principle of reciprocity, but as *strategists* who respond through *time*. Behavior, then, is *strategic* rather than rule or norm conforming, for, as the label suggests, actors in their everyday practices attempt to move through a maze of constraints and opportunities that they grasp imperfectly through past experience and over time.[6] "To substitute *strategy* for the *rule*," writes Bourdieu (1977c:9) "is to reintroduce time, with its rhythm, its orientation, its irreversibility." In contrast, "science has a time which is not that of practice." It is only the social scientist, with the outsider perspective and an intellectual disposition to find patterned regularity in the diversity of human conduct, who sees this macro-structure of gifts and countergifts.[7] Thus, Bourdieu injects the language of strategy into the structuralist model as a way of introducing agency and of marking the difference between everyday practices and their formalized models.

If the notion of strategy is to convey the idea that action is not best understood in terms of compliance to norms or rules, strategies nonetheless involve conduct in normative situations (Bourdieu 1977c:8). Bourdieu does not intend the idea of strategy to suggest that particular types of conduct somehow stand outside normative constraints. Rather, the concept aims to suggest that action involves *uncertainty* even in normative situations and that actions occur *over time* rendering the outcomes seldom clear to the actors involved. Even the most ritualized forms of conduct permit strategies to some extent, since actors can always play on time (Bourdieu 1977c:9, 15, 106). Whether or not actors conform to norms or follow prescribed rituals depends on their interests. As pointed out in the previous chapter, Bourdieu considers all action to be interest oriented.[8]

His language of strategy misleads some critics (e.g. Caillé 1981, 1992),

6. The analogy to a game seems appropriate here, and Bourdieu (1987b:80–81) indeed draws on the game analogy, particularly in his later work.

7. Bourdieu thus departs from the structural-functional interpretation by Gouldner (1973b) of the norm of reciprocity. For Bourdieu, actors strategize to enhance their interests over time in gift exchanges. The overall pattern of regularity observed by the social scientist is an unintended consequence rather than conformity to an underlying norm or rule.

8. This conceptual shift has research consequences for Bourdieu in studying kinship as strategy rather than as rules. He replaces the idea of "rules of kinship" with "matrimonial strategies" (1990c:9, 1990i:i), and redirects attention away from exclusive focus on genealogies to include a much broader array of data, such as age and differences in various types of wealth.

who see it as an indicator of the very kind of utilitarian orientation that Bourdieu opposes. By *strategy*, Bourdieu (1987b:76, 78, 127) does not mean conscious choice or rational calculation. The strategies employed by the Kabyle are not based on conscious, rational calculations but on a "sense of honor" that guides complex maneuvers of challenge, riposte, delay, aggression, retaliation, and disdain. The sense of honor derives from sets of dispositions that internalize in practical form what seems appropriate or possible in situations of challenge, constraint, or opportunity. Thus, choices do not derive directly from the objective situations in which they occur or from transcending rules, norms, patterns, and constraints that govern social life; rather, they stem from *practical dispositions* that incorporate ambiguities and uncertainties that emerge from acting *through time and space*.[9] Bourdieu employs the language, "practical knowledge" and "sense of practice" to describe this fundamentally nonformalized, practical dimension of action that he finds missing in structuralist accounts of human agency. Actors are not rule followers or norm obeyers but strategic improvisers who respond dispositionally to the opportunities and constraints offered by various situations.

The Development of the Concept of Habitus

The idea that actors are practical strategists is then linked to social structures through the concept of habitus.[10] An early [1966] definition of the concept reads as

a system of lasting, transposable dispositions which, integrating past experiences, functions at every moment as a *matrix of perceptions, appreciations, and actions* and makes possible the achievement of infinitely diversified tasks, thanks to analogical transfers of schemes permitting the solution of similarly shaped problems. (Bourdieu 1971c:83)[11]

A somewhat later [1980] and more frequently employed formulation defines habitus as

a system of durable, transposable dispositions, structured structures predisposed to function as structuring structures, that is, as principles which generate and organize practices and representations that can be objectively adapted to their outcomes

---

9. This distinguishes Bourdieu's use of the term from that of Crozier (Crozier and Friedberg 1977), whose strategies seem embedded within the opportunities and constraints presented by situations, whereas Bourdieu stresses as well the role of past socialization.

10. The most in-depth discussions of the concept are to be found in Bourdieu 1977c, chapters 2 and 4, and in Bourdieu 1990h:52–65.

11. In *Algeria 1960* (1979:vii), Bourdieu defines habitus as "a system of durable, transposable dispositions which function as the generative basis of structured, objectively unified practices."

without presupposing a conscious aiming at ends or an express mastery of the operations necessary in order to attain them. (Bourdieu 1990h:53)

Bourdieu has also used the wording "cultural unconscious," "habit-forming force," "set of basic, deeply interiorized master-patterns," "mental habit," "mental and corporeal schemata of perceptions, appreciations, and action," and "generative principle of regulated improvisations" to designate his key concept.[12] The concept has broadened in scope over time to stress the bodily as well as cognitive basis of action and to emphasize inventive as well as habituated forms of action. The variety of designations, nonetheless, all evoke the idea of a set of deeply internalized master dispositions that generate action. They point toward a theory of action that is practical rather than discursive, prereflective rather than conscious, embodied as well as cognitive, durable though adaptive, reproductive though generative and inventive, and the product of particular social conditions though transposable to others.

I noted in chapter 2 that Bourdieu's fieldwork experience among the Kabyle posed the problem of relating individual action to social structure. But the origins of the concept of habitus are also linked to Bourdieu's intellectual strategy for situating himself in French intellectual space in the 1950s and early 1960s.[13] It is primarily in reaction to Lévi-Strauss's structuralism—and the Althusserian variant in French Marxism—and its view of action as a mere reflection of structure that Bourdieu formulates his theory of practice and his concept of habitus.[14] His principal concern was to introduce the idea of agency into structuralist analysis without recourse to the kind of voluntarism he found in Sartre's existentialism (see Bourdieu 1987b:19).

The seminal work of Ervin Panofsky offered Bourdieu crucial conceptual help in developing his concept. Reading and translating in the mid-1960s Panofsky's *Gothic Architecture and Scholasticism*, about the effect of scholasticism on architecture, assisted Bourdieu in his earliest formulation of the concept. In the afterword to his French translation of Panofsky's work (Bourdieu 1967a), we find Bourdieu's earliest use of the term. Bour-

---

12. In his early work, *Un art moyen* (Bourdieu, Boltanski et al. 1965:23), Bourdieu uses "structured praxis" to designate habitus, even though in a more recent interview he sharply differentiates his conceptual language and understanding of action from the Marxist praxis tradition (Bourdieu and Wacquant 1989).

13. Both Durkheim and Mauss employ the term, though neither give it systematic application or elevate it to the explanatory stature that Bourdieu (1980c:134) proposes.

14. Bourdieu (1992:120–21) declares retrospectively that habitus was originally designed to reject all intellectualist versions of action, particularly rational economic maximization models and also positivist materialism.

dieu builds from Panofsky's insights that scholasticism represented a set of implicit cultural assumptions as well as explicit theoretical positions and that these tacit "mental habits" were not only transmitted by institutions, practices, and social relations but also functioned as a "habit-forming force" that generated schemes of thought and action. He draws from Panofsky's ideas of "mental habit" and "habit-forming force" to develop the idea that habitus is a "structuring structure" that generates action. This early formulation emphasizes the manner or mode of thought, or cognitive capacity of action.[15] It is Panofsky's influence that leads Bourdieu to think of school systems as the institutionalized context where the intellectual habitus of a culture develops.

The early conceptualization also bears the imprint of French structuralism, for Bourdieu frequently employs a linguistic analogy to express the concept. He draws from Saussure's (1974) distinction between speech and language to define habitus as a kind of deeply structured cultural grammar for action. With habitus, Bourdieu (1977c:22–30, 1985b:13, 1987b:19–24, 1990h:30–41) develops a "generative structuralism" analogous to Chomsky's (1965) idea of a "generative grammar." As grammar organizes speech, the structures of habitus can generate an infinity of possible practices. Bourdieu sometimes stresses this "innovative" capacity of habitus. In his analysis of precapitalist Algerian peasants and their encounter with the encroaching cash economy imposed by French colonialism, Bourdieu (1979:4) emphasizes that the peasant reaction is *not* a "purely mechanical and passive forced accommodation" to the new economic system. Rather, the peasants respond with "creative reinvention" to the discrepancy between the demands of the new economic rationality and their customary habits.

Unlike Chomsky's generative grammar, however, the inventive capacity of habitus stems not from a "universal mind" but from "an experience and also a possession, a capital" (Bourdieu 1985b:13). Habitus is not an innate capacity, such as the physical operation of the brain posited by Lévi-Strauss or the mentalistic outlook of Chomsky. Habitus is a "structured structure" that derives from the class-specific experiences of socialization in family and peer groups.

Over time, Bourdieu's concept of habitus evolved from a normative and cognitive emphasis to a more dispositional and practical understanding of action (Bourdieu 1980c:133). This shift in emphasis toward the dispositional and practical character of human conduct can be seen in the evolution of his conceptual terminology. An earlier term *ethic* gives way to *ethos*, which

---

15. We see this cognitive emphasis in the 1968 publication of *The Craft of Sociology* (Bourdieu, Chamboredon, and Passeron 1991), in which Bourdieu talks about cultivating a type of research habitus for social scientific inquiry.

eventually becomes absorbed by habitus. The more recent language of "dispositions" suggests a shift from a linguistic analogy to a perspective centered on socialization and body language.

The term "disposition" is key for Bourdieu, since it suggests two essential components he wishes to convey with the idea of habitus: *structure* and *propensity*.[16] Habitus results from early socialization experiences in which external structures are internalized. As a result, internalized dispositions of broad parameters and boundaries of what is possible or unlikely for a particular group in a stratified social world develop through socialization. Thus, on the one hand, habitus sets structural limits for action. On the other hand, habitus generates perceptions, aspirations, and practices that correspond to the structuring properties of earlier socialization. The language of "structured structures" and "structuring structures" captures these two central features of habitus. I next examine in more depth these two faces of habitus.

Structured Structures and Structuring Structures

Habitus tends to shape individual action so that existing opportunity structures are perpetuated. Chances of success or failure are internalized and then transformed into individual aspirations or expectations; these are in turn externalized in action that tends to reproduce the objective structure of life chances. Bourdieu understands this process in terms of a

system of circular relations that unite *structures* and *practices;* objective structures tend to produce structured subjective dispositions that produce structured actions which, in turn, tend to reproduce objective structure. (Bourdieu and Passeron 1977: 203)

Thus, Bourdieu observes that aspirations and practices of individuals and groups tend to correspond to the formative conditions of their respective habitus. What agents judge as "reasonable" or "unreasonable" for people of their station in the social world stems from habitus. Habitus tends to reproduce those actions, perceptions, and attitudes consistent with the conditions under which it was produced. It is "necessity made into virtue" (Bourdieu 1977c:77, 95).

To explain why inegalitarian social arrangements make sense to both the dominant and the dominated, Bourdieu employs the concept to empha-

16. Bourdieu (1977c:214) writes that "the word *disposition* seems particularly suited to express what is covered by the concept of habitus (defined as a system of dispositions). It expresses first the *result of an organizing action*, with a meaning close to that of words such as structure; it also designates a *way of being*, a *habitual state* (especially of the body) and, in particular, a *predisposition, tendency, propensity, or inclination*."

size the class-based character of socialization. Habitus derives from the predominately unconscious internalization—particularly during early childhood—of objective chances that are common to members of a social class or status group. Akin to the idea of class subculture, habitus brings about a unique integration, dominated by the earliest experiences statistically common to members of the same class (Bourdieu 1977c:79). Nevertheless, it is the product of class situations, not their cause. If French working-class youth did not appear to aspire to high levels of education attainment during the rapid educational expansion of the 1960s—and according to Bourdieu they did not—this was because they had internalized and resigned themselves to the limited opportunities that previously existed for their success in school.

Habitus, then, represents a sort of deep-structuring cultural matrix that generates self-fulfilling prophecies according to different class opportunities. And Bourdieu's "cultural" explanation of unequal educational attainment differs from the blaming-the-victim version of culture-of-poverty arguments in emphasizing individuals' adaptation to limited opportunities rather than the cultural origins of deviant behavior. It shows how structural disadvantages can be internalized into relatively durable dispositions that can be transmitted intergenerationally through socialization and produce forms of self-defeating behavior. Bourdieu's habitus thus offers a perspective that sidesteps the recurring debate among culturalists and structuralists on the origins and perpetuating cycles of poverty.

Habitus calls us to think of action as engendered and regulated by fundamental dispositions that are internalized primarily through early socialization. Bourdieu speaks of the internalization or "incorporation" of the fundamental social conditions of existence into dispositions.[17] He describes the fundamental conditions of existence as those that determine materially, socially, and culturally what are probable, possible, or impossible for a given social group. They are similar to Weber's concept of "life chances." These "objective structures" are internalized into corresponding dispositions leading group members to experience them as reasonable or unreasonable, likely or unlikely, natural or unthinkable for people of their own kind. Habitus is

necessity internalized and converted into a disposition. . . . It is a virtue made of necessity which continuously transforms necessity into virtue by instituting

17. He mentions several determining factors in primary socialization, such as "division of labour between the sexes, household objects, modes of consumption, parent-child relations" (1990h:54), but does not offer detailed analyses of what he considers to be the most important ones.

"choices" which correspond to the condition of which it is the product. (Bourdieu 1984a:170)

Habitus transforms social and economic "necessity" into "virtue" by leading individuals to a "kind of immediate submission to order" (Bourdieu 1990h: 54). It legitimates economic and social inequality by providing a practical and taken-for-granted acceptance of the fundamental conditions of existence.[18]

Bourdieu emphasizes the collective basis of habitus, stressing that individuals who internalize similar life chances share the same habitus. While Bourdieu recognizes the singularity of biological individuals' socialization experiences, he argues that " 'personal' style . . . is never more than a *deviation* in relation to the *style* of a period or class so that it relates back to the common style not only by its conformity . . . but also by the difference" (1977c:86). The collective reference is paramount for Bourdieu. Habitus offers the image of "conductorless orchestration" to emphasize the "regularity, unity and systematicity to practices" without conscious coordination (Bourdieu 1990h:59). Bourdieu writes that "the practices of the members of the same group or, in a differentiated society, the same class, are always more and better harmonized than the agents know or wish."

The dispositions of habitus represent an informal and practical rather than a discursive or conscious form of knowledge. This practical evaluation and informal mastery of life chances occurs unconsciously. Bourdieu (1984a:466) writes,

the schemes of the habitus, the primary forms of classification, owe their specific efficacy to the fact that they function below the level of consciousness and language, beyond the reach of introspective scrutiny or control by the will.

One dimension of habitus that Bourdieu emphasizes is the adjustment of aspirations and expectations to what he (adopting the expression from Bachelard) calls the "causality of the probable." Habitus adjusts aspirations and expectations according to the objective probabilities for success or failure common to the members of the same class for a particular behavior. This is a "practical" rather than a conscious adjustment. According to Bourdieu,

18. In an insightful feminist critique of Bourdieu's work, McCall (1992:848) argues that since women in highly stratified societies are obliged to mediate between the "masculine/ public world of paid work and the feminine/personal world of human reproduction" they do not experience the taken-for-granted "fit" between dispositions and positions that Bourdieu's concept presupposes.

if one regularly observes a very close correlation between the scientifically constructed *objective probabilities* (e.g., the chances of access to a particular good) and *subjective aspirations* ("motivations" or "needs") . . . this is not because agents consciously adjust their aspirations to an exact evaluation of their chances of success.

Habitus emerges through primary socialization from a

practical evaluation of the likelihood of the success of a given action in a given situation [which] brings into play a whole body of wisdom, sayings, commonplaces, ethical precepts ("that's not for the likes of us"). (Bourdieu 1977c:77; emphasis added)

The dispositions of habitus predispose actors to select forms of conduct that are most likely to succeed in light of their resources and past experience. Habitus orients action according to anticipated consequences. Unfortunately, Bourdieu gives little insight into the how the process of internalization becomes activated into a process of externalization. We learn little about the triggering mechanism at work or whether certain types of internalization are more easily externalized than others.

Bourdieu emphasizes the stratifying dimension of early socialization. Habitus conveys a sense of place and out-of-place in a stratified social world. Bourdieu (1984a:471) writes that

objective limits become a sense of limits, a practical anticipation of objective limits acquired by experience of objective limits, a "sense of one's place" which leads one to exclude oneself from the goods, persons, place and so forth from which one is excluded.

This social, differentiating dimension of habitus can be seen

in the form of dispositions which are so many marks of *social position* and hence of the social distance between objective positions . . . and correlatively, so many reminders of this distance and of the conduct required in order to "keep one's distance" or to manipulate it strategically, whether symbolically or actually, to reduce it (easier for the dominant than for the dominated), increase it, or simply maintain it (by not "letting oneself go," not "becoming familiar," in short, "standing on one's dignity," or on the other hand, refusing to "take liberties" and "put oneself forward," in short "knowing one's place" and staying there). (Bourdieu 1977c:82)

This puts power and its legitimation at the heart of the functioning and structure of habitus, since habitus involves an unconscious calculation of what is possible, impossible, and probable for individuals in their specific locations in a stratified social order. "The relation to what is possible is a relation to power" Bourdieu (1990h:4) writes.

The virtue-of-necessity dynamic of habitus stresses that not all social worlds are equally available to everyone. Not all courses of action are equally possible for everyone; only some are plausible, whereas others are unthinkable. Bourdieu explains that

agents shape their aspirations according to concrete indices of the accessible and the inaccessible, of what is and is not "for us," a division as fundamental and as fundamentally recognized as that *between the sacred and the profane*. (1990h:64; emphasis added)

Underlying Bourdieu's habitus lies Durkheim's sacred/profane dualism, which at a very fundamental level for Bourdieu divides the scope of agency between the possible and the impossible. Here again we see the influence of the structuralist logic of binary oppositions on Bourdieu's thinking. While insightful, this may render the judgment of habitus too categorical by not exhausting the full range of socialization experiences. There may be gray areas where uncertainties about life chances are internalized that do not fit the fundamentally dichotomous boundaries that Bourdieu's concept of habitus presupposes.

Habitus is fairly resistant to change, since primary socialization in Bourdieu's view is more formative of internal dispositions than subsequent socialization experiences. There is an ongoing adaptation process as habitus encounters new situations, but this process tends to be slow, unconscious, and tends to elaborate rather than alter fundamentally the primary dispositions.[19]

Furthermore, some kinds of class habitus appear to be more durable than others. The French working-class habitus in Bourdieu's analyses seems less adaptable to forms of secondary socialization than does the middle-class habitus. Lower-middle class French families appeared more likely to take advantage of expanding educational opportunities during the postwar period than did working-class families. Thus, the relationship between primary and secondary socialization appears variable by social class, though Bourdieu does not provide a clear directive on this point.

Over time, Bourdieu's conceptualization of the dispositional character of action has increasingly stressed its "embodied" form. The process of internalization of objective structures is not only a mental process but a corporeal one as well. The chances for success and failure common to a

19. Bourdieu talks about "defensive strategies" as a way habitus tends to select for action those terrains that are consistent with its original dispositions.

class are "incorporated" in bodily form as well as in cognitive dispositions. They show up in physical manner and style (e.g., posture and stride) as well as in discursive expression. Bourdieu (1985b:13) finds a classical source of inspiration for his concept of habitus in the Aristotelian idea of *hexis*, "the incorporated and quasi-postural disposition," which subsequently was "converted by scholasticism into habitus."[20] Some of Bourdieu's earliest analyses treat the bodily incorporation of cultural dispositions as a somewhat separate dimension of habitus. In his article, "Célibat et condition paysanne" (1962b), for example, the concept is used to identify an affinity between the bodily comportment of rural French peasants and their attitudes and perceptions of their physical behavior. The bodily and cognitive dimensions of habitus are considered separate but correlated. Yet, both mental and physical dispositions are integrally related, as later formulations of the concept of habitus increasingly stress.[21]

In *Sociology in Question* (1993d:86) Bourdieu argues that "the principles of habitus are *inseparably* logical and axiological, theoretical and practical." The dispositions of habitus represent *master patterns* of behavioral style that cut across cognitive, normative, and corporal dimensions of human action. They find expression in language, nonverbal communication, tastes, values, perceptions, and modes of reasoning.

It is a general, transposable disposition which carries out a systematic, universal application—beyond the limits of what has been directly learnt—of the necessity inherent in the learning conditions. (Bourdieu 1984a:170)

Habitus has the capacity to generalize through analogical transfers its fundamental "generative schemes" to *all* areas of life (Bourdieu 1990h:94). Bourdieu (1989c:387) suggests an analogy to handwriting that embodies a "stylistic affinity" for each individual regardless of form attempted or material used. This key feature of habitus permits Bourdieu, for example, to identify parallel styles of action in arenas as different as family planning, dress, choice of sport, and diet. He writes,

marriage strategies are inseparable from inheritance strategies, fertility strategies, and even educational strategies, in other words from the whole set of strategies for

20. There is some dispute, however, over the original meaning of the term. Boudon (1986: 309), a sharp critic of Bourdieu, claims that the classical notion is not at all what Bourdieu's usage suggests. But, as noted earlier, Bourdieu is more interested in concept development and application than scholarly exegesis. The concept has assumed a range of meanings particular to Bourdieu. See Héran 1987 and Rist 1984 for discussions of the genealogy of habitus.

21. It is noteworthy that the term *hexis* figures more prominently in *Outline of a Theory of Practice* (1977c) than in the later work, *The Logic of Practice* (1990h).

biological, cultural and social reproduction that every group implements in order to transmit the inherited powers and privileges, maintained or enhanced, to the next generation. (Bourdieu 1990h:160–61)

In *Distinction* (1984a) Bourdieu explores how habitus accounts for class differences across a broad range of aesthetic tastes and lifestyles. In the struggle for social distinction in France, we find tastes and lifestyles that correspond to four distinct class habitus: ostentatious indulgence and ease within the upper class, aristocratic aestheticism among intellectuals, awkward pretension by middle-class strivers, and antipretentious ignorance and conformity within the working class. Bourdieu traces manifestations of each of these four sets of dispositions across a gamut of lifestyle indicators. In chapter 7, I will examine more fully these class habitus.

Bourdieu uses his concept of habitus to make conceptually appealing transitions from micro- to macro-levels of analysis and to generalize through quite different domains of human activity. Its originality is to suggest that there may be an underlying connection or common imprint across a broad sweep of different types of behavior, including motor, cognitive, emotional, or moral behaviors. Examples of habitus at work range from "the most automatic gestures or the apparently most insignificant techniques of the body" to very abstract conceptualizations (Bourdieu 1984a: 466). But this very appealing conceptual versatility sometimes renders ambiguous just what the concept actually designates empirically.

The concept may be too encompassing for answering certain kinds of important research questions. Bourdieu resists distinguishing between cognitive, moral, and corporal dimensions of action. His idea is to identify underlying master patterns that represent deep structural patterns that cross-cut and find characteristic forms of expression in all of these dimensions. Yet, for certain research purposes, understanding precisely which of these dimensions seems to be more operative is what interests researchers. It is one thing to say that working-class youth do not enter French universities because they fear failure, and quite another to say that getting a higher education does not belong to their world view or class culture. In the former case, these youths might value higher learning and have hopes of attending the university but choose not to attend because they expect to fail. In the latter case, they would have no desire to attend the university and therefore no expectations. Values and expectations appear to merge in Bourdieu's understanding of habitus as a practical adaptation to the basic conditions of existence. They appear not to internalize as separate, distinguishable dimensions, since the thrust of Bourdieu's argument is to stress the common underlying unity of all practices as stemming from a few underlying master dispositions. Frequently, class values and expectations indeed go together, but not always, and for this reason it is sometimes important to distinguish them.[22]

Bourdieu sees the internalization through socialization of external opportunity structures as a straightforward and nonproblematic process. Habitus faithfully reflects, by definition, the objective conditions under which it was initially formed. Habitus,

> as an acquired system of generative schemes objectively adjusted to the particular conditions in which it is constituted, . . . engenders all the thoughts, all the perceptions, and all the actions consistent with those conditions, *and no others.* (Bourdieu 1977c:95; emphasis added)

If an individual or group were to hold aspirations different from what would seem possible from the objective conditions of their primary socialization, this would stem from subsequent adaptations of habitus to new structural conditions rather than because the early formation of habitus was somehow deficient. Bourdieu tends to assume that the process of internalization of objective chances occurs without flaw. But we lack sufficient evidence that this actually happens in a consistent manner. Are not miscalculation and distortion common occurrences in early socialization experiences? A growing body of research findings from cognitive psychology and survey research suggest such an assumption to be problematic. Individuals and groups persistently misperceive the sentiments, thoughts, and actions of their peers (O'Gorman 1986).[23]

Frequently, Bourdieu writes as if there were an almost exact correlation between hopes and chances, though at other times he recognizes that these

22. The contrast can be seen in the different perspectives offered by Kahl (1953) and Ogbu (1978, 1990) on opportunity perceptions. Kahl argues that working-class values and world view limit their vision for taking advantage of higher education opportunities whereas Ogbu argues that lower-class people—particularly blacks—base their reluctance to pursue advanced schooling on a calculation of limited chances for success.

23. Since I identified a similarity of concern between Bourdieu's effort to relate individual subjectivity and social objectivity and the social construction approach of Peter Berger and Thomas Luckmann, it is appropriate here to note an important difference. Berger and Luckmann see the degree of success of primary socialization as problematic, and connect it to the division of labor and the distribution of knowledge: the internalization of objective realities is likely to be more successful in societies with a relatively simple division of labor and minimal distribution of knowledge than in societies with more complex and inegalitarian structures (Berger and Luckmann 1966:164). Bourdieu theorizes a similar relationship between habitus and the division of labor, but does not conceptualize the possibility of a "deviant habitus." On the other hand, Bourdieu's application of habitus is much more attentive to class-specific forms of socialization than are Berger and Luckmann.

are never completely synchronized. Bourdieu defends the flexible application of his concept against critics who charge that it is applied too mechanistically, warning against universalizing the model of a high correlation between subjective hopes and objective chances that simply reproduces social structure (Bourdieu 1990h:63). Yet if Bourdieu's theoretical intentions are good, the written formulations sometimes fail to convey the intended nuance. An early formulation specifies that

if members of the lower middle and working classes take reality as being equivalent to their wishes, it is because, in this area as elsewhere, aspirations and demands are defined in both form and content by objective conditions which exclude the possibility of hoping for the unobtainable. (Bourdieu 1974c:33)

A systematic distinction between *aspirations* and *expectations* would help give further theoretical refinement to Bourdieu's scheme and at the same time could be easily operationalized in research. Is habitus primarily concerned with expectations or does it include aspirations as well?[24] Bourdieu employs both terms interchangeably.

If Bourdieu's concept of habitus helps describe situations where expectations are adjusted to objective opportunities so that the dominated actually participate in their own domination, the concept also misses the miscalculations of objective probabilities that are also a common feature of group and individual aspirations. Bourdieu gives insufficient attention to the range of conditions under which aspirations fail to synchronize with expectations and expectations with opportunities. Numerous cases suggest that the alignment process of hopes, plans, and chances is problematic. The elevated aspirations among American blacks during the 1960s for high occupational status, despite overwhelming evidence of limited career opportunities, represents just one striking example where disjuncture between hopes and chances occurs (Hout and Garnier 1979, MacLeod 1995). If Bourdieu's capital investment and conversion strategies perspective on class relations insightfully identifies the subtle dynamics of status inconsistency among upper- and middle-class groups, the reproduction dimension of habitus fails to give analogous insight into the complexity and ambiguity of individual perceptions of external realities. The concept of habitus fails to capture the varying degrees of incongruity between hopes, plans, and chances for different groups.

Bourdieu (1984a:143–68) does deal with the issue of disjuncture be-

24. Bourdieu (1984a) seems to describe expectations rather than aspirations, when he writes about "virtue made of necessity" to indicate that expectations are closely correlated with objective probabilities.

tween aspirations and opportunities in a discussion of the effects of diploma inflation. He sees a "structural mismatch between aspirations and real probabilities" caused by educational expansion without parallel expansion and upgrading of job requirements in the labor market. This structural mismatch is the source of an "anti-institutional cast of mind" that translates into worker discontent and forms of adolescent counterculture. He also talks about a "collective disillusionment," saying that it "finds expression in unusual forms of struggle, protest and escapism" (144). But his analysis does not suggest conditions that might help explain why the discontent would take one form rather than another. Moreover, he goes on to sound his familiar theme of reproduction by arguing that "competitive" forms of struggle resulting from "frustrated expectations" are quite compatible with the reproduction of the social order through the "displacement of structure" (164–65).

Under certain conditions, however, there can occur a structural lag, or "hysteresis effect,"[25] between aspirations and changing opportunities (Bourdieu 1977c:78–79). Habitus implies that actors attend to the present and anticipate the future in terms of previous experience.[26] The idea of a "hysteresis effect" is used by Bourdieu to explain why Algerian peasants did not rapidly adapt their notions of time and labor to the new values of economic rationality. It also helps explain why slight improvements over several years in educational opportunity for working-class youth could go largely unperceived in working-class families (Bourdieu and Passeron 1979: appendix). He also uses the idea to explain the contemporary dynamics of the overeducated and underemployed worker in the labor market. Rapid and massive educational expansion without parallel growth in the postwar labor market brought credential inflation and devaluation. Aspirations for higher education credentials that were rewarded by real job opportunities in an earlier period became frustrated by the growing "structural mismatch" between education supply and labor-market demand. Bourdieu (1984a:144) explains the growing evidence of "disaffection towards work" and the "anti-institutional cast of mind" that begins developing in the late '60s and early '70s as the "collective disillusionment which results from the structural mis-

25. The term comes from physical science, and refers to when magnetic effects lag behind their causes.

26. There is some similarity between Bourdieu's understanding of how habitus responds to new conditions and Ogburn's (1922) cultural lag hypothesis. Bourdieu's conceptualization of habitus is not to be conflated with Ogburn's notion of "the adaptive culture." Still, the idea explored by Ogburn that "changes in the adaptive culture do not synchronize exactly with the change in the material culture" is similar to Bourdieu's understanding of habitus as a relatively permanent set of dispositions that enters into tension when it confronts objective conditions quite different from those in which it was originally generated.

match between aspirations and real probabilities."[27] Conditions for change rather than reproduction are set up when habitus encounters objective structures radically different from those under which it was originally formed. Yet, the weight of history shapes decisively our response in those situations.

This is not to suggest that Bourdieu views all behavior as being governed by habitus. He finds (1977c:20) that habitus is most useful for explaining behavioral patterns in situations where normative rules are not explicit. Conduct relies less on habitus in situations that are highly codified, regulated, or threatening to vital material and political interests. Highly ritualized situations reduce (but do not eliminate) opportunities for strategy and innovation by habitus, whereas less ritualized ones enhance strategic opportunities. In discussing certain types of marriage arrangements among the Kabyle, Bourdieu (1990h:182) observes that "the stakes are so high and the chances of a rift so great that the agents dare not rely entirely on the regulated improvisation of orchestrated *habitus.*"

Bourdieu (1990c:108) also acknowledges that habitus "may be superseded under certain circumstances—certainly in situations of crisis which disrupt the immediate adjustment of habitus to field—by other principles, such as rational and conscious computation." Situations of crisis or where the financial stakes are considerable may encourage highly conscious forms of strategizing. But while admitting that strategizing on occasions can be conscious, he is quick to assert that the effects of habitus are nonetheless discernable. As a general rule, where material interests are considerable or the threat of violence eminent, it is less likely that prevailing powers leave the course of action up to the habitus and the more likely that action becomes highly formalized, such as in diplomacy between states (Bourdieu 1987b:96). The thrust of his work, however, is to find evidence of habitus at work in most every situation. The stress Bourdieu places on the role of habitus in shaping action tends to deflect attention away from those situations when other principles governing practices come into play. He does not really consider other organizing modes of conduct in an extensive way.

Habitus seems to work best not only in situations that lack rituals and established protocol but also in relatively undifferentiated societies where the principal mode of domination operates through direct interpersonal relations rather than through impersonal institutions (Calhoun 1993).

27. Bourdieu (1984a:142) sees this collective deception being most likely among social groups who are new to the educational process and who still hold to the traditional value of the credentials—particularly at the lower levels of education. This problem is less likely to occur for those who inherit cultural capital, since that includes information on the changing value of educational credentials.

Thus, the concept seems particularly appropriate for Kabyle society where power is organized through an informal system of honor rather than through formal law. Bourdieu, however, takes the view that the concept applies as well to understanding behavior in advanced societies. In spite of formalized rules and regulations, actors engage in considerable practical strategizing in their everyday interactions that stem more from the dispositions of habitus than from rational choice or norm conformity. Sports in particular can be highly specialized and codified and yet highly regulated by incorporated dispositions (Bourdieu 1988f). Other specialized activities requiring trained bodily movement of habitus include driving, playing a musical instrument, skilled manual labor, dancing, etc. Moreover, specialized mental activities, such as writing, computer programming, and proofreading, evoke a "feel for the game" in their successful accomplishment. Even the daily routines of scientific investigation, Bourdieu reminds us, are shaped by practical mastery of the procedures of science. Nevertheless, the concept shifts level of analysis as Bourdieu moves from Algerian peasant society to modern France. In traditional undifferentiated societies, its conceptual reach is broader, more macro, reproducing the entire societal culture. In highly differentiated societies, habitus becomes more akin to class- and status-group subculture. Bourdieu seems to recognize implicitly the difficulty, as the concept of field—which we will examine in the next chapter—becomes relatively more important in his analyses of highly differentiated societies.

Both adaptation and distinction are two types of agency juxtaposed in the concept of habitus without their exact relationship being clarified. On the one hand, practices appear as a functional adaptation to the necessities of life chances. These practices tend to reproduce social position. On the other hand, habitus generates practices that differentiate actors from their competitors. Here Bourdieu (1989c:9) links the tendency for reproduction to a tendency for habitus to "affirm its autonomy in relation to situations" and thereby tend to "perpetuate a differential identity." This type of agency is more relational, since it emerges from the intersection of the dispositions of habitus and the structures of constraints and opportunities offered by the fields in which it operates. Yet adaptation is the more frequent type of agency in Bourdieu's analyses.

Habitus as Cultural Practices and Habits

On one level, habitus can be understood as Bourdieu's attempt to write a theory of culture as practice. Indeed, he explains his choice of the esoteric term as strategically warranted by the overdetermined character in both lay and scholarly use of the term "culture."[28] Bourdieu (1968:194) theorizes culture as more than a "common code" as in structuralism, more than an ideological system of ideas, beliefs, or values, as in Marxism, or more than a general world view posited by Mannheim's *Weltanschauung*. All of these images of culture, despite their quite different theoretical origins, convey little sense of agency. While the concept of habitus includes all of these features, it privileges the basic idea that action is governed by a "practical sense" of how to move in the social world. Culture is a practical tool used for getting along in the social world.

Bourdieu's concept of habitus, however, needs to be distinguished from Swidler's (1986) "tool kit" view of cultural practices. Though similar in stressing agency and the practical features of culture rather than norms, values, goals, or preferences, Bourdieu is less voluntaristic than Swidler; he stresses the group embeddedness of individual action. Moreover, Bourdieu stresses more than Swidler the power dimension of cultural resources— their capacity to constitute social hierarchies.

If on one level habitus can be read as a way of conceptualizing culture as practice, on another level it associates practice with habit. Bourdieu (1977c:218) explains that the choice of the term habitus stems from "the wish to set aside the common conception of habit as a mechanical assembly or performed programme." He wants to emphasize the generative capacity of habitus (1993d:87). Indeed, Bourdieu's concept, as Camic (1986) insightfully argues, can be viewed as an attempt to revive the meaning given by such classical theorists as Durkheim and Weber to the concept of habit.

Durkheim, and especially Weber, assigned to habitual forms of action an important place in their understanding of agency. Indeed, Weber (1978: 21, 24–25) explicitly conceptualizes habitual action as a pure type, and associates it with traditionalism. Moreover, he observes that "the great bulk of all everyday action" approximates this type. What these nineteenth- and early-twentieth-century social theorists understood by *habit* is quite different from the relatively elementary, skillfully performed, and virtually automatic activities we normally associate with the term today. Camic points out that the classical writers tend to apply the term at a more general level to identify forms of action that emerge apart from an explicitly reflective process. This expanded notion of habit might include "habits of interpersonal interaction; habits of economic, political, religious, and domestic behavior; habits of obedience to rules and to rulers; habits of sacrifice, dis-

28. Bourdieu (1968:706) footnotes an early discussion of habitus by observing that "culture . . . would be a better term than *habitus*. However, this overdetermined concept risks being misunderstood and it is difficult to define exhaustively the conditions of its validity."

interestedness, and restraint." On a still more general level, the term designates a "durable and generalized disposition that suffuses a person's action throughout an entire domain of life or, in the extreme instance, throughout all of life" (Camic 1986:1046). Bourdieu's concept of habitus represents, in part, an effort to revive the idea of habit in the broader and classical sense of the term.[29]

29. Camic's analysis demonstrates that this expanded notion of habit was abandoned by American sociology during the early decades of the twentieth century. A very restricted definition came to be accepted and relegated to the field of psychology in an effort to establish the discipline of sociology as distinct from psychology. Bourdieu's concept of habitus also illustrates his refusal to accept the institutionalized division of intellectual labor between contemporary sociology and psychology.

6 FIELDS OF STRUGGLE FOR POWER

"Field" *(champ)* is a key spatial metaphor in Bourdieu's sociology. Field defines the structure of the social setting in which habitus operates. Bourdieu defines a field as

a network, or configuration, of objective relations between positions. These positions are objectively defined, in their existence and in the determinations they impose upon their occupants, agents or institutions, by their present and potential situation *(situs)* in the structure of the distribution of species of power (or capital) whose possession commands access to the specific profits that are at stake in the field, as well as by their objective relation to other positions (domination, subordination, homology, etc.). (Bourdieu and Wacquant 1992:97)

Fields denote arenas of production, circulation, and appropriation of goods, services, knowledge, or status, and the competitive positions held by actors in their struggle to accumulate and monopolize these different kinds of capital. Fields may be thought of as structured spaces that are organized around specific types of capital or combinations of capital.[1] For example, Bourdieu speaks of the "intellectual field" to designate that matrix of institutions, organizations, and markets in which symbolic producers, such as artists, writers, and academics, compete for symbolic capital. Even science itself—the self-proclaimed highest expression of objectivity—is produced

1. Bourdieu (1980c:138–42) indicates that field means "a certain distribution structure of some kind of capital."

within the framework of a field (Bourdieu 1975b). Other field applications by Bourdieu include studies of social-class lifestyles (Bourdieu 1984a), higher education institutions (Bourdieu 1988b, 1989c), religion (Bourdieu and de Saint Martin 1982), literature (Bourdieu 1983a, 1988a), and housing policy (Bourdieu 1990b).

I begin this chapter with an examination of the origins and metatheoretical objectives of Bourdieu's field analytical perspective. I will then identify several structural features that characterize Bourdieu's fields and their interrelations, and consider the "field of power," which is the principal stratifying force in Bourdieu's analysis of contemporary societies. Finally, I will show how Bourdieu relates his key concepts of habitus, capital, and field to formulate his general science of practices.

Origins of the Concept

The concept of field appears more recently in Bourdieu's work than does habitus. The field analytical method Bourdieu develops represents a gradual shift in his work that occured during the 1970s and '80s. His debates in the '60s with Marxism and structuralism, when he developed his concepts of cultural capital, habitus, strategies, and practices, gave way gradually to an increasing concern with fields. While the early concerns stemming from his philosophical training, his reading of classical sociology, and his fieldwork in Algeria persist, the concept of field receives proportionally more conceptual development and empirical application in more recent work.[2] The concept emerged from the conjuncture in the late 1960s of Bourdieu's research in the sociology of art with his reading of Weber's sociology of religion (Bourdieu 1987b:33). Bourdieu (1971a, 1971c, 1985d, 1992:260) first applied the concept to the French intellectual and artistic worlds as a means to call attention to the specific interests governing those cultural worlds.[3]

Field as Metatheory

As is the case with all of his concepts, the concept of field reflects the metatheoretical dimension of Bourdieu's thought. Bourdieu sees it as an "open concept" designed to correct for the various forms of subjectivism and ob-

2. The concept is hardly mentioned in *Outline of a Theory of Practice* (Bourdieu 1977c) but assumes a prominent analytical role in *The Logic of Practice* [1980] (Bourdieu 1990h), two works that treat his Algerian fieldwork.

3. The term itself is not new to the French intellectual world, since it was employed by both phenomenologists (Merleau-Ponty 1962:462) and existentialists (Sartre 1960:87).

jectivism he criticizes in other prevailing ways of conceptualizing the relationship between social and cultural structures and practices.[4]

The concept of field is first of all a corrective against positivism. Fields are conceptual constructions based upon the relational mode of reasoning. "To think in terms of field is to *think relationally,*" Bourdieu stresses (Bourdieu and Wacquant 1992:96).[5] They illustrate Bourdieu's relational logic by encouraging the researcher to seek out underlying and invisible relations that shape action rather than properties given in commonsense categories. By speaking of fields rather than of populations, groups, organizations, or institutions, Bourdieu wants to draw attention to the latent patterns of interest and struggle that shape the existence of these empirical realities. Positivist conceptions of social location, such as "milieu," "context," or even "social background" fail to highlight sufficiently the conflictual character of social life.

Second, the concept of field is a conduit for Bourdieu's polemic against class reductionism and vulgar materialism. As we shall see in chapter 7, Bourdieu does hold a class perspective of modern societies. But the effects of class background, milieu, or context on individual behavior are never direct for Bourdieu; rather, they are always *mediated* through the structure of fields.

Third, the concept of field is designed to reject idealist interpretations of cultural practices. Field analysis calls attention to the social conditions of struggle that shape cultural production. Even the seemingly most neutral or ivory-tower cultural practices are, according to Bourdieu, embedded in systems of social as well as intellectual distinctions.[6] In these three ways, the concept of field embodies Bourdieu's metatheoretical agenda for sociology.

Beyond Markets and Institutions

Clearly Bourdieu's use of the term differs significantly from its more common use in designating an academic discipline or substantive area of in-

4. Indeed, he suggests that it "offers a coherent system of recurrent questions that saves us from the theoretical vacuum of positivist empiricism and from the empirical void of theoreticist discourse" (Bourdieu and Wacquant 1992:110). For Bourdieu, "the chief merit of the notion of field, . . . is that it allows us to transcend a whole series of methodological and theoretical antinomies" (quoted in Wacquant 1989:41). The oppositions he cites include those already discussed in chapter 3.

5. Bourdieu indicates that fields are to be thought of as a "*pense-bête,* a memory-jogger" to remind researchers to "think relationally" (Bourdieu and Wacquant 1992:228).

6. Bourdieu (1991d:7) criticizes Foucault's "symbolic structuralism," like that of Saussure and Lévi-Strauss, for limiting the search for difference to the realm of discourse without also examining the social conditions in which differential meanings are produced.

vestigation. Moreover, though he uses the terms *field* and *market* inter-changeably, Bourdieu's concept should not be fully assimilated with the neo-classical idea of market. Rather, the concept suggests force field, wherein the distribution of capital in the market reflects a hierarchical set of power relations among the competing individuals, groups, and organizations. Field is a more inclusive concept than market; as a spatial metaphor it suggests rank and hierarchy as well as exchange relations between buyers and sellers. Interactions among actors within fields are shaped by their relative location in the hierarchy of positions.

Field analysis calls attention to the institutional aspects of individual and group action. In a sense, it represents Bourdieu's version of institutional analysis. Yet, Bourdieu (1991d:19) sees the image of "field" as superior to that of "institution" for two reasons: first, he wants to emphasize the conflictual character of social life whereas the idea of institution suggests consensus; second, he wants a concept that can cover social worlds where practices are only weakly institutionalized and boundaries are not well established.[7] Some of the fields that Bourdieu analyses, such as education, do consist of clusters of patterned activities centered around basic social functions. But his concept of field designates arenas of struggle rather than fundamental functions thought to be vital for social life (Bourdieu and Wacquant 1992:103). His framework goes beyond the traditional functionalist conception of institutions.[8]

Since there is a bewildering array of uses of the terms *institution* and *institutionalization* in sociology, it is not surprising to find confusion in Bourdieu's conceptual language. Though a field can designate what is often thought of as an institution, such as the "field" of law, fields are not conceptually equated with institutions. Fields can be inter- or intra-institutional in scope; they can span institutions, which may represent positions within fields (Bourdieu and Wacquant 1992:232). Bourdieu does not confine his attention to particular arenas of agents and activities, such as the family, education, religion, or law, commonly identified as institutions in the functionalist tradition of sociology. Nor does he devote much attention to those political units, such as legislatures or constitutions, commonly treated as institutions in scholarship by political scientists and historians. Yet, many

---

7. Bourdieu (1991d:15) says that one of the key properties of fields is their degree of institutionalization. He talks about the degree of codification to express this characteristic. The field of cultural production, particularly of artists and writers, for example, is considerably less codified or institutionalized than the university field, since admission to the university is more strictly governed than it is to the field of literature.

8. Nonetheless, Bourdieu does stress the latent function of class reproduction by field.

of Bourdieu's ideas find affinity with key themes in neoinstitutional theory, as Powell and DiMaggio (1991:25-26) point out.[9]

If Bourdieu has designed his concept in opposition to consensual views of the social world, he also sees his concept as distinct from views that stress total domination. Bourdieu's fields are *fields of struggle* rather than "total institutions" (Goffman), "ideological state apparati" (Althusser) or orders of "discipline" (Foucault).[10] Fields are sites of resistance as well as domination, one being relationally linked to the other. Yet, as we will see, fields capture struggle within the logic of reproduction; they seldom become sites of social transformation.

The boundaries between fields are not sharply drawn by Bourdieu. He declares that "one of the major points of contention in the literary or artistic field is the definition of the limits of the fields" (Bourdieu 1987b:174). Any effort to establish precise boundaries between fields, Bourdieu argues, derives from a "positivist vision" rather than the more compelling "relational" view of the social world, for boundaries are themselves objects of struggle. This way of looking at fields reflects Bourdieu's relational logic: since in his view social identity is fundmentally referential and oppositional, Bourdieu uses the concept of field to define the broadest possible range of factors that shape behavior rather than delimit a precise area of activity.

One of the advantages of a field perspective is to encourage social scientists not to narrow prematurely the range of their investigation. To illustrate, recent reorientations in the sociology of organizations have considerably enriched organizational theory and our understanding of organizations by refusing to isolate the "environment" from the "internal" structures and processes of organizations. Indeed, DiMaggio and Powell (1983) draw explicitly from Bourdieu's concept of field in their programmatic statement calling for emphasis upon interorganizational contexts.

9. Some critics (e.g., Lamont 1989:782) have suggested that Bourdieu's view of actors as investors in various types of capital lacks a broader institutional perspective. This criticism seems based on the early formulations of his theory of practice and his analyses of the effects of cultural capital on educational attainment. Yet Bourdieu has consistently maintained that practices derive from the *intersection* of habitus with structures, though his exploration of structures did not begin until the early '70s, when he developed his concept of field. While it is true that he has given very limited attention to certain institutional arenas, such as the state, his level of analysis has consistently been one that attempts to guard against reduction of individuals, groups, or organizations to individualistic forms of agency.

10. The principal difference between Bourdieu's concept of field and Althusser's concept of "ideological state apparatus" is that field designates an arena of struggle where there is resistance to the dominant power (Bourdieu and Wacquant 1992:102). (Bourdieu admits that "under certain historical conditions . . . a field may start to function as an apparatus," if the dominant are able to crush effectively all the resistance of the subordinate.)

Bourdieu sees his work as quite different from Foucault's theory of domination in that his framework allows for resistance whereas that of Foucault does not (Bourdieu and Wacquant 1992:167).

Bourdieu uses his field concept effectively to show how boundary questions can function as instruments of struggle, particularly in his analysis of intellectuals (see below, chapter 9). Bourdieu's concern for the boundary problem seems helpful in two respects: first, the very definition of the scope of a research project is not exempt from institutional and professional pressures that can orient research in one direction rather than in another; and second, including or excluding particular components in an investigation can produce symbolic effects that limit one's degree of objectivity.

Yet, in refusing to establish boundaries Bourdieu gives his concept an excessively generous application. Like his types of capital, fields tend to proliferate.[11] Subfields appear as well. And, as in the case of capital, conceptual inflation leads to its devaluation. Further, there is an unresolved and uneasy tension between the priority Bourdieu gives to the internal analysis of fields and his emphasis on boundaries as contested terrain. Finally, the boundary question points to a deeper unresolved problem in Bourdieu's sociology, namely, sociological explanation. If boundaries are themselves the objects of struggle, what hope is there for the sociologist to be able to describe those conflicts in a nonpartisan way? In his effort to discredit positivism by raising social conflict and its ensuing relativism to the status of epistemological privilege, Bourdieu limits drastically chances for the observer to gain an objective grasp of the social world. Indeed, such chances may simply be lost. This is an important and unresolved problem in Bourdieu's approach, and one he attempts to address by calling for a reflexive practice of sociology.

Structural Properties of Fields

Bourdieu (1993d:72) speaks of the "invariant laws" or "universal mechanisms" that are structural properties characteristic of all fields. First, fields are arenas of struggle for control over valued resources. Recall from chapter 4 that Bourdieu (1989c:375) conceptualizes resources as forms of capital when they become the object of struggle and function as a "social relation of power." Field struggle centers around particular forms of capital: economic, cultural, scientific, or religious. Cultural capital, for example, is the key property in the intellectual field, whereas economic capital is the key property in the business world. Scientists compete for scientific capital in the

---

11. Bourdieu admits that there are as many fields as their are interests. Each one has a specific *illusio* (Bourdieu and Wacquant 1992:117). In his study of lifestyles, Bourdieu (1984a:226) writes that there are "as many fields of preference as there are fields of stylistic possibles."

field of science. There are, therefore, as many fields as there are forms of capital.

Actors also struggle over the very definitions of what are to be considered the most valued resources in fields. This is particularly true in cultural fields, where style and knowledge change rapidly. In other words, *fields are arenas of struggle for legitimation:* in Bourdieu's language, for the right to monopolize the exercise of "symbolic violence."

Bourdieu's most striking field analyses are his studies of artists, writers, and teachers, where differences in artistic styles and ideas are viewed as strategies in the struggle for intellectual recognition. These strategies are in turn strongly dependent on the instruments and rules of conflict available in the various cultural fields.[12]

Second, *fields are structured spaces of dominant and subordinate positions based on types and amounts of capital.* Bourdieu stresses time and again that positions in fields are determined by the unequal distribution of relevant capitals rather than by the personal attributes of their occupants.[13] Fields are to be viewed as systems in which each particular element (institution, organization, group, or individual) derives its distinctive properties from its relationship to all other elements.[14] For example, Bourdieu (1971c:161) writes that the intellectual field, which

cannot be reduced to a simple aggregate of isolated agents or to the sum of elements merely juxtaposed is, like a magnetic field, made up of a system of power lines. In other words, the constituting agents or system of agents may be described as so many forces which, by their existence, opposition or combination, determine its specific structure at a given moment in time. In return, each of these is defined by its particular position within this field from which it derives *positional properties* which cannot be assimilated to intrinsic properties.[15]

---

12. Murphy (1988) draws explicitly from Bourdieu's concept to analyze Parkin's (1979) various formulations of closure theory. Camic (1986), who does rely on Bourdieu's concept, carries out in many ways a field analysis in his seminal discussion of why the classical notion of "habit" was expunged during the twentieth century from the active list of concepts in American sociology. Fritz Ringer (1992) draws on Bourdieu's concept for a comparative analysis of German and French intellectual history.

13. This strong structuralist postulate is relaxed somewhat when Bourdieu argues that positions in fields can to some extent be shaped by the habitus that actors bring with them (Bourdieu and Boltanski 1975).

14. This directly reflects Bourdieu's metatheoretical principle of relationality, which he appropriates from Saussure's structural linguistics.

15. Bourdieu's field perspective is similar in ways to Kurt Lewin's (1951) field theory; indeed, Bourdieu references Lewin in his early work. Field theory considers individual behavior to be the product of the lines of force impinging on the individual from others in the field, analogous to the trajectory of a billiard ball as it ricochets off other balls.

Fields are "tightly coupled"[16] relational configurations where change in one position shifts the boundaries among all other positions.

Field struggle pits those in dominant positions against those in subordinate positions. The struggle for position in fields opposes those who are able to exercise some degree of monopoly power over the definition and distribution of capital and others who attempt to usurp the advantages. In general, Bourdieu sees this opposition occurring between the established agents and the new arrivals in fields. Established agents tend to pursue conservation strategies while challengers opt for subversive strategies. Drawing from Weber's description of the opposition between priests and prophets, Bourdieu (1987d, 1991b) depicts this conflict in terms of those who defend "orthodoxy" against those who advocate "heresy." For Bourdieu (1992:289), this fundamental structure of conflict is paradigmatic not only in the religious field but in all cultural fields. The orthodox/heterodox opposition is a struggle for the

monopoly of cultural legitimacy and the right to withhold and confer this consecration in the name of fundamentally opposed principles: the personal authority called for by the creator and the institutional authority favoured by the teacher. (Bourdieu 1971c:178)

Bourdieu sees an analogous opposition in intellectual fields, particularly in academia, between the "curators of culture" and the "creators of culture," between those who reproduce and transmit legitimate bodies of knowledge and those who invent new forms of knowledge. In his study of the Parisian university faculty, Bourdieu (1988b) finds this fundamental opposition between teachers and researchers, or between professors and independent intellectuals.

Crucial for Bourdieu's field analysis is that the two opposing strategies are dialectically related; one generates the other. Orthodoxies call into existence their heterodox reversals by the logic of distinction that operates in cultural fields.[17] Challengers oblige the old guard to mount a defense of its privileges; that defense, then, becomes grounds for subversion.

16. The expression comes from organizational sociology and indicates close linkages between various components of an organizational system. In tightly coupled systems, sectoral disturbance reverberates throughout the system. Though Bourdieu does not see himself as a systems theorist, there are nonetheless certain systemic concepts in his sociology and field is one of them.

17. This symbiotic relationship between orthodox and heterodox views brings to mind Mannheim's (1955) analysis of how ideological and utopian visions of the social world, though radically opposed in their posture toward the status quo, nevertheless become locked into a pattern of complex exchange of critiques, each to an appreciable extent determining the other.

Williams and Demerath (1991) identify a similar dynamic in their study of religion and political process in an American city. They show how logically incompatible themes of civil religion and separation of church and state can coexist and actually "enable" each other in political practice.

Bourdieu in fact speaks of three different types of field strategies: *conservation, succession,* and *subversion.* Conservation strategies tend to be pursued by those who hold dominant positions and enjoy seniority in the field. Strategies of succession are attempts to gain access to dominant positions in a field and are generally pursued by the new entrants. Finally, strategies of subversion are pursued by those who expect to gain little from the dominant groups. These strategies take the form of a more or less radical rupture with the dominant group by challenging its legitimacy to define the standards of the field.[18]

Third, *fields impose on actors specific forms of struggle.* Both the dominant establishment and the subordinate challengers, both orthodox and heterodox views, share a tacit acceptance that the field of struggle is worth pursuing in the first place. Bourdieu refers to this deep structure of fields as the *doxa,* for it represents a tacit, fundamental agreement on the stakes of struggle between those advocating heterodoxy and those holding to orthodoxy.[19] Challengers and incumbents share a common interest in preserving the field itself, even if they are sharply divided on how it is to be controlled. Every field presupposes and produces a particular type of *illusio,* which Bourdieu defines as a belief or acceptance of the worth of the game of a field.[20] In the sociology of religion, for example, contemporary debates occur over trends and types of religious practices, but all assume—including proponents of secularization—that religion is worth talking about in the first place.

Entry into a field requires the tacit acceptance of the rules of the game, meaning that specific forms of struggle are legitimated whereas others are excluded.[21] Thus, entry into professional fields limits struggle to the forms and terms of what is considered legitimate professional procedure. Personal insults and physical violence, for example, are excluded as unprofessional

18. Bourdieu compares the structure of a field to that of a poker game where the pile of chips reflects the unequal distributions of capitals that both summarize the results of previous struggles and orient strategies for the future (Bourdieu and Wacquant 1992:98–99).

19. The idea of the *doxa* resonates with Durkheim's concept of the "collective consciousness." A crucial difference is that *doxa* is field specific rather than the representation of a tacit system of understandings for the entire society.

20. Bourdieu's basic point, as we have seen in his economy of practices, is that behavior in fields is interest driven. Bourdieu wants to stress that actors, regardless of their positions, are complicit in accepting the rules of the game in which they play. Moreover, he stresses that this acceptance goes unacknowledged, or "misrecognized," for the most part (Bourdieu 1991d:22, 45).

21. Bourdieu usually emphasizes that entrants to a field, like opposing players in a card game, pursue the same rewards and follow the same rules while competing to best their opponents. At other times he stresses that knowledge of the rules represents a form of cultural capital that is unequally shared among contending parties.

forms of conflict.[22] But challenging the degree of objectivity in an opposing viewpoint is fair play.

Field analysis, therefore, directs the researcher's attention to a level of analysis capable of revealing the integrating logic of competition between opposing viewpoints. It encourages the researcher to seek out sources of conflict in a given domain, relate that conflict to the broader areas of class and power, and identify underlying shared assumptions by opposing parties.

For fields to operate there must be agents with the appropriate habitus to make them capable and willing to invest in particular fields.[23] New arrivals to fields must pay the price of an initial investment for entry, which involves recognition of the value of the game and the practical knowledge of how to play it.[24]

One important consequence of the competitive logic of fields and their *doxa* is that they help create the conditions for the "misrecognition" of power relations and thereby contribute to the maintenance of the social order. Actors misrecognize the arbitrary character of their social worlds when they take for granted the definition of rewards and of ways of obtaining them as given by fields.[25] An unintentional consequence of engaging in field competition is that actors, though they may contest the legitimacy of rewards given by fields, nonetheless reproduce the structure of fields.

Fourth, *fields are structured to a significant extent by their own internal mechanisms of development* and thus hold some degree of autonomy from the external environment. Bourdieu speaks of the "relative autonomy" of fields to convey the dual character of their interconnectedness with and independence from external factors.[26] Bourdieu uses the language of relative auton-

---

22. Writing about the juridical field, Bourdieu (1987c:831) states that entry "implies the tacit acceptance of the field's fundamental law" and that "to join the game, to agree to play the game, to accept the law for the resolution of the conflict, is tacitly to adopt a mode of expression and discussion implying the renunciation of physical violence and of elementary forms of symbolic violence, such as insults."

23. An important research issue that has not yet received sufficient treatment in Bourdieu's work is identifying the types of habitus that attract individuals to particular fields. More broadly, and outside of Bourdieu's conceptual language, the issue is one of trying to understand the connection between "character and social structure" (Gerth and Mills 1964).

24. Bourdieu argues that those in subordinate positions are there because they have not fully mastered the rules of the game.

25. A corollary to this is that actors situated outside of specific fields can grasp a clear perception of the interests or capitals struggled over in those fields. This evokes Bourdieu's longstanding concern regarding the status of sociological insight as an "outsider" view, yet one that must accommodate insider perceptions in order to avoid producing an objectivist account of the social world.

26. Althusser is generally credited with the idea of the relative autonomy of the cultural instance from economic determination. Bourdieu shares with Althusser the opposition to or-

omy, particularly in his early work on education, to argue that relations between culture and society are complex and mediated, and that the traditional categories of "culture" and "society" are not adequate for describing the increasingly central and complex role that symbolic goods and processes play in the exercise of power in modern societies. The accumulation of educational credentials, and symbolic goods more generally, cannot be fully explained, he argues, in terms of underlying material interests. While the different forms of capital are under certain conditions interchangeable, they are not reducible one to the other.

Culture is a distinct form of power that functions like capital, but with its own specific laws of exercise. Yet, its autonomy is relative, since it is often exchanged for economic capital or positional power in organizations. Historically, Bourdieu sees cultural fields progressively developing and gaining autonomy from the political and economic fields.[27] The driving force of this autonomous development, which he draws from Weber's sociology of religion, is the rise of corps of specialists who are progressively able to develop, transmit, and control their own particular status culture. Thus, fields develop their own organizational and professional interests, which may deviate significantly from external interests. With growing autonomy comes the capacity to retranslate and reinterpret external demands. This capacity varies historically and by type of field.

The relative autonomy of the literary field, for example, suggests that this cultural arena is polarized by two opposing principles of organization. On the one hand, there is the tendency toward autonomy where peer reference and review assumes priority. At the extreme, this results in "art for art's sake." On the other hand is the tendency away from autonomy, where legitimacy and reference are sought outside the field in forms such as book sales, public appearances, honors, etc. (Bourdieu 1991d:12).

Bourdieu associates the autonomy of fields with his concept of symbolic power. As cultural fields grow in autonomy from political and economic power they gain in symbolic power, that is, in their capacity to legitimate existing social arrangements (Bourdieu and Passeron 1977:12). Consequently, fields elicit assent to existing social arrangements and thereby contribute to their reproduction to the extent that they engage actors in field

---

thodox Marxist views of culture and its institutions as mere reflections of underlying economic infrastructure, but Bourdieu's own understanding of the relative autonomy of cultural fields probably owes more to Weber than to Althusser.

27. He writes that "the position of the artist or intellectual within the cultural field developed *in opposition* to market and state bureaucratic control mechanisms within the cultural field" (Bourdieu 1991d:35).

autonomy.[28] The educational system is one example of a cultural field obtaining considerable autonomy as a result of its capacity to control the recruitment, socialization, and careers of actors, and to impose its own specific ideology.

A fundamental methodological principle flows from the posited relative autonomy of fields, namely, the priority given to the *internal analysis* of fields. Bourdieu argues that external influences are always retranslated into the internal logic of fields. External sources of influence are always mediated through the structure and dynamic of fields (Bourdieu and Wacquant 1992:105).[29] The class background of the artist, for example, does not influence the work of art directly. Rather, the effects of class intersect with the patterns of field hierarchy and conflict where the artist is situated (Bourdieu 1984c:6).

In his analyses of changes in French education, Bourdieu repeatedly argues for beginning with an internal analysis of the educational system (Bourdieu and Passeron 1977h; Bourdieu 1988a). External factors, such as demographic expansion, are always retranslated into the terms of the internal logic of the educational field.[30] Contradictions are examined largely from the standpoint of the internal logic of the field. His work thus far has acknowledged but not stressed the importance of *interfield* contradictions.

The priority that Bourdieu accords to the internal analysis of cultural fields reflects three central influences on his thinking: structuralism, his early struggle with Althusserian Marxism, and the substantive areas of his work. The structuralist method stresses internal patterns of systems rather than their origins or connections to external factors. Internal analysis stands as a methodological corrective to Althusser's focus on the logical status of culture within the superstructure/infrastructure dichotomy rather than as an inducement to research into the specific practices of cultural institutions.

---

28. In other words, competitive arenas of practices contribute to the reproduction of the social order as they become more differentiated and autonomous from external influence and capable of capturing agents within their own competitive hierarchies of distinction. In a rough analogy to Durkheim's view of the paradox in organic solidarity where increased specialization and individualism from the growing division of labor actually generate a new basis for social solidarity, Bourdieu sees in the differentiation and development of relatively autonomous social and cultural fields new mechanisms for social reproduction of society.

29. Though Bourdieu argues that field analysis requires analyzing change by giving priority to internal structures and dynamics of fields, he does nonetheless consider that "the struggles that take place within fields, such as the literary field, always depend, in their outcome, happy or unhappy, on the correspondence they can maintain with external struggles" (Bourdieu 1991d:33).

30. One methodological implication that Bourdieu draws from this position is to reject the technique of regression analysis, where a statistical distinction can be made between direct and indirect effects. For Bourdieu (1984c), there are no direct effects. Everything is mediated.

And this methodological principle seems to be an appropriate response for the French system of secondary and higher education which historically has obtained considerable autonomy from outside factors. Nevertheless, at times Bourdieu's work becomes concentrated on the internal analysis of fields, leading one to lose sight of how fields are connected into broader structural patterns. Bourdieu's analysis of the French intellectual field insightfully demonstrates how intellectual positions are shaped by the struggle for intellectual recognition. But they are shaped by more than just professional competition, which Bourdieu acknowledges, but tends to downplay in order to score his methodological point.

Bourdieu finds that the factor analytical technique of "correspondence analysis," described in chapter 3, fits well with the theoretical concerns he invests in the concept of field. Both the concept of field and correspondence analysis permit Bourdieu to situate individuals, groups, organizations, and institutions in terms of multiple axes of differentiation. This helps convey the conflict character of the social world and guards against presenting social hierarchies abstracted from their relations of opposition and proximity. Compared to linear modeling, field analysis shifts attention away from the particularistic characteristics of individuals and groups and toward the struggles and dynamics of arenas of social life that shape their behavior. Bourdieu (1988b:17) rejects single-dimensional scales and cumulative indices that locate individuals and groups by position in social structure in favor of multidimensional analysis, as a way of calling attention to the conflict dimension of social life and guarding against objectivism.

Field Homologies

Bourdieu conceptualizes the relations among relatively autonomous fields in terms of "structural and functional homologies," which he defines as "a resemblance within a difference" (Bourdieu and Wacquant 1992:105–6). Fields are homologous to the extent that they develop isomorphic properties, such as positions of dominance and subordination, strategies of exclusion and usurpation, and mechanisms of reproduction and change. And, Bourdieu stresses, "every one of these characteristics takes a specific, irreducible form in each field." In his early work on French education (Bourdieu and Passeron 1977:63–64, 194–200), Bourdieu emphasized the "structural and functional" homology between French education and the medieval Catholic Church: like the Church, schools not only transmit knowledge and skills but also reproduce themselves by monopolizing the selection and training of their own leadership. Moreover, schools perform another latent function of reproducing social class relations by legitimating the unequal distribution of cultural capital. In *Distinction* (1984a), Bourdieu describes a structural and functional homology relating the Parisian theater scene and fractions of the dominant class, writing that "the social character-istics of the audiences of the different Paris theaters . . . [are] perfectly congruent [with the] characteristics of the authors performed . . . , the works, and the theatrical businesses themselves."

Homology is also depicted in terms of "structures of opposition" in lifestyles that correspond to structures of opposition in the class structure. The opposition between "rare" practices and "vulgar" practices in culture corresponds to the main opposition in social space between those classes with considerable "overall capital value" and those with little (Bourdieu 1984a:175–76). In *La Noblesse d'Etat* (1989c:373) Bourdieu finds a "struc-tural homology" between the field of power and elite higher education in-stitutions in France. There, he observes that "the correspondence is more or less perfect" between the relative locations of French occupational groups and French schools in terms of their respective amounts of eco-nomic capital and cultural capital. In his analysis of the juridical field, Bour-dieu (1987c:822) argues that a "structural correspondence" between the field of law and the field of social classes finds expression in the relations between lawyers and their clients. The position of lawyers in their profes-sional hierarchy corresponds to the position their clients occupy in the so-cial hierarchy.[31] Thus, homology of position among individuals and groups in different fields means that those who find themselves in dominated posi-tions in the struggle for legitimation in one field tend also to find them-selves in subordinate positions in other fields. Finally, there are also homol-ogies in strategies. Consumers in subordinate social-class positions tend to select products produced by producers in subordinate positions within the field of cultural production. Thus, a relation of structural homology obtains between the various categories of cultural producers and consumers ac-cording to their respective positions in the separate fields of struggle (Bour-dieu 1984c).

For Bourdieu, field analysis differs from a *market approach* to consumer practices. Though Bourdieu superficially resembles a growing number of social scientists who use economic imagery in their analytical language (Warner 1993:1051), he does not work within a rational choice framework. Field analysis does not analyze cultural consumption in terms of a supply-demand function. Cultural tastes are not simply imposed by cultural pro-

31. Bourdieu (1987c:850) writes that "those who occupy inferior positions in the field (as for example in social welfare law) tend to work with a clientele composed of social inferiors who thereby increase the inferiority of these positions."

ducers on unwitting consumers; neither do cultural tastes stem from cultural producers attempting to respond directly to patterns of consumer demand. Field analysis posits that the relation of supply and demand, of artists and their public, and more generally, of the field of cultural production and the field of social classes, is *mediated* by field structures and processes. Producers struggle within the field of cultural production and their cultural products reflect more their respective positions of dominance or subordination in that struggle than they do the demands of consumers.[32] Consumers, in turn, select from these cultural products according to their own positions of dominance or subordination within the struggle for distinction among the social classes. Thus a relation of "structural homology" rather than one of conscious adjustment is established between the various categories of cultural producers and the various categories of consumers according to their respective positions in the separate fields of struggle. Bourdieu writes that

The logic of objective competition at the core of the field of cultural production leads each of the categories of producers to offer, without any conscious search for adjustment, products that are adjusted to the preferences of the consumers who occupy homologous positions within the field of power. (1984c:14)

Bourdieu holds that a symbolic isomorphism parallels the structural isomorphism among fields,[33] and that the cardinal semantic oppositions, such as high/low, light/heavy, and refined/crude, in cultural fields function to reinforce analogous social distinctions. He contends that

the categories of perception and appreciation (e.g. obscure/clear or easy, deep/light, original/banal, etc.) which function in the world of art are oppositions that are almost universally applicable and are based, in the last analysis, through the opposition between rarity and divulgation or vulgarization, uniqueness and multiplicity, quality and quantity, on the social opposition between the "elite" and the "masses," between "elite" (or "quality") products and "mass" products. (Bourdieu 1980b:157)

An example from his research is the light/heavy opposition that he observes functioning in the education field to simultaneously produce a "social discrimination" in terms of the field of social classes (Bourdieu 1989c:385).

32. An example of research in the United States that illustrates this point is Peterson's (1985) study showing that literary production is shaped more by the constraints of the publishing industry than by producer–consumer market relations.

33. The "objective basis" for the isomorphism in symbolic oppositions is the isomorphism in structural oppositions in the volume and structure of different types of capital across different fields (Bourdieu 1989c:384).

Teacher evaluations of students' written work that differentiates writing styles in opposing terms, such as elegant/labored, simultaneously discriminates between students with different amounts of cultural capital.

Bourdieu sometimes identifies homologies *within* fields. For example, within cultural fields he posits "a homology . . . between the space of positions within the field of production and the space of works defined in terms of their strictly symbolic content, notably their *form*" (Bourdieu 1988a:544). The conceptual terminology of *field* and *social space* often interweave in Bourdieu's account without clear distinction. At other times fields suddenly become differentiated into subfields (Bourdieu 1991c:230). In general, he thinks of the space of field positions in terms of the distributions of different types of capitals. The space of works includes all the stylistic features that differentiates works.

Thus, Bourdieu uses the language of homology to explain the effects of class relations on various cultural domains (Bourdieu and Wacquant 1992:106). Struggles in one field have homologous effects (never direct ones) in other fields.[34] Bourdieu (1980b:147) writes that "through the logic of homologies, the practices and works of the agents in a specialized, relatively autonomous field of production are necessarily *overdetermined;* the functions they fulfill in the internal struggles are inevitably accompanied by external functions, which are conferred on them in the symbolic struggles among the fractions of the dominant class and, in the long run at least, among the classes." Struggles in cultural fields produce cultural distinctions that are simultaneously social distinctions. They create social ingroups and outgroups as well as schools of thought or style. For Bourdieu, the opposition "between orthodoxy and heterodoxy" in the cultural field finds homology in the struggle for "maintenance or subversion of the symbolic order" in the field of social classes. Struggle in the cultural field produces "*euphemized* forms of ideological struggles between the social classes" (Bourdieu and Wacquant 1992:106). Field homologies reinforce patterns of conflict across different fields. The general overall effect is the *reproduction* of common patterns of hierarchy and conflict from one field to another.

Bourdieu thus draws different kinds of analogies between fields. Some point to an underlying function of social reproduction. Others point to

---

34. The emphasis Bourdieu places on the dynamics of struggles within fields tends to overshadow other important processes that can occur. For example, in their examination of organizational fields, DiMaggio and Powell (1991:67) find processes of imitation and professionalization as well as coercion and competition. Bourdieu, however, speaks virtually always of competitive struggle. Yet, isomorphism can emerge through other institutional processes as well as competition.

isomorphic patterns of hierarchy in positions and strategies of agents.[35] As
a conceptual strategy, Bourdieu's idea of homologous relations between
fields is directed against an *instrumental* view of interfield relations.[36] It re-
states the key theme found in his theory of action and the concept of habitus
that social structures are not the aggregate result of conscious, rational calculation. Nor do they refer to patterns of interaction or mutual awareness.
There can be, according to Bourdieu, an "objective orchestration" of the
fields of cultural production and social classes without thinking of their
connection in terms of some "conscious adjustment" to consumer demand.
Rather, the "quasi-miraculous correspondence prevailing at every moment
between the products offered by a field of production and the field of socially produced tastes" stems from the "functional and structural homology" between fields rather than from some expression of instrumental design. Bourdieu (1984a:233–34) writes of this relationship in discussing the
social-class basis of tastes in the following way:

The logic of the functioning of the fields of cultural-goods production, together
with the distinction strategies which determine their dynamics, cause the products of their functioning, be they fashion designs or novels, to be predisposed to
function differentially, as means of distinction, first between the class fractions and
then between the classes. The producers can be totally involved and absorbed in
their struggles with other producers, convinced that only specific artistic interests
are at stake and that they are otherwise totally disinterested, while remaining un-
aware of the social functions they fulfill, in the long run, for a particular audience,
and without ever ceasing to respond to the expectations of a particular class or class
fraction.

35. There is a certain affinity between Bourdieu's search for functional and structural homologies and Merton's concept of "functional equivalents." Neither advocates a form of functional analysis that posits a series of system needs that are indispensable for system survival.
Rather, both focus attention on the *"range of possible variation* in the items which can . . .
subserve a functional requirement" (Merton 1968:106). Like Merton, Bourdieu is interested
in the idea of equivalent positions in differing settings. But for Bourdieu the question of positionality in different settings leads to a more fundamental issue, namely, whether the structure
of class relations is reproduced. Forms of class differentiation may change, but the idea of
structural and functional homology is compatible with the claim that changes in form are not
incompatible with underlying structural continuity in class relations.
36. In his analysis of fields of cultural production and their relationship to the class structure, Bourdieu (1980b:147) explains the empirical observation of a close connection between
the "artist's position in the field of production and the position of his audience in the field
of the classes and class fractions" as a "structural and functional homology" rather than the
"product of a conscious calculation." The one exception Bourdieu (1991d:31) mentions is the
sector of the field of cultural production that is most closely associated with the field of power
and is most oriented toward the commercialization of culture. Here Bourdieu seems prepared
to recognize a greater role for conscious strategizing.

Thus, the connections between fields, like the oppositions within fields, stem from structural factors, not the intentions of actors.

Bourdieu's field analytic perspective, then, is intimately connected to his conception of class legitimation. The idea of field autonomy, mediation, and homology ties in with his theory of symbolic power and violence. It builds on the idea that legitimation of social class inequality is not the product of conscious intention but stems from a structural correspondence between different fields. Class distinctions become translated into euphemized forms specific to other fields. Actors unwittingly reproduce or change those class distinctions simply by pursuing their own strategies within the sets of constraints and opportunities available to them. When cultural producers pursue their own specific interests in fields, they unwittingly produce homologous effects in the social class structure.[37] Most importantly, intellectuals of various kinds play a key role in that process. By competing in cultural fields, intellectuals help to legitimate the dominant cultural order and reproduce the class structure. In serving the interests of their particular fields, intellectuals *also* serve the interests of the class structure.

Though Bourdieu's homologies between fields are structural and functional, they are not intended to suggest objective properties independent of the practices of agents. Indeed, in the final analysis Bourdieu falls back on the concept of habitus to explain homology among fields. It is because of habitus that actors display similar dispositions across a broad range of domains. Habitus is "the unifying principle of practices in different domains" (Bourdieu 1977c:83).[38] Field analysis, then, does not imply a kind of objectivism that would separate the function of a particular domain from the practice of individuals and groups. It is the practical logic of habitus that makes the underlying connection across fields. Hence, habitus is "the real principle of the structural homologies or relations of transformation objectively established between [fields]" (Bourdieu 1977c:83–84).

Bourdieu claims he does not think of the ensemble of fields and their functional and structural homologies as constituting a unified social sys-

---

37. Indeed, he suggests this process is most successful when it is not a direct, conscious objective. In a study of French Catholic bishops, Bourdieu attributes the effectiveness of communication and interaction styles between clergy and laity to their "affinity of habitus" rather than to conscious design (Bourdieu and de Saint Martin 1982:43).

38. Habitus and the related composition of capital help Bourdieu explain the sense of orientations that actors assume within fields. They help answer such questions as "do actors attempt risky bold ventures or settle for safe, secure strategies?" or "do actors manifest modesty or audacity in their practices?" Bourdieu (1991d:16) suggests that such orienting patterns of habitus can help situate actors in analogous positions across different fields as well.

tem.[39] Though he stresses the *doxa* dimension of field participation, he resists positing the existence of a kind of Parsonian *shared normative order* at the societal level. Since fields vary historically in their degree of autonomy from the economy, the polity, and class structure, Bourdieu claims that one cannot establish a universal classification system connecting the various fields. While recognizing them as arenas of struggle, Bourdieu does not, for example, root them in a deeper transhistorical process, such as capitalist development.

But in his zeal to distinguish his work from grand social theory in the tradition of Parsons and Althusser, Bourdieu downplays the systemic character of his own thought and work. As fields gain in autonomy they develop the systemic properties that I identified in the last section. Moreover, Bourdieu does make two general claims that represent broad historical trends: the increasing autonomy of cultural fields from the economy and polity and the ultimate dominance of the economic field. In addition, he applies field analysis only to differentiated societies. He did not use it in his studies of Algerian or French peasants nor does he appear to advocate its use for the study of such societies.

This underscores a tension in the complex relationship between habitus and field. While he wants to identify the "invariant laws" of fields and their interrelations, he resists conceptual claims that represent the kind of objectivist theorizing he denounces. Ultimately, his conceptual strategy falls back on habitus as the fundamental source for homologous connections among fields. As a result, the distinctiveness of the concept of field is thrown into doubt.

The idea of structural homology represents an important methodological and at times explanatory principle in Bourdieu's field analysis. Bourdieu employs the idea with great versatility and imagination. Yet the conceptual power of this principle may be less than would first appear. Homology in terms of just what? Though Bourdieu rejects functionalist theory but retains the idea of social functions in his work, the functionalist implications for fields of structural homology need clarification. Furthermore, if one were to grant that structural homology exists between individuals or groups across different fields, we still need to know the *social process* through which this "objective" alliance or opposition obtains. I will examine in chapter 9 how Bourdieu (Bourdieu 1991c:245) uses the idea to explain the capacity for political alliance between intellectuals and workers. Both intellectuals

---

39. In contrasting his framework to structuralist Marxist concerns about the articulation of the various instances in a social formation, Bourdieu declares: "I believe indeed that there are *no transhistoric laws of the relations between fields*, that we must investigate each historical case separately" (Bourdieu and Wacquant 1992:109).

and workers find themselves in subordinate positions, though in different fields. Yet it is likely that many different groups occupy homologous field positions without forming alliances. What are the processes as well as resources that help us understand why some groups but not others form strategic linkages?[40] Bourdieu's notion of structural homology unfortunately stops short of shedding light on this important question. Indeed, all too often it tends to act as a form of explanation that finds sufficiency in its own right. In this way, explanation by homology becomes a form of "structural mystification." While structural location may indeed help explain the reciprocal relationship between groups, a fuller understanding of such connections must be sought in factors such as status group co-membership, network ties, and common world views. What is needed in addition is a politics of collective mobilization.

The Field of Power: Economic Capital versus Cultural Capital

The principal field in Bourdieu's work is the *field of power*. He puts this concept to two distinct but overlapping uses. On the one hand, it functions as sort of "meta-field" that operates as an organizing principle of differentiation and struggle throughout *all* fields. This is the most important usage. On the other hand, the field of power can designate for Bourdieu the dominant social class.[41]

Bourdieu considers conflict to be the fundamental dynamic of all social life. At the heart of all social arrangements is the struggle for power. One of Bourdieu's key claims is that this struggle is carried out over symbolic as well as material resources. Moreover, it is Bourdieu's fundamental claim that cultural resources, such as education credentials, have come to function as a kind of capital, and thereby have become a new and distinct source of differentiation in modern societies. Indeed, according to Bourdieu (1989c: 373–85), *two* major competing principles of social hierarchy—what Bourdieu calls a "chiasmatic structure"—shape the struggle for power in modern industrial societies: the distribution of *economic capital* (wealth, income, and

40. This question is important since Bourdieu (1991d:18) remarks that the structural homology of fields is something quite different from networks that channel flows of information among specific actors.

41. Bourdieu prefers "field of power" to "dominant class," "ruling class" or "elite" to signal that the term is a relational construct rather than a designator for a specific population (Bourdieu and Wacquant 1992:76; Wacquant 1993b:20–21). He sees this terminological choice as a means of guarding against a "realist concept designating an actual population of holders of this tangible reality that we call power" (Bourdieu and Wacquant 1992:229). For discussion of this second usage of the concept in Bourdieu's analysis of social stratification, see below, chapter 7.

property), which Bourdieu calls the "dominant principle of hierarchy," and the distribution of *cultural capital* (knowledge, culture, and educational credentials), which Bourdieu calls the "second principle of hierarchy." This fundamental opposition between cultural capital and economic capital delineates Bourdieu's field of power.[42]

Individuals, families, groups, and organizations, in Bourdieu's analysis, tend to draw disproportionately from either cultural or economic resources in their struggle to maintain and enhance their positions in the social order. In the case of France, Bourdieu sees the field of power emerging in the late nineteenth century as the opposition between "artists" and "bourgeois" (Bourdieu 1989c; Wacquant 1993b:22–23). Yet, for Bourdieu (1984a:115, 123) this is the fundamental opposition that structures most cultural, political, and social conflict in all the advanced societies.[43]

Much of Bourdieu's work is devoted to examining the various forms the opposition between economic and cultural capital can assume. The distinctive lifestyles and political preferences of individuals and groups—indeed almost all of their practices—can be understood largely in terms of their distribution according to these two opposing types of capital.[44] As a general rule, Bourdieu finds that the greater the difference in asset structure of these two types of capital, the more likely it is that individuals and groups will be opposed in their power struggle for domination.

The fundamental cultural capital/economic capital opposition delineates as well other arenas of struggle organized around different forms and combinations of capital. Bourdieu (1989c:381) argues that the chiasmatic structure of economic capital and cultural capital distributes and ranks *all*

42. A recent definition by Bourdieu (1992:229–30) defines the field of power as "the relations of force that obtain between the social positions which guarantee their occupants a quantum of social force, or of capital, such that they are able to enter into the struggles over the monopoly of power, of which struggles over the definition of the legitimate form of power are a crucial dimension."

43. He in fact sees the field of power as a "transhistorical" structure whose existence predates the rise of modern industrial societies. At its most general level, this chiasmatic structure represents the "fundamental opposition of the division of labour of domination" across all societies that occurs "between temporal and spiritual powers (Wacquant 1993b: 24).

44. Bourdieu (1984a:124) does note that factors like geographical region can also play a role in determining how individuals and groups are distributed in terms of economic and especially cultural capital. Those situated near cultural centers, such as Paris or New York, have cultural resources more readily available for accumulation. In the case of France, Bourdieu notes the opposition between engineers and private-sector executives and between industrial and commercial employers in terms of differences in economic and cultural capital that stem in part from the fact that the former tend to be associated with large firms in the Paris region whereas the latter work in smaller firms in the French provinces.

other fields of struggle (e.g., economic, administrative, university, artistic, scientific, religious, intellectual). Figure 1 illustrates how Bourdieu (1983a: 319, 1984a:128–29) maps the field of power relative to class structure and to the literary and artistic fields. At the most general level, Bourdieu depicts the field of social classes (rectangle 1) as a two-dimensional space structured around the axes of volume and type of capital. The vertical axis measures the total volume of capital and the horizontal axis measures relative amounts of economic and cultural capital. The field of power (rectangle 2) is situated above the X-axis, in that portion of the social space with the greatest volume of capital, and is itself internally differentiated according to the poles of economic and cultural capital. Within the field of power the literary and artistic field (rectangle 3) is situated relatively nearer the pole of cultural power in the upper left quadrant of figure 1 (positions with considerable total capital but a negative ratio of economic to cultural capital). It thus occupies a "dominated position" within the field of power but a "dominant position" within the broader field of class relations. Finally, the literary and artistic field is itself internally differentiated by the economic/cultural capital opposition pitting the more commercialized art forms against those destined for peer consumption (Bourdieu 1983a:320).

Fields vary, then, in terms of their respective proximity to the competing poles in the field of power. At one end stands the economic field, where economic capital predominates. At the opposite end lies the artistic field centered around cultural capital. The administrative and university fields occupy intermediary positions, with the administrative being situated closer to the economic and the university closer to the artistic.[45] The juridical field, Bourdieu (1987c:851) observes, obtains less autonomy than the artistic and scientific fields, since it is more closely tied to the political field.

45. Until very recently Bourdieu has said little about his conception of the state. In recent work (Bourdieu 1989c:371–559, 1993a; Bourdieu and Wacquant 1992:111–15) he suggests that with the rise of the bureaucratic state there emerges a new form of capital, "statist capital," which is the object of struggle within the field of power. Whereas earlier conceptualizations of the field of power focused on economic capital and cultural capital, Bourdieu's more recent thinking appears now to include this other power resource. Statist capital is a form of power over the different fields and different types of capital that circulate within them. It functions as a kind of "meta-capital," in that it exercises power over other forms of capital and particularly over their exchange rate. This new capital derives from the growing concentration of various fields in the state. He writes, "it follows that the construction of the state goes hand in hand with the constitution of the field of power understood as the space of play in which holders of various forms of capital struggle in particular for power over the state, that is, over the statist capital that grants power over the different species of capital and over their reproduction (via the school system in particular)" (Bourdieu and Wacquant 1992: 114–15).

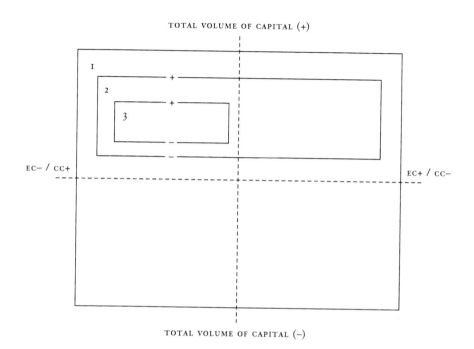

TOTAL VOLUME OF CAPITAL (+)

EC− / CC+

EC+ / CC−

TOTAL VOLUME OF CAPITAL (−)

NOTE
Rectangles represent arrays of positions
on Cartesian coordinates where the Y-axis
measures the total volume of economic and
cultural capital and the X-axis measures the
ratio of economic to cultural capital

KEY
1. Social Space or Field of Social Classes
2. Field of Power
3. Artistic Field
EC = Economic Capital
CC = Cultural Capital

This means that art and science are less dependent upon the economy and
polity than is law for rewarding careers and developing symbolic systems.
The religious field is situated near the artistic field since it too organizes
around a struggle for noneconomic legitimation. The journalistic field, in
contrast, is the most dependent upon the administrative and political circles.[46] Thus, cultural fields vary in their degree of autonomy from economic

46. See Bourdieu 1996. There is nonetheless some overlap in Bourdieu's conceptual terminology, which may reflect usage in different contexts. We find, for example, at one point he
specifies that "'political field' refers to specifically political institutions and actors ('champ
politique') *and also* to the whole field of power relations in politics and society ('champ du
pouvoir')" (Bourdieu 1988a:545), emphasis added.

and political authority.[47] A central objective of Bourdieu's sociology consists of situating fields of cultural activity relative to the field of power.[48]

Each field is internally differentiated by a "homologous structure" of an economically dominant and culturally dominated pole and a culturally dominant and economically dominated pole (Bourdieu 1989c:383). Bourdieu's field analytic approach to the study of the social world consists of identifying the various forms that this oppositional structure takes in specific arenas of struggle. His is a structuralist analysis that searches for transformations of this deep structure of all social and political conflict. For example, even within the economic field Bourdieu (1989c:383; Bourdieu and de Saint Martin 1978) finds that one can identify a fundamental opposition between two groups: (1) technocratic big business leaders, whose training, careers and firms are closely connected to public sector institutions, and (2) owners of large family firms that operate primarily in the private sphere. The former are inheritors of cultural capital and accumulators of scholastic capital whereas the latter are inheritors primarily of economic capital.[49] This same opposition occurs at the level of the large corporation where it in fact is the basis of the classic struggle over manager or owner control (Bourdieu and de Saint Martin 1978:58). And in the university field, Bourdieu finds the economic capital/cultural capital opposition taking on the form of the familiar tension between teaching and research.

The chiasmatic structure of economic capital and cultural capital functions, therefore, both as the bedrock of Bourdieu's field analysis and his approach to the topic of social stratification. It is an organizing principle both *between* and *within* fields. As we will see in chapter 7, it also functions as an organizing principle of the social class structure.

Toward a General Science of Practices: A Research Program

Having presented Bourdieu's key concepts of habitus, capital, and field, I will now summarize the overall conceptual framework of his general science of practices and its methodological agenda. If the dispositions of habitus

47. Bourdieu sees this variation as both historical and societal. Cultural fields vary in their autonomy from economic and political power in different historical periods and across different societies. He suggests that the variation can depend on two factors: (1) on the value accorded to works of art by the various fractions of the dominant class, and (2) on the "production and reproduction of economic capital" (Bourdieu 1983a:322).

48. For example, *La Noblesse d'Etat* gives Bourdieu's analysis of the relations between the field of power and the *grandes écoles*. His 1982 study with Monique de Saint Martin of the French Catholic bishops situates them relative to the field of power.

49. Bourdieu indicates that since the business bourgeoisie is increasingly acquiring cultural capital, this traditional opposition is attenuating to some degree (Bourdieu and de Saint Martin 1978).

are the product of class-specific conditions of primary socialization, the action they generate is not, however, a direct expression of this prior class socialization and the accumulation of specific forms of capital it provides. Rather, action is the product of class dispositions *intersecting* with the dynamics and structures of particular fields. Practices occur when habitus encounters those competitive arenas called fields, and action reflects the structure of that encounter. The relationship is dialectical, and includes an important temporal dimension. Bourdieu's sociological analysis therefore calls for constructing *both* the structure of the relevant field and the class habitus of the agents involved. In *Distinction* (1984a:101), Bourdieu offers the following equation as a summary formula of his model:

[(habitus) (capital)] + field = practice.

Bourdieu's complete model of practices conceptualizes action as the outcome of a relationship between habitus, capital, and field.[50] He warns that practices cannot be "deduced either from the present conditions which may seem to have provoked them or from the past conditions which have produced the habitus . . . [but from their] interrelationship" (Bourdieu 1990h:56).[51] Practices are not to be reduced to either habitus or field but

50. The formula makes it clear that Bourdieu resists reducing practice to the independent effects of either habitus, capital, or field. It is their *combination* that produces practices. Unfortunately, the formula confuses more than clarifies the exact relationship among the terms. Are habitus and capital interactive terms whereas field is additive? Or does the formula simply recommend that every empirical inquiry take into account all of these factors?

In Bourdieu's early work, his theory of practice focuses essentially on habitus. It is made to do practically all of the conceptual work. As he develops the concept of field, however, his theory of practice increasingly becomes one corresponding to the formula. From the outset, it was clear that habitus alone was not the sole source of practices but rather a sort of triggering and mediating force. Practices emerged not simply from habitus but from the *intersection* between habitus and the objective structures of situations. Still, it was habitus that seemed to be the driving force as Bourdieu (1977c:78) suggests when he writes "in practice, it is the habitus, . . . which accomplishes practically the relating of these two systems of relations, in and through the production of practice." Just what habitus intersects with to produce practices does not receive extensive theorization until Bourdieu develops the concept of field. We are told, for example, that practices emerge out of a "dialectical relationship" between habitus and an "objective event" (82–83). He also writes of the "conjuncture" to specify the conditions in which habitus is operating to produce practices. We know that what habitus encounters are "objective structures," "systems of relations," "events," "conjunctures," but we are given little theoretical insight into the exact character of these macro realities until the idea of field is developed. With the concept of field, we see increasing evidence of Bourdieu's fundamental claim that the social world is structured by polarities. Yet, it is habitus that creates the homologies of practices across different fields. So while the development of the concept of field gives new insight into how Bourdieu thinks about macro structures, the central concept of habitus continues if somewhat less visibly to be the central pillar of Bourdieu's conceptual edifice.

51. To emphasize the point that he thinks of practices as emerging from the encounter between habitus and fields, Bourdieu (1991d:20) stresses that in his model practices do not

grow out of the "interrelationship" established at each point in time by the sets of relations represented by both. In chapter 8, I will critically assess that relationship in discussing how Bourdieu deals with the problem of social change.

Bourdieu (1984c:5–6, 1987b:176; Bourdieu and Wacquant 1992:104–5) indicates that his approach to the study of intellectual and artistic works consists of three necessary step. (1) Research must relate the particular field of practices to the broader field of power. This first step illustrates the commanding place that stratification and power have in Bourdieu's sociology. In the case of artists and writers, we find the literary field embedded within the field of power where it occupies a dominated position (Bourdieu 1983a). The legal field, in contrast, is situated much closer to the dominant pole of power. (2) Research should identify the structure of objective relations between the opposing positions occupied by individuals or groups as they compete for intellectual or artistic legitimation. What are the forms of economic and cultural capital that are specific to the field under investigation? How are they distributed relative to other forms of capital? This means identifying the dominant and subordinate positions for all the participants in the field. And (3) research must analyze the class habitus brought by agents to their respective positions and the social trajectory they pursue within the field of struggle.

These three analytical steps might be said to constitute the general research method in Bourdieu's sociology. The analysis of practices involves the construction of the fields where they occur and the habitus of the agents brought to those fields. The next chapters will examine Bourdieu's field analysis in three key areas of substantive concern in his work: social-class structure, the system of higher education, and intellectuals in France.

---

mechanically flow from the various forms of capital held by agents. Such a view is precisely what he criticizes as characterizing the status-attainment research tradition. Nevertheless, Bourdieu (1991d:16–17) himself relies heavily on his concepts of capital and habitus in explaining the style of investment strategies that agents employ in various fields.

7 SOCIAL CLASSES AND THE STRUGGLE FOR POWER

Perhaps Bourdieu's greatest inspiration for the practice of sociology is his uncanny eye for the subtle but powerful forms of social distinction. We find this talent roving widely across detailed ethnographic observations, statistical tables, literary texts, photographs, interviews, questionnaire surveys, and census reports. By professional social scientific standards, Bourdieu's research style is unorthodox, combining as it does methods and types of data that are usually objects of specialized analysis with little cross-over. It is quintessential Bourdieu to find in a single paragraph literary and philosophical references interspersed with percentages from a survey. In the view of one critic (Collins 1989:460), this style earns him the title of "the world's most successful survey researcher." Not all, of course, would agree. In this chapter I attempt to flesh out the central features of Bourdieu's theory and method in stratification research.

A central objective of Bourdieu's work is to show how culture and social class correlate. Cultural practices, he argues, are markers of underlying class distinctions. This view sets him apart from many contemporary postmodern voices (e.g., Jean Baudrillard [1988a, 1988b]) who stress the uncertain, contingent and socially diverse character of cultural life.[1] Yet, he proposes to demonstrate this connection between culture and social class without

---

1. Bourdieu (1984a:561) juxtaposes his general argument in *Distinction* against the earlier claim by Daniel Bell (1976:33–84) that distinct class cultures have dissipated in modern postindustrial societies.

treating the former as a mere epiphenomenon of the latter. In order to demonstrate that thesis, Bourdieu reformulates the concept of social class. Class, like capital, habitus, and field, is a master concept in Bourdieu's sociology. In his own words, class is a "universal principle of explanation" (Bourdieu 1984a:114).[2] The "original class situation" represents "the point from which all possible views unfold and on which no view is possible" (Bourdieu and Passeron 1977:89). Yet, how Bourdieu conceptualizes social class is not well understood, in part because of the range, tensions, and ambiguities to be found in his use of the term.

This chapter is intended to clarify how Bourdieu thinks of social class. I will begin by reviewing the meta-sociological issues that Bourdieu sees as crucial in approaching the topic of stratification. These center primarily on objectivist and unidimensional images of stratification that Bourdieu rejects. They also concern essentialist conceptions of social class that Bourdieu rejects in favor of a relational approach. Since Marxism has been a central theoretical reference for Bourdieu, I explore how Bourdieu differentiates his concept of class from Marxist versions. Bourdieu also draws substantially from Weber, and I describe Bourdieu's modification of Weber's understanding of the relations between class and status before summarizing Bourdieu's own conception of social class as a multidimensional and relational theoretical construct that he sharply distinguishes from realist conceptions of social classes. Next, I examine Bourdieu's portrayal in *Distinction* (1984a) of the three-class structure in contemporary France, and devote particular attention to his analysis of various intra-class fractions. Since Bourdieu argues that each social class and class fraction has a characteristic habitus that generates specific sets of practices, I present the most salient of these class habitus and illustrate the types of distinctive lifestyles that Bourdieu claims they produce. Finally, I turn to Bourdieu's understanding of the dynamics of conflict and reproduction that characterize class relations.

Bourdieu's Metatheory of Social Class

Bourdieu's research enterprise is guided by two central meta-sociological concerns: transcending the fundamental antinomy between subjectivist and objectivist approaches to the study of social life and substituting relational for substantialist concepts of social reality. He considers that the debate

---

2. The existence of social classes and their importance for ordering social life in advanced societies are starting presuppositions for Bourdieu, not hypotheses to verify. Debating the existence and importance assigned to social class divisions, Bourdieu argues, is part and parcel of class struggle.

over the existence of social classes is filtered through the distorted lens of the subjectivism/objectivism antinomy. Indeed, he writes that

the problem of social classes is one of the sites *par excellence* of the opposition between objectivism and subjectivism, which locks research in a series of fictitious alternatives. (Bourdieu 1990h:289)

His approach to stratification research therefore needs to be understood as an effort to transcend the forms that he sees this antinomy taking in various approaches to the problem of social class. He also considers the concept of social class to be one par excellence where one sees substantialist thinking and essentialist ideology. He therefore offers an alternative relational understanding of class relations.

Bourdieu holds a highly stratified view of the social world in which individuals and groups struggle to maintain or enhance their relative standing within a hierarchically structured social space. For him, social inequality is rooted in objective structures of unequal distributions of types of capital. He thus rejects what he calls subjectivist approaches to the topic of stratification. Under the heading subjectivism, Bourdieu groups three different views. The first includes micro-level analyses, such as symbolic interactionism, ethnomethodology, and phenomenology, which view social differentiation as emerging directly out of micro-interaction processes. These harbor the "subjectivist illusion" in that they fail to recognize that agents bring the properties of their location in a hierarchically structured social order into each and every situation and interaction (Bourdieu 1984a:244).[3] Second, under subjectivism, Bourdieu includes approaches that reduce social-class existence and identity to individual or collective consciousness. And third, he also includes the view of class as a cognitive construct without objective roots in social reality.[4]

Though Bourdieu grounds social distinctions in objective structures, he also rejects strictly objectivist approaches to social inequality. Under

3. Bourdieu (1984a:578–79) writes that "the notion of situation, which is central to the interactionist fallacy, enables the objective, durable structure of relationship between officially constituted and guaranteed positions which organizes every real interaction to be reduced to a momentary, local, fluid order (as in accidental encounters between strangers), and often an artificial one (as in socio-psychological experiments). Interacting individuals bring all their properties into the most circumstantial interactions, and their relative positions in the social structure (or in a specialized field) govern their positions in the interaction." See Bourdieu 1977a, wherein he elaborates the opposition between "situation" and the broader context of structural factors.

4. Bourdieu attributes this position to political conservatives who oppose any form of class analysis that challenges the legitimacy of the status quo.

objectivism in stratification research, he groups Marxism, mainstream status-attainment research, network analysis, and all other structuralist theories of social inequality. These vastly different approaches all share one key feature: they focus on macro-level structures, often in the form of statistical regularities, that are rarely visible to the engaged actors and which must be constructed by the social scientist.[5] But, Bourdieu argues, actors act on their practical knowledge of the social world, whereas objectivist approaches tend to reduce actors to simple reflections of overarching structures. In stratification analysis as elsewhere, Bourdieu presents his "structuralist constructionist" approach as one that includes *both* actor perceptions of objective reality and objective measures of aggregate behavior.

One expression of objectivism in stratification research that Bourdieu singles out for criticism is Marxist social-class theory. Bourdieu criticizes Marxists for offering economistic interpretations of social class.[6] He is sharply critical of all attempts to conceptualize class primarily in terms of position in the social relations of production (Bourdieu 1985e:723). Though an affirmed materialist, Bourdieu believes that position in the social relations of production is only one of several sources of power that shape the social order in capitalist societies. Following the thinking of Weber, Bourdieu (1985e) argues that social space is multidimensional and does not reduce to a single causal mechanism such as the economy. He argues that

social class is not defined solely by a position in the relations of production, but by the class habitus which is "normally" (i.e., with a high statistical probability) associated with that position." (Bourdieu 1984a:372)

Moreover,

a class is defined as much by its *being-perceived* as by its *being*, by its consumption—which need not be conspicuous in order to be symbolic—as much as by its position in the relations of production (even if it is true that the latter governs the former). (Ibid., 483)

5. Bourdieu suggests that political leftists who favor social transformation through class politics tend to adopt one of these approaches. They see their role as social scientists as one of providing the necessary empirical documentation of the class structure in order to increase class consciousness and mobilization for political change.

6. Bourdieu includes the Althusserians in this critique even though they see themselves as rejecting earlier orthodox versions of Marxism that treat culture as a mere reflection of underlying economic relations.

Forms of symbolic and social accumulation and differentiation also constitute an important dimension of social-class relations. Property ownership or the lack of it cannot account for the importance of the accumulation of noneconomic goods and resources that occur in the exercise and perpetuation of power, including economic power. Bourdieu criticizes Marxist class theorizing for neglecting the *symbolic* dimension of class relations. There needs to be a political economy of symbolic goods.[7] Bourdieu includes in his class analysis lifestyle indicators, tastes, educational credentials, gender, and age, as well as occupation and income. Bourdieu's classes are constellations of stratifying factors; just as the whole is greater than the sum of its parts, so for Bourdieu it is the ensemble of pertinent stratification factors that constitute social classes rather than any single determining factor.[8]

Bourdieu (1987f:3) further argues that *both* objectivist and subjectivist approaches harbor fundamental "substantialist" assumptions about social classes. They assume that if social classes exist they are simply out there waiting for the social scientist to identify and describe them. Moreover, both approaches offer an "essentialist" view of class by attributing to classes intrinsic and universal attributes—whether they be subjective or objective in character. Yet, Bourdieu argues that social classes are not simply given in reality but are contested identities that are constructed through struggle over what is the "legitimate vision of the social world and of its divisions." In sharp reproach of positivism, Bourdieu declares that "in the reality of the social world, there are no more clear-cut boundaries, no more absolute breaks, than there are in the physical world."[9] There is only an immense

7. Bourdieu's criticisms of Marxist conceptualizations of class harbor two limitations. First, they do not acknowledge the considerable diversity among Marxists themselves on the class question. Like Bourdieu, many contemporary Marxists stress the symbolic as well as objective component of classes, emphasize their relation dimension, and acknowledge their historically contingent character (McCall 1992). Second, his criticisms do not acknowledge the growing overlap in Marxian and Weberian approaches of which Bourdieu himself is a prime example.

8. Bourdieu's multidimensional approach to forms of power also stands in opposition to those non-Marxist studies of stratification that tend to reduce social differentiation to a single dimension. This would include mobility studies that consider only occupational changes. Such is also the case of stratification analyses that elaborate an abstract hierarchy of social strata based on a composite index of different forms of capital, such as the Warner studies (Warner and Lunt 1941). Bourdieu (1984a:125) wants to move away from this kind of demonstration by emphasizing the *differences* in configuration of several different capital holdings and how one of the key factors in class struggle is the "exchange rate" between the different types of capital.

9. He suggests that the image of a flame—which he likely borrows from Bachelard— "whose edges are in constant movement" best conveys the idea that in the social world there are no "clear-cut boundaries," no "absolute breaks" (Bourdieu 1987f:13).

plurality of possibilities. Collective identity emerges through the mobilization of both material and symbolic resources. Class identities are constructed "relationally" as they reflect the oppositional character among existing classes. Indeed, it is this political reality of symbolic struggle over the very identities of classes as social groups that Bourdieu defines as the proper object for stratification research.

This leads Bourdieu to insist on a sharp distinction between social classes as *scientific constructs* and social classes as *real mobilized social groups*. Constructing a model of the social-class structure yields a theoretical representation of "probable classes" rather than real social groups. The objectivist moment of research must then be supplemented with the subjectivist moment of inquiry to see if the theoretically constructed classes of the social-scientific model actually correspond to real mobilized social groups. Bourdieu's stratification framework includes measures of both objective resources and of symbolic representations of social classes.

If economism represents one important objectivist flaw in Marxist theory of social classes, its preoccupation with the issue of class boundaries represents an underlying substantialist assumption. Structural Marxism focuses on delineating clear-cut logical and empirical boundaries between classes and classifying individuals according to their location in the social relations of production. The work of Poulantzas (1975) and Baudelot, Establet, and Malemort (1973) in France, and Erik Olin Wright (1985) in the United States are prime expressions of this type of class analysis. Bourdieu is sharply critical of all attempts to delineate the boundaries between classes and class fractions. Since for Bourdieu (1987b:64–65) class definition is itself an object of social conflict, class boundaries are objects of struggle that cannot be mapped definitively by social scientists. Class boundaries take shape only through the mobilization of individuals into groups.

Bourdieu also argues that the degree of institutionalization of social boundaries varies according to the state of conflict between classes. Class-boundary institutionalization depends on the relative symbolic power of particular groups to impose as legitimate their vision of the social divisions in society. This points to the need to study the symbolic dimension of class struggle, since class identity is itself a matter of perception and conception as well as being materially constituted.

Bourdieu believes that Marxist class theory is particularly prone to conflate theoretical constructs of classes with real social groups. Marxism commits the "theoreticist fallacy," he argues, "when it grants reality to abstractions." Because of its political project, Marxism tends to assume "the movement from probability to reality, from theoretical class to practical class" and thereby conflate "classes on paper" or "logical classes" with real, mobilized classes (Bourdieu 1987f:7).[10]

For Bourdieu, however, if the shared conditions of existence associated with property ownership or the lack thereof constitute necessary conditions for class formation, they by no means represent sufficient conditions for class identity. Here Bourdieu addresses the classical debate within Marxism over what conditions would most likely provoke a shift from a "class-in-itself" to a "class-for-itself" to generate class politics.[11] Bourdieu argues that both those who emphasize the class-in-itself conditions for class formation and those who stress the voluntarism of the class-for-itself are simply trapped in another form of the objectivism/subjectivism dichotomy. "More often than not," Bourdieu claims, Marxist theory conceptualizes this shift "in terms of a logic that is either totally deterministic or totally voluntarist" (1985e:726).[12] The determinist view depicts class action as flowing directly from the underlying contradictions in the objective relations of production. The voluntarist view identifies class action in terms of a subjective "prise de conscience" that is generally elicited through the enlightened leadership of the Party. In contrast, Bourdieu tries to offer a conceptualization of social class that relates class consciousness and action to underlying conditions of existence without falling into either a determinist or voluntarist account.[13]

According to Bourdieu, neither voluntarist or determinist views takes into account the relationship between life chances and their symbolic representations, and in particular the *symbolic labor* of leadership that is required

10. Bourdieu writes (ibid.) that "by equating constructed classes, which only exist as such on paper, with real classes constituted in the form of mobilized groups possessing absolute and relational self-consciousness, the Marxist tradition confuses the things of logic with the logic of things."

11. The dispute Bourdieu carries on with Marxism regarding this aspect of class theory is one of emphasis rather than of fundamental difference, for it has long been recognized that only under certain conditions does a class-in-itself become a class-for-itself. See Giddens (1973:29–30) for a presentation of Marx's two models of social class.

Bourdieu's repeated claim that real classes are not "classes on paper" does not appear to make a conceptual break with Marx. Marx's own thinking on classes is variable. Sometimes he thinks of class as any grouping of individuals that share the same relationship to the means of production, regardless of their consciousness. At other times, he emphasizes that groupings of individuals can be called classes only when their shared interests lead to collective awareness and action. Bourdieu wishes to emphasize this dimension of social class.

12. To make this point Bourdieu does not acknowledge the considerable variety of positions in this debate. His extremes would seem to pit the "critical Marxists" against the "scientific Marxists" (See Gouldner 1980, 1985). But a number of Marxists, including some classical theorists like Gramsci (1971), have taken up positions between these two extremes.

13. In his effort to conceptualize social class in terms of both actor representations and life chance indicators and to emphasize that class awareness and mobilization requires symbolic and organizational work, Bourdieu (1987f:6, 8) indicates some affinity to the works of Centers (1949), Halbwachs (1959), and Thompson (1963).

to generate class identity and action.[14] "Classes-on-paper" can become "classes-in-reality" *only if* there is symbolic and political work to give them identity and mobilization. It is in fact the symbolic labor of intellectuals that represents the important factor in developing class identity and generating class action. Trade union and political party leaders, who are directly responsible for class organizations, and social scientists and state officials, who produce scientific and bureaucratic classifications that become official categorizations, all play key roles in generating the social identity of classes (Bourdieu 1985e:727). For Bourdieu, then, intellectuals play a central role in his understanding of class relations.

Class and Status

Another way in which Bourdieu attempts to transcend the subjectivist/ objectivist antinomy in class analysis can be seen in how he appropriates and modifies Weber's concepts of class and status. Bourdieu (1984a:xiii) indicates that he wants to "rethink Weber's opposition between class and *Stand.*" For Weber, the concept of class is a statistical construct describing one's market situation in the distribution of life chances. Status groups, by contrast, denote real social groups based on common lifestyles. Weber sees considerable overlap between one's life chances and status group membership but not a necessary one. Status groups could coincide with classes. "But," Weber (1978:932) points out, "status honor need not necessarily be linked with a class situation. On the contrary, it normally stands in sharp opposition to the pretensions of sheer property." From this idea Bourdieu develops a general argument that status functions to disguise underlying class interests.

In an early article, "Condition de classe et position de classe," Bourdieu (1966) makes an analytical distinction between "class condition" and "class position." He associates class condition with the fundamental conditions of existence (Weber's "class") but ascribes the properties of class position (Weber's "status") to symbolic distinctions that emerge from the oppositions and affinities among classes. "Situational properties" are life chances

---

14. The idea stressed by Bourdieu that class behavior does not automatically follow from class situation certainly parallels Weber's position on the relationship between class situation and class action. Weber (1978:929) writes that "the emergence of an association or even of a mere social action from a common class situation is by no means a universal phenomenon. . . . For however different life chances may be, this fact in itself, according to all experience, by no means gives birth to "class action" (social action by the members of a class)."

The social closure theorist Raymond Murphy (1988) also sees this conceptual intention by Weber, and calls for recognition of the difference between constructed class and mobilized class.

for basic living standards, whereas "positional properties" emerge out of the dynamic of status competition. Class position (i.e., status distinction) represents that form of class struggle emerging from ostensibly nonmaterial distinctions. Class situation (i.e., economic power) represents the material conditions that set the broad parameters for class position.

Bourdieu points out that for Weber the possession or lack of possession of property is the fundamental determinant of class situation. Status groups, however, are defined by the *distance* they are able to establish from the underlying class situation—that is, by a search for distinction from underlying economic necessity.[15] Bourdieu (1966:213) argues that instead of thinking of Weber's distinction as opposing "two types of *real* unities" that vary in relative importance from society to society, one should think of them as "*nominal* unities" that

result from the *choice to accentuate the economic or symbolic aspect*, since these two aspects always coexist in reality (in different proportions that vary by society and by class) because the symbolic distinctions are always second to the economic differences they express and transfigure.

Bourdieu (1980a:214) thus appropriates Weber's conceptualization of status groups as based on "lifestyles," but argues they are *not* "a different kind of group from classes, but are rather dominant classes denied as such, or, so to speak, sublimated and thereby legitimated." Thus, classes take on the appearance of status groups in everyday life.[16]

This reformulation of the relationship between social class and status permits Bourdieu to integrate culture, tastes, and lifestyle indicators into a social-class framework. It marks his distance from Marxist class analysis by conceptualizing culture as a constituent feature of social class and by identifying status as a source of false consciousness. Bourdieu offers a class-symbolization model of status where cultural differences serve as markers of class differences. Class differences find expression in status distinctions that rank individuals and groups on scales of social honorability rather than in terms of economic interest alone. They go misrecognized, however,

15. Weber (1978:927) writes that " 'property' and 'lack of property' are . . . the basic categories of all class situations." Bourdieu (1966) notes that Weber (1978:937) specifies the following contrast between class and status groups: "With some over-simplification, one might thus say that classes are stratified according to their relations to the production and acquisition of goods; whereas status groups are stratified according to the principles of their *consumption* of goods as represented by special styles of life.

16. Here we see the complexity of Bourdieu's thought on the relationship between economic capital and symbolic capital. The relationship is both positively and negatively correlated. Just as the status distinctions associated with class position both deny and yet signal class condition, so symbolic capital is economic capital denied.

since they are legitimated through the powerful ideology of individual qualities of talent, merit, and giftedness.[17]

Bourdieu's reformulation of the relationship between class and status is complex, and not without ambiguity and tension. He acknowledges that the relationship itself varies by social class.[18] For some classes, such as the underclass (sous-proletaires), positional properties may directly reflect the socialization incurred by extremely limited material resources. Here class position and class situation are practically identical. For the middle classes, in contrast, positional properties are less directly determined by class situation, as they derive more from the dynamics of interclass distinctions more available to economically privileged groups (Bourdieu 1966:205). He therefore sees the limited material conditions of existence as having a more direct bearing upon attitudes and behavior of very economically disadvantaged classes whereas positionality assumes relatively more importance for the materially advantaged groups. The underlying explanatory principle seems to be that symbolic distinctions grow as distance from necessity increases.

Finally, the class/status distinction correlates with another distinction Bourdieu sometimes makes between "intrinsic" and "relational" features of class.[19] Intrinsic features signal "material conditions of existence, of primeval experiences of the social world" whereas class-position characteristics

17. See Gartman's (1991) neo-Marxist, Frankfurt school critique of Bourdieu's class-distinction model of cultural practices. Gartman accuses Bourdieu of establishing a "tautological relation" between class and culture by integrating culture into his definition of class. For Marxists, class is fundamentally determined by location in production relations, which, in turn, determines lifestyles and culture (superstructure). Gartman further contends that with the emergence of mass consumer society cultural differences no longer signal underlying class differences. Differences in consumer choices reveal, not status distinctions of individual or social honor, but income differences. These perceptions deflect attention away from class inequalities at the point of production and from the sphere of social honor into a realm of competition for income where effort and perhaps luck operate.

Two sets of empirical questions separate Bourdieu from Gartman's perspective. First, there is disagreement over the magnitude of actual empirical differences in consumer preferences between social classes. Gartman minimizes these differences whereas Bourdieu emphasizes them. Second, there is disagreement over how consumers really perceive lifestyle differences. Gartman argues that these are perceived in sheer quantitative terms of income differences stemming from the competitive market whereas Bourdieu sees them as perceived in noneconomic status distinctions.

18. In the 1966 article Bourdieu (205) acknowledges that the explanatory strength of his structural approach will "vary considerably according to the position of the social classes to which it is applied and according to the degree to which the properties of position are irreducible to situational properties."

19. This distinction appears in the 1966 article, "Condition de class and position de class," but also reappears in his more recent statement on the concept of social class, "What Makes a Social Class?" (1987f). In Bourdieu 1985e (724–25) actors are defined by their "relative positions" within social space, but there actors have both "intrinsic properties (their condition) and their relational properties (their position)."

are relational (Bourdieu 1987f:6). Here he associates class situation with the intrinsic features of class that convey a fundamentally "materialistic" image of class. But he also talks about the "relational" features of class position whose effects stem from comparative advantages or disadvantages relative to other classes "as being above or below them, or between them" (ibid.).[20]

This "intrinsic/relational" distinction stands in tension with his recurring demands for the eradication of all "substantialist" assumptions from sociological analysis. Are the intrinsic material conditions to be explained relationally as well as all the positional properties? Are we to conceptualize relationally class situation as well as class position? Doesn't the distinction between situation and position imply that the relational logic applies to the latter rather than the former? If relational logic applies to class situation, so that even the material conditions of existence of a class are to be seen in comparison with other classes, then how much more relational and comparative could one be in thinking about class position?

Bourdieu's Constructed Social Class

If social class is the fundamental sociological grouping for Bourdieu, his use of the term creates some confusion. At times his usage is clearly Marxist, as when it points to position in productive relations. More frequently, Bourdieu's usage approaches Weber's "market situation." At other times, "social class" is used as a broad classificatory category. "Class" sometimes refers to a specific group, such as laborers, the elderly, or women. At other times it is an instrument of cognitive and social distinction. It can receive quite diverse designations, and Bourdieu seldom offers definitions to clarify his intent for the reader.

In light of Bourdieu's meta-sociological considerations, what alternative conception of social class does he offer? How does Bourdieu construct his "theoretical" classes? Like both Marx and Weber, Bourdieu thinks of social class in terms of power and privilege. But as Brubaker (1985:761–62) perceptively points out, Bourdieu's concept of class differs from that of both Marx and Weber. Though an affirmed materialist, Bourdieu does not define social class primarily in terms of location in the social relations of production. Nor does his social class represent Weber's "market situation." His constructed classes are defined in terms of "similar positions in social space" that provide "similar conditions of existence and conditioning" and therefore create "similar dispositions" which in turn generate

20. In this article, he does not specify whether this "relational" feature is fundamentally symbolic or whether it includes the material dimension as well.

"similar practices" (Bourdieu 1987f:6). Classes are sets of "biological individuals having the same habitus" (Bourdieu 1990h:59). In other words, he defines social classes as any grouping of individuals sharing similar conditions of existence and their corresponding sets of dispositions. He also assimilates the idea of social classes with the symbolic and social classification struggle for the "monopoly of the legitimate representation of the social world" (Bourdieu 1990c:180).[21]

Thus, Bourdieu's conceptualization of class is not tied to the specific historical development of capitalism, as it is for Marx. And though similar to Weber's life chances, it includes dispositions as well as market power. Social class becomes a generic term for all social groups sharing similar life chances and dispositions. In this respect, classes, for Bourdieu, resemble a Durkheimian category of groups sharing experiences and collective representations (Durkheim 1965; Durkheim and Mauss 1963:81–88).[22]

What, then, for Bourdieu, are the important constituent factors of social classes? He defines social-class position in terms of the volume and structure of various forms of capital and how they are changing over time. The most basic capitals are economic, cultural, social, and symbolic. While their interrelationships can vary from society to society, the important factors always appear to be those most directly related to the fundamental "material conditions of existence" (Bourdieu 1984a:106). With regard to France and the United States, he explicitly ranks economic capital as the most important, followed by cultural capital. But this need not be the case in every society (Bourdieu 1987f:3–4).

Bourdieu's concept of class also takes into account other stratifying factors, such as gender, race or ethnicity, place of residence, and age. These are "inseparable" features of class, along with economic factors. At times they appear constitutive of social classes. Yet they do not appear to be primary forms of capital. In *Distinction* (1984a:102–9) Bourdieu treats them as "secondary" to those capitals directly affecting the fundamental material conditions of existence. Bourdieu's thinking on this matter is complex, and is open to both misunderstanding and legitimate criticism.

Consider how he deals with the relationship between social classes and gender. Bourdieu (1984a:107–8) holds that

sexual properties are as inseparable from class properties as the yellowness of lemon is from its acidity: a class is defined in an essential respect by the place and value it gives to the two sexes and to their socially constituted dispositions. This is why

21. He sees the struggle over symbolic classifications as a central feature "of every kind of struggle between classes, whether of generations, of gender, or of social rank" (ibid.).
22. In a seminal review of Bourdieu, DiMaggio (1979:1470) calls attention to this Durkheimian dimension of Bourdieu's thought.

there are as many ways of realizing femininity as there are classes and class fractions, and the division of labour between the sexes takes quite different forms, both in practices and in representations, in the different social classes. So the true nature of a class or class fraction is expressed in its distribution by sex or age, and perhaps even more, since its future is then at stake, by the trend of this distribution over time.

Here he affirms the importance of gender as a constituent feature of social class. Gender characteristics are "inseparable" from class and define it in an "essential respect." To illustrate, Bourdieu (105, 108) notes that certain occupations, such as medical and social services, are highly feminized, or, though from the same social class, males are more likely to study science and females more likely to study literature in French schools.

Nevertheless, gender creates social divisions that occur *within* classes rather than cross-cut them. Indeed, Bourdieu (107) specifies that "the volume and composition of capital give specific form and value to the determinations which the other factors (age, sex, place of residence, etc.) impose on practices."

In a later article on social class, Bourdieu (1987f:7) echoes the same line of thought when he refers to other principles of "ethnic, racial or national" stratification that compete with class principles in the struggle to define and understand the social world. Certain formulations by Bourdieu suggest that gender could be considered a form of capital and itself constitute a social class. Occasionally he refers to gender classes on par with social classes (Bourdieu 1984a:468, 1987f:15). More frequently he suggests that gender can function as a stratifying mechanism capable of creating gender classes. Indeed, it is the secondary social divisions based on gender, race, region, or nationality that compete with the "real underlying principles" (Bourdieu 1987f:7) of class formation and prohibit the transition from "probable" classes that are founded in objective determinants of social space into real classes. There can be real mobilized social groups that Bourdieu is willing to call classes, even though they are rooted in what he labels "secondary" sources of social division. Yet they seem to become classes only when they mobilize economic and cultural capital as well. Gender as a secondary factor constitutes one of the "potential lines of division" that if mobilized can "split [social classes], more or less deeply and permanently" (Bourdieu 1984a:107). But though a "potential" source of mobilization, gender is less likely to be an enduring and forceful social division like social class.[23] Thus, the secondary factors of sex, race, age, or region, while to be

23. Bourdieu writes (ibid.) that "groups mobilized on the basis of a secondary criterion (such as sex or age) are likely to be bound together less permanently and less deeply than those mobilized on the basis of the fundamental determinants of their condition."

included in the constructed class, appear to have less potential for class mobilization than do material factors.

Bourdieu's (1984a:468) treatment of gender as a "secondary" constituent of class seems to contradict claims elsewhere in his work that gender is a major social division; indeed, that gender is the paradigmatic form of symbolic violence. This claim, which we find in his early anthropological work and reaffirmed more recently in an article on sexual domination (Bourdieu 1990e), and which presents the male/female dichotomy as representing a fundamental and universal ordering principle, is not integrated into his class analysis. There in fact seems to be two different roles for gender at work in different portions of Bourdieu's work, and their interrelations remain unclear. On the one hand, when Bourdieu writes in *Distinction* about the "fundamental conditions of existence," he evokes a materialist image of "distance from necessity" and defines gender as a secondary variable in this stratification framework. Yet, in other parts of his work, he refers to the gender symbolism of the binary male/female opposition as a form of domination in all social hierarchies. How the two views interact is not clear.

This complex line of argument suggests that Bourdieu is trying to chart a position somewhere *between* the importance accorded by Marxists to class and the importance accorded by feminists to gender.[24] Against Marxism, Bourdieu argues for a multidimensional understanding of class by holding that key features of class include stratifying features like gender, race, region, and nationality. But are there objective gender classes on par with objective social classes as certain formulations suggest? Here there is ambiguity. More certain is Bourdieu's acknowledgement that gender can constitute a competing source of social division to social class. But his claim that gender is ultimately less capable than class of sustaining mobilized social action shows his distance from most contemporary feminists.[25]

The complexity and ambiguity in Bourdieu's position is exacerbated by his methodology. Bourdieu reasons more in terms of ensembles of variables

24. Though feminism has never been as significant an intellectual reference for Bourdieu as has Marxism.

25. See McCall (1992) for an insightful feminist critique of Bourdieu's use of gender. After criticizing Bourdieu for relegating gender to a "secondary" social division relative to social class, she identifies a possible "second reading" of Bourdieu that would consider gender as a form of embodied capital. Moreover, she finds a powerful "cross-class gender symbolism" in Bourdieu's claim that the male/female dichotomy is a fundamental binary opposition in any social order. Yet she also criticizes Bourdieu for defining this gender symbolism "too rigidly and deterministically" (ibid., 847). McCall (851) sees Bourdieu as accepting gender division as a "universal and natural" category that structures all of social life, rather than acknowledging that masculinities and feminities are constructed and contested identities, and that individuals can experience ambiguities around gender identity boundaries.

rather than separating out individual variables for precise measurement. He thinks of classes as structured ensembles or constellations of factors, and resists abstracting out individual traits as key indicators. Bourdieu's structuralist and antipositivist data-analytic method calls for focus on the "complete system of relationships which constitutes the true principle of the specific strength and form of the effects registered in any particular correlation" (1984a:102–3, 106–7). This permits him to criticize more conventional multivariate modeling techniques for attempting to measure the relative importance of various independent variables. He affirms the relative importance of the different forms of capital, but only in structured combinations—never as individual variables. Furthermore, he offers no demonstration of how much better his preferred statistical model fits the data than any others.

If classes are sets of individuals who share similar objective opportunities and subjective dispositions, how are they to be represented empirically? Is not one recurrent research finding that individuals equal in education and occupation often differ considerably in attitudes and behavior? Bourdieu (1984a:106) acknowledges this difficulty, but places much of the blame for it on prevailing methods employed in sociology:

Social class is not defined by a property . . . nor by a collection of properties (of sex, age, social origins, ethnic origin . . . income, educational level etc.), nor even by a chain of properties strung out from a fundamental property (position in the relations of production) in a relation of cause and effect . . . but by the structure of relations between all the pertinent properties which gives its specific value to each of them and to the effects they exert on practices.

No single indicator of class is sufficient, and Bourdieu stresses the limitations of purely statistical analyses. Rather, class analysis calls for a particular method. It is

the work of construction and observation . . . to isolate (relatively) homogeneous sets of individuals characterized by sets of properties that are statistically and "sociologically" interrelated. (Bourdieu 1984a:259)

Class analysis involves the "work of construction" in an effort to assemble two total systems of factors: the conditions of external existence and their corresponding dispositions. Bourdieu generally relies on data about the resources, activities, and attitudes of members of different occupations. But he also emphasizes "secondary properties" including place of residence, gender, and age.

For Bourdieu, therefore, social class is always a "constructed class," forged from imaginative combinations of statistical evidence and ethno-graphic description—frequently supplemented with interviews, photo-graphs, and extracts from advertisements and the popular press. Bour-dieu's "work of construction" resembles what Brubaker (1985:768) calls a "Webero-Proustian method": it resembles an ideal-type of capital configu-rations that is garnered with observed subtleties in manner and style that individuals employ to mark social rank. *Distinction* illustrates best how Bourdieu employs this method. There he offers a portrait of the class struc-ture of contemporary France that distinguishes classes in terms of differ-ences in economic and cultural capital, habitus, and lifestyle. It is to that description that we now turn.

The French Social-Class Structure

Bourdieu thinks of social classes as structured configurations of the various forms of capital that define a field. The field of social classes, as described in chapter 6, figure 1, is structured by amounts and types of capital, "under-stood as the set of actually usable resources and power" (Bourdieu 1984a: 114). The most important are economic capital and cultural capital.[26] In order to construct the most homogeneous groupings of individuals in terms of their fundamental conditions of existence, he constructs a three-dimensional social space. The three fundamental dimensions of this space are: total volume of capital, composition of capital, and social trajectory.[27] Using this framework, Bourdieu outlines in *Distinction* his view of the class structure in contemporary France.

Differences in the *volume* of total capital demarcate interclass divisions. In the case of France, differences in total volume of capital define an overall three-tier stratification structure that includes a dominant class, a middle class, and a working class.[28] The substantial possession of almost every kind of capital sets apart the dominant class—the focus of most of Bourdieu's work—from all other groups in the stratification order. In terms of occupa-

26. Sometimes Bourdieu (1986a) joins "social capital" to economic and cultural capital as one of the *three* main forms of capital. Social capital is a "capital of social connections, honour-ability and respectability" that can be converted into economic, political, and social advantages (Bourdieu 1984a:122). Nevertheless, it is economic capital and cultural capital that form the basis of Bourdieu's model of the class structure in modern France.

27. The most concise statements of this conceptualization are to be found in Bourdieu 1984a:114–32 and 1985e:723–24.

28. Bourdieu (1984a:345–46) uses interchangeably the Marxist terminology of "bourgeoi-sie" to designate the dominant class and "petite bourgeoisie" to designate the middle class. He also will speak of the dominant, middle, and working classes in the plural as well as in the singular depending upon whether he wishes to emphasize inter- or intraclass relations.

tional categories, Bourdieu's (1984a:128, 1989c:379–83) dominant class includes the liberal professions, university teachers, senior state officials, big-
business owners and executives, and artists and writers. At the opposite end
of the interclass spectrum stands the working class, which holds very little
capital. Bourdieu includes within the working class the several types and
skill-levels of manual laborers, whether in modern industry or agriculture.
Between these two extremes lie the broad middle class, with modest
amounts of capital accumulation.[29]

Differences in the *composition* of capital holdings delimit several *intraclass* fractions. The dominant class is internally differentiated by unequal
distributions of economic capital and cultural capital.[30] At one extreme
stand those occupations, such as writers, artists, and university professors,
rich in cultural capital but less well endowed in economic capital. At the
opposite extreme, stand big-business owners and financiers whose economic wealth is not matched by their cultural capital. In between one finds
the liberal professions and senior managers in the private and public sectors
who tend to have a more balanced composition of economic and cultural
capital.[31] These three dominant class fractions struggle for access to valued
resources and positions of power, and over definitions of cultural legitimacy
in the advanced industrialized societies.[32] They are the principal contenders
in the field of power.

29. Though Bourdieu does not try to delimit class boundaries in his own work, it is clear
from his use of occupational categories that he does not see, as does, for example, Alain Touraine (1973), the emergence of a new and expanded working class that would include a broad
range of lower-level white-collar positions. Bourdieu's analyses show that the traditional division between blue- and white-collar workers remains in force across a broad range of lifestyle
indicators.

30. Bourdieu's most comprehensive statement of this conceptualization of the dominant
class is to be found in *Distinction* (114–15), but an early statement identifying the unequal
distributions of economic capital and cultural capital as the principal source of stratification
within the dominant class is to be found in "Cultural Reproduction and Social Reproduction"
(Bourdieu 1973a).

31. Bourdieu's conceptualization of intraclass groupings in terms of the composition of
their different types of capital has a certain affinity with Lenski's (1952, 1954) analysis of status
discrepancies. Both call attention to the multidimensional character of stratification and the
discrepancies in attitudes and behavior that can be caused by the different types of capital.
Bourdieu and Lenski differ, however, in their choices of methodology employed to demonstrate discrepancies in valued resources. Reflecting his antipositivist position and his desire
to highlight subtle intraclass social divisions, Bourdieu (1984a:572) refuses to use a composite
index as a proxy for social class.

32. The idea of the dominant class divided against itself did not of course originate with
Bourdieu. As Mannheim (1956:156) put it already in 1936, "the modern bourgeoisie had from
the beginning a twofold social root—on the one hand the owners of capital, on the other
those individuals whose only capital consisted in their education. It was common therefore
to speak of the propertied and educated class, the educated element being, however, by no
means ideologically in agreement with the property-owning element."

Bourdieu (1984a:122–23, 339–41) finds the same "chiastic structure" in cultural and economic capital distribution within the middle class. It opposes, for example, primary school teachers to small-business employers (e.g., shopkeepers and craftsmen) since the former are relatively richer in cultural capital whereas the latter hold relatively more economic capital.[33] Junior executives, technicians, clerical personnel, and paramedicals, media personnel, and health and social service occupations hold intermediate positions between these two extremes. Bourdieu (1984a:354–71) devotes particular attention to these intermediate, or "semi-bourgeois," positions, which he labels the "new petite bourgeoisie."[34] Bourdieu characterizes these new positions as being cultural-capital-intensive yet relatively unregulated or standardized, and specialized in the production of symbolic goods and services. They permit the maximum of "cultural pretension" since they do not represent types of knowledge with well-established standards through professionalization and formal education. They have become the "new taste-makers" of the "art of consuming, spending and enjoying." They include

all the occupations involving presentation and representation (sales, marketing, advertising, public relations, fashion, decoration . . . in all the institutions providing symbolic goods and services. These include the various jobs in medical and social assistance (marriage guidance, sex therapy, dietetics, vocational guidance, paediatric advice) . . . and in cultural production and organization (youth leaders, play leaders, tutors and monitors, radio and TV producers and presenters, magazine journalists), which have expanded considerably in recent years. (Bourdieu 1984a:359)

They have emerged in recent years with the growth of the service and communication sectors in the technologically advanced societies. They are symptomatic of the new mode of domination through symbolic violence, the imposition of dominant-class culture on subordinate groups.

In France, Bourdieu (357) finds that the new petite bourgeoisie recruits from two different social origins: (1) educated individuals from working-class origins who do not accumulate the most prestigious educational credentials and who are unable to convert their credential capital into well-established, prestigious positions; and (2) individuals of dominant-class origins who also do not obtain prestigious educational credentials but who are able to avoid downward mobility by converting their inherited cultural

33. At an even more disaggregated level of analysis, the same differentiating principle distinguishes art and crafts retailers from heads of other kinds of small businesses.

34. Bourdieu (150, 153) uses the labels of "new bourgeoisie" and "new petite bourgeoisie" interchangeably to designate such "semi-bourgeois" positions.

capital as well as social and economic capital into the symbolic goods and services that are easily marketable.

These new occupations offer dominant-class individuals without much education "an honourable refuge to avoid social decline" (358). Since these semi-bourgeois positions become a common ground for different class recruits (150), class conflict takes on the form of a competitive struggle for distinction and emulation that is based on perceptions of the social worth of different kinds of lifestyles.[35]

The lowest volume of total capital assets describes the working class. Bourdieu defines the working class by its relative lack of economic and cultural capital, compared to the dominant and middle classes. In particular, he suggests that the significantly greater economic constraints facing the working class limit its range of cultural capital accumulation. Relative differences in economic and cultural capital can be found among such working-class occupations as skilled, semi-skilled, or unskilled manual workers and farm labors (114). But Bourdieu has devoted little attention to analyzing intraclass differences within the working class. The focus of his work is on the dominant classes.

Bourdieu's focus on configurations of various forms of capital stimulates reconsideration of the significance of occupational categories, which are frequently used in social science as measures of social class. Bourdieu is sharply critical of using occupational categories in this way, arguing that they are "bureaucratic" rather than "scientific" categories, and therefore tend in fact to represent quite socially heterogeneous groupings. But since they are readily available measures, Bourdieu himself employs occupational titles as the principal indicator of positionality within his three-dimensional space. He conceptually deconstructs them, however, in terms of the underlying volume and composition of capital they represent. This provides a more disaggregated and multidimensional view of actors situated in multiple social hierarchies than is found in mainstream status-attainment research.

Unfortunately, the interpretative power of his approach is not matched by the degree of empirical precision that many sociologists would desire. Social capital in particular is seldom measured. Thus Bourdieu's work points to the urgent need to collect data on the variety of valued resources that constitute class position, to interpret existing data categories such as occupation in a structural rather than empiricist manner, and to present

---

35. Bourdieu's portrayal of the new petty bourgeoisie differs significantly from recent French Marxist accounts (Baudelot, Establet, and Malemort 1973, Poulantzas 1977) in that he stresses the social, cultural, and ideological diversity of this middle range in the class structure.

data in a format that will more adequately communicate the complex, oppositional, and tentative character of class relations.

The third dimension in Bourdieu's model refers to how the volume and composition of capital for groups and individuals change over time.[36] Changes in capital volume and composition determine the collective future of the group. Bourdieu argues that the social trajectory of a class decisively shapes the attitudes and practices of its members. The social mobility chances for a group are another important kind of objective structure that is internalized in habitus.[37]

Bourdieu (1984a:123) speaks of three possible social trajectories: upward mobility, downward mobility, or stagnation. Movement upward or downward will tend to give respectively optimistic or pessimistic views regarding one's future chances. Whether a class is rising or declining numerically will shape its outlook toward the future. Bourdieu finds that the pessimism of French shopkeepers and farmers reflects their decline as a class, whereas the rising numbers of technicians accounts for their relatively greater degree of optimism. Habitus reflects fairly distinctly the three different kinds of movement: growth, decline, or status quo.

Compared with mainstream status-attainment research in sociology, Bourdieu's multidimensional class analysis provides a more comprehensive structural reading of social position in the stratification order. Location in social space, he argues, cannot be adequately captured by such unidimensional measures as father's occupational prestige or family income. He calls for looking at a broader range of social background factors that likely shape individual attitudes and behavior. The concept of cultural capital, in particular, taps dimensions of unequal advantage not fully appreciated by measures of parental income, occupation, and education. We are already beginning to see a growing body of studies inspired by Bourdieu's concept that provide new insights into the cultural components of social inequality (e.g., DiMaggio and Mohr 1984, Lareau 1989).

The three dimensions of stratification—volume and composition of the forms of capital and social trajectory—provide the general framework for Bourdieu's analysis of class structures in contemporary societies. He argues that individuals who share similar positions on all three dimensions also share similar conditions of existence or class condition. Where they

36. This dimension is first identified in Bourdieu's 1966 article "Condition de classe et position de classe," but does not receive elaboration until his 1974 article "Avenir de classe." The concept is used throughout his subsequent work, particularly in his analysis, in *Distinction*, of class-based lifestyles and consumption patterns.

37. For Bourdieu, individual trajectories are always derivative from the collective trajectories of class (Bourdieu 1984a:112).

do, one can anticipate observing corresponding similarities in all forms of cultural and social practices. Where they do not, incongruities in practices will occur. We will see in the next section how Bourdieu identifies important intraclass differences where similarity in volume but differences in composition of capital occur or where similarity in both volume and composition are clouded by differences in social trajectory.

Class, Habitus, and Tastes

Of particular interest to sociologists is how Bourdieu integrates his conceptualization of social space with his concepts of habitus and field to explain aesthetic preferences, consumer behavior, and lifestyles. He argues that the class structure of society, as defined by the three dimensions of social space, becomes internalized in distinct class habitus. Each habitus embodies both the material conditions of existence of the class and the symbolic differentiations (e.g., high/low, rich/poor) that categorize and rank its relation to other classes. Individuals then enter the various fields of taste with dispositions that predispose them to make lifestyle choices characteristic of their class habitus. Lifestyles are practical expressions of the symbolic dimension of class relations.

Having constructed the three-dimensional social space in which he conceptualizes social-class relations, Bourdieu (1984a:208) then argues that the patterns of cultural consumption and lifestyle distribute along similar sets of axes demonstrating that there is a "structural homology" between the field of social classes and the space of lifestyles. By "structural homology" Bourdieu thinks of this relationship between class and lifestyles less in terms of "correspondence" between specific classes and particular consumer traits than in terms of "structures of opposition." Rather than posit that particular consumer products or practices correspond to intrinsic characteristics of specific classes, Bourdieu offers his structural and relational approach to the class/culture nexus. It matters little whether professionals prefer tennis, hockey, rugby, boxing, or cricket. What matters is that their preferences express systematic opposition to those of other classes. Thus, whether in sports, interior decorating, clothing, food, or leisure, one should be able to find systematic oppositions differentiating the various classes. His demonstration is designed to argue against three alternative views: postmodern cultural fluidity, income explanation, and conscious status-seeking.

By stressing the connection between lifestyle distinctions and social structure, Bourdieu stands apart from most postmodern consumer-culture theorists claiming that rapidly changing production, marketing, and consumption patterns have lead to a profusion and proliferation of status symbols that no longer correspond to enduring social-class divisions. For example, Bourdieu shifts the focus from the high level of generality pursued by Baudrillard (1988a, 1988b) to argue that the current inflation of lifestyle tastes stems from a structured social space where particular classes and class fractions compete to impose their own particular tastes as legitimate. Bourdieu emphasizes that social classes differentiate themselves across a broad and changing array of consumer practices.

If Bourdieu sees a clear connection between class and many consumer practices, he also sees his approach as distinct from an income explanation. While he acknowledges that much consumer behavior is associated with level of income, Bourdieu insists that this association is *mediated* by the dispositions of habitus.[38] He argues that "income tends to be credited with a causal efficacy which it in fact only exerts in association with the habitus it has produced" (1984a:375). The primacy of habitus rather than sheer number of dollars in shaping consumer choice "is clearly seen when the same income is associated with very different patterns of consumption."[39] Or, it can be seen

whenever a change in social position puts the habitus into new conditions, so that its specific efficacy can be isolated, it is taste—the taste of necessity or the taste of luxury—and not high or low income which commands the practices objectively adjusted to these resources. (175)

He thus sharply criticizes supply–demand models of consumer behavior that limit explanation of consumer choice to one of purchasing power. Bourdieu contends that actors choose products for reasons of taste rather than because of careful cost–benefit analysis. "The real principle of preferences is taste, a virtue made of necessity" (177). And taste stems from the deeply rooted expectations that individuals internalize from their experiences of abundance or scarcity in the social world.

Bourdieu also rejects the idea that consumer practices stem from a conscious strategy of status-seeking à la Veblen (1979). If consumer practices are socially differentiated in ways that are homologous to social-class distinctions, this nexus emerges through habitus rather than through conscious calculation. Bourdieu (1984a:172–73) stresses that

38. Here we see the recurring theme in Bourdieu's work of the *cultural mediation of practices*. Though a materialist, Bourdieu is sharply critical of crude economistic accounts of practices, including consumer behavior.

39. Unfortunately, he does not adequately back up this claim with convincing empirical support from either his own research or that of others.

all the practices and products of a given agent are objectively harmonized among themselves, without any deliberate pursuit of coherence, and objectively orchestrated, without any conscious concertation, with those of all members of the same class.

Thus, Bourdieu rejects class-based rational-actor modes of individual behavior.

We next turn to examples of how he sees class habitus intersecting with particular lifestyle fields to generate class-based consumer practices in France.

Bourdieu (176) theorizes differences in volume and composition of capital as the two fundamental organizing principles that link cultural consumption and lifestyle to social-class conditions.[40] These differences in class condition generate distinct and mutually differentiating class habitus that in turn produce lifestyle distinctions.[41] They differentiate a dominant-class habitus of distinction from a working-class habitus of necessity. Differences in total volume of capital distinguish as rare and therefore more desirable those practices that presuppose considerable economic and cultural capital from those common vulgar practices that are readily available to individuals with little capital. Actors with abundant capital enjoy considerable freedom from the practical constraints and temporal urgencies imposed by material scarcities and the consequent necessities of earning a livelihood. Those with meager capital find little respite from the practical demands of making a living. This relative "distance from necessity" produces different class habitus, which in turn generate distinct sets of tastes.[42] Since habitus produces

40. Though in *Distinction* (114) Bourdieu defines the three stratification dimensions of volume of capital, composition of capital, and social trajectory, he draws unevenly upon them in his analysis of French class structure and consumer practices. If differences in total volume of capital delineate the three principal classes (dominant, middle, and working), differences in composition and their changes over time are found only in the dominant and middle classes. Indeed, at one point in his analysis Bourdieu (171) neglects the third dimension altogether and reduces in summary form his own analysis to the first two dimensions. His (339–65) exploration of the dimension of change in capital holdings over time is most developed in the case of the subtle differences in lifestyle among the various fractions constituting the middle class.

41. Bourdieu (172) writes that "life-styles are thus the systematic products of habitus, which, perceived in their mutual relations through the schemes of the habitus, become sign systems that are socially qualified (as 'distinguished', 'vulgar' etc)."

42. Here Bourdieu (54) draws a close connection between cultural practices and economic necessities. He presupposes that economic necessities must first be met before cultural activities can occur, as least as they are defined by legitimate dominant culture. His argument here is consistent with how he elaborates a materialist understanding of status and subjective dispositions. Positively advantaged groups are more likely to generate status distinctions. And dispositions are "engendered . . . in the last analysis, by the economic bases of the social formation in question" (Bourdieu 1977c:83).

practices adjusted to the regularities of the conditions of existence, taste becomes

a practical mastery of distributions which makes it possible to sense or intuit what is likely (or unlikely) to befall—and therefore to befit—an individual occupying a given position in social space. It functions as a sort of social orientation, a "sense of one's place," guiding the occupants of a given place in social space towards the social positions adjusted to their properties, and towards the practices or goods which befit the occupants of that position. It implies a practical anticipation of what the social meaning and value of the chosen practice or thing will probably be, given their distribution in social space and the practical knowledge the other agents have of the correspondence between goods and groups. (Bourdieu 1984a:466–67)

Through the working of habitus, taste

transforms necessities into strategies, constraints into preferences, and, without any mechanical determination, it generates the set of "choices" constituting life-styles. . . . It is a virtue made of necessity which continuously transforms necessity into virtue by inducing "choices" which correspond to the condition of which it is the product. (Bourdieu 1984a:175)

As the distance from economic necessities grows,

life-style increasingly becomes the product of what Weber calls a "stylization of life," a systematic commitment which orients and organizes the most diverse practices—the choice of a vintage or a cheese or the decoration of a holiday home in the country. (55–56)

Differences in basic conditions of existence produce, therefore, a "basic opposition between the tastes of luxury and the tastes of necessity," between actors whose economic circumstances permit the pursuit of status distinctions and those who can afford no such luxury (183). This opposition pits members of the dominant classes against those of the working class (industrial laborers and peasants). It generates two corresponding and opposing types of class habitus: the taste for freedom and taste for necessity.

TASTE FOR FREEDOM

Since the dominant class possesses a high volume of capital, it develops a "taste of freedom" from the mundane material necessities and practical urgencies of everyday life. This "sense of distinction" is characterized by

an "aesthetic disposition" in its "distant, detached or casual disposition towards the world of other people" (Bourdieu 1984a:376).[43] It

proposes the combination of ease and asceticism, i.e., self-imposed austerity, restraint, reserve, which are affirmed in that absolute manifestation of excellence, re-
laxation in tension. (176)[44]

Though this aesthetic disposition finds its fullest expression in the field of
art,

there is no area of practice in which the aim of purifying, refining and sublimating
primary needs and impulses cannot assert itself, no area in which the stylization of
life, that is, the primacy of forms over function, of manner over matter, does not
produce the same effects. (Bourdieu 1984a:5)

Thus, the dominant class's freedom from material constraints permits it to
stylize and formalize natural functions in order to invest them with a sense
of distinction. In art, the aesthetic disposition elevates form over the content of a work. Abstract organization, which must be decoded intellectually,
rather than the representative image, which can be appreciated by the uninitiated eye, becomes the mark of artistic sensibility. Similarly, dominant-
class taste in clothing stresses form and style rather than simply covering the
body to make it comfortable. In eating, the mundane function of satisfying
hunger is formalized into a ceremonial ritual governed by rules of etiquette
and sociability. Even care of the body becomes stylized in elaborated forms
of attention given to its strength, health and beauty.

CHOICE OF NECESSITY

The dominant-class taste for freedom is defined in opposition to the
working-class taste for necessity. Holding little capital, industrial laborers
and rural peasants must confront directly and continuously the practical
needs and urgencies of making a living. The working class experiences this
"forced choice of necessity" not, however, as a deprivation but as a preference—a "taste for necessity" that privileges substance over form, the infor-

43. For Bourdieu (54), the structural precondition for the development of the aesthetic
disposition is a class condition "characterized by the suspension and removal of economic
necessity and by objective and subjective distance from practical urgencies."

44. Goffman (1950–51) points to the quality of "restraint" as a form of cultivation used
to symbolize class status. Since a disposition of discipline requires time for development, it
functions as a "restricting mechanism" for those who wish to usurp this form of social distinction through quick acquisition.

mal over the formal, the sensual over the intellectual. Thus, workers eat beans not because they cannot afford anything else but "because they have a taste for what they are anyway condemned to" (Bourdieu 1984a:178). Their choice of less expensive foods is explained by the reasoning that these foods are more substantial and filling.

It is noteworthy that Bourdieu views his argument here as quite different from that of economic determinism. He argues that the experience of material constraints is transformed into a distinct habitus.[45] Working-class consumer behavior is *not* directly determined by sheer material scarcity. If income directly determined consumer choice, then one would expect significant increases in income, such as winning the lottery or career mobility into small business, to transform radically the consumer practices of workers. That it does not, Bourdieu argues, justifies his argument. He suggests that

having a million does not in itself make one able to live like a millionaire; and parvenus generally take a long time to learn that what they see as culpable prodigality is, in their new condition, expenditure of basic necessity. (Bourdieu 1984a: 374)

Moreover,

the specific effect of the taste for necessity, which never ceases to act, . . . is most clearly seen when it is, in a sense, operating out of phase, having survived the disappearance of the conditions which produced it.

The contrast between the dominant-class taste of freedom and the working-class taste of necessity is conceptualized relationally by Bourdieu. These tastes are not simply reflections of two distinct sets of conditions of existence. Rather, the aesthetic disposition of the dominant class "is defined, objectively and subjectively, in relation to other dispositions," notably that of the working class (55). Bourdieu (56) contends that

the tastes of freedom can only assert themselves as such in relation to the tastes of necessity, which are thereby brought to the level of the aesthetic and so defined as vulgar.

---

45. Bourdieu's habitus explanation distinguishes him from a variety of materialist perspectives on culture and tastes. In an interesting variation on the materialist thesis, David Halle (1991) finds materialist underpinnings in working-class preferences for landscape paintings that relate, not to Bourdieu's "culture of necessity," but to the "material context of the house and neighborhood."

Working-class lifestyles thus serve as a negative reference for the dominant class.

> Perhaps their sole function in the system of aesthetic positions is to serve as a foil, a negative reference point, in relation to which all aesthetics define themselves, by successive negations. (57)

Dominant-class attitudes toward this working-class preference is to judge it as they do their own, namely, as a choice freed from economic necessity. They thereby commit what Bourdieu (178) labels a form of "class racism" by condemning the working-class lifestyle as one of ignorance, conformity, or bad choices rather than as one that is adjusted to underlying material necessities.[46] Here Bourdieu returns to his recurrent criticism of substantialism. In the area of lifestyles, he sees substantialist views as those that depict group preferences as natural inclinations, inherent in groups rather than stemming from the logic of mutual distinction.

In contrast, dominant-class lifestyles serve as a "positive" reference for the working class; indeed, they exercise symbolic power. The stylization of life affirms "power over a dominated necessity" and hence

> always implies a claim to a legitimate superiority over those who, because they cannot assert the same contempt for contingencies in gratuitous luxury and conspicuous consumption, remain dominated by ordinary interest and urgencies. (56)

The relationship between the two class habitus is one of domination. Dominant-class tastes are legitimated in that they appear to originate from qualities of charisma, knowledge, and aptitude rather than from distance from necessity. Though working-class individuals have internalized from their limited means of existence a taste for necessity, they acknowledge the superiority of dominant-class tastes for freedom. When asked to express their opinions about high-brow art forms, working-class individuals respond with "That's not for the likes of us" or "I wish I were better informed about that" (Bourdieu, Boltanski et al. 1965). Schooling, Bourdieu stresses, plays a central role in inculcating this acknowledgement of the superiority of dominant-class standards of taste.

Class identity is thus oppositional. The two habitus of distinction and necessity are dialectically related, as one finds its identity in contrast to the other. Bourdieu thinks of habitus as reflecting not only the underlying

---

46. Bourdieu (178) charges that the dominant class view of taste "consciously or unconsciously . . . naturalizes the taste of necessity . . ., converting it into a natural inclination simply by dissociating it from its economic and social raisons d'être."

conditions of existence but also the relative position of an individual and group in the class hierarchy. Dispositions reflect both class conditions and the relational rank or position in the class hierarchy (Bourdieu 1984a:246). Bourdieu's study of cultural practices and lifestyles identifies numerous instances where he finds evidence of this double opposition. For example, as regards the use of language he finds it

> between popular outspokenness and the highly censored language of the bourgeois, between the expressionist pursuit of the picturesque or the rhetorical effect and the choice of restraint and false simplicity (litotes). (176)

The same opposition

> is found in body language: here too, agitation and haste, grimaces and gesticulation are opposed to slowness—"the slow gestures, the slow glance" of nobility, according to Nietzsche—to the restraint and impassivity which signify elevation. (177)

Bourdieu treats the popular classes as homogeneous in their habitus, driven by material necessity, lacking in cultural capital, and hence dominated by dominant culture. Because they have no distance from necessity and no cultural capital, French workers are exempted from the invidious struggle for distinction. This image of the French working class raises three sets of issues that point to difficulties in Bourdieu's work. Can there be a genuine form of working-class culture outside the purview of dominant class culture? Are there important sources of differentiation in consciousness and practices that Bourdieu's working-class habitus does not reveal? And, is the "forced necessity" of working-class taste a fully "relational" conceptualization, or does it suggest a deeper essence of the working-class experience? I will address briefly each of these concerns.

Bourdieu argues that all dominated groups are inseparably tied to dominant culture. Subordinate groups are "always subject to the domination of the dominant cultural arbitrary" (Bourdieu and Passeron 1977:23). Bourdieu claims that there are no authentic popular class cultures freed from the imprint of dominant culture. Rather, arguments for the existence of "popular cultures" are but intellectualized productions that look as if they were genuine representations of autonomous cultural forms.

> Populism is never anything other than an inverted ethnocentrism, and if descriptions of the industrial working class and the peasantry almost always vacillate between miserabilism and millenarian exaltation, this is because they leave out the relation to class condition which is part of a complete definition of that condition,

and because it is less easy to state the actual relation to the condition one is describing (without necessarily being able to feel it) than to put one's own relation to it into the description. (Bourdieu 1984a:374)

The problem occurs because intellectuals confound their own relationship of identification with or support for the working class—a relationship established by the habitus of choice rather than by the habitus of necessity—with the working-class condition itself.[47] Intellectuals who celebrate popular culture do not take into account the differences in habitus between themselves and the working class. For Bourdieu, the problem of popular culture is a problem of intellectuals.

Bourdieu sees working-class domination by dominant culture in the following ways: by substituting cheap goods for luxury consumer items and by the lack of cultural capital. He observes that the working-class lifestyle is characterized by both "the absence of luxury goods, whisky or paintings, champagne or concerts, cruises or art exhibitions, caviar or antiques" and by

the presence of numerous cheap substitutes for these rare goods, "sparkling white wine" for champagne, imitation leather for real leather, reproductions for paintings, indices of a dispossession at the second power. (386)

Because they lack the forms of cultural capital that drive the new modes of automation and communication in the advanced societies,

ordinary workers are dominated by the machines and instruments which they serve rather than use, and by those who possess the legitimate, i.e., theoretical, means of dominating them. (387)

In cultural practices in particular, Bourdieu (394) sees French working-class families as completely dominated.[48] He concludes pessimistically that

there is no realistic chance of any collective resistance to the effect of imposition that would lead either to the valorization of properties stigmatized by the dominant

47. Bourdieu (372) writes that "the *narodniki* of all times and all lands, by identifying with their object to the point of confusing their relation to the working-class condition with the working-class relation to that condition . . . present an account of the working-class condition that is statistically improbable, since it is not the product of the relation to that condition which is ordinarily associated with the condition."

48. Bourdieu observes that even in the political arena, where struggles in the trade-union movement "might provide the one genuine principle of a counter-culture," the working class in fact acquiesces to the "effects of cultural domination" (395).

taxonomy (the "black is beautiful" strategy) or to the creation of new, positively evaluated properties. Thus the dominated have only two options: loyalty to self and the group (always liable to relapse into shame), or the individual effort to assimilate the dominant ideal which is the antithesis of the very ambition of collectively regaining control over social identity (of the type pursued by the collective revolt of the American feminists when it advocates the "natural look"). (384)

Nevertheless, the French working class does find a limited measure of autonomy from dominant-class standards in a few selected practices, namely, attitudes toward the body, food, and language. Bourdieu (ibid.) suggests that the "popular valorization of physical strength," which is a "fundamental aspect of virility," is "perhaps one of the last refuges of the autonomy of the dominated classes." It is this "capacity to produce their own representation of the accomplished man and the social world" which represents "one of the most autonomous forms of their self-affirmation as a class."

Rather than view expressions of physical prowess from the standpoint of dominant-class norms and therefore judge them as fundamentally retrograde or sexist, Bourdieu here asks that we view them as an expression of the working-class condition, one that depends on a "labour power which the laws of cultural reproduction and of the labour market reduce, more than for any other class, to sheer muscle power." The working class is "only rich in its labour power" and therefore as a class "can only oppose to the other classes—apart from the withdrawal of its labour—its fighting strength, which depends on the physical strength and courage of its members, and also their number, i.e., their consciousness and solidarity or, to put it another way, their consciousness of their of their solidarity." Physical strength is the one form of capital over which the working class is able to exercise some monopoly power. Indeed, it is the social foundation for working class political power.

In the case of food, Bourdieu (179) writes that "the art of eating and drinking remains one of the few areas in which the working classes explicitly challenge the legitimate art of living." In contrast to the dominant-class style of sobriety and restraint, the French working class maintains an "ethic of convivial indulgence," perhaps best captured by the popular expression, "bon vivant" (ibid.). This style associates indulgence and conviviality. Similarly, in speech one finds an "efficacity and vivacity" in a highly contextualized use of "ellipses, short cuts and metaphors" that is "freed from the censorship and constraints of quasi-written" language use found in the upper classes (395).

Bourdieu (376) sees in the working-class taste of necessity not only an adaptation to necessity but also a kind of defensive strategy against it, one that resists middle-class pretension and dominant-class distinction:

The submission to necessity which inclines working-class people to a pragmatic, functionalist "aesthetic," refusing the gratuity and futility of formal exercises and of every form of art for art's sake, is also the principle of all the choices of daily existence and of an art of living which rejects specifically aesthetic intentions as aberrations.

In another place (394–95), he writes of working-class autonomy as a

realistic (but not resigned) hedonism and skeptical (but not cynical) materialism which constitute both a form of adaptation to the conditions of existence and a defence against them.

Bourdieu (380) thus finds a measure of working-class autonomy in the "principle of conformity," which is the "only explicit norm of popular taste." It expresses itself in "calls to order" such as "who does she think she is?" or "that's not for the likes of us." The aim of this norm is

to encourage the "reasonable" choices that are in any case imposed by the objective conditions [which] also contain a warning against the ambition to distinguish one-self by identifying with other groups, that is, they are a reminder of the need for class solidarity. (380–81)[49]

But these spheres of partial autonomy of working-class practices from dominant-class standards hardly constitute for Bourdieu resources for an offensive strategy that might forge a distinct, collective social and cultural identity. Moreover, because of the cultural socialization effects of mass edu-cation,

the most politically conscious fraction of the working class remains profoundly sub-ject, in culture and language, to the dominant norms and values, and therefore deeply sensitive to the effects of authority imposition which every holder of cultural authority can exert, even in politics. (396)

Bourdieu emphasizes how subordinate groups unwittingly follow the terms set forth by the dominant class. This certainly taps one important

49. This leads Bourdieu to admit that the "low interest which working-class people show in the works of legitimate culture to which they have access—especially through television—is not solely the effect of a lack of competence and familiarity" (ibid.). It is also an expression of the social norm of conformity, of social closure that resists the "pretension to distinguish oneself."

dimension of relations between workers and dominant-class standards. Yet, it hardly exhausts our understanding of the historical experiences of subordinate groups in the Western democracies. Even the most powerless groups are able on occasion to disrupt the system of domination. The vote, for example, can permit subordinate groups to help determine which fraction of the dominant class will have the greatest influence on policy. Moreover, subordinate groups have the greatest opportunity for resisting dominant-class control when there is disagreement and sharp conflict within the dominant class itself (Domhoff 1983:2). Bourdieu does not devote much attention to situations where subordinate groups are able to place restraints on the actions of dominant groups.

Bourdieu's focus on the dominant class tends to miss the considerable internal working-class differentiation that exists. In their survey of dietary practices among French workers, Grignon and Grignon (1980:550) conclude that if one takes into account residence, job, family structure, and origins, it is "unthinkable" to speak of a unitary popular taste and lifestyle among the popular classes in France. Bourdieu's treatment in *Distinction* of French working-class lifestyles and tastes does not give sufficient attention to fundamental differences between urban workers and the peasantry. The most striking difference is the ability of the peasantry to resist mass-marketing trends in food products because of their own high degree of self-sufficiency (Grignon and Grignon 1980:538). This is made possible to a considerable degree by the domestic labor in food preparation provided by rural women (537). By contrast, urban worker dietary practices are much more closely constrained by income (545) Moreover, the manual nature and physicality of life for the peasantry—which is paradoxically reinforced in many instances with modernization—is reflected in peasant tastes and tends to shock dominant lifestyle sensibilities (543). Furthermore, differences occur among urban workers, notably between those from peasant origins who tend to retain important elements of the peasant lifestyle, and those whose origins are urban (552) Bourdieu's account in *Distinction* of French working-class lifestyles glosses over these differences. In contrast to the refined dissection of differences internal to the dominant class and to the various fractions of the petty bourgeoisie, Bourdieu gives scant attention to this fragmented existence and its impact upon consciousness within the French working class.[50] The stress on habitus suggests just the opposite analytical thrust, namely, the tendency to look for an underlying unity

50. Mann (1970:33) argues that workers develop a *"dualistic* consciousness" that corresponds to their segmented experience in which "control and money, work and non-work become separated."

across a wide diversity of practices. But more stress on Bourdieu's idea that practices emerge from the *intersection* of habitus and field could potentially take into account the diversity of practices within the working class.

The key concept of cultural capital appears limited for generalized use. It does not really apply to the working class except to say they have none. The concept seems predicated on dominant culture experiences and practices and perhaps imports an ethnocentric view when applied outside of that social milieu. This is suggested by the apparent need to talk of the working class solely in terms of the "lack" of cultural capital, which would reflect a dominant-class view of working-class practices (Grignon and Passeron 1985). Bourdieu (1984a:387) sees working-class domination in terms of the lack of *internalized cultural capital* which means that "ordinary workers are dominated by the machines and instruments which they serve rather than use, and by those who possess the legitimate, i.e., theoretical, means of dominating them." This "dispossession" seems to be for Bourdieu the underlying social relation connecting the working class to the social world.[51]

Grignon and Grignon (1980:551) argue that a more refined analysis of the different fractions of the working class reveals different types of resources that can be employed strategically and hence thought of as forms of capital. For example, the craft tradition and skill training that helps constitute what is often referred to as the "labor aristocracy" clearly differentiates internally the French working class. While in certain respects this "professional culture" can give legitimacy to dominant cultural hierarchies, it can be—and often is—employed as a collective capital in struggle with employers. In this respect, it does not simply reflect the relations of domination (Bourdieu 1984a:551). While Bourdieu does not deny that subordinate groups can mobilize some resources in struggle against dominant groups, the overwhelming thrust of his analysis is directed to showing how limited that capacity indeed is.

Most of these criticisms focus on *Distinction*, which is not first and foremost a study of working-class culture. Rather, *Distinction* is directed against the dominant-class aesthetic, particularly the intellectuals who specialize in it. The thrust of Bourdieu's criticism in *Distinction* is to expose the "strategies of distinction" that shape tastes and life-styles, notably in the dominant and middle classes. It is an effort to "expose" symbolic power of domination. But Bourdieu stresses that classes are constituted relationally and that the "culture of necessity" functions as a negative reference to the dominant aesthetic. Nevertheless, the emphasis Bourdieu places on the idea that

51. This reflects the fundamental division that Bourdieu (1984a:387) sees between practical knowledge and theoretical knowledge that translates into social-class differences.

working-class lifestyles are driven by the force of necessity evokes a kind of Halbwachsian perspective on popular taste as one "without taste"—for this lifestyle is highly constrained by primary necessities (Grignon and Grignon 1980:551). Though Bourdieu rejects all universals, whether biological, physical, or spiritual in his definition of dominant-class culture,[52] his analysis nonetheless suggests an implicit assumption that cultural practices become possible *only after* primary needs are satisfied. This implies a set of universal primary needs that must be met before cultural practices can occur. Such a view would embody the classic opposition of nature and culture, and it is hence surprising that Bourdieu, who wishes to transcend all received intellectual dichotomies, would consciously or unconsciously rely on this one. Judging from his frequent denunciations of all forms of substantialism, including those forms attributing intrinsic characteristics to social groups, it is doubtful that Bourdieu would want to embrace the image of the French worker as a sort of "noble savage," freed from the invidious entrapments imposed by formalized culture. Yet it is strange that his zealous attention to all conceivable forms of conceptual dichotomies that can carry unwanted social and ideological baggage fails to guard against this one.

PRETENSION AND GOOD WILL

Bourdieu (1984a:339) writes of opposition between the bourgeois habitus and the petit bourgeois habitus as "a bourgeois ethos of ease, a confident relation to the world and the self . . . with a petit-bourgeois ethos of restriction through pretension." More generally, he summarizes the petite bourgeoisie habitus as one of "asceticism, rigor, legalism, the propensity accumulation in all its forms" (331). These are dispositions of "tension" and "pretension" which convey the fundamental ambiguity of a class that wishes to escape identification with the working class yet lacks the requisite resources to cultivate the lifestyle of the dominant class it emulates.[53] Reflecting the dynamics of upward mobility aspirations, the petit bourgeois displays "thrift, acquisition, accumulation, [and] an appetite for possession inseparable from permanent anxiety about property" whereas the bourgeois exhibits "ostentation, big spending and generosity" (330).

Unlike the working class, the petite bourgeoisie enters the game of

---

52. This is the meaning intended when he speaks of the *arbitrary* character of dominant-class culture (see Bourdieu and Passeron 1977:8).

53. The most complete embodiment of the petit-bourgeois habitus is found in what Bourdieu (351, 354) calls the "executant petite bourgeoisie," which includes junior executives, office workers, and primary school teachers.

distinction but has neither the capital nor the corresponding habitus to appropriate fully dominant-class lifestyles. It attempts to emulate the standards set by the dominant class, but its "striving towards distinction" betrays an awkward pretension where the dominant aesthetic displays ease and familiarity in the world of culture (58). It is caught in the opposition between its upward mobility ambitions and actual possibilities and therefore produces practices "which are perceived as pretentious, because of the manifest discrepancy between ambition and possibilities" (176).

Bourdieu writes of the petit bourgeois habitus in its relationship to high culture as one of "cultural goodwill" that signals an "undifferentiated reverence" toward high culture, one that leads to a

concern for conformity which induces an anxious quest for authorities and models of conduct and leads to a choice of sure and certified products (such as classics and prize winners). (331)

Moreover, the petit bourgeois delights

in all the cheap substitutes for chic objects and practices—driftwood and painted pebbles, cane and raffia, "art" handicrafts and art photography. (58)

In this way, it reveals a set of dispositions that "betray the gap between acknowledgement and knowledge" (323). "The petit bourgeois," Bourdieu writes,

do not know how to play the game of culture as a game. They take culture too seriously to go in for bluff or imposture or even for the distance and casualness which show true familiarity. (330)

The same habitus betrays its identity in language usage by the tendency to hypercorrection, a vigilance which overshoots the mark for fear of falling short and pounces on linguistic incorrectness, on oneself and others. (331)

In the area of ethics one finds an almost insatiable thirst for rules of conduct that subjects the whole of life to rigorous discipline. And in politics one finds "respectful conformism or prudent reformism."

Some critics (e.g., Hoffman 1986) charge that Bourdieu gives a demeaning account of the French middle class. Is Bourdieu simply reporting the middle-class lifestyle of "pretension" or is he also condemning it? Certainly, some of his formulations are hardly endearing. But these need to be interpreted within the framework where Bourdieu situates them. The pretension of the middle class is seen from the standpoint of dominant-class culture. It reflects the ambiguous condition of being caught between two classes, one from which it is trying to escape and the other to which it is trying to gain access. Bourdieu's labels are designed, not to suggest intrinsic features of this class, but to convey the desperate ambiguity of the middle position. It would therefore seem more fruitful to ask whether there are middle-class cultural forms that escape to a greater extent than Bourdieu believes the imprint of dominant-class tastes? Mouriaux (1980), for example, suggests that the French petite bourgeoisie has its own proper culture and distinctive lifestyle which may actually exert some influence over that of the working class and the dominant class, rather than reducing the middle class to a relationship of dependency on the dominant class.

ARISTOCRATIC ASCETICISM VERSUS BOURGEOIS HEDONISM

Within the dominant and middle classes, Bourdieu identifies subtypes of habitus that correspond to different class fractions. Differences in capital composition generate distinct patterns of consumer behavior and lifestyles for class fractions that are relatively richer in economic capital from those who are relatively richer in cultural capital. Within the dominant class, those relatively richer in economic capital adopt a "hedonistic aesthetic of ease and facility" toward arts consumption, which is "symbolized by boulevard theatre or Impressionistic painting" (Bourdieu 1984a:176). In contrast, the dominated fractions of intellectuals and artists, who are relatively richer in cultural capital but poorer in economic capital, reject the "ostentation and the bourgeois taste for ornament" of the dominant fraction, and adopt an "ascetic" aesthetics that leads them to "support all artistic revolutions conducted in the name of purity and purification" (ibid.). These contrasting sets of dispositions are sharpest where the asymmetries in economic and cultural capital are greatest, notably between teachers and employers, where they are "clear-cut, total [and] comparable to the gap between two 'cultures' in the anthropological sense" (283). Teachers, who have the greatest asymmetry between their cultural capital and economic wealth, are particularly "inclined to ascetic consumption in all areas" (185). In the area of leisure, for example, Bourdieu (219) makes the colorful observation that

the aristocratic asceticism of the teachers finds an exemplary expression in mountaineering, which, even more than rambling, with its reserved paths (one thinks of Heidegger) or cycle-touring, with its Romanesque churches, offers for minimum economic costs the maximum distinction, distance, height, spiritual elevation, through the sense of simultaneously mastering one's own body and a nature inaccessible to the many.

This kind of habitus stands in sharp contrast to

the health-oriented hedonism of doctors and modern executives who have the material and cultural means of access to the most prestigious activities, far from vulgar crowds, is expressed in yachting, open-sea swimming, cross-country skiing or under-water fishing.

It also contrasts with employers who

expect the same gains in distinction from golf, with its aristocratic etiquette, its English vocabulary and its great exclusive spaces, together with extrinsic profits, such as the accumulation of social capital.[54]

In the area of culture, the ascetic aristocratism of teachers leads them to adopt "serious and even somewhat severe cultural practices," such as museum visits. By contrast, the hedonistic aesthetic of professionals leads them to the most expensive and prestigious activities, such as "visiting antique dealers, galleries and concert-halls" (286).

Thus, within the dominant class one finds two opposing types of habitus that correspond to their respective configurations of economic and cultural capital: an aristocratic asceticism or disposition for austerity and purity and a hedonistic taste for luxury, ornament, and ostentation. These differences in habitus are rooted in the underlying material conditions of existence. But—and this is Bourdieu's main point—these material differences are experienced and represented dispositionally as cultural distinctions. It is this practical translation of material conditions into symbolic distinctions that for Bourdieu represents the social functions of culture.

THE EFFECTS OF MOBILITY

Variations in both capital composition and social trajectory differentiate middle-class lifestyle patterns as well. Bourdieu (339) argues that a more refined analysis of the petit bourgeois habitus reveals that

this system of dispositions takes on as many modalities as there are ways of attaining, staying in or passing through a middle position in the social structure, and that this position itself may be steady, rising or declining.

54. Some national cultural differences are obvious if one compares many of the lifestyle indicators Bourdieu uses for France to other national settings. "English vocabulary" is fairly removed from the afternoon golf match among American executives. In the American context, the choice between golf, squash, and bowling undoubtedly point up important social distinctions. And changes may well have occurred in France since these data were gathered. Bourdieu's general argument, however, is unaffected by national differences and changes over time. What is required is that systematic differences across classes be found regardless of what those differences might be.

Bourdieu (346, 351) gives particular attention to two variants from the modal petit bourgeois habitus: an "optimistic progressivism" toward their future chances in the modern world and a "pessimistic, regressive conservatism" that embraces "most austere and traditional values."[55] The former tends to be found among those who are younger, investing in education credentials, of lower social origins, and moving up into the rapidly growing sector of new culturally intensive occupations.[56] The latter tend to be found among the craftsmen and small shopkeepers, whose numbers and general standard of living in France are declining, and who lack the economic capital and cultural capital they need for conversion into more valued capital, such as higher education credentials.

The new petty bourgeois tend to be carriers of postmodern consumer culture that caters to and promotes a particular interest in style itself. This variation of the middle-class habitus consists of calculating hedonism in a search of stylistic effects in all aspects of life. It is in this particular class fraction that one finds the greatest effort to customize lifestyle and make it a life project through a zealous quest for all the new and latest in relationships, experiences, and consumer goods.

Class Conflict and Social Reproduction

We next examine how Bourdieu understands the dynamics of stratification processes in advanced societies. He sees competitive struggle as representing the fundamental dynamic of all social life. Individuals, families, and groups struggle to maintain or improve their relative market positions within the stratified social order. Competition occurs (1) over valued forms of capital, and (2) over definitions of what is legitimate capital. I will first explore Bourdieu's understanding of conflict over types of capital and then examine his view of class struggle as a classification struggle.[57]

CAPITAL REPRODUCTION STRATEGIES

Bourdieu thinks of class struggle in terms of actors pursuing, consciously and unconsciously, social reproduction strategies that maintain or improve their positions in the stratification order. These strategies involve ways of

---

55. In Bourdieu's analysis, several different factors contribute to the differentiation of these two subtypes of petit bourgeois habitus. But they tend to cluster into distinct ensembles.

56. Bourdieu observes that there tends to be a significant proportion of women in this condition in France.

57. Additional considerations regarding his views on conflict, reproduction, and change are taken up in chapter 8.

investing various types of capital to maintain or enhance positions in fields (Bourdieu 1984a:125–68). To illustrate, class fractions richest in cultural capital, such as secondary school teachers and university professors, invest heavily in the education and general cultural enrichment of their children. In contrast, class fractions richest in economic capital, such as industrial and commercial employers, downplay educational and cultural investments for their children in favor of direct transfers of economic wealth.[58] And the economically and culturally well-endowed liberal professions, such as law and medicine, invest heavily in education and especially in those cultural activities that provide a social capital of connections, reputation, and respect that are useful for professional careers (120–22). Thus, reproduction strategies depend largely on the total volume and composition of capital to be maintained.

They also depend on the "state of the instruments of reproduction (inheritance law and custom, the labor market, the educational system etc.)" (125). Bourdieu devotes particular attention to "reconversion strategies" where groups restructure their capital holdings by exchanging one currency for another in order to maintain or improve their relative positions in the class structure.[59] He argues that study of how individuals and groups convert one type of capital into another and at what rate of exchange provide important insight into the character of class relations (Bourdieu 1980c:57). Reconversion strategies are necessitated by changes in the economy, the growth of bureaucracy, and, most significantly for Bourdieu, the growth of cultural markets. Educational credential markets, in particular, he argues, have become a new important source of stratification in industrial society by providing vital resources for status distinctions among segments within upper- and middle-class groups (Bourdieu and Boltanski 1977).[60] Bourdieu contends that economic, political, and legal changes have precipitated a shift in upper-class inheritance practices from one of direct transfer of property to reliance upon the cultural transmission of economic privilege: investment in education gives upper-class offspring the chance to appropriate family privilege and wealth through access to the more powerful and remunerative institutional positions. The growing value of educational credentials as currency for giving access to and legitimation in most labor markets makes higher education an attractive investment for middle-class

58. Bourdieu (120) observes, however, that upper-level managers in the private business sector favor investing in the cultural as well as economic futures of their children.
59. See in particular his discussion in *Distinction* (125–68).
60. Here Bourdieu joins the "credential society" theories that developed in the 1970s (Collins 1979, Miller 1976).

groups as well.[61] Bourdieu describes these changes as a shift from a "family" mode of reproduction to a "school" mode of reproduction where the educational system increasingly replaces families in mediating the class reproduction process (Wacquant 1993b:27, 32).

Bourdieu (1984a:131) adopts the analytical language of class reproduction and reconversion strategies to distinguish his approach from mainstream social mobility research. Conceptualizing social classes in terms of their volume and composition of capital and social trajectory through fields permits Bourdieu to shift attention to multidimensional components of class hierarchies that cannot be captured in additive linear models or one-dimensional mobility scales. His (1980c:57, 1984a:125) model emphasizes the *differences in configuration* of different types of capital and how one of the key factors in class struggle is the "exchange rate" between the different types of capital.

Bourdieu's perspective of social mobility as capital investment and conversion strategies distinguishes "vertical" from "transverse" movements. The former designates upward or downward movement within the same field whereas the latter indicate movement across fields (Bourdieu 1984a: 131). Intrafield vertical mobility (e.g., from primary school teacher to college professor) involves capital accumulation strategies with one type of capital. Interfield movements require capital reconversion, as when shopkeepers invest in the higher education of their children rather than simply passing on the family business.

One recurring theme in Bourdieu's work on stratification is the continuity of class position within the hierachy amid change in class condition. Occupational mobility, he argues, does not necessarily imply class mobility. Class groups can improve their condition by increasing their standard of living yet remain in the same relative position within the social hierarchy. Bourdieu sees this happening where strategies of capital accumulation occur in fields that are declining in importance or where reconversion strategies traverse fields of similar rank order. Occupational mobility in France from small land owners to low-level civil servants or from small artisans to office workers illustrate that occupational change is not incompatible with the reproduction of social class structure (Bourdieu 1984a:131).

Bourdieu makes a forceful argument that the shift from earlier forms of capitalist to contemporary industrial or postindustrial societies has brought reproduction rather than transformation of the social class structure. Though Bourdieu (1973a) admits that a limited and "controlled mobility"

---

61. A second major change in French dominant-class reproduction strategies is the switch from technical training, such as engineering, to degrees in management and public administration (Bourdieu 1989c:386).

can occur to provide meritocratic legitimation to an inegalitarian social structure, the general findings from occupational mobility research in several Western countries, including France, indicate that Bourdieu underestimates the amount of mobility that actually occurs (see Bénéton 1975, Boudon 1974, Goldthorpe 1980, Hout and Garnier 1979).[62] Mobility studies indeed show rigidities at the extremes of the social stratification structure as Bourdieu's theory predicts. But a large number of mobility studies also show considerable movement, particularly short-range movement, across the broad middle range of the class structure. Moreover, some of Bourdieu's own data show that there is more occupational mobility in France than his analysis suggests.[63]

Bourdieu challenges the thesis of considerable mobility in the advanced societies he studies by debunking empirical measures of occupational status categories. He points to instances where changes in occupational titles signify no real shift in relative class position and to cases where intergenerational transfer of occupation from father to son actually represent a decline in class position, as in declining economic sectors like farming. He is generally quite dismissive of mobility data, and does not really draw from them to make his reproduction argument.[64] Moreover, whatever intergenerational improvement there has been can be understood in terms of the key distinction we observed earlier in the chapter that Bourdieu makes between the situation (or condition) of the individual members of a class and the position of the class in the social hierarchy. He has consistently argued that while there have been changes in the general living conditions of all classes (class situation), no group seems to have really improved its relative position in the stratification order (class position). Every group has moved up in terms of living standards (class situation), but the pecking order (class position) remains unchanged. For Bourdieu (1984a:185, Bourdieu and Passeron

62. Bénéton (1975) shows that by using statistical independence as the normative reference the rate of intergenerational occupational reproduction falls approximately between 40 and 50 percent. Bourdieu's claim for the reproduction of the class structure implies that this rate should be much higher.

63. Table 9 on page 121 of *Distinction* shows that each of the principal fractions of the dominant class recruit no more than two-fifths of their membership from among individuals sharing dominant-class origins.

64. Bourdieu's early claims of the reproduction of social structure in France were based in part upon educational opportunity data, not occupational mobility data. He argued that by the mid-1960s educational opportunities were still strongly class-based and only slowly changing despite years of higher education expansion. Early key statements of his reproduction position (Bourdieu 1973a; Bourdieu and Passeron 1977, 1979) suggested that reproduction and mobility where antagonistic processes in social structure. In his more recent work, Bourdieu (1984a) seems more willing to admit that there can be considerable intergenerational movement in the broad middle range of the class structure, though he continues to maintain that the French class structure remains intact.

1979:79–80), therefore, change in class situation is not incompatible with the reproduction of class position. By employing a conceptual language of "field of power," "systems of social differences," "class reproduction strategies," and "structural homologies" among fields, Bourdieu (1989c:191–96) wants to expand the range of empirical data beyond the standard occupational and educational indicators most frequently found in mobility analysis. It permits him to focus on relations between the dominant class and elite sectors of French higher education to stress their disproportionate impact in shaping the intergenerational transmission of power in French society.

It is one thing to dismiss the uncritical use of occupational categories in mobility tables and to counsel caution in determining the proper sociological significance in changing occupational titles, but quite another to offer a plausible empirical test of just what change in social structure might look like. This, Bourdieu has not sufficiently done. (I will consider his limited treatment of social change in chapter 8.) If the mode of class reproduction has switched from that of the family to the school, as Bourdieu claims, then it would seem that the argument should find support across a range of data on educational and occupational opportunity and rewards in income. Bourdieu's reproduction argument finds partial support in many such data currently available but not to the degree that his claims suggest.

CLASS CONFLICT AS CULTURAL CONFLICT

Bourdieu analyses the nature of class conflict in postindustrial societies as one that increasingly takes the form of investments in cultural and symbolic distinctions. If parents invest in good education for their children it is to increase their "scarcity value" on the job market. Bourdieu sees evidence of considerable class conflict in French education, and we will examine this conflict in chapter 8.

More generally, Bourdieu argues that social classes tend to invest in symbolic distinctions that give them the appearance of status groups. As we have seen, status groups for Bourdieu are social classes in disguise. He connects this phenomenon to the growth of the new consumer-oriented economies

whose functioning depends as much on the production of needs and consensus as on the production of goods [and has generated] a social world which judges people by their capacity for consumption, their "standard of living," their life-style, as much as by their capacity for production. (Bourdieu 1984a:310)

In more recent writings Bourdieu gives increased emphasis in his analysis of social-class relations to the dynamics of struggle over the representations and definitions of the social world as well as over access to valued material resources.[65] Class struggle, according to Bourdieu, occurs not only over valued resources or for access to positions of power in fields. The very definition of what is valued and the understanding of one's position in fields are themselves objects of struggle. "Classification struggle," Bourdieu (1987b:164) contends, "is a fundamental dimension of class struggle."

Bourdieu's most insightful demonstration of social classification patterns is to be found in *Distinction*. There he explores how the practices of symbolic distinctions ranging from mundane everyday preferences in food and clothing to displays of the more refined aesthetic tastes embody an underlying logic of inclusion and exclusion. Bourdieu (1984a:56) sees lifestyle differences as "perhaps the strongest barriers between the classes." Taste implies distaste. Symbolic distinctions are simultaneously conceptual and social. Our practical everyday preferences are organized around primary forms of conceptual classifications such as high/low, brilliant/dull, unique/ordinary, and important/trivial. These primary conceptual classifications are simultaneously social classifications that serve to rank individuals and groups in the stratification order. Class struggle as classification struggle, then, involves the various practical uses we make of these primarily conceptual classifications. They dictate a "sense of place" in the social order and thereby fulfill the social closure functions of inclusion and exclusion. Bourdieu writes that

principles of division, inextricably logical and sociological, function within and for the purposes of the struggle between social groups; in producing concepts, they produce groups, the very groups which produce the principles and the groups against which they are produced. What is at stake in the struggles about the meaning of the social world is power over the classificatory schemes and systems which are the basis of the representations of the groups and therefore of their mobilization and demobilization. (479)

Bourdieu calls attention to the struggle over occupational titles as a particularly salient expression of this classification struggle. Individuals and groups attempt to enhance the perception and social honor of their jobs by selecting labels and titles most likely to increase social recognition. He cites as examples "technicians who claim to be engineers" or "physiotherapists *(kinesitherapeutes)* who count on this new title to separate them from mere masseurs and bring them closer to doctors" (481).

65. This represents a shift in emphasis in Bourdieu's work, not a change in direction. Even his early article, "Condition de classe et position de classe" (Bourdieu 1966), which stresses the analytical distinction between class condition and class position, also includes a section devoted to the importance of the symbolic dimension of class relations.

This emphasis on the classification dimension of class relations finds expression in Bourdieu's (1987b:92) claim that a central concern throughout his work is to develop a "genetic theory of groups." How do groups come into existence and how do they reproduce? (Bourdieu 1985e:741). For Bourdieu, the possibility of collective existence depends on *both* shared life chances and their symbolic representations. He stresses, however, that it is the struggle over representations that shapes whether or not groups develop a significant social identity (Bourdieu 1987b:92–93). Group power depends largely on the capacity of individuals to organize around a name for which they are able to obtain some official recognition (Bourdieu 1984a: 480–81).[66] Bourdieu emphasizes that groups emerge in reality only if there is symbolic work to form group identity.

Class power is nomination power. The classification struggle among groups centers around the capacity to appropriate and impose as official and legitimate group names and categorizations.[67] The ultimate source of public and legal power of nomination resides with the State, which holds the "monopoly of legitimate symbolic violence" (Bourdieu 1987b:163). Bourdieu offers as examples of this state power the establishment of official occupational classifications and codes that confer positive or negative status on job roles. He calls attention to struggles between employers and unions over definitions of job titles (Bourdieu and Boltanski 1981). He also points to the symbolic effect of educational credentials. Like titles of nobility, educational credentials are institutionalized symbolic capital that confers entitlement on the holders.

Processes of group formation require the delegation of symbolic powers as well as the creation of group identity. There must be agents capable of imposing themselves as legitimate spokespersons and delegates for the class. In recent work Bourdieu (1984b) has shown interest in classes as collective, mobilized entities, and explores in particular the processes of delegation of authority by class members to spokespersons.[68] His objective is to orient sociological analysis not just to the specific interests of authorized spokespersons but to the processes by which they assume the mandate for

66. A seminal application of this general perspective is to be found in Boltanski's (1987) study of the French "cadres."

67. A particularly interesting illustration of classification power is to be found in David Karen's (1990) study of elite college admissions policies and processes in the United States. Karen notes that political mobilization by blacks and women during the 1960s and '70s led to special categories for these groups in elite college admissions and hence increased chances for access to elite schools. In contrast, applicants form working-class families, which did not mobilize politically during this same period, do not receive special consideration.

68. He has not, however, explored other aspects of collective organization or social movements.

group representation. Group origins and existence, Bourdieu (1985e:739) maintains, derive not only from the self-interests of group spokespersons or from the structural linkages between group leaders and followers, but also from the process of symbolic delegation "in which the mandated representative receives from the group the power to make the group." In short, he points to the importance of processes of institutionalization of authorized leadership of social classes.[69] Of particular interest to Bourdieu is the dynamics of charismatic leadership.

Bourdieu's interest in the powers of nomination and delegation shows that he links the possibility of class action to the accumulation of symbolic power. Class mobilization does not flow automatically from differences in life chances; those differences also need to be symbolically represented. It is through the symbolic labor of specialized agents that class identity and hence action become possible. One important implication of this analysis is that it assigns a key role to intellectuals in the conduct of the class struggle.[70] I will take up this crucial point of Bourdieu's analysis in chapter 9, which is devoted to his theory of intellectuals.

Bourdieu stresses the importance of class conflict in modern social life. Yet class conflict in his work appears largely in the form of individual and group investors (particularly families) in competitive markets. This perspective insightfully calls attention to the pervading influence of market competition in most areas of contemporary social life. But Bourdieu has little to say about what *collective* forms of class struggle look like. One gains little sense of social class as an organization at work. Most of Bourdieu's investigations look at forms of status distinctions attached to individuals and families. When he does consider organized labor, for example, he emphasizes the importance of the symbolic delegation of group identity and interests to leadership as a necessary condition for collective mobilization. This kind of analysis tends to reduce collective conflict to one of competition among the leaders of different organizations. As Bourdieu insightfully shows how party and union leadership can become caught up in a relatively autonomous world of jockeying for distinctive positions, the groups they actually represent fade into the background.

69. "The working class," Bourdieu writes, "exists in and through the corps of mandated representatives who give it material speech and visible presence, and in the belief in its existence that this corps of plenipotentiaries manages to enforce, by its sheer existence and by its representations, on the basis of the affinities objectively uniting the members of the same 'class on paper' as a probable group" (742).

70. Bourdieu's analysis of the necessary conditions for class action parallels one of those identified by Weber (1978:929), who writes that "the degree in which 'social action' and possibly associations emerge from the mass behavior of the members of a class is linked to the general *cultural* conditions, especially to those of an *intellectual* sort" (emphasis added).

Further, he devotes little attention to the actual processes of conflict. His analyses are limited largely to the distributions of the various forms of capital that he asserts to be the outcomes of conflict among individuals and groups. It would be helpful to have greater focus on the actual processes of conflict, especially for organizations. Case studies of contract negotiations between employers and unions might, for example, reveal sets of conditions that either limit or free leadership initiatives in their relatively autonomous worlds of interleadership posturing for distinctive positions.

The focus on individual competition as the predominant form of conflict in modern stratified societies certainly taps an important dimension of differentiation in the modern period. However, this focus may also disproportionally reflect Bourdieu's own professional milieu and his choice of areas of investigation. Education and high-brow culture are supreme instances of individual competitiveness and distinction. These preferred substantive areas of investigation may have excessively shaped his view of class conflict. While the individual race for academic credentials has certainly broadened its scope in the postwar period, it is not clear that individual mobility is the only game in town. If Bourdieu had concentrated more on the workplace, or the state, or on social movements, he might have stressed more the collective and organizational dimension of class struggle. Relatedly, if his empirical work had included case studies of situations where the struggle over definitions and classifications did indeed alter the stratification hierarchy, then he might have developed his theory differently. Finally, seen from a broad historical perspective, Bourdieu's portrayal of social conflict as almost exclusively one of market competition seems odd in a country that produced the French Revolution.[71]

Thus, for Bourdieu, class struggle in the advanced countries tends to follow the logic of market competition rather than one of collective mobilization. Class struggle is an "integrative struggle" and a "reproductive struggle" (Bourdieu 1984a:165). Bourdieu's understanding of the dynamics of social life in advanced societies is one of structural permutations rather than of structural transformation; one of market competition, not collective organization; and one of reproduction, not revolution.

71. In selected passages Bourdieu implies that collective struggle and mobilization would be a desirable alternative to endless reproduction through individual competition. But that alternative would appear to be exceedingly elusive for subordinate groups.

8 EDUCATION, CULTURE, AND SOCIAL INEQUALITY

Education occupies a central place in Bourdieu's work. His concern with exploring the intimate connections between class, culture, and power in modern stratified societies ultimately leads him to study educational institutions. Pursuing his central theme of the importance of culture in social stratification, Bourdieu sees the educational system as the principal institution controlling the allocation of status and privilege in contemporary societies. Schools offer the primary institutional setting for the production, transmission, and accumulation of the various forms of cultural capital. More importantly for Bourdieu, schools inculcate the dominant systems of classification through which symbolic power is expressed.[1] Moreover, schools are the key institutional base for the symbolic work of intellectuals.

Bourdieu (1982) explains in his Collège de France inaugural lecture that the field of education—as well as the study of intellectuals—receives "primordial status" in his work because it gives insight into the unconscious categories of thought that shape the dominant modes of understanding the modern world. Thus, for Bourdieu, the sociology of education is not a subspeciality of sociology but rather the foundation for a sociology of sym-

---

1. Bourdieu (1967b) writes that "the school system is one of the sites where, in differentiated societies, the systems of thought, which are the apparently more sophisticated equivalent of the 'primitive forms of classifications,' are produced."

bolic power.[2] Indeed, it is no exaggeration to say that, with the exception of his anthropological work, virtually all of Bourdieu's investigations of French society connect with some aspect of French education.[3]

Bourdieu was one of the first sociologists to take a critical look at the popular post–World War II public policies of expanding educational opportunity in order to reduce social inequality. Though educational levels in all Western democracies have seen tremendous improvement during the last forty years, glaring inequities in wealth, income, and status persist. Bourdieu argues that education actually contributes to the maintenance of an inegalitarian social system by allowing inherited cultural differences to shape academic achievement and occupational attainment. One of Bourdieu's first works on French education, *The Inheritors* (Bourdieu and Passeron 1979), documents the persistent overrepresentation of middle- and upper-class students in French universities despite years of education expansion. In subsequent work, Bourdieu consistently emphasizes the socially stratified character of French education.

As I point out in the beginning of this book, a key question animating Bourdieu's work is, how do inequalities of privilege and power persist intergenerationally without conscious recognition and public resistance? The answer, he contends, can be found by exploring how cultural resources— especially educational credentials, selection mechanisms, and cognitive classifications—can be used by individuals and groups to perpetuate their positions of privilege and power. Bourdieu maintains that the educational system—more than the family, church, or business firm—has become the institution most responsible for the transmission of social inequality in modern societies. The task of the sociologist, therefore, is to "determine the contribution made by the educational system to the reproduction of the structure of power relationship and symbolic relationships between social classes" (Bourdieu 1973a:71).

The education system, Bourdieu argues in *Reproduction* (Bourdieu and Passeron 1977:177–219), performs three central functions. It first of all performs the "function of conserving, inculcating and consecrating" a cultural heritage. This is its "internal" and most "essential function." Schooling provides not just the transmission of technical knowledge and skills,

---

2. He writes, "the sociology of education is a chapter, and not a less important one at that, in the sociology of knowledge and also in the sociology of power—not to mention the sociology of the philosophies of power" (Bourdieu 1989c:13).

3. Indeed, five of Bourdieu's books are devoted to French education (Bourdieu 1988b, 1989c; Bourdieu and Passeron 1977, 1979; Bourdieu, Passeron, and de Saint Martin 1992). In addition, several issues of *Actes de la recherche en sciences sociales* have been devoted to education.

but also socialization into a particular cultural tradition. Analogous to the Catholic Church, the school is "an institution specially contrived to conserve, transmit and inculcate the cultural canons of a society" (Bourdieu 1971c:178). It performs a cultural reproduction function.

When this first function combines with traditional pedagogy, the education system performs a second, "external" function of reproducing social-class relations. It reinforces rather than redistributes the unequal distribution of cultural capital. It also performs a social reproduction function. The education system performs yet a third function, "legitimation." By consecrating the cultural heritage it transmits, the education system deflects attention from and contributes to the misrecognition of its social reproduction function.

Bourdieu was an early and key architect of the widely influential theory of social reproduction—a theory that has led many to see that, in spite of formal meritocratic practices, educational institutions can actually enhance social inequalities rather than attenuate them. Bourdieu differs, however, from other reproduction theorists in that he does not see education as directly determined by the state, the economy, or social classes. In contrast to both functional and Marxist theories, Bourdieu argues that "relative autonomy" rather than close correspondence characterizes the relationship between the education system and the labor market.[4] Bourdieu's particular contribution is to show that schools are neither neutral nor merely reflective of broader sets of power relations, but play a complex, indirect, mediating role in maintaining and enhancing them. Finally, Bourdieu was one of the first social reproduction theorists to examine how internal school processes of selection and instruction, school culture, and tracking structure actually do this.

Since Bourdieu's early work on education is already widely known, more attention in this chapter will will be devoted to his more recent contributions, particularly those found in *Homo Academicus* (1988b) and *La Noblesse d'Etat* (1989c). His early work on education focused on student culture, the transmission of cultural capital, pedagogy, and academic selection processes. His more recent work charts the field of French education and its relation to the field of power. While the broad outlines of this perspective of

4. Bourdieu does not see modern universities as subservient to private economic or public political interests, as does Smith (1974). He does not posit a "correspondence" between education and the economy, as Marxists like Bowles and Gintis (1976) do for the United States or Baudelot and Establet (1973) do for France. Bourdieu also rejects non-Marxian technical functional views (e.g., Clark 1962) that posit a tight fit between labor-market demand and education supply.

institutional stratification are present in his early work (see *Current Research* 1972), they receive more development in later publications on the *grandes écoles* and the university professorate.

I will begin by examining how Bourdieu situates the French education system in relation to the field of power. (As was noted in chapter 6, this is consistent with the sequence of methodological steps Bourdieu outlines for research.) The fundamental opposition of cultural capital and economic capital creates a highly stratified system of higher education in France. Next I consider how he uses his concepts of cultural capital and habitus to explain how individuals distribute throughout that system. Bourdieu also looks at school processes, and we will observe how he sees them as mediating the effects of cultural capital and habitus to explain educational attainment. The chapter continues with a look at Bourdieu's view of educational institutions as powerful labeling systems that subtly translate social distinctions into academic evaluations, and then takes up his analysis of the socialization experience in the high tracks of French education as formative of an elite whose authority assumes quasi-sacred qualities. I will consider how Bourdieu sees the French educational system as relatively independent from the class structure, the state, and the economy, and examine how Bourdieu sees educational expansion through his perspective of class-based capital investment strategies. Since much of the criticism of Bourdieu's work for neglecting social change and transformation stems from his analyses of education, I conclude the chapter with an assessment of his thinking in this important area.

Education and the Field of Power

I observed in chapter 6 that for Bourdieu two major competing principles of social hierarchy shape the struggle for power in modern industrial societies: the distribution of economic capital (wealth, income, and property), which Bourdieu calls the "dominant principle of hierarchy," and the distribution of cultural capital (knowledge, culture, and educational credentials), which Bourdieu calls the "second principle of hierarchy." Substantial possession of both types of capital distinguish the dominant class from all other groups. The dominant class, however, is internally differentiated by unequal distributions of economic capital and cultural capital. It is Bourdieu's thesis that these two competing claims to power internally differentiate French higher education as well. French higher educational institutions— disciplines, professors, and students—are all polarized by differences in *total volume* of capital and by differences in the *relative amounts* of cultural and economic capital. *La Noblesse d'Etat* and *Homo Academicus* offer a detailed social map of how Bourdieu sees French higher education institutions internally stratified by these two competing principles of hierarchy.

Bourdieu observes that *type* and *prestige* of educational institution attended are as influential for later careers as are number of years spent in schooling. A major theme of his work is that French educational institutions are socially as well as academically tracked.[5] Of particular significance is the elite sector of post-secondary professional schools *(grandes écoles)* that parallel the French universities.[6] The *grandes écoles* stand at the pinnacle of French higher education: they are academically more selective than the universities; they prepare graduates for leadership roles in government and the economy; and they provide their graduates with valued alumni networks that help advance students' careers. A rough equivalent in the United States would be the most prestigious business, law, and graduate schools. Whereas entrance to a university in France requires no more than the successful completion of the *baccalauréat*, entrance to the academically prestigious *grandes écoles* requires intensive and specialized post-secondary preparation (usually two years) for passing the highly competitive entrance examinations. Thus, the *grandes écoles* represent the institutional embodiment of the French meritocracy. Bourdieu's work, however, demonstrates that the sharp status distinction between the universities and the *grandes écoles* is *social* as well as academic, for these professional schools recruit in large measure from the dominant social class.

Bourdieu's most comprehensive demonstration of the socially segmented character of French higher education is to be found in *La Noblesse d'Etat*. In that work, Bourdieu (1989c:185–264) assembles the results of a vast and multifaceted data collection project on the *grandes écoles* initiated in 1967 by Bourdieu and several collaborators, particularly Monique de Saint Martin. It documents the social origins of students at 84 French institutions of higher learning and offers a more in-depth analysis of social and academic background for 21 of the *grandes écoles*, exploring cultural practices, political attitudes, and religion at 15 of them. The documented differ-

5. Research on the social consequences of tracking is by now well established in American sociology of education (Oakes 1985). Pioneering work by Karabel (1972), Brint and Karabel (1989), Cookson and Persell (1985), and Dougherty (1994) on community colleges and prep schools, demonstrate that *type* of school attended and curriculum studied decisively shapes career outcomes. Bourdieu was one of the first sociologists to emphasize this point. His argument was perhaps more radical in France than in the United States, since, in France, a nationally centralized and standardized system of education is supposedly designed to reduce regional and social differences.

6. In addition to the universities and *grandes écoles*, French higher education includes a broad range of vocational and technical schools that for the most part do not require the *baccalauréat* (roughly equivalent to the high school diploma) and recruit most of their students from the lower middle class and the working class.

ences in total volume of economic and cultural capital reveal two broad institutional tracks.[7] At one extreme, stands such top-tier schools as the Ecole Nationale d'Administration, the Ecole des Hautes Etudes Commerciales, the Ecole Normale Supérieure, and the Ecole Polytechnique, whose graduates can choose from a broad range of career possibilities at the highest echelons of government, business, and education. They recruit students largely from the dominant class. At the other extreme, one finds the university faculties of science and letters and a broad variety of other schools that offer specialized technical and vocational training, which recruit students from distinctly less elite social backgrounds.[8] There is therefore in France a bifurcated higher education system that is stratified in its relationship to the field of power. According to Bourdieu (1972:17),

> the function of the dualist structure of higher education, in which the *grandes écoles* stand opposed to the Faculties, is to distinguish the members of the ruling class from members of the other classes and, in particular, from the middle classes.

Differences in composition of capital further differentiate 21 of the top-tier schools between two opposing poles: schools such as the Ecole Normale Supérieure (rue d'Ulm), the Ecole Normale Supérieure de Jeunes Filles de Sèvres, and the Ecole Normale de Saint-Cloud, represent the scientific and intellectual pole, since they recruit students from the same social milieu for which they prepare their graduates, namely, the teaching, artistic, and scientific professions. In these schools, academic excellence, or the accumulation of scholastic capital, is the principal hierarchy that ranks these institutions and the students within them. In contrast, schools such as the Ecole Nationale d'Administration, the Ecole Polytechnique, and the Institut des Sciences Politiques de Paris and Ecole des Hautes Etudes Commerciales, represent the administrative and economic pole, since they both recruit from and channel their students into the higher echelons of business and state administration. Together, these institutions are ranked not only in terms of academic excellence but also according to the "dominant hierarchy outside of the academic establishment"; that is, "according to their position in the hierarchy of economic capital and according to the power of the

7. These results stem from an analysis of correspondence based on the social origins of the students (Bourdieu 1989c:199).

8. A second axis of differentiation revealed in the correspondence analysis of the 84 institutions distinguishes "private" from "public" schools. Business, art, and architecture schools connected to private industrial and commercial interests charge tuition and offer fairly rigorous training but are not as selective academically as the tuition-free public sector engineering, agronomy, teaching, and research schools that prepare students for public-sector careers (Bourdieu 1989c:213).

positions to which they lead" (1972:18). Thus, these two elite educational tracks tend to serve two distinct fractions of the dominant class: the fraction relatively richer in cultural capital and the opposing fraction relatively richer in economic capital.[9]

Among the university faculties, Bourdieu also finds a similar socially segmented structure.[10] He identifies an analogous bipolar structure with "at one pole the scientifically dominant but socially subordinate faculties, and, at the other, the scientifically subordinate but temporally dominant faculties" (1988b:54).[11] In examining the population of tenured professors in Parisian university faculties during the late 1960s, Bourdieu finds that their social profile varies according to this bipolar structure. Broadly speaking, the faculties of natural sciences, arts and social sciences, law, and medicine are situated respectively on a continuum between the poles of cultural power and of economic and political power. Dominant-class representation in terms of social background and a number of indicators showing the degree of participation in instances of economic and political power increases as one moves from science to medicine.[12] Professors from the economically rich fractions of the dominant class tend to be located more frequently in the law and medical faculties than in the science and humanities faculties.[13] To illustrate, professors in the law and particularly the medical faculties

9. Another differentiating factor in the correspondence analysis of the 21 schools distinguishes those offering a "generalist" preparation for administration from those offering "technical" training for highly specialized positions (Bourdieu 1989c:216). A third correspondence analysis on 15 of the most elite *grandes écoles* reveals a similar pattern. Schools leading to careers in administration, such as Ecole Nationale d'Administration and Institut des Sciences Politiques de Paris, are more likely to recruit students from the Parisian bourgeoisie who have a literary background in secondary schools and who attended prestigious private schools, whereas schools leading to technical positions, such as Ecole Centrale, Ecole des Mines, and Institut National Agronomique, recruit more students from the middle classes and who have followed the scientific tracks in secondary schools (ibid., 221).

10. This analysis is found in *Homo Academicus* (1988b:38–40, 271–75), which is based on a random sample of 405 tenured faculty members from the medical, law, arts and social sciences, and natural sciences faculties in the Paris area, and in which he observes that "the structure of the university field reflects the structure of the field of power, while its own activity of selection and indoctrination contributes to the reproduction of that structure" (40–41).

11. Bourdieu writes, "the university field is organized according to two antagonistic principles of hierarchization: the social hierarchy, corresponding to the capital inherited and the economic and political capital actually held, is in opposition to the specific, properly cultural hierarchy, corresponding to the capital of scientific authority or intellectual renown" (ibid., 48).

12. Indicators include father's occupation, type and prestige of secondary and higher education institutions attended, listing in the French *Who's Who* or *Bottin Mondain*, decorations, and participation in various government or university administrative bodies.

13. Bourdieu (1988b:38) writes that "the professors of the different faculties are distributed between the pole of economic and political power and the pole of cultural prestige according to the same principles as the different fractions of the dominant classes."

are more likely to live in socially exclusive Parisian neighborhoods than are professors in the arts and sciences (44). Thus, a fairly clear distinction between sciences and letters, on the one hand, and law and medicine, on the other hand, can be made.[14] The French university world broadly divides into two camps if one looks at it in terms of the key characteristics that distinguish the principal fractions of the dominant class.

Bourdieu finds that these structures have remained remarkably stable throughout the 1970s and '80s. If May 1968 brought reform and greater access to the French universities, it also brought dominant-class flight from them. Competition for entry to the top-tier schools has increased considerably as has the gap between the top- and lower-tier institutions. Today, top-tier schools tend to recruit even more from the dominant class than before (Bourdieu 1989c:271). Further, the phenomenal development and expansion of specialized professional schools offering training in management, advertising, journalism, and business tend to attract students with considerable inherited economic capital (278). Bourdieu considers these schools to be refuges for dominant-class youth who are unable to gain access to the academically most selective *grandes écoles* and yet who refuse the alternative of going to less prestigious university faculties or to one of the second-tier schools.

Bourdieu thus points to a fundamental paradox between two simultaneous developments in French higher education: the increase in options in higher education, offering a broader range of educational opportunities than before; and a reinforcement of class-based social stratification within the higher educational system.

Bourdieu also observes a shift in power away from the intellectual pole in French higher education toward the administrative and economic pole. The Ecole Nationale d'Administration has replaced the Ecole Normale Supérieure in the struggle to define the most legitimate and prestigious form of higher education in France today. Indeed, the Ecole Nationale d'Administration has come to impose itself as the standard for the entire field of the French *grandes écoles* (282). This shift, Bourdieu suggests, parallels a decline in the traditional prestige of the intellectual professions (teaching and research), which are being more and more eclipsed by the increased prestige associated with top positions in state administration, big

---

14. Bourdieu (1989b:376–77) locates the discipline of sociology closer to "law and to the temporally dominant disciplines" than to the scientific disciplines. Sociology is a field of symbolic production that is divided by "two radically discrepant logics: the logic of the political field . . . and the logic of the scientific field." The scientific logic in sociology dictates that communication be based on scientific criteria. Yet, sociology is infiltrated with the logic of the political field, where communication is shaped by the "*social* force of its advocates."

business, political party leadership, and the media—particularly television. This shift, Bourdieu sardonically suggests, gives rise to a technocratic vision of intellectual practice, one that also contributes to the decline of the famous French tradition of autonomous intellectuals, exemplified by Jean-Paul Sartre, and elevates in standing the "intellectual journalism" of Raymond Aron, which Bourdieu deplores.

Habitus, Cultural Capital, and Selection Processes

In order to show how individuals distribute throughout this stratified field of French education, Bourdieu calls on his concepts of habitus and cultural capital. As was pointed out in chapter 5, habitus, which is akin to the idea of class subculture, refers to a set of relatively permanent and largely unconscious ideas about one's chances of success and how society works that are common to members of a social class or status group. These ideas or, more precisely, dispositions, lead individuals to act in such a way as to reproduce the prevailing structure of life chances and status distinctions. The concept of habitus permits Bourdieu to stress that educational choices are dispositional rather than conscious, rational calculations.

An important theme in Bourdieu's work on education is his assertion that academic selection is shaped by class-based *self-selection*. Whether students stay in school or drop out, and the course of study they pursue, Bourdieu argues, depends on their practical expectations of the likelihood that people of their social class will succeed academically. Bourdieu believes there is generally a high correlation between subjective hopes and objective chances. A child's ambitions and expectations with regard to education and career are the structurally determined products of parental and other reference-group educational experience and cultural life.[15] Working-class youth do not aspire to high levels of educational attainment because, according to Bourdieu, they have internalized and resigned themselves to the limited opportunities for school success that exist for those without much cultural capital.[16] In contrast, upper-middle-class youth internalize their social advantages as expectations for academic success, and stay in school. Bourdieu, thus, insightfully demonstrates how much educational selection in fact occurs through self-selection.

15. This echoes in part the widely accepted view in American status-attainment research that stresses the importance of student expectations on educational achievement (Sewell, Hauser, and Portes 1969). With his concept of habitus, Bourdieu emphasizes how expectations derive from early class socialization.

16. See Ogbu (1978, 1990) for a similar discussion of the sources of the lower college expectations of American blacks.

Bourdieu's analysis of student self-selection through a habitus involving a high positive correlation between objective possibilities and subjective aspirations is insightful but not entirely convincing. Numerous cases suggest the alignment process of aspirations to chances to be problematic. The high aspirations among American blacks after World War II for a college education, despite overwhelming evidence of limited career opportunities in the professions, represents just one striking example of a disjuncture between hopes and real chances (Hout and Morgan 1975; MacLeod 1987; Michelson 1990; Ogbu 1978, 1990).[17] Even Bourdieu's own account of middle-class participation in the postwar expansion of enrollment in French higher education suggests that this alignment comes more easily for some groups in given circumstances than for others. While Bourdieu's formulation of the "causality of the probable" may helpfully describe the attitudes of working-class youth who do not continue their education and upper-class youth who take for granted their completion of university degrees, it does less well in explaining why middle-class families began investment in the credential market, where traditionally their chances for success had not been great. Suddenly the tacit and practical implementation of the effects of early socialization, so well captured by the concept of habitus, gives way to a more consciously rational class reconversion strategy that conveys the sense of a highly future-oriented perspective of class behavior.

In addition to class habitus, class differences in *cultural capital* also affect educational attainment. Cultural knowledge and style operate as carriers of social inequality. As was pointed out in chapter 4, Bourdieu finds it useful to think of culture—especially in the form of educational credentials—as a kind of capital ("scholastic capital") that can be purchased with time, energy, and money and then exchanged for occupations with high status and incomes. His concept of cultural capital covers a wide variety of resources, including verbal facility, general cultural awareness, information about the school system, and educational credentials. Bourdieu points to an *unequal distribution of cultural capital*. Social classes differ greatly in levels of educational attainment and patterns of cultural consumption. Bourdieu finds that students' academic performance is strongly related to parents' cultural background. Parents pass on their cultural heritage to their children. Most higher education degrees in France, for example, are held by children of professionals; very few are held by children of farmers and factory work-

---

17. See Rosenbaum 1976 for evidence of a similar disjuncture in which students misperceive the consequences of secondary school tracking, and Karabel 1972 for misperceptions of community college tracking.

ers.[18] Thus, Bourdieu sees class distinctions as mediated by both aspirations and expectations and cultural style and knowledge into differential educational performance and attainment.

Bourdieu focuses on how the higher-educational system reproduces, rather than redistributes, the unequal distribution of cultural capital. This leads him to examine the structural features of curriculum, pedagogy, and evaluation for an explanation of how this occurs. He argues that formal schooling contributes to the maintenance of an unequal social system by privileging certain cultural heritages and penalizing other. Even prolonged exposure to university instruction does not fully compensate lower- and middle-class youth for their initial handicap in cultural capital. French schools, he finds, emphasize the forms of knowledge and cultural ideals and styles dominant social groups in particular cherish. He suggests that the traditional program of humanist studies, which until recently dominated the preparatory track for entrance to the university and elite professional schools in France, does not provide the technical skills needed in the broadest sectors of the job market.[19] The humanities appeal less to those students whose lack of economic security motivates them to seek out technical and vocational options. Moreover, this program of study acts as a selection device: academic success in the humanities requires general cultural awareness and a refined and elegant style of language. Curriculum content and style, then, offer advantages to those who possess the "educationally profitable linguistic capital" of "bourgeois language": its tendency "to abstraction, formalism, intellectualism and euphemistic moderation" reflects a literary and cultured disposition that is found most often among the dominant classes. This socially valued and academically revered linguistic style contrasts sharply with the "expressiveness or expressionism of working-class language, which manifests itself in the tendency to move from particular case to particular case, from illustration to parable" (Bourdieu and Passeron 1977:116). It further differs from the distinctive features of lower-middle-class language, with its "faulty hypercorrectiveness and proliferation of the signs of grammatical control," which betrays its "anxious reference to the

18. Bourdieu's concept of cultural capital has stimulated an important body of research into the cultural dimensions of unequal education attainment. Apple 1982, Apple and Weis 1985, Cookson and Persell 1985, DiMaggio 1982, DiMaggio and Mohr 1984, Lamont and Lareau 1988, Lareau 1989, and Robinson and Garnier 1985 are just a few noteworthy examples.

19. The curricular content of the high track in French lycées has switched to mathematics and science since Bourdieu began his research on French education in the early 1960s. But the formal rather than practical orientation of their instruction hardly appeals to lower-class dispositions.

legitimate norm of academic correctness" (134).[20] Because of the emphasis placed on the spoken as well as written word, the traditional preference in French schools for the eloquent lecture helps secure the privileges of those rich in cultural capital. Bourdieu makes the interesting ethnographic observation that even the physical organization of the traditional French university—lecture halls and amphitheaters rather than small seminar rooms or even libraries—testifies to the preeminence of the spoken word (Bourdieu and Passeron 1977:120). The formal lecture elevates the role of the professor as the legitimate transmitter of cultural goods.

The use in France of a traditional pedagogy that stresses the refined mastery of a literary linguistic style discriminates in favor of those rich in inherited cultural capital. By failing to provide compensatory coursework adapted to meet the language deficiencies of those without cultural capital, traditional pedagogy fulfills the function of serving dominant-class interests by demanding "uniformly of all its students that they should have what it does not give": namely, a practical and informal mastery of language and culture that can be acquired only in the dominant-class family (128).[21] Style as much as content becomes the mechanism whereby cultural privilege is reinforced and cultural disadvantage is left unattended.[22]

The classic oral and essay examinations, like the traditional form of instruction, present advantages to those richest in cultural capital. Such examinations tend to measure ability in linguistic expression as much as mastery of subject matter. For example, Bourdieu's secondary analysis of reports of *agrégation*[23] juries finds clear preference for candidates who distinguished themselves by spoken and written eloquence (Bourdieu 1989c: 19–47; Bourdieu and de Saint Martin 1974). These national examinations represent the highest level of achievement within the French educational system and symbolize the triumph of democratic, secular, and state-controlled education over the interests of church, region, and social class. While they promulgate the ideals of democratic equality and meritocratic

---

20. Bourdieu's suggestion that distinct linguistic styles stemming from class-based socialization shape academic performance is echoed in Basil Bernstein's work (1971–75), which Bourdieu helped introduce into France.

21. Cultural and linguistic styles labeled "cultivated" or "distinguished" by the school system in fact reference a *particular mode of acquisition* which is "only possible in families whose culture is scholarly culture" (Bourdieu and de Saint Martin 1974:354).

22. Bourdieu's scathing attack on traditional pedagogy reflects the particularity of the French case in contrast to other national educational systems that are more open to business and science instruction and compensatory programs.

23. A highly competitive national examination leading to teaching posts in French *lycées* and universities.

achievement, Bourdieu forcefully argues that, in practice, they favor the culturally privileged.

Another theme in Bourdieu's work is that education mediates the effects of class background in complex ways. He systematically relates the selective process of education to social-class structure without reducing this relationship to one of simple class determinism. Social-class background is filtered through a complex set of factors that interact in different ways at different levels of schooling. For instance, Bourdieu explains that the reason a strong correlation between social-class background and school performance at the lower levels of schooling may gradually weaken or even disappear at higher levels is because of how class background and academic selectivity intersect: differential performance according to class will appear less pronounced at the higher levels of schooling because the surviving lower-class students represent a highly select subgroup (Bourdieu and Passeron 1977).

Bourdieu's analysis of results from a language test administered to university students illustrates how the educational system translates the student's initial degree of educational opportunity and amount of cultural capital into characteristically academic traits (Bourdieu, Passeron, and de Saint Martin 1965; Bourdieu and Passeron 1977:74–89). Cultural capital and "degree of selection" are the fulcrum concepts used to interpret the test results. Students of dominant-class origin obtain high test scores on all types of vocabulary questions, from the definition of scholastic concepts to those that presuppose a more general cultural background. By inheriting the most socially valued forms of cultural activity from parents who usually have some university education, these cultural heirs are able to cash in cultural capital on good academic performance.

The mediation process is particularly visible for academically successful lower-class students who rely more heavily on the school for their acquisition of cultural capital than do upper-class students. The few lower-class students taking the exam score just as well as upper-class students on questions involving academic concepts, since these lower-class students themselves represent a highly select academic group. Lower-class survivors have compensated for their initial lack of capital by acquiring a scholastically based cultural capital through exceptional intellectual ability, individual effort, and unusual home or social circumstances. However, these lower-class students do not score as well on questions requiring broad cultural knowledge, because they lack the background of their upper-class schoolmates. Though academically successful, lower-class students bear the mark of their initial cultural disadvantage by being too "scholastic" in their cultural style.

Meanwhile, the large number of middle-class students receive the lowest scores, because they represent a less highly select academic group and because they come from a class milieu in which major investment in higher education has only recently begun. Student performance and achievement, therefore, can be seen as the outcome of a complex interplay of expectations, cultural capital, and the degree of selection.

Thus, Bourdieu's approach establishes structural linkages between educational processes and social stratification. Macro-level patterns of social-class inequality and unequal distribution of cultural capital are linked to micro-level processes of pedagogy, evaluation, and curriculum.

Academic Classifications as Social Classifications

Bourdieu (1989c:19–98) argues that the struggle for economic and cultural capital not only differentiates socially French institutions of higher learning, it also structures and differentiates French mentalities. The educational system instills a system of widely used cognitive classifications that reinforce social distinctions. For Bourdieu, this is its most insidious function. He draws this basic thesis from Durkheim and Mauss (1963) to argue that there is a fundamental though unrecognized connection between institutional structures and the cognitive dispositions they inculcate within individuals. Rather than limit this demonstration to the social and mythical worlds of "primitive" peoples, Bourdieu applies it as well to his own milieu—modern French academe.

In a study of successful secondary school candidates on a highly competitive national examination (lauréats du Concours général), Bourdieu (1989c:19–47) finds that the categories such candidates use to characterize the intellectual qualities for success in various academic disciplines correspond to qualities the candidates attribute to themselves and which are attributed to them by their examiners. Students and examiners alike were more likely to attribute success in literature, language, philosophy, and mathematics to innate talent whereas hard work and study were more likely to be mentioned for geography and the natural sciences. Indeed, Bourdieu (31) finds a whole series of bipolar oppositions, such as brilliant/dull, gifted/motivated, distinguished/vulgar, cultivated/academic, eloquent/awkward, original/common, and refined/crude, that both students and teachers employ to differentiate success in the various academic disciplines. These dichotomies point to two underlying ideal types of academic success: the most highly valued type evokes an image of charismatic qualities of individual talent, while the other suggests success that comes through hard work and determination. However, Bourdieu (33) also finds that the different representations of success observed for the different disciplines are paralleled by differences in social origins and amounts of inherited cultural capital. Students in literature, language, philosophy, and mathematics are more likely to come from higher social-class origins; their representations of success in terms of individual talent in fact reflect greater advantages in inherited cultural capital. Thus, the very representations of success in French academe express euphemized social-class distinctions. These bipolar "scholastic forms of classification" function analogously to what Durkheim and Mauss called "primitive forms of classification," as they represent the incorporation of institutional structures, such as discipline and tracks, that are in a homologous relationship with the social-class structure (49). The academic meritocracy is a form of aristocracy. It is rooted in the notion of "natural" rights and abilities of individuals, which masks inherited cultural advantages.

Bourdieu extends this kind of analysis by arguing that cognitive polarities parallel the hierarchy of institutional tracks in French education and thus reflect the underlying inequalities established in the struggle for economic and cultural capital. For example, the division between those schools recruiting students with considerable capital and those with less capital becomes the institutional basis for the familiar distinctions between mental and manual labor, or between conceptual and applied tasks, that distinguish senior managers from middle managers and engineers from technicians. Moreover, the cultural capital/economic capital opposition becomes the institutional basis for the conceptual distinction between pure and applied orientations toward knowledge, science, and culture. Bourdieu (1984a:387) writes that

the educational system, an institutionalized classifier which is itself an objectified system of classification reproducing the hierarchies of the social world in a transformed form, with its cleavages by "level" corresponding to social strata and its divisions into specialities and disciplines which reflect social divisions ad infinitum, such as the opposition between theory and practice, conception and execution, transforms social classifications into academic classifications, with every appearance of neutrality, and establishes hierarchies which are not experienced as purely technical, and therefore partial and one-sided, but as total hierarchies, grounded in nature, so that social value comes to be identified with "personal" value, scholastic dignities with human dignity.

Educational institutions, Bourdieu therefore argues, operate as an "immense cognitive machine" that under the appearance of technical neutrality impose primitive intellectual classifications that ratify existing social classifications (1989c:51–81).[24] This process goes misrecognized at a tacit level. Indeed, it can only operate tacitly, since widespread awareness of this "latent function" would make the system inoperative. Social and personal insults, such as "you are only a worker's son" or "you are crude," which would be judged unacceptable in academic culture, can nonetheless be expressed euphemistically as academic judgements in the "misrecognized form": "correct but nothing more," "lacks style," or "unremarkable work" (Bourdieu 1989c:61). The classification function of schooling is buttressed by its legitimation function. Schools "consecrate social distinctions by constituting them as academic distinctions" (Bourdieu and Passeron 1977). Because actors believe these classifications to be academic, they employ them as legitimate labels without full awareness of their social consequences. Through socialization, they have been incorporated as practical instruments that actors employ practically without conscious reflection. Yet, these academic judgments are also social judgments that ratify and reproduce social class distinctions.

Technical Training as Elite Formation and Consecration

Bourdieu argues that the professional training provided by the academically selective *grandes écoles* imparts not only technical knowledge and skills but even more importantly a status culture.[25] He sharply criticizes the technical-functional view of education, and draws notably from Durkheim's sociology of religion to stress the ritual and symbolic aspects of elite schooling. Indeed, Bourdieu (1989c:164) draws an explicit analogy between modern secular educational institutions and religion when he writes that "the school is in fact a religious instance, in the Durkheimian sense." By this Bourdieu means that the French *grandes écoles* separate out a social elite and bestow on the elected "all the properties ordinarily imparted to sacred beings." These schools create a kind of secular priesthood—what he calls a "state nobility"—for positions of power in modern France. This status culture legitimatizes the inter-institutional track system examined earlier by creating a kind of "sacred/profane" opposition between the elite *grandes écoles* and all other post-secondary educational institutions in France. Through an

24. Bourdieu's argument here overlaps somewhat with Meyer's (1970, 1977) discussion of the "chartering effects" of schools, which stress the institutional impact of education on social structure by defining and conferring rights, responsibilities, and roles in the larger society. Both Bourdieu and Meyer draw on Durkheim to make their respective arguments, but Bourdieu stresses the cognitive and social stratifying effects of the institutionalizing process of education on larger society more than does Meyer.

25. His argument is similar to the one made by Randall Collins (1979) who, like Bourdieu, draws many of his insights from Weber's discussion of the role of education in society.

intensive and elaborate socialization process of ritual and ceremony, these secular and technical schools in fact set apart and sacralize a power elite. They create a kind of new secular religious order, endowed with quasi-sacred qualities, that characterize technocratic leadership in modern France.[26]

Bourdieu (101–81) documents this "consecration" aspect of French elite education by looking at the socialization experience in the *class prépara-toires*, which represents the very competitive high track in French secondary schooling leading to the *grandes écoles*.[27] Bourdieu considers the French *classes préparatories* as "total institutions" analogous to the boarding-school experience in the British public schools and American prep schools.[28] The socialization in the *classes préparatories* amounts to a "vast consecration ritual." Physical as well as mental exercises instill an ascetic culture of self-control in preparation for control over others. All activities are designed to nurture a charismatic quality of entitlement. Students experience a highly regimented social and intellectual life that fosters social homogeneity, a common culture, a shared sense of entitlement and a common symbolic capital.

But, for Bourdieu, even more important than the regimented organization of everyday life is the pedagogy that forms a regimented intellectual habitus. The constant preparation for competitive exams, the use of textbooks rather than original works (even in the humanities), the large number of problem sets and regular drills, the intensive pace, and the competitive atmosphere create an instrumental, pragmatic, and narrowly calculating orientation toward culture and intellectual work. Rather than nourishing a critical spirit that might encourage research, this pragmatic orientation motivates students to confine their interests to what will help on the competitive examinations. Bourdieu observes that, while this is perhaps useful for professional managers of the state and the economy, it does not foster an interest in more probing intellectual exploration that is important for training teachers and researchers. Paradoxically, then, those students who

---

26. The polemical import of Bourdieu's recourse to the language of Durkheimian sociology of religion can be better appreciated if one recalls that one of the crowning legacies of the French Revolution was to create free, public, and secular education institutions where religion would no longer play a central role.

27. He bases his observations on extensive data from questionnaire surveys, interviews with both students and faculty, and by examining a variety of written testimonials of experiences from graduates of the *classes préparatoires*.

28. The concept of "total institution" comes from Goffman (1961). Bourdieu's analysis of the socialization experience identifies many of the same mechanisms that Cookson and Persell (1985) describe in their study of American elite boarding schools. However, Bourdieu stresses the homogenizing experience of the French *classes préparatoires* whereas Cookson and Persell devote attention to the various forms of deviance and alienation in boarding schools.

are most highly selected academically find themselves in an organized academic setting that is least likely to encourage an interest in research or intellectual development as an end in itself. The *grandes écoles* give students a competitive culture but not one that encourages critical thought.

The Relative Autonomy of the Education Field

Another central theme in Bourdieu's work is that educational institutions are not simply an adjunct of more decisive institutions in society. As I noted in chapter 6, Bourdieu speaks of the "relative autonomy" of cultural fields from outside interests. He uses the idea of relative autonomy to theorize a complex relationship between the education system, the economy, and the social class structure (Bourdieu and Passeron 1977:177–78). It is through the logic of relative autonomy that Bourdieu sees the education system being capable of carrying out its "*external function* of social conservation."

The relative autonomy of the education system refers to its capacity to develop a distinct status culture and its own organizational and professional interests, which may deviate significantly from labor-market demands or dominant-class interests. Bourdieu emphasizes that the educational system obtains relative autonomy from outside institutions through its self-reproductive capacity and its vested interest in protecting the value of scholastic capital. Referring to Durkheim, he points to the educational system's capacity to recruit its leadership from within its own ranks as the reason for its unusual historical continuity and stability, analogous more to the church than to business or the state (Bourdieu and Passeron 1977:195–98).[29] Education's virtual monopoly over recruitment, training, and promotion of personnel allows the educational system to adapt its programs and activities to its own specific needs for self-perpetuation. For example, the intergenerational transmission of a humanist cultural tradition in the traditional French university has stood at cross-purposes with the more contemporary concern for utilitarian knowledge encouraged by industrialization. This has undoubtedly been one important source of anticapitalist sentiment among well-educated French men and women. It also helps explain why the French academic profession has strongly resisted repeated efforts by state planners to align the curriculum more closely with the practical needs of business. The combination of an internally generated body of knowledge

29. The reference to Durkheim concerns his little-known, but perhaps most significant work in the sociology of education, *The Evolution of Educational Thought* (1977).

and professional and organizational interests form the basis for the relative autonomy of the educational system from state control and corporate pressure.

Bourdieu's idea of the relatively autonomous status of the educational system provides a desirable alternative to both technical-functional and instrumentalist class domination views of the education-society nexus.[30] By calling attention to the organizational proclivity for self-perpetuation, the internal labor market, and the institutional basis of meritocratic ideology, Bourdieu correctly argues that the educational system mediates external demands.

The term *relative autonomy* can be used, however, to emphasize two quite opposite tendencies, and this property reflects both its ingenuity and its ambiguity. The term can refer to a deeper level of relationship and function that goes ill-perceived. Bourdieu draws upon this aspect of dependency when he discusses the relationship of education to the class structure. "Relative autonomy" captures the ill-perceived dimension of the educational transmission of social inequality: formal equality of opportunity and reward based on merit permit the subtle transfer of privilege through cultural capital. *Reproduction*, for example, emphasizes the idea of a close but ill-perceived connection between social structure and the school. Attainment, performance, and tracking are all presented as being heavily class based, albeit in mediated form. And though every attempt is made to argue that social-class reproduction occurs by various forms of cultural and institutional mediation rather than through more conscious and instrumental means, still, the social reproduction process seems to occur without great difficulty: schooling seems to assure the privileged of success and the less fortunate of failure. Risks of downward mobility for upper-class individuals are only mentioned, not explored. And the chances for upward mobility for lower-class youth are suggested to be minimal.

But "relative autonomy" implies autonomy as well as dependency. The term can emphasize the system's capacity to resist external demands. Bourdieu in fact draws upon this aspect of the term when he discusses the way French teachers have resisted attempts by state technocrats to modernize and render French secondary and higher education more relevant to the demands of business and advanced technology (Bourdieu, Boltanski, and

30. Clark's *Educating the Expert Society* (1962) is a classic statement representing the technical-functional perspective and Smith's *Who Rules the Universities?* (1974) presents an instrumental view of class domination. Bowles and Gintis's *Schooling in Capitalist American* (1976) offers a structural view of class and school relations that also allows little institutional autonomy from class interests.

Maldidier 1971). Here he correctly captures the idea (absent in human capital theory and most radical theories) of organizational and professional interests that emerge and, to some extent, are able to transform outside constraints according to their own terms. But the emphasis changes depending on whether he is discussing the relationship of education to social structure, or to the labor market and the state.

Additionally, the degree of autonomy from the labor market varies according to type of education and type of labor market in Bourdieu's analyses. Vocational education, for example, seems more closely attuned to job entry and performance in the skilled manual labor market than liberal arts programs are to white-collar jobs. Moreover, there appears to be a better "fit" in Bourdieu's analysis between the *grandes écoles* and elite job positions than there is for either vocational education or the liberal arts programs. This kind of variation is not well captured by the language of relative autonomy.

While the idea of relative autonomy captures an important historical development of the French educational system, it does less well accounting for change itself. The notion works best for Bourdieu when he refers to the resistance of the traditional emphasis in French secondary and university education on the classics to curricular reform more in line with knowledge and skill needs of industrialization. Nevertheless, the rise in importance over the past thirty years of mathematics and modern foreign languages in the high track of French secondary education and the growth in vocational programs suggest a growing alignment of educational programs with modern technological needs. The notion of relative autonomy, however, is unable to give an adequate description of such changes.

Bourdieu's use of the term does not permit him to specify the conditions under which educational institutions can achieve autonomy, the degree to which they do, the limits of that autonomy, and how it might change. Yet, these are important considerations if one is to gain a richer understanding of the complex relationship between a stratified educational system and a segmented labor market. The term gives Bourdieu conceptual maneuverability but at the considerable price of lack of empirical precision.

Bourdieu speaks of the relative autonomy of the educational system to refer to its capacity to undermine government instituted reforms. The idea that the relationship between policy objectives and actual consequences is mediated by divergent organizational and professional interests is not novel, but is frequently unappreciated by critical theories of education. Nevertheless, the interests of teachers, school administrators, and those of state managers may well coincide under certain conditions and on certain issues, such as expanding state resources for increasing student aid, building additional science facilities, and increasing instruction in the humanities.[31] Bourdieu does not explore such cases. A complete assessment of the relationship of educational institutions to state agencies would also require an assessment of such conditions. Moreover, it would call for a study of the politics of educational reform, one that would look at the actors, organization, and objectives that are subject to contention.

The emphasis on relative autonomy leaves Bourdieu with very little to say about the relationship of schooling to the state and organized interest groups. Yet, educational planning and policy making are carried out more by government officials than by relatively autonomous teachers and professors. Moreover, organized labor and teachers' unions can act as important pressure groups. And business interests, even in France, are not entirely absent from universities, as the switch in curriculum to scientific and business-oriented studies over the last thirty years suggests (Isamberg-Jamati and Segré 1971). In stressing the autonomy of cultural institutions, Bourdieu's analysis tends to downplay the importance of these other factors.

Since Bourdieu considers educational field autonomy to be a matter of degree rather than an either/or condition, his work on France invites cross-national comparisons. National differences in particular would seem to demand some modification of the model. American universities, for example, are very much constrained by economic interests, such as research funding, student enrollments, and alumni relations. Significant political influences often impinge on the allocation of research funding, grants, and at times on the expression of faculty views. In the case of the United States, at least, there would seem to be much more interaction and less autonomy between the academic field and the economic and political fields than Bourdieu's framework suggests to be the case in France.

Education, Reproduction and Change

In this concluding section, I take up Bourdieu's treatment of education and social change and the criticism his thinking on this important topic has received.

EDUCATION EXPANSION: CLASS REPRODUCTION STRATEGIES

In chapter 7, I pointed out that Bourdieu analyzes the dynamics of the contemporary class structure in terms of capital investment strategies by

---

31. Dougherty (1994), for example, shows that community college leaders find their own organizational interests favored in policies that appeal to business and government interests as well.

individuals and families who compete to maintain or enhance their positions in the social order. Bourdieu (in Bourdieu and Boltanski 1977:198)
analyzes the postwar expansion of the French educational system in terms
of social-class "strategies of reproduction" through which middle- and
dominant-class groups try "consciously or unconsciously, to maintain or
improve their position in the structure of class relations by safeguarding
or increasing their capital." Individuals and groups protect or advance their
positions within the social hierarchy by preserving, reinforcing, or transforming their stock of capital.

In order to maintain or improve their positions in the stratification
order, different classes pursue different kinds of educational investment
strategies. Middle-class groups (e.g., shopkeepers) started investing in
higher education after World War II in order to obtain economic security
in a job market that increasingly required formal qualifications. Traditionally low in cultural capital, these groups began investing in the expanding
universities. Frustrated by the traditional emphasis upon the humanities
and by forms of instruction that do not aid students with little inherited
cultural capital, middle-class groups demanded that curriculum and instruction be oriented toward the acquisition of usable knowledge and skills for
the increasingly professionalized job market.

A second kind of strategy is pursued by the intellectual elite who traditionally invest in education and thus already hold considerable cultural capital. This dominant-class fraction has assured the reproduction from generation to generation of professors, writers, and artists in France. As the main
carriers of the humanist tradition in France, this culturally elite group
works to protect its cultural capital from devaluation; it resists bending
academic requirements to the changing skill needs of the labor market.
These wealthy cultural capitalists strongly defend the merits of liberal arts
instruction, oppose reform measures that would give a greater vocational
emphasis to the university curriculum, and argue for the complete autonomy of the university. They also orient their own children toward the
grandes écoles, particularly the highly prestigious and selective Ecole Normale Supérieure, which prepares teachers for secondary schools and universities.

Other dominant-class fractions pursue different strategies in order to
maintain their positions of power and privilege. In the face of democratic
ideals of equality and new administrative and legal restrictions, it has become increasingly difficult simply to inherit economic wealth and power.
Big-business leaders, who are wealthy in economic capital but only moder-
ately wealthy in cultural capital, have responded to the decline of the family
firm by "converting" their economic capital into cultural capital in the form

of academic degrees for their children. These degrees allow them easy, but also legitimate, access to top managerial positions in large French firms (Bourdieu 1989c:371–481; Bourdieu and de Saint Martin 1978). On the other hand, those quite wealthy in both cultural and economic capital, such as doctors and lawyers, have intensified their accumulation of cultural capital in order to compete successfully for the same top business positions and to protect their professional positions against newly successful middle-class *arrivistes*. Both of these privileged class fractions dominate the prestigious professional schools, such as the Ecole Polytechnique and the Ecole Nationale d'Administration, whose graduates are channeled directly into top leadership posts in government administration and large corporations.[32]

Bourdieu's analysis of the varying and often conflicting educational investment strategies of different class groups demonstrates that the stakes in education are not the same for everyone. He perceptively suggests that the increased demand for academic credentials represents more than a response to increased skill demands in the labor market. Rather, Bourdieu ties postwar higher educational expansion to changes in the cultural and economic capital of social classes and to conflicts over access to positions of power and privilege.[33] His analyses also suggest that the biggest beneficiaries of the expanding educational meritocracy are not the capitalists, as Marxists argue, but those richest in cultural capital, namely, the professions.

BOURDIEU'S THEORY OF CHANGE

Numerous critics have argued that the strong social reproduction emphasis in Bourdieu's early work on French education, particularly in *Reproduction*, does not sufficiently anticipate situations of social crisis and change.[34] The difficulty stems from the central role that Bourdieu assigns to his concept of habitus in explaining social action. Critics charge that despite Bourdieu's claim to insert agency into his structuralist analysis, habitus harbors an inescapable structural determinism. In the last analysis, habitus is unable to account for innovation and change, for it reduces action to the interests of the types of capital it internalizes in dispositions and generates only practices corresponding to those interests.

32. As Bourdieu (1988b) notes, the elite status of the Ecole Normale Supérieure has waned whereas that of the Ecole Nationale d'Administration has waxed to become the current apex of the French *grandes écoles* hierarchy.
33. There is a clear affinity between Bourdieu's perspective on education expansion and Collins's (1971) status-group conflict explanation. Both draw inspiration from Weber.
34. See, for example, Berger 1986; Collins 1981a; Connell 1983; DiMaggio 1979; Gartman 1991; Giroux 1983; Jenkins 1982, 1992; Joppke 1986; Prost 1970; Sewell 1992; Sulkunen 1982; Swartz 1977; Swartz 1981.

Bourdieu strongly rejects this criticism, charging that it is based on a superficial and partial acquaintance with his total oeuvre, that it downplays the "inventive" side of habitus, that it in fact amounts to "reactions of hostility, if not rage" by intellectuals who defend the professional ideology of "creators," and that habitus is not a closed but an "open" concept, including to the problem of change (Bourdieu and Wacquant 1992:132–37).[35] Only recently has Bourdieu acknowledged that some of his formulations might lend themselves to the perception that he is a "hyperdeterminist" (Bourdieu and Wacquant 1992:132).[36] When he writes of habitus as "an acquired system of generative schemes objectively adjusted to the particular conditions in which it is constituted the habitus engenders *all the thoughts, all the perceptions, and all the actions* consistent with those conditions *and no others*" (Bourdieu 1977c:95; emphasis added), the concept does seem deterministic. Numerous similar formulations that reduce to "structures producing habitus, which generates practices that in turn reproduce structures" lend credence to critics' concern.

My own view is that habitus represents a mediating concept between practices and structures rather than a structurally determinative construct.[37] Since its operation occurs through time and across situations that can differ in structural conditions from those in which habitus was formed, there is room for modification and change, as Bourdieu claims.[38] Yet, as Bourdieu admits to his critics and states forcefully in numerous places in his work (e.g., Bourdieu 1989c:9), the tendency to perpetuate structures is built into his socialization model of action. Habitus tends to reproduce those actions consistent with the conditions under which it was produced (Bourdieu 1977c:95). For example, Bourdieu (1990h:60–61) speaks of "avoidance strategies" generated by habitus "to protect itself from crises and critical challenges" by "rejecting information capable of calling into question its accumulated information" and by "avoiding exposure to such information" by tending to "favour experiences likely to reinforce it." The tendency for

35. Wacquant (1992) stresses the openness of Bourdieu's framework to accommodate a theory of change, even though Bourdieu himself has not systematically formulated such a theory.

36. Bourdieu writes (ibid., 136): "I can understand such misinterpretations: insofar as dispositions themselves are socially determined, one could say that I am in a sense hyperdeterminist. It is true that analyses that take into account both effects of position and effects of disposition can be perceived as formidably deterministic."

37. I join here several other critics (Harker 1984, 1990; Miller and Branson 1987; Schiltz 1982; Sulkunen 1982; Thapan 1988; Wacquant 1992) who think of habitus as a mediating concept.

38. Several other critics (Calhoun 1993; Powell and DiMaggio 1991) also see that habitus contains *both* dimensions: determinism and the possibility for modification and change.

reproduction built right into the concept is strong indeed.[39] Moreover, technically the critics are right in that habitus *itself* cannot account for change. In Bourdieu's full model, however, practices result from the *intersection* between habitus and fields. As was noted in chapter 6, the scope of Bourdieu's theory of action is not complete without the idea of fields, since fields are able to impose their own particular logic upon the propensities of habitus. Structural reproduction occurs only if habitus operates in conditions similar those that produced it in the first place (Bourdieu 1990h:63). Indeed, as Bourdieu (1974a:5) understands the dialectical relations between habitus and field, three different kinds of situations can occur. In situations where opportunities and constraints are quite similar to the situation in which the dispositions of habitus were first internalized, habitus will tend to produce practices that correspond to existing structures. This results in social reproduction. In situations where the opportunities and constraints of fields change gradually, habitus tends to adapt, though there will be some degree of "mismatch." These are situations Bourdieu has in mind when he talks about the "hystersis" of habitus. Though habitus is an adaptive mechanism, it always addresses present situations in terms of past experiences. Change comes about when traditional strategies are deployed in relation to novel phenomena.[40] When the discrepancies between new situations and those in which habitus was formed are slight, only a gradual modification of structures occurs. In Bourdieu's analyses, the rate of this adaptive process appears to vary according to location in fields and according to amount and structure of capital. For example, French middle-class families were much quicker to take advantage of increasing higher educational opportunities during the 1950s and '60s than were working-class families. But where discrepancies are considerable, rapid transformation can ensue. Where there is a sharp, rapid change in opportunity structures, the expectations of habitus are frustrated, creating the potential for social crisis. Bourdieu writes that, in crisis situations

the dialectic of mutually self-reproducing objective chances and subjective aspirations may break down. Everything suggests that an *abrupt slump in objective* relative to subjective aspirations is likely to produce a break in the tacit acceptance which the dominated classes . . . previously granted to the dominant goals, and so to make

---

39. In fact, Bourdieu (1986a:241) sees a tendency toward reproduction in his concept of capital as well as in his concept of habitus when he writes that capital "contains a tendency to persist in its being" and "to reproduce."

40. See Sahlins 1981 for a particularly striking example of this type of change in a traditional society.

it possible to invent or impose the goals of a genuine collective action. (Bourdieu and Passeron 1979:97)

In this third kind of situation, reproduction gives way to either resignation or revolt.

Thus, Bourdieu's overall view of action permits considering situations where existing opportunities no longer correspond to the expectations from primary socialization. Such situations oblige habitus to generate nonadaptive forms of behavior. The source of change is rooted in the *encounter* between habitus and structures when they lack perfect fit. This observation notwithstanding, the general use of the concept by Bourdieu has been to emphasize the adaptive nature of most action and its social reproductive consequences. The disjuncture between habitus and field is treated more in terms of structural lag or imperfect synchronization than in terms of structural contradictions that would generate change (Bourdieu and Boltanski 1981:96). There is discontinuity and adjustment in Bourdieu's work but not contradiction and revolution.

MAY '68: A STRUCTURAL HISTORY

Bourdieu takes up the important issue of social change and gives it his fullest development to date in *Homo Academicus*, where he proposes a "structural history" of the May 1968 crisis in France. Just as the logic of social reproduction implies a close alignment of expectations with opportunities, the possibilities for social crisis, it follows, are most likely to occur where a sharp disjuncture occurs between expectations and actual rewards. Bourdieu sees May 1968 as the unfolding drama of frustrated expectations that stemmed from the central role that educational credentials have come to play in French society.

The rapid expansion of the educational credential system in French society had the effect of creating disjunctures between expectations and rewards in three areas: faculty careers, student plans, and manual labor. Bourdieu argues that prior to the 1960s—the period of rapid educational expansion—the higher educational system in France was characterized by a high degree of harmony between teachers and students, because both held considerable cultural capital and represented highly select social groups. It was a world of shared habitus. Educational expansion, however, fundamentally altered this traditional harmony, creating a gap between expectations and rewards for both teachers and students. In the universities, the traditional faculty career system (a sponsorship system based on cooptation and long preparation) was upset by the expanding ranks of junior faculty who brought heightened expectations for quick advancement to a very limited number of senior positions. Teachers found themselves facing increased numbers of less highly selected, middle-class students who did not possess the cultural background that teachers traditionally took for granted. Middle-class students, in turn, found that the humanistic and scholastic orientation of much university instruction gave them little assurance of obtaining the practical skills needed to compete in a tight job market. Increasing the number of graduates devalued the university degrees they were counting on to secure high-status jobs. Moreover, the French university was unable to impose selection, or "cooling off," mechanisms to adjust student expectations to the reality of the limited number of good job opportunities. Finally, manual workers were frustrated to find that the upgrading of their skills through vocational training came precisely at a time of declining labor-market demand for manual skills. The conjunction of these different crises in expectations represents for Bourdieu the underlying structural factors that led to May 1968.

Bourdieu's analysis of the May 1968 crisis in France needs careful comparative inspection with other national contexts. It may not, for example, generalize well to the United States. Unlike the French student movement, the American student movement of the 1960s was not precipitated by an "abrupt slump" in professional opportunities. On the contrary, these were actually increasing during this period.

It is also noteworthy that Bourdieu's university field analysis of May 1968 says nothing about the social movement and organizational aspects of the May events.[41] Nor does it offer insight on possible international contagion factors, such as the potential mobilizing force of the Vietnam War and of student uprisings in other countries. Though Bourdieu acknowledges that broader changes in the postwar economy helped shape the conditions leading to the 1968 social crisis, those economic changes do not figure directly into his analysis. The focus of his analysis—and the methodological point he wishes to score—is on how external factors are filtered through and mediated by the internal logic of cultural fields such as the French university.

Since Bourdieu's field approach holds that as fields gain in autonomy they retranslate external influences in terms of their own internal logic, analytical priority is therefore given to the internal structures and dynamics of fields. For Bourdieu, the most important features of May 1968 are to be found *within* the French university system. Moreover, Bourdieu locates the site of the crisis in the French higher-education system within the facul-

41. See Touraine 1968 for a discussion of the French May 1968 from a social movement perspective.

ties of arts and social sciences, precisely that part of French higher education where postwar expansion had been greatest, where academic selection was lowest, and where the connections with labor markets were weakest. In those areas where enrollments were limited, admission was highly selective, and good job prospects following graduation were assured, May 1968 brought little disruption. This was notably the case of the *grandes écoles*, particularly the Ecole Polytechnique and the Ecole Nationale d'Administration. Yet this insightful contrast paradoxically suggests that the politics of education expansion and the sheer increase in numbers of students and faculty may have had more to do with the crisis than Bourdieu's analysis acknowledges. He notes that the *grandes écoles* also had a sponsorship mobility system for faculty recruitment and promotion. This system, however, was preserved from the crisis because the institutions did not expand. Moreover, these elite schools enjoyed close ties with elite sectors of the French labor market. Thus, the structural linkages between the different types of educational institutions and the political economy in France are central for explaining their different experiences in May 1968. Bourdieu acknowledges the importance of these linkages between external and internal factors, making his focus on the internal factors only partially successful.

As a theoretical framework for understanding change, Bourdieu's idea of disjuncture between habitus and field leaves unanswered some important questions. First, it is not certain in Bourdieu's framework what exactly might bring about a sudden downward shift in opportunities, especially when they seem so solidly undergirded by the proclivity of habitus to reproduce them. Second, it is not clear under what conditions frustrated expectations would lead to resignation or revolt—two radically different responses. Since one can probably find frustrated expectations to some extent in all historical periods, what constitutes a breaking point? Here Bourdieu's social action view of change seems vulnerable to criticism addressed to "relative deprivation" theories of social crisis.[42] Bourdieu (1979:77–97, 1984a: 143–47) attributes expressions of anti-institutional attitudes and behavior among middle-level French white-collar workers in the 1970s to the frustrated expectations of the overeducated. But under what conditions might frustrated expectations lead to self-blame rather than revolt? Conditions under which one would occur but not the other need further specification. Crucial types of conditions to consider would include the amount of resources and capacities of a group to act as an organized unit, and the relative strength and degree of organization of its oppositions (Tilly 1978). And

---

42. Gurr's *Why Men Rebel* (1970) is representative of relative deprivation analyses of social turmoil. See Skocpol 1979 for a concise critique of relative deprivation theories of social crisis.

what role should be attributed to state agencies, university administrations, and organized interest groups? Bourdieu has very little to say about organizational capacities and practices of groups; yet these would seem crucial to any analysis that explores the question of order and disorder in society.

Beyond the idea of disjuncture between expectations and objective chances, there are other elements in Bourdieu's work that indicate potential sources of change: intrusion of external events into fields, increase in sheer numbers of field participants, uneven development and conjuncture of crises among different fields, growth in types of capital, and social struggles that expose field *doxa* necessitating new forms of symbolic domination and new reproduction strategies by agents (Wacquant 1987).[43] They appear in different places in his work and have yet to be assembled into a general theory of social change.

43. For example, Bourdieu (1989c:482–86) discusses the impact of general structural transformations in the field of power on cultural production. These transformations, however, are not theorized, but attributed to changes in economic concentration and the bureaucratization of large firms.

9

INTELLECTUALS AND INTELLECTUAL FIELDS

The role of intellectuals in modern societies occupies a central place in Bourdieu's work, but one that goes largely unnoticed despite the rapidly growing interest in Bourdieu. Bourdieu's understanding of intellectuals stems from his general view of practices, of the dynamics of cultural capital and symbolic violence, of fields of cultural production, and of the stratification order in modern societies. Indeed, an implicit—and sometimes quite explicit—theory of intellectual practices interweaves with each of these theoretical and empirical interests. In order to extrapolate a richer understanding of Bourdieu's sociological project, I begin this chapter by observing how a concern for intellectuals intersects with key themes in his overall social scientific enterprise, notably his theory of symbolic power and violence. I then consider how Bourdieu approaches the problem of defining intellectuals as an object of sociological investigation; how Bourdieu situates intellectuals relative to the social class structure; and, in the light of Bourdieu's key concept of intellectual field, how intellectuals are stratified by their participation in fields of cultural production. I will examine Bourdieu's view of intellectuals in politics to see how he understands intellectual political roles as fundamentally ambiguous, and present his most comprehensive study of intellectuals to date, his analysis of Parisian university professors. Attention in this chapter is confined to Bourdieu's critical analysis of existing intellectual practices and institutions. Chapter 10 takes up his normative vision for the kind of role he believes intellectuals—sociologists in particular—should play in modern societies.

The Importance of Intellectuals

There are at least three important reasons for why it is useful to look at Bourdieu's work from the standpoint of a theory of intellectuals. First is national tradition. Bourdieu writes in a country where the ideal of the detached and critical intellectual who intervenes actively in the political life of the nation is particularly strong. Beginning with Emile Zola and the Dreyfusards, artists, writers and teachers have frequently played significant political roles in France. Jean-Paul Sartre perhaps best epitomizes this national tradition where "men of letters became the leading political figures since they spoke with authority, despite the fact that they did not hold the reins of government" (Huszar 1960:8). As a consequence, the role of intellectuals has, perhaps in France more than in any other country, been the object of both emulation and critical reflection. Indeed, it is difficult to imagine a leading French thinker who is not concerned with intellectuals. Pierre Bourdieu is certainly no exception.

Second is substantive areas of research. A considerable portion of Bourdieu's work centers on fields of intellectual production.[1] Bourdieu (1993d: 132) indicates explicitly his intention to "make a contribution to the sociology of intellectual production." And he acknowledges that the study of intellectuals falls within his initial project of investigating the "whole set of dominant positions," though he has not yet completed their systematic study (Wacquant 1993b:20).

Third, and most important, is that the topic is central to his intellectual and political project. For Bourdieu, the study of intellectuals is crucial for an understanding of the character of stratification, political conflict, and the perpetuation of inequality in modern societies. We can see this central concern at the very heart of his theory of symbolic power and violence.[2] As I observed in earlier chapters, Bourdieu's theory of symbolic power holds that class relations are mediated through symbolic struggle. A key dimension of class relations is the struggle to legitimate particular definitions and classifications of the social world. This struggle for symbolic power involves the capacity to name and to categorize, indeed the capacity to make social groups (Bourdieu 1985e:731–35, 1988a:23). It calls for symbolic labor, which is precisely the work of intellectuals who, as symbolic

---

1. A selected list of his field analyses of intellectuals includes Bourdieu 1971c, 1975b, 1980b, 1983a, 1984a, 1985d, 1988b, 1991a, 1991b, 1991d, and 1993c.
2. Garnham 1986 also highlights the centrality of a theory of intellectuals in Bourdieu's work.

producers,[3] are strategically situated for shaping the character of class relations.[4]

The importance Bourdieu accords to symbolic producers in modern
societies raises serious questions, however. Intellectuals can be key players
in the mediation of class relations to the extent that the operation of power
requires legitimation and misrecognition. Yet, as I noted in chapter 4,
power can operate on many occasions more through compliance or brute
force than through tacit consent (Mann 1973). Power relations can be
clearly understood and still not contested where individuals do not see via-
ble alternatives without tremendous risks. In order to highlight the symbolic dimension of power relations, Bourdieu's theory of symbolic power
may underestimate the capacity of nonspecialists to develop in certain situations appropriate understandings of the true character of power relations. If
such were the case, then the central role that Bourdieu assigns to specialized
symbolic producers would seem less persuasive.

While it is certainly the case that political and economic elites rely
more today on the highly credentialed than they did earlier in the century,
care must be taken not to assign an unwarranted importance to intellectual
roles. Indeed, too much importance may be attributed to intellectuals in
general. Ruling elites can choose to ignore their highly educated advisors
and managers as often happens in the United States (Wood 1993). Bourdieu challenges effectively the self-image of intellectuals as outsiders to the
established order. But he does not go so far as to challenge their assumed
self-importance.[5]

3. Bourdieu (1990c:146) writes that "culture producers hold a specific power, the properly
symbolic power of showing things and making people believe in them, of revealing, in an
explicit, objectified way the more or less confused, vague, unformulated, even unformulable
experiences of the natural world and the social world, and of thereby bringing them into
existence."

4. Though Bourdieu (1990c:27) claims only a recent acquaintance with the work of
Gramsci, there is a similarity in their views regarding the functions they see intellectuals playing in developing group identity. Gramsci (1971:334) writes: "A human mass does not distinguish itself, does not become independent in its own right without, in the widest sense, organizing itself; and there is no organization without intellectuals, that is without organizers
and leaders, in other words, without the theoretical aspect of the theory-practice nexus being
distinguished concretely by a group of people 'specialized' in conceptual and philosophical
elaboration of ideas."

Intellectuals are also key actors for Touraine's (1973) action approach to the study of society
as the cultural domain is emphasized in his concept of "historicity." The struggle over cultural
orientations by those who create and manipulate the symbols of society occupies a central
place in his analysis of the "self-production of society." But the focus of Touraine's work is
on actors in social movements, whereas Bourdieu is concerned more with providing a map
of their structural location.

5. This critical observation reflects perhaps better the American context than the French,
where leading intellectuals have often played greater roles in national policy making and where

The Problem of Definition

Bourdieu's (1987b:171, 1988b:269, 1990c:143) approach to the study of intellectuals poses at the outset the problem of who is an intellectual—how the sample for a sociological study of intellectuals is to be defined. For Bourdieu (1988b:256–70), who is an intellectual and what are specifically intellectual traits are themselves objects of struggle within cultural fields. Defining who is an intellectual is inseparably linked to the question of who has the authority to do the defining and ranking.[6] The object of sociological investigation must be this struggle itself.[7] The task of the sociologist, Bourdieu stresses, is not "to set himself up as the judge of the judges, and of their right to judge. He merely points out that this right is the object of conflicts whose logic he analyses" (269). The researcher must grasp the field as a whole rather than from the standpoint of just one position within it. For Bourdieu, then, the definition of who really is an intellectual and how that definition has changed is fundamentally a question of how the intellectual field is constituted (Bourdieu and Wacquant 1992:107). For Bourdieu, the sociology of intellectuals is in reality a sociology of cultural fields.

This distinguishes his approach from those that begin with *a priori* definitions of intellectuals in terms of some idealized cognitive quality or particular social or political commitment. Shils (1972:3), for example, characterizes intellectuals by their "unusual sensitivity to the sacred, an uncommon reflectiveness about the nature of the universe and the rules which govern their society."[8] The idea that an "unusual sensitivity to the sacred" or an "uncommon reflectiveness" about the nature of the social universe conveys fundamentally what is distinctive about today's vast array of cul-

---

a highly education senior civil service enjoys greater power than in the United States. It invites cross-national comparisons.

6. Bourdieu (1988b:269) writes that "the question of the definition of the intellectual, or, rather, of specifically intellectual work, is inseparable from the question of defining the population which can be allowed to participate in this definition. The true objective of the struggle which is engaged at the heart of the field of cultural production . . . is in fact the attribution of the right to judge in the matter of cultural production."

7. Bourdieu (256–70) illustrates this point with a critical secondary analysis of a 1981 survey of leading French intellectuals by *Lire*, a review of commentary on French cultural life. Claude Lévi-Strauss, Raymond Aron, Michel Foucault, and Simone de Beauvoir head the list of forty-two names. Bourdieu himself is ranked at the bottom of the list. He finds that both the respondents sampled and their responses overrepresent a specific group of cultural producers who have particularly close ties to the mass media. The sample was determined by media visibility more than by quality of intellectual production.

8. Coser (1965:viii) offers another normative definition when he identifies intellectuals as "men who never seem satisfied with things as they are" and those who "live for rather than off ideas."

tural producers, ranging from artists, writers, and professors to lawyers, engineers, managers, and state officials, reveals the danger of generalizing on the basis of some hypothetical existential condition.[9] Nor would Bourdieu's intellectual field perspective necessarily posit that political and social dissent constitute a universal characteristic of the intellectual (Nettl 1969).[10] This too would prejudice the treatment of the topic, since it narrows the range of possibilities from the outset.

Bourdieu is not alone in suggesting that an initial definition of the object of research can prejudice the investigation. We can no longer assume that intellectuals share common social or political commitments or display a characteristic cognitive propensity (Brint 1984). Neither can we assume that intellectuals are a fairly cohesive and self-conscious "intelligentsia" that opposes the status quo (Gagnon 1987:5). Bourdieu adds to this critical awareness by showing that the label "intellectual" is itself a form of symbolic capital whose value and possession are objects of struggle.[11]

Bourdieu's own empirical work focuses primarily on artists, writers, and academics—the humanistic intelligentsia—rather than on law, medicine, or the technical intelligentsia (engineers, technicians, and managers). He in fact confines most of his analyses to those who have considerable cultural capital and who are therefore members of what he calls the dominant class. Yet his conceptualization aims to cover all types of cultural producers who invest primarily in cultural markets. This permits the researcher a broader conceptual and empirical sweep than what is traditionally associated with the word "intellectual." It resists universalizing selected attributes of a collection of individuals and invites examination of the specific features of every historical context.

Yet, despite the field perspective, Bourdieu also advocates a particular type of critical intellectual role that includes a strongly *normative* vision of what intellectuals should be. Intellectuals—particularly those armed with science—are to be critics rather than servants of power. This ideal stands in tension with his methodological claim that the object of sociological inquiry should be field struggle rather than advocacy of one particular posi-

9. Shils (1972:154) is on firmer historical and sociological ground when he observes in another passage that "the intellectual classes differ from society to society in composition and structure . . . [and in] their beliefs about intellectual actions and roles."

10. Indeed, many highly educated individuals, including those in the traditional humanist occupations, have supported the status quo. The recent work by Brint (1984, 1994) on the political attitudes of the highly educated in the United States casts doubt on the general claim that intellectuals as a whole tend to contest the status quo.

11. Jacoby's (1987) critical lament for the decline of public intellectuals in American culture, for example, represents a position within the struggle for what American academics on the political left should be doing.

tion. I will examine this normative component in more detail in the next chapter.

Intellectuals and the Stratification Order

Bourdieu's analytical strategy for the study of intellectuals begins with his analysis of the field of power. He first situates the various fields of cultural production, such as the literary field (Bourdieu 1983a) and the academic field (Bourdieu 1988b) in relation to the field of power. He then identifies the structural location of the various types of symbolic producers within their respective fields of cultural production (*Current Research* 1972:39).

As I observed in chapter 7, Bourdieu distinguishes the dominant class from all subordinate social classes by virtue of its advantages in total volume of valued resources. However, Bourdieu's (1973a) dominant class is internally differentiated by unequal distributions of economic capital and cultural capital. Wealthy cultural capitalists, such as lawyers, top managers, and professors, compete for position with industrial owners who base their claims to power, not on cultural capital, but on economic capital. Since, for Bourdieu, intellectuals are cultural capitalists whose form of capital is subordinate to economic capital, he assigns to them the status of a "dominated fraction" of the dominant class.[12] For Bourdieu, therefore, intellectuals are in the contradictory position of being both dominant and dominated in terms of their class location. They are in the dominant class because they enjoy the power and privileges that come with the possession of considerable cultural capital. That power comes from their capacity to provide or withdraw legitimation of the social order. Yet, they are dominated in their relations with the holders of political and economic power. In the final analysis, the autonomy of cultural capital from economic capital is only *relative*, not absolute, as is the working assumption in mainstream intellectual history (Caute 1964).

The significance of Bourdieu's idea of intellectuals as being located within the dominant class, albeit in a dominated position, is to be measured against the common self-conception among intellectuals, particularly in France, as being in opposition to the dominant class. In France since the

12. Bourdieu writes, "the producers and transmitters of symbolic goods owe their most essential characteristics to the fact that they constitute a dominated section of the dominant classes" (*Current Research* 1972:23). Since the publication of *Distinction* in 1979, Bourdieu increasingly refers to intellectuals as the "dominated pole of the field of power" rather than as the "dominated fraction of the dominant class." This rhetorical shift accompanies his increased use of the language of "social space" rather than social structure, and probably reflects the decline of structuralist Marxism as a key intellectual reference for Bourdieu (see his 1984a: 260–67, 283–95, 315–17; 1989a; 1989c:373–85, 482–86; 1990c:140–49).

time of Zola and the Dreyfus affair, being an intellectual has generally meant being associated with the political left and working-class parties and labor organizations. Bourdieu's position challenges that self-conception by suggesting that the intellectual posture derives more from a situation of privilege and its specific professional interests than from a genuine solidarity with the working class. Indeed, it is the basis for an ambiguous and fragile alliance with subordinate groups.

Though intellectuals play an important role in the power struggle, they do not for Bourdieu constitute a social class. While certain cultural resources can provide a power base for relatively autonomous and competitive fields of struggle against economic capital and political power, they do not create a social class. Moreover, Bourdieu sees intellectuals as highly differentiated by their participation across different fields requiring different configurations of capital and by their stratification within particular fields. He proposes methodologically that we examine the beliefs and conduct of intellectuals in terms of their strategies for distinction *within* intellectual fields. Intellectual fields are key mediating arenas between the social-class location of intellectuals and their ideas, professional ideology, and political conduct. This view demarcates his position on intellectuals from that of a number of New Class theorists—notably Gouldner (1979)—who see in the development of a highly educated segment of the work force the beginnings of a new social class.[13] Bourdieu has nonetheless contributed—particularly via his concept of cultural capital—to some of the more recent advances in New Class theorizing (Collins 1979, 1981a; Cookson and Persell 1985; Eyerman, Svensson, and Soderqvist 1987; Featherstone 1987; Martin and Szelenyi 1987; Szelenyi and Martin 1988/89).[14]

Recent changes in the economy, Bourdieu notes, have had an impor-

13. Gouldner sees the possibility of the ensemble of humanist intellectuals and the technical intelligentsia forming a distinct social class by virtue of a common identity and culture ("Culture of Critical Discourse") as shaped by their experience of higher education and their common relation to the means of production. In contrast, Bourdieu emphasizes the internal differentiation mechanisms of cultural fields that leave little chance for those in the intellectual professions to achieve something like class unity. By rejecting the idea of intellectuals as forming a separate social class, Bourdieu joins the Marxist tradition, which, for the most part, has seen intellectuals as unable to generate a set of common interests and forced to choose between the two main social classes: capital or labor. This was notably Gramsci's (1971) position. Though strategic actors in shaping class relations, intellectuals as a whole, Gramsci thought, had neither a common institutional basis nor a set of common interests that would permit them to constitute a separate social class.

14. Bourdieu (1984a:12–13) suggests that the debate surrounding the political inclinations of intellectuals must itself be situated within the competitive field in which it occurs, and that attributions of essentially left or right political inclinations to intellectuals reflects most likely the position of the theorist in that field. Bourdieu has not, however, actually submitted the New Class debate to field analysis.

tant influence on intellectual roles. The shift toward a service economy, where an increasing proportion of the labor force is employed in technologically advanced and large bureaucratic organizations, has brought about radical changes in the conditions of cultural production. Bourdieu sees in this broad transformation of the occupational structure a decline in traditional independent cultural producers, like Sartre, and an increase in the power of technocratic-type intellectuals (e.g., graduates of the Ecole Nationale d'Administration).

The Intellectual Habitus

I observed in chapter 7 that, for Bourdieu, the economic capital/cultural capital opposition translates into fundamental differences in life chances that generate distinct types of habitus among the social classes. In particular, the rise of culture as capital and the development of relatively autonomous cultural markets tend to generate a distinct intellectual habitus of "aristocratic asceticism" that is constructed against the "bourgeois" habitus of "temporate hedonism." The habitus of "aristocratic asceticism" is "oriented towards the least expensive and most austere leisure activities and towards serious and even somewhat severe cultural practices . . . and is opposed to the luxury tastes of the members of the professions" (Bourdieu 1984a:286). Especially characteristic of teachers and public-sector executives, Bourdieu sees the habitus of aristocratic asceticism as stemming from their efforts for "maximizing the profit they can draw from their cultural capital and their spare time (while minimizing their financial outlay)" (287). Teachers, in particular,

hardly ever have the means to match their tastes, and this disparity between cultural and economic capital condemns them to an ascetic aestheticism (a more austere variant of the "artist" life-style which "makes the most" of what it has. (Ibid.)

Aristocratic asceticism is not an intrinsic but a relational characteristic of the more intellectually oriented professions, for it grows out of the conflict between economic capital and cultural capital, the two principles of classification that are at the center of the struggle for power in contemporary societies.

Intellectuals as Producers in Cultural Fields

A central theme in Bourdieu's work is that intellectual attitudes and behaviors do not reduce to class position. Nor do they stand independent of social structure. Bourdieu (1972:33) posits that "all intellectuals are defined, primarily, by the fact that they occupy determinant positions in the intellectual field." As was noted in chapter 6, Bourdieu speaks of the intellectual field to designate that matrix of institutions and markets in which artists, writers, researchers and academics compete over valued resources to obtain legitimate recognition for their artistic, literary, academic, or scientific work.[15] Intellectual fields are primarily arenas of struggle over who has the authority to define what are the legitimate forms of cultural production. Bourdieu focuses on positions within intellectual fields, not on individuals or particular occupational groups. Intellectuals stake out positions that are constituted oppositionally and reflect the unequal distribution of types of cultural and symbolic capital involved in the struggle (Bourdieu 1983a:213). In general, Bourdieu sees this opposition as occurring between established intellectuals and their challengers; the established intellectuals tend to pursue conservation strategies whereas the challengers opt for subversive strategies. Bourdieu depicts this conflict in terms of those who defend "orthodoxy" and those who advocate "heresy."[16]

Bourdieu (1987d) elaborates this orthodoxy/heresy opposition from Weber's (1978:399–634) distinction between priests and prophets. Priests and prophets struggle for the

monopoly of cultural legitimacy and the right to withhold and confer this consecration in the name of fundamentally opposed principles: the personal authority called for by the creator and the institutional authority favoured by the teacher. (Bourdieu 1971c:178)

In contemporary French academic life, Bourdieu (1988b) sees this opposition between the "curators of culture" and the "creators of culture," between those who reproduce and transmit legitimate bodies of knowledge and those who invent new forms of knowledge, between teachers and researchers, between professors and independent intellectuals.

In Bourdieu's hands, field analysis offers a structural interpretation of the rise of cultural markets and the modern intelligentsia.[17] Field analysis

15. Ross (1987, 1991) analyzes the contemporary French intellectual world in terms of investments in various intellectual markets. Ross bases some of his analysis on the work of Debray (1981) who has been influenced by Bourdieu. Ringer (1992:4–5) also adopts Bourdieu's concept of the intellectual field in his comparative study of intellectual cultures among French and German academic historians and social scientists between 1890 and 1920.

16. Hofstadter (1963:430–31) identifies a similar distinction between the "clerisy" and the "avant garde," between those who legitimate dominant values and those who question them.

17. While Bourdieu (1992:75–200) has paid particular attention to the late-nineteenth-century origins of the modern literary field in France, he has not sketched out the broad

posits that with the emergence of a specialized corps of cultural producers there also emerges a parallel cultural arena in which the production, circulation, and consumption of symbolic goods become increasingly autonomous from the economy, the polity, and religion. It is Bourdieu's basic research hypothesis that as cultural fields gain in autonomy from external factors the intellectual stances assumed by the agents increasingly become a function of the *positions* occupied by the agents *within* these fields.[18]

If the intellectual field is structured by hierarchically ordered positions, it is also governed by the dynamic "law of the quest for distinction" (Bourdieu 1972:35). The struggle for individual distinction is particularly acute among intellectuals, since, in intellectual life, "to exist is to differ, i.e. to occupy a distinct, distinctive position" (Bourdieu 1983a:338).[19] This struggle involves career interests that shape intellectual interests. Book contracts, reviews, citations, honorary rewards, leadership positions in professional organizations, academic posts, and the arduous route to tenure all involve fundamental decisions regarding one's position in the intellectual world (Bourdieu 1980c:70). Moreover, intellectual interests are simultaneously "political" stances in that they result from strategies by agents to maintain or enhance their positions in fields.[20] According to Bourdieu,

the theories, methods, and concepts that appear as simple contributions to the progress of science are *also* always "political" maneuvers that attempt to establish, restore, reinforce, protect, or reverse a determined structure of relations of symbolic domination. (1971c:121)

---

historical development in Western countries of relatively autonomous intellectual fields more generally. He has nonetheless noted (in his 1971c, 1971d) several factors he sees important in that historical development: the increasing division of labor correlated with the development of capitalism, the Industrial Revolution and the Romantic reaction against it, the expansion of mass public education that helped create a mass consumer market for symbolic goods, the growth of a variety of organizations for dissemination and consumption (salons, publishing houses, theaters, etc.) outside of religious and political control, and above all the development of groups of specialists of symbolic production. See Charle's (1987, 1990) work employing Bourdieu's framework on the historical development of the intellectual field in France.

18. Bourdieu (1971d:166) notes that the structural features of a cultural field are historically contingent. He writes that it is the "historic and social conditions which make possible the existence of an intellectual field" and "at the same time define the limits of validity of a study of a state of this field."

19. Another factor contributing to the intensively competitive character of intellectual fields is that the consumers are also the competitors.

20. Bourdieu (1971c:179–80) writes that "the ultimate cause of the conflicts, real or invented, which divide the intellectual field along its lines of force and which constitute beyond any doubt the most decisive factor of cultural change, must be sought at least as much in the objective factors determining the position of those who engage in them as in the reasons they give, to others and to themselves, for engaging in them."

Theories, methods, and concepts are therefore weapons of struggle for intellectual recognition. Their selection, whether fully conscious or not, are governed by the "search for distinction."[21] Hence, intellectuals are strategists who aim to maximize their influence within cultural fields.[22] The relationship between intellectuals and social classes, therefore, is mediated by intellectual field strategies.

DIVIDED WORLDS: THE INTERNAL DIFFERENTIATION OF INTELLECTUALS

Far from constituting a unified social class, Bourdieu considers that intellectuals are highly stratified in their struggle for symbolic legitimation. They are stratified by the type of cultural markets where they invest and by the type and amount of cultural capital they have been able to inherit or accumulate. In any intellectual field, one can identify dominant and dominated positions, conservatives and avant garde, those who pursue strategies of reproduction and those who pursue strategies of subversion. Bourdieu (1983a:333) identifies two fundamental oppositions among cultural producers: the first distinguishes two types of cultural markets and the second identifies a legitimation struggle within one of those markets.

Bourdieu (1971d:54–100, 1983a:319–20, 1985d) identifies the most fundamental source of differentiation among intellectuals between two different fields of cultural production: (1) the field of restricted production and its dependence on the educational system for its reproduction, and (2) the field of "mass-audience" production. Fields of restricted symbolic production, whether in art or science, are highly specialized cultural markets. Participants struggle over the criteria for determining the most legitimate cultural forms and direct their efforts toward peer approval (Bourdieu 1971d:55, 62). These specialized cultural markets tend to be structured around specific forms of symbolic capital that are relatively autonomous from economic and political capital. These are the markets for "pure science" or "art for art's sake" that reject commercial or political criteria (Bourdieu 1992:202–20).

In contrast, Bourdieu thinks of the less specialized fields of symbolic production as being more oriented toward external criteria of commercial success and popular demand. They produce what can readily and rapidly

21. Bourdieu writes that "intellectual, artistic or scientific stances are also always unconscious or semi-conscious *strategies* in a game where the stakes are the conquest of cultural legitimation or in other terms for the monopoly of the legitimate production, reproduction, and manipulation of symbolic goods and the correlative legitimating power" (118).

22. Bourdieu further argues that individuals in the field of cultural production most inclined to take the most risky positions of the avant guard are those who have enough economic capital to give them sufficient "distance from necessity" to disregard material concerns (1991d: 40).

be transformed into economic capital. This pits those cultural producers more able to sell their work to dominant-class fractions against those less able to do so. In the struggle for intellectual legitimation, the field of restricted production represents the dominant position and the field of mass-audience production represents the dominated position.[23] Intellectual types roughly parallel the contours of this structural divide.

Another source of differentiation between intellectuals occurs within the field of restricted production itself. There, Bourdieu finds conflicting interests between those who occupy institutional positions for conserving and reproducing the existing order in symbolic fields and those who contest that order by proposing new forms of symbolic capital. In his analysis of artists and writers, this polarity occurs between the new and the old guards, between those who accumulate positions of cultural authority—those with significant positional property in the cultural field—and challengers who are trying to gain entry and rise up in the field. Bourdieu suggests that this tension is often intergenerational in that age frequently separates the representatives of the cultural establishment from those who are seeking to change its legitimating criteria.

Though Bourdieu acknowledges the growing importance of mass-audience fields of cultural production in contemporary societies, he maintains that it is the fields of restricted cultural production that establish the most legitimate cultural forms, and that it is above all the university that conserves and consecrates these forms.[24] He argues that

the Academy claims the monopoly of consecration of contemporary creators. It contributes to the organization of the intellectual field in respect of orthodoxy by a type of jurisprudence which combines tradition and innovation. (179)

Moreover,

the university claims the monopoly of transmission of the consecrated works of the past, which it sanctifies as "classics" as well as the monopoly of legitimation and consecration (by granting degrees amongst other things) of those cultural consumers who most closely conform.

23. In the literary or artistic field, Bourdieu (1983a:321) sees this struggle manifested in terms of those more closely connected to the economic and politically dominant groups and who do "Bourgeois art" compared to those who advocate "art for art's sake."
24. Bourdieu (1971c:179) maintains that "every intellectual brings into his relations with other intellectuals a claim to cultural consecration (or legitimacy) which depends, for the form it takes and the grounds it quotes, on the position he occupies in the intellectual field. In particular the claim depends on his relation to *the university, which, in the last resort, disposes of the infallible signs of consecration*" (emphasis added).

The intellectual field depends, therefore, on the educational system for the functions of conservation, consecration, transmission, and reproduction of legitimate culture.[25]

The relationship between intellectuals and the educational system is, however, wrought with tension. According to Bourdieu (1971d:74–75), one source of tension within the intellectual field is the time lag between the consecration function and intellectual production. The unending search for distinction that drives the field continually yields new competing forms of knowledge. Competitive struggle between cultural producers generates innovation. Yet efforts by producers to receive legitimation for their new cultural forms are frustrated by the power of consecration of the educational system and the inertia of that system for giving legitimacy to new cultural forms. Bourdieu observes that this tension accounts for the ambivalent attitude he finds among marginal intellectual producers, such as journalists and media people, toward the educational system.[26] Quick to denounce scholarly knowledge as too "academic" they yet relish the idea of their own viewpoints becoming recognized as legitimate within academic circles. Bourdieu claims that this testifies to the power of the educational system to legitimize dominant culture. It also testifies to the relation of domination the educational system establishes even with those cultural producers who are on the fringes of the intellectual field. He observes that

several of the attacks against academic orthodoxy come from intellectuals situated on the fringes of the university system who are prone to dispute its legitimacy, thereby proving that they acknowledge its jurisdiction sufficiently to reproach it for not approving them. (Bourdieu 1971c:179)

Such intellectuals seek recognition from the very institution they are contesting, and hence paradoxically reinforce its legitimacy.

Bourdieu (1963) is sharply critical of mass culture and mass-media theorists who emphasize the impact of advertising and television on social and cultural tastes. He charges that they underestimate the continuing role of schooling and social-class influences in shaping both cultural production and consumption. Still, the issue remains open to debate. Some critics (e.g.,

25. Bourdieu argues that a sociology of intellectuals needs to be connected to a sociology of education, notably to an analysis of the structures and functions of the educational system. Ringer (1992) concurs with this view, and his work on German and French academics is cast within this perspective.

26. He writes that "this type of ambivalent attitude is particularly widespread among the lower strata of the intelligentsia, among journalists, popularizers, disputed artists, radio and television producers, etc.: many opinions and modes of conduct have their origins in the relationship which these intellectuals have with early education and thereby with the educational establishment" (Bourdieu 1971c:188).

Garnham 1993) charge that Bourdieu himself underestimates the degree of shift in cultural influence from schools to extrascholastic forms of mass culture—particularly television. It is no longer clear that the traditional importance Bourdieu assigns to the academy and its specialized cultural markets in shaping the agenda for symbolic struggle between classes continues today to play the role that it once did in France or in other countries. The growing importance of the electronic media may be more pronounced in Great Britain and the United States than in France, though the work of Debray (1981) stresses the extent to which the Parisian intellectual milieu appears to have become more media oriented since the 1970s. In recent work, Bourdieu (1996) also emphasizes the growing negative effects of mass-media markets in the intellectual field.

Another line of internal differentiation is based on relative proximity to the field of power. This opposition occurs between experts and technicians who offer their services to the dominant fractions and the unattached, independent intellectuals—more frequently found in the humanities—who take advantage of the autonomy given them by the intellectual field to intervene as critics in the political field. Within the artistic field he sees this polarity occurring between those artists who do "bourgeois art" and the avant garde.

Finally, Bourdieu (1971d:119, 1972:35) suggests that conflict between intellectuals is more intense for those holding neighboring positions in the intellectual field. This is explained by the "law of the search for distinction" that governs field activity. Participation in competitive cultural markets requires adopting a strategy of differentiating one's position from all others. Of all the stratifying mechanisms among intellectuals, it is this "search for distinction," the incessant jockeying for better and more distinctive positions, that Bourdieu emphasizes most.[27]

THE INTELLECTUAL *DOXA*

If the struggle for legitimation in cultural fields generates oppositions between orthodox and heterodox views, these oppositions are nonetheless framed by an underlying consensus on topics deemed worthy of discussion and debate (Bourdieu 1971d:96). As was noted in chapter 6, Bourdieu refers

27. Bourdieu's identification of key axes of differentiation of French intellectuals invites comparisons with other national contexts. The public/private axis of internal stratification, for example, may be more salient elsewhere. Within the private sphere, a further split may appear between those oriented toward for-profit activities and those oriented toward volunteerism and community service. Similarly, within the public sphere there may be a split between those sectors more in contact with and supportive of business and those more concerned with providing social services.

to this common grounding of orthodox and heterodox views as the *doxa*.[28] Similar to the Durkheimian concept of a cultural unconscious,[29] the *doxa* refers to the fundamental assumptions and categories that shape intellectual thought in a particular time and place and which are generally not available to conscious awareness of the participants.[30] Bourdieu (1971d:96) sees the educational system as playing a decisive role in establishing this *doxa* of topics for the different fractions of the dominant class and for intellectuals in particular. He (1971c:185) posits that

in a society where the transmission of culture is the monopoly of a school, the underlying affinities uniting works of learned culture (and at the same time behavior and thought) are governed by the principle emanating from the educational institutions.[31]

Bourdieu's idea of a far-reaching intellectual *doxa* may reflect a period of cultural and intellectual consensus in France after World War II that no longer exists. While it is probably the case that some hidden *doxa* exists in every intellectual period, the concept runs the risk of obscuring the variations in degree of cultural unity that may also exist in different periods and in different national settings. The fragmentation of the Western intellectual world—a postmodernist theme—suggests the emergence of a more diversified intellectual field than Bourdieu's concept would anticipate.

INTELLECTUAL FIELDS AND THE REPRODUCTION OF CLASS RELATIONS

Though intellectual attitudes and behavior do not reduce to social-class position, Bourdieu argues that their location within fields of symbolic pro-

28. Bourdieu (1971c:182–83) writes that "the cultivated men of a given age may have different opinions on the subjects about which they quarrel but they are at any rate agreed on quarrelling about certain subjects. What attaches a thinker to his age, what situates and dates him, is above all the kind of problems and themes in terms of which he is obliged to think."

29. While not to be equated with Bourdieu's concept of *doxa*, Gouldner's (1970) concept of "infrastructure" resembles the basic point.

30. Bourdieu (1967b:116) suggests that "the open conflicts between tendencies and doctrines tend to mask from the participants themselves the underlying complicity which they presuppose and which strikes the observer from outside the system, that consensus within the dissensus which constitutes the objective unity of the intellectual field of a given period."

An illustration of Bourdieu's point can be found in Ringer's (1992:7) study of German academics, which shows that the "orthodox" majority and the "modernist" minority actually shared many assumptions regarding their common cultural heritage. Murphy's (1988) field analysis of Parkin's (1979) polemical attack against structural Marxism is another example. Though both Parkin and structural Marxists hold in common a number of objections to structural functionalist views of stratification, their underlying similarities are masked in Parkin's work because it is an intellectual strategy designed to attack the prominent position held by Marxism among academics in the 1970s.

31. In discussing the case of philosophy, Bourdieu (1983a:314) states that "academic routine and perhaps above all . . . school manuals (an unmentionable reference), . . . perhaps do more than anything else to constitute the 'common sense' of an intellectual generation."

duction nonetheless reproduce the stratification order. Intellectual fields serve to mark, and thus reinforce, social-class relations.[32] Even the "ultimate basis" of intellectual fields for specialists is their relationship to the social-class structure (Bourdieu 1971d:126). Yet, Bourdieu understands this social-class reproduction function in structural rather than in instrumental terms. Simply by pursuing their specific interests as specialists in cultural production intellectuals *also* legitimate the class structure. Intellectual practices are organized almost exclusively according to the logic of status distinction, which Bourdieu (1984a) depicts as a social practice defined by its "distance from material necessity." To play the intellectual game means that one has to transcend the demands of basic economic necessity. This imposes two conditions: it requires an intellectual disposition (habitus) that is able to bracket off from immediate concern the needs of everyday existence in order to work with ideas; it also requires the requisite cultural capital as a form of competence for engaging in the intellectual field competition. Both conditions are facilitated by conditions of existence that offer freedom from material needs. Both serve, therefore, as mechanisms of social closure by excluding those unable to make the substantial investments of time, effort, and resources required to compete. In this way, intellectual fields contribute to the reproduction of the social-class structure.

For Bourdieu, the concept of intellectual field links the symbolic work of intellectuals to those structural conditions it both constitutes and reflects. In this way, Bourdieu sees his concept as transcending both idealist (e.g., Caute 1964; Eisenstadt 1973) and materialist (e.g., Brym 1987; Wright 1985) conceptualizations of intellectuals, which stress either the power of ideas or the determining role of political and economic interests to the exclusion of the other.[33]

Intellectuals and Politics

Much of the sociology of intellectuals, inspired particularly by the Marxist tradition, is ultimately concerned with the political role of intellectuals in modern societies. Beginning with Marx himself, Marxists have tried to connect the political attitudes and behavior of intellectuals to their location

32. Bourdieu (1983a:337) writes, "without ever being a direct reflection of them, the internal struggles depend for their outcome on the correspondence they may have with the external struggles between the classes or between the fractions of the dominant class and on the reinforcement which one group or another may derive from them."

33. Ross (1987) takes a similar view, by questioning the pertinence of the materialist/idealist dichotomy that has shaped much of the debate on the role of intellectuals. He works with the idea of "intellectual markets" where intellectuals find or create opportunities for investments in cultural capital.

within the social-class structure. This effort has not been entirely success-ful. Because of their privileged access to valued resources, intellectuals, Marxists have argued, tend to defend their advantages by siding with capi-talists in the class struggle. Nevertheless, Marx and Engels (1978:481) con-sidered that "a portion of the bourgeoisie . . . who have raised themselves to the level of comprehending theoretically the historical movement as a whole" would join the proletariat in its struggle against the capitalist class. What might trigger such an act of enlightened class consciousness is far from clear, however, both in the writings of Marx and Engels and in subse-quent Marxist work (see Karabel 1994).

The contemporary Marxist, Erik Olin Wright (1985), for example, ar-gues that intellectuals are highly educated workers who occupy "contradic-tory class locations"; at the economic level, they are located between the petite bourgeoisie and the proletariat, whereas, at the ideological level, they occupy a contradictory position between the bourgeoisie and the proletar-iat. This leads to contradictory political attitudes and behavior as intellectuals vacillate between support for capitalists or workers depending on the issue.

At the opposite extreme, among non-Marxists, one finds the view that intellectual attitudes and behavior have little if anything to do with the social origins or current class position of intellectuals. Caute (1964:17, 19), for example, takes this view when he writes that

the sociological approach to communism, while of cardinal importance in analyzing proletarian or peasant behaviour, is of strictly limited use when applied to intellectu-als. . . . The act of [intellectuals'] political affiliation remains one of personal convic-tion, personal psychology, personal choice.

Mannheim's (1955) classic view of intellectuals as "relatively classless" be-cause of their mobility is a variant of this position.

Bourdieu is sharply critical of the idealized view of the intellectual as a "creator" who transcends the constraints of social location. But if much closer to the Marxist view than that of Caute or Mannheim, Bourdieu none-theless argues that the connection between position in the class structure and political activity is mediated by participation within cultural fields. He criticizes attempts to derive politics directly from class location as "short-circuit" efforts, for they neglect the symbolic dimension of the class strug-gle, which Bourdieu wishes to highlight.[34]

34. In his analysis of cultural fields Bourdieu (1988a:544) criticizes Lucian Goldmann's Marxist-inspired theory of literature for committing the "short-circuit effect" by reducing literary works "directly to the world vision or to the interests of the social group which are supposedly expressed through the artist acting like some sort of medium."

A central issue in the sociology of intellectuals is one of identifying what tilts some intellectuals to the left and others to the right in their political commitments. A variety of explanations for leftist politics among intellectuals have been proposed: ideas (Eisenstadt 1987) and ideology (Marxism), resentment and discontent from the experience of blocked upward social mobility (Schumpeter 1975:152–53), membership in a critical subculture (Hollander 1987), and political resources and communication networks (Brym 1987).[35] Bourdieu's explanation, as we shall see, does not fall neatly into any one of these frameworks.

Bourdieu (1985e) attributes the willingness of many intellectuals to support dominated groups to their own dominated status within the field of power. His theory of the relationship between economic capital and cultural capital suggests a predicting hypothesis: the greater the investment in cultural capital and the greater the incongruity between cultural capital and economic capital, the more likely individuals are to contest the established order.[36] This has certainly been the case in France where since the turn of the century a particularly important political market has developed with a fairly consistent left opposition coalition of organized labor, political parties, and affiliated intellectuals (Debray 1981, Ory 1986, Ross 1991). Intellectuals in France, as is well known, tend to vote left (Bourdieu 1984a: 438).[37] This line of reasoning permits Bourdieu to account for why French school teachers and university professors have been particularly supportive of the French Left. Teachers, he argues, may be more inclined toward political radicalism than other highly educated professionals, especially if they come from working-class or petit-bourgeois origins. Their disparity between economic capital and cultural capital is perhaps greatest, since teachers rarely have the means to match their tastes, and because their meritocratic accomplishments are not sufficient for entry into bourgeois

35. Gagnon (1987) provides a good review of the prevailing theories of intellectuals and their political involvements in liberal democracies.
36. He also suggests that intellectuals with less capital are more inclined to support the status quo, when he writes that "intellectuals are, other things being equal, proportionately more responsive to the seduction of the powers that be, the less well-endowed they are with specific capital" (Bourdieu 1983a:322).
37. This general pattern can be found in most Western European countries as well. Lipset (1991) argues that this may be particularly the case in the United States, where the degree of alienation of intellectuals from dominant institutions and their elites has historically been greater than in Western European countries. Brint (1984, 1991), however, provides evidence showing that whatever political left propensities there may be among highly educated Americans, they hardly approach the significance of an "adversary culture" that neoconservatives fear. Nonetheless, there are important national variations, and Bourdieu's capital asymmetry framework needs empirical testing beyond the French case.

circles, where economic and social capital as well as cultural capital are needed.[38]

With the exception of his study on Heidigger (Bourdieu 1991f), Bourdieu has devoted little attention to those intellectuals who openly embrace right-wing politics. Nevertheless, he has sketched out three types of politically conservative intellectuals with distinct origins (Bourdieu 1992:385–90). First, are those who originate from "dominant positions in the field of power" but who cultivate strategic positions between dominant institutions, their elites, and intellectual institutions. These intellectuals function as critics of both. Bourdieu identifies Raymond Aron and Joseph Schumpeter as representative of this type. Second, are the high ranking civil servants—what Bourdieu calls the "state nobility"—who by virtue of their legitimation through the elite sector of French higher education and the positions they occupy within the state bureaucracy see themselves as neutral technocrats who stand above the particularistic interests of both labor and capital. Third, are what Bourdieu (1987b:60; 1992:40, 110–11), adopting the term from Weber, calls "proletaroide intellectuals." These are first-generation, petty bourgeois intellectuals whose origins are rooted in subordinate forms of economic and cultural capital and who find themselves in subordinate positions within the intellectual field. Put off by the lifestyle of the more privileged cultural heirs, these first-generation intellectuals become a key source of anti-intellectualism.

Bourdieu's capital asymmetry perspective seems to be a useful explanation for why French teachers have traditionally been located on the political left. As an explanation for why intellectuals contest the status quo, it overlaps with the blocked mobility framework but incorporates the idea of intellectuals as investors in cultural markets rather than members in a critical subculture. Although as a general research proposition one might find significant cross-national differences, it merits further exploration. Moreover, it needs to be complemented with consideration of the actual organizational base or communication networks that organize such political propensities (Brym 1987).

Bourdieu enhances our understanding of this structural propensity for

38. Bourdieu (1984a:287–91) writes, "the disparity between economic capital and cultural capital, or, more precisely, the educational capital which in its certified form, is undoubtedly one of the foundations of their propensity to contest a social order which does not fully recognize their merits because it recognizes other principles of classification than those of the educational system which has classified them. This meritocratic (and therefore, in a sense, aristocratic) revolt is intensified when it is combined with the loyalties, refusals and impossibilities, or refusals of the impossible, which are linked to a petit-bourgeois or working-class origin and which, together with purely economic constraints, prevent full membership in the bourgeoisie."

leftwing politics among French intellectuals by emphasizing its ambiguous character. Though he notes that the basis for the alliance can be a "felt and sometimes real solidarity with the dominated classes" (1984a:316), he sees intellectuals' alliance with the working class as a fragile one. The alliance is tenuous because it is based on a *structurally homologous position* of class domination rather than a *common experience* of class subordination, that is, an identity of habitus (Bourdieu 1985e:737, 1987b:174).[39] Intellectual professions of solidarity with disenfranchised groups, therefore, reflect a "sort of structural bad faith" (Bourdieu 1984c).[40]

Bourdieu finds this ambiguity to be particularly striking among those in the lowest positions of the intellectual field, and contends that intellectuals who speak in the name of the "people" or "popular culture" are generally those who are in the lowest positions (1987b:179–80). One finds them among first-generation intellectuals who have relatively less cultural capital than their peers and who are put off by some aspects of the intellectual lifestyle (181). They are in a sense doubly dominated; they hold subordinate positions within the dominated fraction of the dominant class. Bourdieu suggests that these "proletaroide intellectuals" (60) tend to play a very dangerous anti-institutional and violent role in social movements. His concern appears to be less that they "turn towards reformist or revolutionary movements," than that they "frequently . . . import into them a form of anti-intellectualism" (1988b:178).[41] Examples can be found in the excellent study by Jeannine Verdès-Leroux (1981) of the French Communist Party. She finds that first-generation entrants to the intellectual world from modest origins made up most of the intellectuals of the party at the time of Maurice Thorez.[42] Intellectuals affiliated with the French Communist Party

39. Bourdieu (1984a:372) is dismissive of efforts by left-leaning social scientists who try to identify with the working-class condition through participant observation.

40. Bourdieu (1991d:32–33) cites Tom Wolfe's controversial *Radical Chic* as illustrative of the precarious and disingenuous quality of alliance by intellectuals with disadvantaged groups in the American context.

41. Bourdieu is particularly severe in his criticism of intellectuals who express anti-intellectual sentiments. This reflects his criticism of attempts to portray and celebrate selected forms of popular culture as autonomous from contamination by dominant intellectual culture.

42. More recently Bourdieu (1991d:33) has characterized the "intellectuels proletaroides" as those who identify with the political cause of dominanted groups and attempt to subvert the established order, not only in terms of their structurally homologous position of domination, *but also* in terms of "an identity or a least a similarity of condition." Here we observe a shift and tension in his thinking about the politics of this type of intellectual. These intellectuals appear to share *both* a similar condition and position with dominated groups. In earlier analyses he seemed to be saying that political alliance with the working class was precarious precisely because the common link was limited to an homology of position but *not* a shared condition. Now he seems to be pointing to a group of intellectuals he feels does indeed share a common condition as well as position. But this shared habitus is no assurance for Bourdieu

have a long history of subordinating intellectual production to party approval.

Bourdieu is also critical of the propensity of intellectuals to usurp broader collective interests for the sake of their own vested interests in cultural and political markets. He suggests that the origins of their opposition politics lie more in their own fields of competition for political and intellectual recognition than in the broader interests of groups they represent.[43] For Bourdieu, the false political consciousness of intellectuals lies in their tendency to conflate uncritically their own field interests with the broader collective interests of those they represent. Bourdieu (1985a) has devoted particular attention to the dynamics of symbolic "delegation" in which the interests of a collectivity are refracted through the field interests of their intellectual leaders.

One might question, however, whether all intellectual behavior that purports to entail some form of solidarity with outside groups reduces to one of posturing in competitive fields? Might it not be shaped in distinct ways by the particular demands imposed by the types of groups intellectuals attempt to represent? Do capitalists and labor impose similar demands and constraints on the intellectuals they call upon to represent them? Bourdieu's emphasis on the determining influence of intellectual fields tends to give short shrift to differences in intellectuals' behavior that may derive from the character of the groups they represent.

Another reason why Bourdieu considers that the homology of class positions that generates alliances between intellectuals and the working class proves fragile is because the intellectual habitus of aristocratic asceticism, which rejects bourgeois materialism, spurns "popular materialism" as well. The struggle against economic capital in the name of cultural capital renders political strategies focused on bread-and-butter issues difficult for intellectuals to embrace fully. It is the intellectual's investment in idealism, spiritualism, intellectualism, or cultural pursuits, that makes it difficult for him or her to support any political strategy that is fundamentally concerned with making money.[44] Thus cultural capital and the fundamental mental dispositions that accompany its accumulation appear to militate against in-

---

of the kinds of political engagements he would like to see intellectuals undertake. Indeed, it provides further evidence of Bourdieu's deep pessimism regarding the possibility of intellectuals playing any genuine progressive political role outside of their own intellectual fields.

43. Bourdieu's idea that intellectuals pursue their own interests is not of course new. Schumpeter (1975:154) noted that intellectuals can develop interests relative to career and standing that may clash with those of groups they represent.

44. Intellectuals, Bourdieu (1984a:316) writes, "are obliged to recognize the supreme affirmation of their spiritual point of honour in the negation of popular materialism implied in the artistic negation of 'bourgeois' materialism."

terclass alliance between high-status cultural producers and economically subordinate groups.

Bourdieu further argues that the propensity among cultural producers to contest the established order grows out of their efforts to substitute cultural markets for control of economic markets rather than out of a desire to seek genuine policies of equality of cultural opportunity. This helps Bourdieu (1987b:61, 62) explain why some French intellectuals could have progressive politics in general but be very conservative when it comes to university or cultural policies. They can both support nationalization of large private firms yet resist efforts to modernize the traditional humanities curriculum. Thus, Bourdieu argues, the politics of intellectuals bear the mark of the conflict between cultural capital and economic capital. The scope of their political commitment is limited to one of increased market share in the struggle for power. As such, it tends to reproduce the very social order that the intellectual's vision for advancing the ideals of culture pretends to contest.

Finally, Bourdieu points to changes in the conditions of intellectual production as a source of ambiguity in political attitudes and behaviors among highly educated workers. He notes a significant decline in the numbers of French intellectuals working as self-employed artisans or entrepreneurs and their increasing integration as salaried employees within large bureaucratic organizations where they no longer claim full control over the means of their intellectual production (Bourdieu 1984a). His analyses echo the familiar theme of "intellectual proletarianization." This shift in the conditions of intellectual production, Bourdieu argues, tends to generate contradictory attitudes among large numbers of cultural producers toward this new relationship to the means of intellectual production. On the one hand, Bourdieu sees this change as increasing the chances of protest against the status quo. These "new cultural intermediaries" are likely to support criticism and challenges to established cultural and social hierarchies because they themselves occupy dominated positions as salaried employees in their work settings. On the other hand, he feels that this transformation tends "to encourage the emergence of intellectual producers more directly subordinated to economic and political demands" (152). Bourdieu sees in the emergence of private corporate and public administrative demand for applied social research the creation of a "new kind of cultural producer" whose intellectual agenda and style are increasingly set by market and bureaucratic priorities. These new wage earners of research, he charges, become more attentive to the norms of "bureaucratic reliability" than act as guardians of the "critical detachment from authority" afforded by the relative autonomy of the university. Moreover, their intellectual products bear the imprint of the "standardized norms of mass production" rather than those of the book or scientific article or the charismatic quality traditionally attached to the independent intellectual (Bourdieu 1988b:123–25, 1989c:484). It is this ambiguous location in the field of power that, according to Bourdieu (Bourdieu and Boltanski 1977), "underpins the ambiguity of the consciousness and political practice, hesitating between 'participation' and 'revolt'" that he finds among salaried intellectuals.[45]

PROFESSORS, POLITICS, AND MAY 1968

In order to illustrate Bourdieu's central thesis that cultural fields mediate the political attitudes and behavior of intellectuals, we turn to *Homo Academicus* (Bourdieu 1988b), his most detailed research into the institutional basis of intellectuals' politics. This study offers a field analysis of political divisions among Parisian university professors in May 1968.[46] *Homo Academicus* demonstrates how the structural differentiation Bourdieu finds within the field of power also internally differentiates the French academic intelligentsia. This work offers a multi-leveled analysis of how the fundamental cultural capital/economic capital opposition is refracted within French academe. Further, Bourdieu argues that the interests of these intellectuals are not simply class based; indeed their most immediate and determining interests may not be class interests at all—so he claims—but those of the academic field itself. Indeed, he advances the fundamental claim that

45. Bourdieu's analysis of the sources of ambiguity in intellectual politics suggests a superficial resemblance to Wright's (1985) theory of contradictory class locations. Both paint a more complex picture of the relationship of intellectuals to social classes than can be found in most earlier Marxist analyses. There are, however, fundamental differences. Whereas Wright thinks of social-class location in terms of position within the social relations of production, Bourdieu thinks of it in terms of market location. Further, Wright's view of intellectuals is rather monocausal. Current class position, albeit a contradictory one, accounts exclusively for political orientation. Non-class-influences are ignored. For Bourdieu, however, positions in relatively autonomous cultural fields can be the source of political orientation. And there can be a broad range of cultural fields differing in types of capital, size, and importance where intellectuals invest their cultural resources. This permits Bourdieu to explore a greater range of cultural and structural conditions potentially able to shape the political conduct of intellectuals.

46. The work is based on two groups of tenured professors in Parisian institutions of higher learning during the late 1960s. First, a stratified random sample of 405 tenured faculty members was drawn from the schools of medicine, law, arts and social sciences, and natural sciences. Second, the population of all 170 tenured faculty members comprising the principal institutions of higher learning in the arts and social sciences was selected. An impressive body of information from the public record was gathered on social and educational background, faculty and administrative positions held, participation in various government commissions, honorific titles and positions, and forms of political participation, such as signing political petitions (see Bourdieu 1988b:39–40, 227–42, 271).

it is not, as is usually thought, political stances which determine people's stances on things academic, but their position in the academic field which inform the stances that they adopt on political issues in general as well as on academic problems. (xvii–xviii)

This claim might suggest that Bourdieu in fact substitutes a field reductionism for a class reductionism in explaining political attitudes and behavior. Certainly the strong emphasis he gives in *Homo Academicus* to the effects of field position on academic politics suggests this. Yet, in his (1991d:7) analysis of the literary field he seems to guard against this kind of field position reductionism. There he suggests that stances are mediated more by strategies than by positions alone, since strategies of differentiation can take on their own autonomy. The exact relationship of strategies to positions and their constitutive capital configurations, however, needs conceptual clarification. It appears to vary by type of field.

Using correspondence analysis on a variety of measures of economic, social, and cultural capital, and of political and economic power, Bourdieu (1988b) shows that French higher education institutions, faculties, disciplines, and professors are all differentiated along the axes of the economic capital/cultural capital opposition that characterizes the field of power. The social profile of teachers and students varies by type of school. The law and medical faculties are situated closer to the pole of economic and political power whereas the natural and social science and arts faculties stand closer to the pole of cultural power. The analysis reveals two different relationships among faculty to the dominant class: knowledge for service to economic and political power and knowledge for its own sake.

Among the arts and social science faculties a similar opposition distributes institutions, disciplines, and professors in terms of two different kinds of power. First, there is *academic power*, which refers to the degree of control over the organizational mechanisms for teacher training, selection, promotions, and careers in the French university.[47] In addition, there are *scientific power* and *intellectual renown:* the former indicates degree of control over research resources and prestige within the scientific community; the latter refers to recognition by the broader educated public for published work. Professors, therefore, are differentiated in terms of the cultural markets where they make their principal investments. Professors who accumulate academic power are found disproportionately at the Sorbonne. They also tend to be located in the traditional disciplines of philosophy, French litera-

47. The concept is similar in meaning to Collins's (1979) concept of "positional property" which indicates a degree of control over the flow of valued resources in an organization by virtue of a position held in that organization.

ture, and the classics. Within this sector of the French academy, the struggle for institutional positions and symbolic capital pertain largely to the consecration, conservation, and transmission of legitimate culture and to the reproduction of the institution that performs these cultural functions. Professors struggle for academic power by accumulating capital in the form of administrative and honorific positions within the academy. They deliver lectures, publish textbooks, and compile dictionaries and encyclopedias, activities which are valued primarily within the academic market (Bourdieu 1988b:98). Here is where *homo academicus* resides—the teacher who specializes in the classification of existing types of knowledge and who consecrates certain forms as legitimate for transmission to future generations. The ideal-typical route to academic power begins with graduation from the Ecole Normale and continues by an assistant professorship, completion of the state doctoral thesis, and promotion to a chair at the Sorbonne (87).

In contrast, professors who accumulate intellectual or scientific capital tend to be found at the Collège de France, the Ecole des Hautes Etudes en Sciences Sociales, and in newer social-scientific disciplines, such as linguistics and sociology.[48] These individuals invest in the intellectual and scientific fields, where they attempt to accumulate symbolic capital in the form of recognition by peers for their contribution to scientific knowledge, or in the form of prestige and influence among the broader educated public. If the production of knowledge in the academic field is largely intended for classroom consumption, in the scientific field, knowledge production occurs in laboratory and research centers and is destined largely for peer review in specialized publications. In the intellectual field, knowledge production is destined to influence the opinions of the broader educated public opinion—and especially the media—as well as for peer review in specialized publications. While some French professors are more oriented toward the intellectual field and others more oriented to the scientific field, both stand in opposition to *homo academicus*, who invests primarily in the reproduction of the educational institution.

Bourdieu also finds that a power struggle *within* each faculty pits those professors more oriented toward the accumulation of academic power against those more oriented toward the accumulation of intellectual or scientific capital. In short, Bourdieu's field analysis of the French academy locates the familiar tension between teaching and research within a broader institutional framework of power relations between opposing

---

48. Today Bourdieu is himself at the Collège of France, but when the data were gathered in the late 1960s and early '70s he was at the Ecole Pratique des Hautes Etudes (renamed in 1975 the L'Ecole des Hautes Etudes en Sciences Sociales).

groups.[49] It also can be viewed as Bourdieu's version of the familiar position/expertise opposition that constitutes two distinct claims to authority in bureaucratic organizations.[50] According to Bourdieu, the struggle for power in the French academe pits those with positional power in terms of control over allocation of valued organizational resources against those who base their claims to power on new and valued forms of knowledge.[51]

Another line of internal differentiation is age; it opposes younger against older professors who have had more time to accumulate various forms of academic, scientific, and intellectual power. At a third level, Bourdieu distinguishes those research-oriented professors who are highly specialized within particular disciplines from those who have considerable academic power but who also enjoy considerable intellectual renown. This source of differentiation opposes a small group of university "mandarins" who have accumulated considerable intellectual and scientific capital as well as academic capital against those specialists in circumscribed bodies of knowledge whose authority derives more from peer review internal to the area of specialization than from either institutional position or public notoriety (Bourdieu 1988b:81). The alumni status of a *normalien* is decisive in the accumulation of academic power and particularly in achieving mandarin status. Bourdieu (87) writes that

. . . the social capital represented by *Ecole Normale* connections when they are duly maintained by sustained exchange, is one of the sole bases of transdisciplinary solidarity; which explains why it plays a decisive role every time that someone has to obtain and hold positions of university power which are situated beyond the little local fiefs, limited to the scale of a disciple, and even positions of prestige such as those offered by the Collège de France. . . . the fact of being a *normalien* exercises a multiplier effect on all the social powers held.

This opposition pits the university establishment mandarins against the specialists. Thus one finds a few professors at the Sorbonne who have considerable intellectual renown and who also dominate an entire discipline

49. Bourdieu's analysis resonates with the Gouldner's (1957) classic ideal-types of "locals" and "cosmopolitans." But Bourdieu (1988b:13) rejects Gouldner's types as "semi-scientific" because he contends that Gouldner's ideal-types focus on familiar professorial types in the university rather than directing attention to the underlying matrix of institutional arrangements that make these types possible.

50. Critics (e.g., Gouldner 1954:22–23, and Parsons 1947:58–60) have long noted that these two forms of bureaucratic authority were conflated in Weber's analysis of bureaucracy but have since been distinguished and much researched.

51. A version of this fundamental opposition characterizes Szelenyi and Martins' (1988/89) analysis of the recent struggle for power in Eastern Europe and the former Soviet Union.

and control access to teaching and research positions in it. At the opposite pole one finds specialists in disciplines marginal to the traditional French university curriculum, such as economics and social psychology (109).[52]

In terms of their social origins and habitus, Bourdieu finds that Parisian university professors distribute unevenly across this segmented university map. Bourdieu writes that

the professors of the different faculties are distributed between the pole of economic and political power and the pole of cultural prestige according to the same principles as the different fractions of the dominant classes. (38)

Professors from the economically rich fractions of the dominant class tend to be located more frequently in the law and medical faculties than in the science and humanities faculties. Those professors who have relatively more scientific capital or intellectual renown also tend to come from higher social origins, notably Parisian bourgeois origins (79). The security of inherited privilege gives them the confidence and freedom to choose more risky cultural investments in scientific research or in those least institutionalized cultural sectors (108–9).

In contrast, Bourdieu finds that those professors with positional property in academe but with little symbolic capital in either the scientific or intellectual fields tend to come from the lower middle class. In particular, they tend to recruit from families of primary school teachers, and to a lesser extent from secondary or higher education teachers, particularly from the provinces (78–79, 83–84). Here is the heart of the "cultural aristocracy," those of modest social origins whose families have invested intergenerationally in education. It is to the educational system that they owe their upward social mobility and their ideological allegiance. These are the secular "oblates" who, like their religious counterparts, are

inclined to think that without the [school] there is no salvation—especially when they become the high priests of an institution of cultural reproduction which, in

52. Despite his position at the Collège de France, Bourdieu does not consider himself a "mandarin," as he is sometimes labeled. In the French universities, his influence on appointments in sociology has never been equal to that of Raymond Boudon. At the Ecole des Hautes Etudes en Sciences Sociales, his struggles—often unsuccessful—with Alain Touraine and the *Annales* block of historians over resources and appointments are legendary. Entry to the Collège de France brought him considerable symbolic capital, but also isolated him from any significant positional power within the universities or the Ecole des Hautes Etudes en Sciences Sociales. As was discussed in chapter 1, Bourdieu thinks of himself as an "outsider" to the world of academic power. He sees himself as a scientific specialist.

consecrating them, consecrates their active and above all passive ignorance of any other cultural world.

Their "deserving, but miraculously lucky" election into the academic elite and their exclusion from the nonuniversity world of privilege creates a "curious mixture of arrogance and inadequacy." As a consequence, it is among these "survivors" that one finds the staunchest unwavering support for the academic meritocracy and defense of the academic establishment against all outside intrusion.[53]

Bourdieu's field analysis reveals that stances taken by Paris university professors with regard to the May 1968 student movement correspond almost exactly to their positions along the axes of intellectual, symbolic, economic, and political power that differentiate the French university system (125–27).[54] Professors investing almost entirely within the academic market by devoting their energies primarily to teaching were most hostile to the student movement, since the call for fundamental reforms threatened to devalue their valued currencies. But those whose investments included broader markets of cultural production, or who concentrated on scientific research, reacted more favorably.

Professors within the law and medical faculties who were much more closely associated with the economic pole of power tended to oppose the student movement whereas many professors within the arts and science faculties openly embraced the movement. Within the medical faculty, Bourdieu (61) finds that medical researchers tended to be situated to the political left whereas clinical practitioners, and especially surgeons, tended to be situated to the political right; these political dispositions were manifested during the May events. More generally, Bourdieu finds that if one factors out those professors who were already political activists, professors in the natural sciences tended to situate themselves more to the political left than did those in the arts and social sciences. His analyses seem to suggest that professors whose distance from the economic pole of the field of power is greatest, who do scientific research or who invent new forms of knowledge, are more inclined to question the status quo than are those

53. Bourdieu writes that the survivors "offer to the academic institution which they have chosen because it chose them, and vice versa, a support which, being so totally conditioned, has something total, absolute, unconditional about it" (100–101).

54. He observes (xvii) that "there is an almost perfect homology between the space of the stances . . . and the space of the positions held by their authors in the field of production . . . [and that] . . . the distribution in the academic field . . . corresponds very closely to the distribution in terms of political positions or trade-union affiliations and even stances adopted during the events of May 1968."

who preserve and transmit the cultural heritage of a social order. As we shall see in the next chapter, this political orientation corresponds to Bourdieu's vision for the scientific intellectual in modern society.

Bourdieu's criticism of both the intellectual and political attitudes and behavior of his fellow intellectuals is severe. Still, his criticism is accompanied by a vision for the intellectual vocation—one that suggests that social scientists can practice a self-critical and progressive politics. We turn in the next chapter to an examination of Bourdieu's vision for the social scientist in the modern social order.

10 THE SCIENTIFIC INTELLECTUAL AND POLITICS

In France, the questions of who is an intellectual and what intellectuals should do have evoked keen interest and intense debate (Ory and Sirinelli 1986). Bourdieu's field analytic perspective proves useful in capturing the dynamics and scope of that experience. As was noted in chapter 9, Bourdieu is critical of universal definitions of intellectuals, since he sees the very idea of modern intellectuals as being historically contingent—that is, inseparably tied to the historical development of relatively autonomous cultural fields. His field analytical perspective stresses that all definitions of intellectuals are at once historical and fundamentally political, emerging as they do from struggles among symbolic producers for legitimation. Yet, despite his admonition that the task of the sociologist is to analyze fields of struggle rather than take up positions within them—including the field of struggle over who is an intellectual—Bourdieu also works with a *normative* definition of the intellectual vocation.[1] This points to a paradox and

---

1. In assessing the contribution of *Homo Academicus*, Loïc J. D. Wacquant says that Bourdieu's analysis "discloses the *totality of the game* that engenders both the specific interests of intellectuals and the one-sided vision that each participant has of the interests to others" (Bourdieu and Wacquant 1989:679). This stretch for inclusivity in analyzing actors within the academic field is not incompatible with my claim that a strong normative dimension underlies Bourdieu's work. Value orientation and objectivity are not mutually exclusive, especially when a study is done reflexively. It is possible to offer a reasonably objective field analysis of existing intellectual positions and still hold a normative commitment to a particular one. It is clear in *Homo Academicus* that Bourdieu does not attach the same values to each of the positions he describes in the academic field. Clearly, he is more favorably predisposed to the researcher

unresolved tension in Bourdieu's thought, one that reflects his position as a politically committed social scientist in postwar France.[2]

In this chapter I examine the normative dimension of Bourdieu's thinking about social scientists as intellectuals. What key underlying values inform Bourdieu's understanding of their intellectual vocation? What values should intellectuals defend and how should they relate to politics? I will address these questions by asking how Bourdieu conceptualizes sociology as a science and with what consequences. I will then examine what Bourdieu believes should be the role of the social sciences and the social scientist in the modern world; how the intellectual vocation and the political vocation combine. The chapter concludes with a brief look at Bourdieu's own political engagements.

Between Politics and the Ivory Tower

The classic dilemma faced by all modern intellectuals is whether they should participate "in political and social movements or whether they should refrain from doing so and be responsible only for what they write" (Huszar 1960:214). One finds a variety of responses to this question ranging between two opposing extremes: (1) the "classic" position articulated by Julien Benda (1927) that the "clerks" should not betray their vocation to timeless and transcendent truths by taking up the cause of historically limited projects and politically contingent truths;[3] and (2) the Sartrean image of the "total intellectual" who takes a public stance on all the salient issues of the day. Both extremes, Bourdieu (1989a:102) argues, express a fundamental and invariable property of all intellectual life, namely, the *will to autonomy*. Depending on historical circumstances, this thrust for intellectual freedom finds expression in either retreat from outside involvements that threaten its autonomy or in other outside engagements to enlarge it. It is this desire for intellectual freedom, that Bourdieu wants above all to foster.

Thus, Bourdieu is a staunch defender of intellectual freedom. Critical inquiry is a historically achieved value that can be preserved and enhanced only by struggling to free intellectual life from all economic and political

---

who accumulates intellectual capital through published research than he is to the professor who accumulates and transmits scholastic capital simply by teaching. While I would agree with Wacquant that the analysis of *Homo Academicus* is not fundamentally distorted by partisanship, Bourdieu's value orientation is nonetheless visible.

2. Pels (1995) captures well this normative dimension of Bourdieu's thinking about intellectuals.

3. Benda reversed his position in later years by embracing a more politically engaged role for intellectuals.

constraints. In the contemporary period, as we shall see, Bourdieu finds its highest expression in science. Yet he also believes that it is only by freeing the practice of science from all political contamination that one can hope to achieve a politically effective practice of science. This strategy, he believes, indicates a way of transcending the classic opposition between "pure culture and engagement" (99). Yet, this same strategy poses a key problem for Bourdieu: since he also stresses the interested and political character of scientific practices, how can he hope to intervene in politics in a disinterested way as a social scientist?[4]

As was discussed in chapter 9, Bourdieu sees modern intellectuals as a distinct historical type of symbolic producers that emerged in the late nineteenth and early twentieth centuries. Emile Zola represents the best historical embodiment of Bourdieu's ideal intellectuals who enter politics "with authority rooted in the autonomy of their disciplines" (Bourdieu 1989a:101, 1992:185–89, 461–72). Intellectuals are to be "bi-dimensional" in character, as they must meet two necessary conditions: (1) "they must belong to an intellectually autonomous field, one independent of religious, political, economic or other power, and they must respect that field's particular laws"; and (2) "they must deploy their specific expertise and authority in their particular intellectual domain in a political activity outside of it" (Bourdieu 1989a:99, 103). To grasp how he sees this paradoxical claim for both intellectual detachment and public involvement to be possible, we must turn to his understanding of science for the answer.

Vive la Science

Though the autonomy of science has come under sharp attack since Kuhn's widely influential work *The Structure of Scientific Revolutions* (1962) and the development of a strong critical tradition in the sociology of science (Bloor 1976; Latour and Woolgar 1979; Woolgar 1988), Bourdieu readily embraces science as the model for sociology. Indeed, he casts his strategy to transcend all forms of the subjectivism/objectivism antinomy in the language of "true scientific theory and practice" (Bourdieu 1988g:782). His sharp criticism of prevailing sociological practices and his call for a reflexive practice of sociology are all made in the name of a "genuine scientific field"

4. Bourdieu's article "The Corporatism of the Universal" (1989a) provides his most comprehensive statement of how the social scientist should relate to politics. I draw principally but not exclusively on the central themes in this paper for the discussion that follows. Other key references that show Bourdieu's thinking on the role of the social scientist in politics include Bourdieu 1975b, 1981, 1986c, 1987e, 1988b, 1988c, 1988e, 1988g, 1989a, 1989b, 1990d, 1990g, 1991; Bourdieu, Casanova, and Simon 1975.

(Bourdieu and Wacquant 1992:176). Even his (1975b) piercing criticism of science as an intellectual field, with interests, conflicts, and hierarchies analogous to other cultural fields, distinguishes between a "false" or "official" science and a "genuine" science.[5] References to "objectivity" and "laws" abound in his work.

This is not a new turn for Bourdieu. His early methodological work *The Craft of Sociology* [1968] (Bourdieu, Chamboredon, and Passeron 1991) stresses the need to lay a firm epistemological foundation for a *scientific* practice of sociology. Yet, Bourdieu has less to say about the exact nature of science than he has about its social effects. Just as he is less interested in proposing a theory of culture than a theory of the social uses of culture, so also he seems less interested in proposing a theory of science than of the social effects of science. Nevertheless, there is ambiguity in how he actually conceptualizes science. Moreover, how he conceptualizes science corresponds to the kind of political practice he envisages for critical social scientists.

On the one hand, he continues the Durkheimian legacy of positing continuity between natural science and social science. Indeed *The Craft of Sociology* (20) strongly echoes the theme that "sociology is a science like others" in order to differentiate it from commonsense reasoning and speculative social theory. On the other hand, Bourdieu is a sharp critic of empiricism and positivism. As I observed in chapter 2, he draws on Bachelard to stress the historical, constructionist, and agonistic character of scientific reason. Science is empirical but not positivist. Like Bachelard, Bourdieu argues that evidence is not simply there waiting to be discovered. Social-scientific knowledge is consciously constructed against taken-for-granted knowledge of the social world (Bourdieu and Wacquant 1992:235). For Bourdieu, science progresses from new critical insights into the taken-for-granted world of power relations rather than by an accumulation of facts.

Moreover, Bourdieu (1975b; Bourdieu and Wacquant 1992:176) contends that science is a field of struggle for intellectual legitimation. He in fact subscribes to a competition model for scientific innovation.[6] In the "agonistic logic of science" the struggle among competing field interests

5. His (1990a:299) critical guns thunder even louder, however, against those critics of science (e.g., Bloor, Latour, and Woolgar) who he believes completely relativize scientific knowledge by reducing it to politics.

6. He posits that "scientific reason realizes itself when it becomes inscribed not in the ethical norms of a practical reason or in the technical rules of a scientific methodology, but in the apparently anarchical social mechanisms of competition between strategies armed with instruments of action and of thought capable of regulating their own uses, and in the durable dispositions that the functioning of this field produces and presupposes" (Bourdieu and Wacquant 1992:189).

for scientific recognition turns self-interested pursuit into the development of new scientific knowledge. Bourdieu (1989b:384) is sharply critical of consensual views of science, as he envisions a "space of regulated confrontation" rather than consensus as the key condition for scientific innovation.[7] Preferring what he calls a *"working dissensus . . .* [of] critical acknowledgment of compatibilities and incompatibilities" (1989b:384, 1995:10), he writes that "a genuine scientific field is a space where researchers agree on the grounds of disagreement and on the instruments with which to resolve these disagreements and on nothing else" (Bourdieu and Wacquant 1992: 176).[8]

Furthermore, the emphasis Bourdieu gives to symbolic power and violence strongly suggests that the study of "social" facts is quite different from the study of "natural" facts. Sociological knowledge is fundamentally historical and political rather than natural. Theoretical propositions originate from the position of the researcher in the intellectual field as well as from the conceptual boundaries of the intellectual discipline. Bourdieu (1975b) admits that social science can never reach the degree of autonomy from external forces that natural science obtains.[9] Yet, the natural-science model remains present in his thinking. We see Bourdieu synthesizing and attempting to transcend two quite opposing views of sociology: the empiricist/positivist and the constructionist. This reveals a tension in his thought, for it is not clear just how Bourdieu relates these two quite different concepts of social science.

This tension reflects Bourdieu's paradoxical posture towards the Western Enlightenment tradition of rationality more generally. Bourdieu main-

7. Though Merton (1973) also points out the importance of competition in the world of science, Bourdieu criticizes Merton's emphasis on the normative structure that governs scientific practice. According to Bourdieu (1990a:298), Merton is insufficiently critical of the official norms espoused by scientists themselves. Bourdieu (1975b) sees the scientific field as a market rather than a moral community where various so-called normative stances are viewed as strategies for struggle within the scientific field. For Bourdieu (1990a:300), it is the material and symbolic reward structures, not the normative ideals, that more decisively shape scientific behavior.

Bourdieu nonetheless speaks of the "regulated competition" that is institutionalized in the autonomous practice of science so that certain forms of struggle (physical violence, the use of nonscientific methods) are not permitted. Thus, in spite of his criticism of Merton, Bourdieu's intellectual market perspective rejoins Merton's analysis at another level.

8. A couple of pages later he concludes his criticism of a consensual view of science with the following declaration: "If nothing else, let us at least have conflicts!"

9. In his article "The Specificity of the Scientific Field," Bourdieu (1975b) argues that the social sciences can never achieve the degree of autonomy that natural sciences like biology and physics enjoy because "internal struggle for scientific authority" in the social sciences is connected to "external struggles" between social classes in the political field "for the power to produce, to impose, and to inculcate the legitimate representation of the social world."

tains there are *both* historical and universal qualities in Enlightenment rationality.[10] On the one hand, he affirms a radically historicized view of scientific reason by arguing against the idea that "reason lies in the structure of the mind or of language [rather than] in certain types of historical conditions, in certain social structures of dialogue and nonviolent communication" (Bourdieu and Wacquant 1992:189). He resists identifying this transcendent possibility as a universal property rooted in mind or language.[11] Contrasting his view to that of Habermas (1970, 1979), Bourdieu writes that "reason itself has a history: it is not Godgiven, already inscribed in our thinking or language" (Bourdieu and Wacquant 1992:189). Rather than positing certain transhistorical, universal communicative structures, Bourdieu joins with deconstructionists like Derrida in affirming the historically contingent and relative character of the most fundamental scientific categories.

On the other hand, he embraces the Enlightenment tradition by contending that, even if reason is historical, it also has a capacity to produce forms of knowledge that transcend its own historical limitations. Bourdieu speaks of the "universal" value of a mode of understanding, discovery, and communication which he calls science. This mode of discourse follows certain rules of evidence and logic that permit a collective body to discern the better demonstration without prejudicing the process by including power factors relative to ownership, politics, and status. The practice of scientific reason, therefore, makes possible a valued mode of communication that Bourdieu believes is less available in other types of cultural practices.[12] In this respect, it is *normative*. But rather than being intrinsic to mind or language, reason is viewed as a "field property" that emerges as the universe of cultural practices gradually gains some autonomy from competing forms of economic, political, or religious power. In short, Bourdieu's sense of the transcendental character of scientific reason is an emergent historical one.

One can understand Bourdieu's thinking here as a positioning strategy that gives him critical leverage against Foucault and deconstructionists like Derrida at one extreme and Habermas at the other. Vis-à-vis the poststructuralists, Bourdieu affirms the method and norms of the Enlightenment tradition of rationality. He sees this tradition as offering a form

10. Bourdieu thus differs sharply from Foucault, who is a major critic of the Enlightenment tradition.

11. This also separates Bourdieu from Chomsky's (1965) view of innate language/knowledge capacities.

12. In its ideal form, scientific communication differs from political communication in that the importance that science assigns to arguments, problems, and solutions is based solely on scientific criteria, that is, "how well propositions and procedures conform to the rules of logical coherence and compatibility with observational evidence" (Bourdieu 1989b:376).

of knowledge that is self-referential and capable of some degree of self-transcendence. He eschews radical relativist views (e.g., Feyerabend 1978) that depict science as simply some alternative form of knowledge on a par with religion, magic, etc. Vis-à-vis Habermas, however, Bourdieu associates the claim for a transcendental reason with an interested position within the intellectual field. But it is also a type of interest that Bourdieu wants to institutionalize and develop. To distinguish his position from that of Habermas, Bourdieu (1989a:104) proposes, not a "universal pragmatics," but a *politics of the universal, a Realpolitik* of Reason [to promote] socially instituted forms of communication favoring the production of the universal."[13] Bourdieu wants to institutionalize this ideal mode of scientific communication where "competition . . . is organized in such a manner that no one can succeed over anyone else, except by means of better *arguments, reasonings* and *demonstrations,* thereby advancing reason and truth."[14]

In sum, rather than positing a universal reason or a rational subject like the Cartesian *cogito,* Bourdieu suggests that there is developing a historical possibility of something like a universal reason or a rational subject, that this would be a desirable event, and that every effort must be made to encourage its development. In place of the idea of a freely choosing subject embodied in human nature, Bourdieu thinks of human rationality as a historical possibility that is not innate but must be conquered bit by bit in an unending struggle against the world of social determinations. Bourdieu's position, therefore, is paradoxical: he affirms both a historicized view of reason and a normative, universalizing one.[15]

There also is a *moral/ethical* dimension to Bourdieu's understanding of science and the role that social science is to play in the modern world. Bourdieu embraces the Enlightenment belief that increasing rational

13. The difference on this point between Bourdieu and Habermas is perhaps one of emphasis. While Habermas presents his ideal in formal terms, Bourdieu (1989a) stresses the sociological conditions most likely to foster this idealized type of human communication.

14. There is striking similarity between Bourdieu's view of scientific communication and Gouldner's (1985:30) "culture of critical discourse (CCD)." Gouldner defines CCD as "any assertion—about anything, by anyone—[that] is open to criticism and that, if challenged no assertion can be defended by invoking someone's authority. It forbids a reference to a speaker's position in society (or reliance upon his personal character) in order to justify or refute his claims. The CCD is the special ideology of intellectuals and intelligentsia, and it is essentially an ideology about how discourse should be conducted."

Both Gouldner and Bourdieu suggest a mode of rational discourse that is critical, self-reflective, and inattentive to social distinctions among speakers. A principal difference is that, whereas Gouldner sees CCD as formative of a New Class among the highly educated, Bourdieu sees scientific rationalism as confined to a more limited professional arena.

15. He admits that "the universal subject is a historical achievement that is never completed once and for all. It is through historical struggles in historical spaces of forces that we progress toward a little more universality" (Bourdieu and Wacquant 1992:190).

awareness of social life enhances possibilities for human freedom.[16] Bourdieu believes that by increasing conscious awareness over the conditions that determine ones behavior, one is able to gain, not only satisfaction from pushing back the boundaries of the unknown, but also a margin of maneuverability whereby one can more clearly discern what is possible and what is not possible to change (Bourdieu and Wacquant 1992:198–99). By exposing the arbitrary character of the principles by which we unwittingly construct social life, we gain some measure of possibly shaping sociology, the university, society, and ultimately ourselves in ways that permit a greater space for human freedom.[17] In short, there is in Bourdieu a vision of personal emancipation from the grips of misrecognized forms of social domination.

Yet, the margin of freedom for alternative constructions seems very small indeed. The bulk of his work points to the ongoing reproduction of relations of domination. Perhaps it is Bourdieu's sharp reaction to the ideology of individualism and subjectivity of the intellectual world that leads him to be exceedingly cautious in talking about the liberating potential of sociology.

Bourdieu's general conception of science is shaped by the French historical context wherein a broadly positivist philosophy of science and French republicanism found mutual reinforcement. Beginning in the late nineteenth century, to be scientific meant breaking with a purely literary approach to intellectual work by employing systematic methods of empirical investigation. It also meant believing in a general unity underlying the various sciences, and holding the conviction that the advance of democracy depended on the progress of science (Ringer 1992:207–25). The French scientific tradition that emerged in the late nineteenth century, and of which Bourdieu is an intellectual heir, stood sharply opposed to the humanistic and generalistic notion of belles lettres. It was also profoundly anticlerical in that it reflected a profound suspicion of all forms of authority not rooted in positive knowledge. It expressed the need to find a secular replacement for the moral authority once represented by the Catholic Church. This view of science certainly animated Durkheim, and it shapes Bourdieu's thinking as well. Thus, it is not surprising to find in Bourdieu normative elements that associate science with freedom, equality, and the

16. He writes (1990c:183) that "knowledge by itself exercises an effect—one which appears to me to be liberating—every time the mechanisms whose laws of operation it establishes owe part of their effectiveness to misrecognition." As Wacquant (Bourdieu and Wacquant 1992:194) points out, Bourdieu embraces the "modernist project of the *Aufklärung*."

17. This can be seen in Bourdieu's conception of sociological research as socioanalysis, where sociology reveals the social unconscious of our practices.

belief that the practice of science can enhance the chances for human emancipation.

For Intellectual Autonomy: Members of the Scholarly Guild Unite!

Bourdieu contends that intellectual freedom for rational inquiry is a historical and collective value whose defense should be the first concern of all intellectuals. He declares: "Yes, I am a resolute, stubborn, absolutist advocate of scientific autonomy . . . [and] . . . the sociologist has no mandate, no mission, other than that which he or she assigns herself by virtue of the logic of her research" (Bourdieu and Wacquant 1992:187).[18] Rather than justify the raison d'être of sociology in terms of serving some outside interests, Bourdieu (ibid.) contends that "sociology must first assert its autonomy." Social scientists must join in "efforts to guarantee the *social conditions of the possibility for rational thought*" (Bourdieu 1989a:103).[19] Bourdieu (1989b:374) wants to enhance scientific progress by "controlling the purely social effects of domination" in the social organization of scientific production and communication. The first and most important task for social scientists, therefore, is "to work collectively towards the defense of their own interests and towards the means necessary for the protection of their autonomy" (Bourdieu 1989a:103).[20]

Bourdieu's call for defending the interests of intellectual autonomy from all forms of political and economic influence demands *collective* as well as individual action. He sees intellectual freedom as a field property rather than an individual moral attribute. Bourdieu calls for intellectuals to practice a "Realpolitik" of individual freedom by doing everything possible to establish the social and political conditions that preserve and enlarge a social space for intellectual freedom (Bourdieu and Wacquant 1992:190). One of the first concerns should be gaining control of the means of intellectual production. Examples of this defense of intellectual guild interests would include making publication of scholarly work less dependent on commercial

18. By "field autonomy" Bourdieu does not have in mind the kind of "value-free" sociology extrapolated from Weber by American professional sociology during the 1950s (Gouldner 1973a). Bourdieu is a sharp critic of the positivist fact/value distinction in sociology.

19. Similarly, Gouldner (1973c:96, 98) writes that "an emancipatory sociology's first task is to establish the social and human conditions required to *sustain* rational discourse about social worlds . . . and the conditions of its own existence as a practical rational discourse."

20. Gouldner (1973c:96) too envisions the need to create "new *communities*" of intellectuals as autonomous and "liberated social space" to "support rational discourse in sociology and social theory." But as Pels (1995:103) perceptively points out, Gouldner follows Habermas in separating an ideal rational speech community from interest whereas Bourdieu connects rationality and interest.

interests and resisting the use of political criteria—including identity politics—in hiring and promotion of university faculty (ibid.). Other techniques for enhancing the autonomy of scientific practices from social distortions would include using international rather than strictly national peer review groups, creating alternative publications and research centers to rival monopolistic ones, and raising minimum training requirements for entry positions in the social sciences (178).

Since firmly establishing his symbolic power in French sociology with his ascension to the Collège de France, Bourdieu has shown more interest in establishing his niche in international intellectual markets. He has shown increasing interest in combatting regional and national differences that limit the free exchange of ideas, and has proposed the need "to establish the ends and means of a worldwide collective action by intellectuals" (1989a:99). The social space for rigorous scientific inquiry and debate that Bourdieu (1989b:374) seeks to create would foster cross-disciplinary and cross-national confrontations of different theories, methods, and bodies of data. He sees the creation of *Liber*, his European-oriented review of scholarly work, to be an expression of this kind of vision.

Bourdieu considers the quest for intellectual freedom to be a formidable struggle against powerful obstacles: against administrative power and authority of the state, against the commercial interests of publishing, and especially against the concentration of power in the media. He is particularly critical of journalism, which he sees as a key threat, for it introduces anti-intellectual forms of cultural production into the intellectual field. The media undermine the power of peer review, which for Bourdieu is a fundamental condition for intellectual autonomy, by substituting "readability, topicality, 'novelty,'" and good telegenic qualities for the proper criteria of intellectual competence (Bourdieu 1989a:106, 1996; Bourdieu and Wacquant 1992:58).[21] He sees the greatest threat to intellectual autonomy coming from inside impostors who play what he calls "intellectual journalist" or "journalist intellectual" roles by creating an amalgam of journalistic and intellectual criteria in their work. The autonomy of peer review becomes compromised by criteria and interests external to the scientific field, and dependency on public, and particularly private, funding can reduce autonomy if intellectuals shape their work accordingly.[22] He suggests that those

21. He warns that "the most serious danger . . . is in the tendency to strip intellectuals of their prerogatives to evaluate themselves and their production according to their own criteria" (Bourdieu 1989a:106).

22. Most of Bourdieu's work has been supported through the public sector and he admits (Bourdieu and Haacke 1994:75) that he would find it hard to secure financial support from the private sector for the kind of work he does.

most likely to use outside resources from the media or from commercial, political, or religious fields, are in fact weak contenders in the intellectual competition who compensate for their weakness by appealing to interests outside of the intellectual field (Bourdieu 1989a:104–5).[23] They are marginal cultural producers who play fundamentally anti-intellectual roles and pose a threat to intellectual freedom by politicizing the scientific field (Bourdieu 1990c:185). Bourdieu's vision for enhancing the autonomy of the scientific field requires imposing barriers of entry that would oblige individuals, whatever their motives, to play by the rules of science.[24]

Bourdieu's call for pursuing sociological practice entirely in terms of its own standards, without any external political, economic, and social distortions, reveals a striking commitment to professionalism, as well as a fundamental tension in his thought. This call sits uneasily with the basic assumption of sociology—one that Bourdieu has applied with particular rigor to the intellectual profession—that the beliefs and actions of all men and women (including social scientists) are shaped by social influences.[25] It is difficult to see how this basic sociological insight can be replaced by an ideal that contradicts it. If, as Bourdieu argues, the scientific field functions like any other social field fraught with social divisions and hierarchies, it is not clear how such a field can progressively become oriented exclusively around the sole criteria of rational inquiry. Bourdieu does not believe that a genuinely scientific field of world sociology currently exists, because of all the internal and external factors that inhibit the practice of pure science (Bourdieu 1989b:385). That Bourdieu believes it can, that it is a vision worth striving for, points up an underlying idealism that generally goes unnoticed in his world of interest, domination, strategy, and reproduction.

A related problem posed by Bourdieu's call for complete intellectual autonomy from outside influences is whether in the final analysis scholars

23. He writes, "there is a social law applicable to all the fields of cultural production . . . that heteronomy is introduced by those agents who are dominated according to the specific criteria of the field," and adds that "there are always people who, being scientifically dominated, are spontaneously on the side of the preconstructed, who have vital interests in deconstructing the constructed, in misunderstanding the understood, and thus in trying to bring everybody back to the starting line" (Bourdieu and Wacquant 1992:184).

24. It is noteworthy that Bourdieu's criticism of "disloyal competition" is not directed at self-interest or other individual motivations. He is not critical of self-interested behavior per se, provided that it is channeled into "scientifically proper behavior" (Bourdieu and Wacquant 1992:177). He stresses that "we must create conditions such that the worst, the meanest, and the most mediocre participant is compelled to behave in accordance with the norms of scientificity in currency at the time" (178).

25. Gouldner (1970:54), for example, points out this contradiction between the sociologist's desire for objectivity and his or her fundamental assumption that we are determined in countless ways.

can indeed operate by a law unto themselves. Is not the validity of truth-claims for the scientific community ultimately dependent on whether they win the approval and financial support of some external social group? Bourdieu's desire to protect peer review from all external influences would seem to work only to the extent that the products of rational inquiry find favor and support outside of the scientific community. The conditions for scientific autonomy would seem to require broader legitimation of the value of science.

More importantly, Bourdieu may underestimate the threat to intellectual freedom that can come from *within* the autonomous intellectual world itself. The problem may not be compromises with the external powers of markets and states, as Bourdieu emphasizes, but from the internal capacity of intellectuals to impose symbolic violence and monopolies of method and resources that stifle rather than liberate intellectual inquiry.[26] Bourdieu of course believes that the critical orientation of rational scientific thought within an institutionalized framework that fosters the competitive exchange of ideas will provide sufficient guard against this. But the historical record thus far does not inspire complete confidence in this belief that intellectuals are their own best guardians of free inquiry.

Finally, it is not apparent how the kind of intellectual autonomy Bourdieu idealizes would be financed (see, e.g., Ansart 1990:248–49). Bourdieu (1990c:51) observes that those subordinate groups most interested in having existing power relations exposed tend not to read the sociological literature and cannot afford it. Critical sociology "is a social science without a social base." He talks about the mode of conduct that should govern the scientific community, the kind of agenda it should follow, but he says little about financially supporting it. Most French sociologists are civil servants, working either as university teachers or researchers at the Centre National de Recherche Scientifique. This secure career status gives them a certain liberty from student demands, market pressures, and intellectual fashions, as it has Bourdieu himself. Does he assume this kind of civil-servant status as a basis for scientific field autonomy even though it may not be available in all national contexts? Does he assume extensive state support for the kind of intellectual autonomy he advocates?

---

26. Though he hoped for the development of a New Class, Gouldner may not have shared Bourdieu's faith in the *Realpolitik* of scientific autonomy. For Gouldner (1970:488–89) doubted the capacity for intellectuals to escape the fetters of professionalism, writing that "professional courtesy stifles intellectual curiosity; guild interests frown upon the washing of dirty linen in public; the teeth of piety bite the tongue of truth."

Science and Politics

The struggle to establish autonomous intellectual fields has, for Bourdieu, a deeper purpose. They will provide the institutional base for his vision of the scientific intellectual who intervenes in politics but in the name of science and free, critical inquiry.

Bourdieu believes that social scientists can bring not only their expertise but also a moral and ethical force to their engagements in public life. Growing out of the autonomy gained in the literary, artistic, and particularly scientific fields by the end of the nineteenth century, Bourdieu (1989a: 101) sees there developing in the most autonomous sectors of these cultural arenas core values of "ethical integrity and competence" that become the basis for a *politics of purity.* These values fundamentally oppose the "objectives and values such as money, power and honors predominant" in the fields of economics and politics.[27] They are the "unwritten laws of ethical and scientific universalism in order to practice moral leadership." The interest in disinterestedness he exposed as a misrecognized feature of intellectual practices now becomes a conscious value worth pursuing. The intellectual values of freedom and autonomy become juxtaposed to commercial and political interests in the struggle for power in the advanced societies. For Bourdieu, these values are rooted in the development of autonomous cultural fields like science.

We recall that Bourdieu argues that the proper task of social science is not to take sides in social conflict but to make the struggle itself the object of investigation. In the 1975 inaugural issue of *Actes de la recherche en sciences sociales* (vol. 1, p. 6), he specifies that the proper objective of social scientific research

does not oppose one value judgment to another but takes account of the fact that the reference to a value hierarchy is objectively inscribed in practices and in particular inscribed in the struggle over this hierarchy itself and is expressed in the antagonistic value judgments.

By revealing the social world as one of conflict and struggle over valued resources and definitions that are hierarchically ordered, sociology debunks

27. We return here to the fundamental opposition Bourdieu draws between culture and the economy, between culture and politics. We see, however, a shift in attitude toward culture. The fundamental opposition of cultural capital and economic capital that Bourdieu sees differentiating the dominant class is no longer conceptualized here in terms of resources. Now cultural capital becomes a value worth struggling for.

the taken-for-granted character of social worlds that "conceal power rela-tions" (Bourdieu 1993d:12). For Bourdieu, this disenchantment of the so-cial order is profoundly political, for it strikes at the very efficacy of power relations. Socioanalysis has political effects.

In a 1970 interview, Bourdieu outlines the kind of political impact he believes science can have. Quoting Bachelard, who wrote that "there is science only of the hidden," Bourdieu says that by demasking taken-for-granted power relations "genuine scientific research embodies a threat for the 'social order'" (Bourdieu and Hahn 1970:15). Scientific research, there-fore, "inevitably exercises a political effect." This, he argues, is not some political ideology one can choose since "science of society is inherently critical" (19). Genuine scientific research, by its very nature, embodies a "threat" to the established powers. It is this political effect that distinguishes pure science from "art for art's sake" (Bourdieu 1993d:14). Since the power relations that sociology reveals owe part of their strength to the fact that they do not appear to be power relations, "all sociological discourse has a political effect, even by default" (Bourdieu and Hahn 1970:19). Thus, "so-cial science necessarily takes sides in political struggles" with the interests of subordinate groups (Bourdieu and Wacquant 1992:51). And he points (in Bourdieu and Hahn 1970:20) to the key role that the sociologist can play in modern societies: "The sociologist unveils and therefore intervenes in the force relations between groups and classes and he can even contribute to the modification of those relations."[28]

This reasoning points to an extraordinary idealism in Bourdieu's think-ing about the role of the social scientist in the modern world. That Bour-dieu believes that a critical and professional sociology can potentially mod-ify relations between social classes amounts to a phenomenal claim for the power of sociological knowledge in modern stratified societies. It also points to a remarkable faith in the emancipatory effects of science, a view that is no longer widely shared in the post-Kuhnian era. Moreover, it does not explain why many sociologists who also subscribe to a nonpositivist understanding of sociology as science (Talcott Parsons is a notable exam-ple) do not side with subordinate groups. Clearly, Bourdieu invests in his understanding of science a progressive political project that he tries to legit-imate in the name of scientific authority.

In the interview alluded to above, Bourdieu admits that even though sociology can weaken power relations by unveiling them, sociology can be

---

28. Bourdieu's view of a political dimension inherent in social scientific practice is not dissimilar from Althusser's (1970) justification for doing theory: doing social science becomes a form of politics just as doing theory becomes a form of political practice.

accommodated and recuperated by dominant groups for their own interests. In revealing the hidden mechanisms of power, science may be of service to dominant groups in that it may lead to better and alternative modes
of manipulation and social control. Those in dominant positions are better
situated to benefit from the existing hierarchical order and thus meet the
threat from science of having their privileged positions exposed. Their advantaged resources also give them opportunities to find alternative sources
of legitimation for their privileged positions. But Bourdieu is banking on
the other possibility, namely, that when prevailing power mechanisms are
exposed, they will lose their efficacy to the benefit of those subordinate
individuals and groups who have access to and are able to use this knowledge. For Bourdieu, science is on the side of subordinate individuals and
groups.

There is, therefore, a political dimension to Bourdieu's conception of
science and what sociology should do in the modern world. It is political
in the sense that for Bourdieu a key objective of social-scientific research
is to struggle against all forms of symbolic domination. He thinks of the
intellectual vocation of social scientist in an activist sense. Acts of research,
no matter how seemingly mundane, are acts of struggle, conquest, and victory over taken-for-granted assumptions about social life: scientific research
is a struggle against all forms of symbolic domination. By exposing through
research arbitrary mechanisms that maintain power relations, the social scientist is able to challenge the legitimacy of the status quo. As existing power
relations lose their taken-for-granted character, this opens up the possibility for alternative ways of constructing social relations. Thus for Bourdieu
politics and science combine in the very objective of the social scientific
vocation. "Acts of research" are for Bourdieu fundamentally political acts.[29]

This points up a tension in Bourdieu's thinking about the nature of
science, between science as description and science as political intervention.
On the one hand, he recurringly warns social scientists against partisanship
in the social struggles they study. Social conflicts are to be objects of study
not occasions for partisanship. The field analytic perspective offers a more
comprehensive view than any one of the parochial interests involved. On
the other hand, Bourdieu believes that science necessarily sides with the
interests of subordinate groups, since by exposing the mechanisms of power
science renders them less effective for dominant groups.

This line of argument points again to the central role that Bourdieu

29. Indeed, the preamble of the first issue of *Actes de la recherche en sciences sociales* (1975)
identifies this dual character in his conception of social scientific research. Accardo (1983),
Pels (1995), Robbins (1991), and Wacquant (1992) are others who have caught this activist
sense of Bourdieu's conception of social scientific research.

assigns to legitimation in the exercise of power. It presupposes that science holds considerable authority in order to produce this kind of political effect. It also presupposes that scientific authority comes with the accumulation of symbolic power, by increasing field autonomy from outside interests. As scientific field autonomy increases, so also do the potential political effects that science can produce.[30] Indeed, the kinds of political effects he seeks would seem possible only so long as science enjoys a legitimacy superior to politics. Here, however, is the rub. Once knowledge of the interested character of scientific practice becomes widely known, science itself encounters legitimacy problems. Just as gift exchange becomes intolerable when participants come to view the practice as fundamentally self-interested, so science loses its claim to superior objectivity when it comes to represent parochial rather than universal interests. The ideology of disinterestedness would seem essential for science to have the kind of moral authority Bourdieu would like for it to exercise in the political area. But when that ideology becomes no longer believable, then science loses its symbolic power to intervene with effectiveness in political life. When the emperor goes without clothes, the parade may continue—but not for long. Even small children can see the difference!

This points to a complex if not ultimately contradictory position in which Bourdieu finds himself. To achieve the desired political effects, belief in science as a form of disinterested knowledge and inquiry must exist. Yet, the thrust of Bourdieu's own work on the scientific field emphasizes the very political character of that social universe. And though intellectual politics are undoubtedly different than electoral politics, they nonetheless are politics.

*   *   *

Bourdieu's model scientific intellectual who intervenes in the political arena but in the name of science contrasts sharply with several other intellectual role models. Though he resolutely defends academic freedom from all outside intrusion, Bourdieu clearly has no sympathy for the university as "ivory

---

30. Bourdieu (1989a:100) advances the following proposition to speak of the political effects of increased field autonomy: "The greater the intellectuals' independence from mundane interests because of their specific expertise (e.g., the scientific authority of an Oppenheimer or the intellectual authority of a Sartre), the greater their inclination to *assert* this independence by criticizing the powers that be, the greater the *symbolic effectiveness* of whatever political positions they might take."

Thus membership in a relatively autonomous field of cultural production is crucial, for, in Bourdieu's thinking, it seems to generate a propensity to contest the power of holders of economic and political capital and to do so with greater effectiveness.

tower," with its guardians of elite cultural traditions (see, e.g., Allan Bloom's *The Closing of the American Mind* [1987]). Against the traditional role of the professor who preserves, transmits, and consecrates an elite cultural tradition, Bourdieu casts his lot with researcher, the creator of new forms of knowledge.

Bourdieu is equally critical of the researcher who offers his services to dominant groups or the state. He rejects (1989c:486) the role of intellectual as expert in service to dominant group interests. He is sharply critical of the modern technocratic state and its use of science for political purposes. Bourdieu would use science to intervene in the political world, but in the name of science and the scientific agenda as set by scientists themselves rather than by government bureaucrats, politicians, or business leaders.

He also opposes for intellectuals a role of service to subordinate groups. Bourdieu's normative view of advocating increased autonomy of the professional guild from outside influence contrasts sharply with commonly held views among politically left-leaning intellectuals. Intellectuals on the political left tend to see themselves in leadership positions or as providing some kind of service to subordinate groups—often the working class—whom they support politically. But Bourdieu (1985c) rejects this model of political activism.

The "fellow traveler" image has been a particularly important one among leftist intellectuals, especially during the Cold War. In France, the fellow-traveler role permitted leftist intellectuals to play a highly visible support role for leftwing politics and yet retain a certain distance from the communist-dominated labor and political organizations. It permitted some criticism of Communist Party organizations and yet legitimated their existence as the only serious game in town.[31] Sartre was undoubtedly the most prominent French intellectual who assumed this role in the 1950s.[32] Bour-

---

31. The "fellow traveler" label has come under particularly harsh criticism in recent years by conservative intellectuals who want to stress the complicity of leftist intellectuals with the horrors of Stalinism. See Caute 1964, Hollander 1981, Johnson 1988, and Judt 1992.

It is difficult in the contemporary post-Marxist political climate to appreciate the intellectual and political climate of France in the 1950s, when the French Communist Party was perceived to be the only effective organized voice for the French working class. To be on the left meant to be in solidarity with the working class and therefore to accept the legitimacy of its formal organization.

There is debate over just how much "critical distance" many fellow travelers actually showed. Ory and Sirinelli (1986:164) remark that the perceived need to show solidarity with the largest and most powerful leftwing organization in France paradoxically made it more difficult for them to criticize the party than it was for former members who had left it.

32. Though in his later years Sartre became openly hostile to the French Communists and the established French left.

dieu's (1985c) vision of scientific intellectuals breaks rank with the image of intellectuals as advocates for subordinate groups.

Bourdieu's scientific intellectuals also oppose Gramsci's (1971) idea of "organic intellectuals."[33] Where Gramsci sees the development of worker-intellectuals who share and can "understand" and "feel" their connections with the working class and thereby give symbolic expression to the collective identity and interests of workers, Bourdieu sees marginal participants in intellectual fields who are bound by their own particular professional interests and who tend to inject their position of domination into their understanding of subordinate group interests. Political alliance between intellectuals and the working class becomes one of structural homology for Bourdieu rather than one of shared habitus.

Both the fellow-traveler and organic intellectual models share the idea that intellectuals should subordinate their own particular interests to those of the working class, which is deemed to be the historical carrier of social transformation from capitalism to socialism.[34] Bourdieu (1985c:93, 1989a: 109) rejects this kind of support role. Intellectuals, as we have already noted, must pursue first of all their own corporate interests, and only then intervene in politics as intellectuals rather than as subordinate group representatives. By defending their own interests of protecting critical inquiry, intellectuals establish the grounds for debunking the legitimacy of dominant power relations and thereby actually advance the interests of subordinate groups. Though Bourdieu resists speaking of intellectuals as representative of universal interests, as does Gouldner, his analysis in fact leads to an ultimate correspondence between the critical debunking function by intellectuals of dominant power relations and the interests of subordinate groups. This sort of "intellectual trickle-down effect" is a matter of faith, however, since, following Bourdieu's own line of thought, defining exactly what are the "objective" interests of subordinate groups is itself an object of struggle. Bourdieu does not deal with cases where the kind of universal scientific

33. Organic intellectuals function to give symbolic expression to the collective identity and interests of the groups they represent. They perform legitimating and organizing roles for particular social groups. Gramsci (1971) saw the traditional sector of the humanist intelligentsia (e.g., artists, writers, scholars, clergy, philosophers) as lending its support to bourgeois groups and a newer developing technical intelligentsia (e.g., engineers and scientists) as capable of providing a collective vision for the emerging industrial working class. The "organic" relationship between the working class and its intellectuals would be dialectical: intellectuals would stimulate the formation of the working class, which would give birth to its own intellectuals, who in turn would act upon that class to give it further development.

34. At least in theory. One of the contributions of Bourdieu's field analysis of intellectuals is to show the "bad faith" of leftist intellectuals who conflate those two sets of interests by projecting the interests of their own particular intellectual field positions onto those of the subordinate social groups they support.

interest he advocates might conflict with the interests of subordinate groups. This is an important if complex issue and needs further consideration.

Bourdieu's model of the scientific intellectual differs from other views on the *range of issues* to be addressed by intellectuals. He rejects the model of the "total intellectual" (Bourdieu 1980d) as exemplified by Jean-Paul Sartre. Following the example set by Emile Zola, Sartre established a paradigmatic form of prophetic denunciation that became a tradition within the French intellectual world and imposed itself as a normative model for anyone entering the French intellectual field (Bourdieu 1991d:36).[35] To be a total intellectual meant to be able to speak critically to all the issues of the day. Bourdieu scornfully denounces this role of speaking as a sociologist to all the current issues (Bourdieu and Wacquant 1992:185–86). For him, this is not the proper role of the sociologist as scientist for three reasons: (1) it generally means overstepping the bounds of the particular competence of the sociologist; (2) it casts the sociologist in the image of a social prophet whose charismatic style of leadership further mystifies power relations; and (3) while presenting the appearance of responding to public needs, it in fact serves the interest of the intellectual by attempting to improve his or her position within the intellectual field. Bourdieu objects to all intellectual strategies that try to improve one's position by using nonscientific means of media popularity, political correctness, etc.

Like Bourdieu, Foucault also criticizes the Sartrean image of the universal intellectual. But Bourdieu (1989a:108) distinguishes his position from Foucault's (1980:126–33) model of the "specific" intellectual as one who confines his or her political activity to limited domains of expertise. Bourdieu wants his "large collective of intellectuals" to roam more broadly than across a few limited domains. The principal difference between Bourdieu and Foucault here is that Bourdieu wants to create the social conditions that would permit the collective intervention of intellectuals over a broader spectrum of issues. As Wacquant (Bourdieu and Wacquant 1992:190) suggests, therefore, Bourdieu's position represents a sort of synthesis of Sartre and Foucault.

Bourdieu (1990c:184) likewise rejects the image, associated with Karl Mannheim, of the free-floating intellectual.[36] Bourdieu objects to idealizing

35. Bourdieu's criticism of Sartre is extended and elaborated by Anna Boschetti (1988), one of Bourdieu's students and collaborators.

36. Though commonly attributed the image of the free-floating intellectual, Mannheim (1956) himself believed that intellectuals were only "relatively" free of their class interests—a point he stressed in response to criticism of *Ideology and Utopia*. Mannheim did envisage a kind of self-critical though technocratic vision of the intellectual role that would be sufficiently

intellectuals as free from class and intellectual field interests.[37] Bourdieu's sociology of intellectuals stresses how they are bound to particular field interests, yet his vision for the critical intellectual does share with Mannheim the hope that, by affirming their own corporate interests, intellectuals can play a guiding role in modern societies.[38]

Finally, though Bourdieu argues that scientific intellectuals should pursue first of all their own interests to advance the cause of science, he does not embrace Gouldner's (1979) New Class project. Bourdieu (1985c:94) sees an urgent need to "create an international of artists and scholars capable of proposing to or imposing reflections and recommendations on political and economic powers." Yet, Bourdieu's vision for enhancing the autonomy of scientific practice from external distortion does not appear to lead to anything like class-wide consciousness, organization, and mobilization. Bourdieu focuses much more on the intellectual guild whereas Gouldner was centrally concerned with the role of intellectuals in broader social transformation.

Bourdieu's Own Political Practice

Bourdieu's political activities parallel his vision of the scientific intellectual. Three general types of political activity can be identified: a few highly visible political engagements, choice of research topics, and criticism of intellectual practices.

Given Bourdieu's criticism of the fellow traveler, the total intellectual, and other specific intellectual roles, it is not surprising that he should avoid certain highly visible types of political expression frequently found among French intellectuals. Bourdieu rarely signs political petitions or joins demonstrations and political rallies, and does not work openly for or affiliate with a leftwing political party or labor union. Among French sociologists, Alain Touraine and Edgar Morin are considerably more visible on political

freed from political commitments and parochial interests to grasp a view of the social totality and thereby be better able to represent the general interest. Mannheim seems more willing to accept some form of the technocrat role whereas Bourdieu is categorically critical. Even in his own political practice, Bourdieu has shown relatively little inclination to be a "service intellectual" to the state—including the French Socialist state from 1981 to 1994. Bourdieu does share with Mannheim, however, the idea that the social scientist can obtain a vision of the totality. Field analysis is precisely an attempt to grasp a total vision of a particular arena of conflict.

37. We see this criticism in his study of Heidegger (Bourdieu 1988d) and of contemporary philosophy (Bourdieu 1983b).

38. Like Bourdieu, Mannheim (1956:170) argues that intellectuals should not assume the posture of a service class toward the working class but rather should be true to their own intellectual vocation.

matters in the French media, despite Bourdieu's intellectual renown and his position at the Collège de France.[39] Nor is Bourdieu known as an advocate for particular social groups or causes, such as ecology, feminism, race, or peace, as was Foucault on mental health and prisons.

Unlike a number of French intellectuals who were committed communists in the 1950s (e.g., Emmanuel Le Roy Ladurie) or ultra-leftists in the '60s (e.g., André Glucksman) and then became fervent anti-communists in the '70s and '80s, Bourdieu has remained on the political left and has been a sharp critic of the conservative parties that ruled France until 1981. He has been generally situated with the Rocardian current in the French Socialist Party and the French Socialist trade union (CFDT) for many years. However, he has consistently resisted the fellow-traveler mode, even when a Socialist, François Mitterrand, gained the presidency in 1981. In fact, to the consternation of many on the left, Bourdieu signed a petition of support for the right of the French comedian Coluche to oppose Mitterrand in the 1981 presidential elections. For Bourdieu, the Coluche candidacy represented a protest against the enclosed world of French political leadership, both left and right, against the technocratic organization of political life in France.[40] Then, in December 1981, Bourdieu initiated contact with Foucault to launch a public protest against the French Socialist government's policy of noninvolvement in reaction to Jaruzelski's military crackdown against Solidarity in Poland.[41] And his 1993 publication of *La misère du monde*, on social exclusion and suffering, represents a sharp critique of the neglect by French Socialists of social welfare needs in France.

Despite his criticism of intellectuals as experts serving power, Bourdieu did help the Mitterrand government on a few occasions. In response to Mitterrand's request to the Collège de France, he authored in 1985 a series of educational reform guidelines. When Michel Rocard became Prime Minister in 1988, Bourdieu accepted the presidency of a commission to study educational curriculum and issued a series of recommendations for changing the curriculum ("Report of the Collège de France on the Future of Education" [1990]).

In the late 1980s and early 1990s we see increased political activism with more media attention. His criticism of media-oriented intellectuals persists (see Bourdieu 1996), but he himself has become more visible in the media by granting interviews, appearing on television, and making

39. Touraine, for example, frequently writes opinions on a wide variety of topics for *Le Monde*.

40. Interview with Bourdieu (Paris, November 1993).

41. See Eribon (1991:298–308) for an account of this collaborative effort by Bourdieu and Foucault.

statements in the French press.[42] In addition, Bourdieu has increasingly lent his public support to various progressive causes. He joined with numerous Arab intellectuals against the American initiative in the 1991 Iraqi War. He has joined in protests against repression against Algerian intellectuals. He has been active in antiracism struggles in France, though without formally joining any group.

Bourdieu's most significant area of public engagement is undoubtedly reflected in his research and writing. In choosing a research topic he seems guided by the degree to which he believes that the scientific examination of a situation will have some political impact.[43] His early research on peasant cultures in Algeria spoke to both the horrors of the colonial war and the unintended social and cultural dislocations that would follow the war of liberation. *The Inheritors* [1964] (Bourdieu and Passeron 1979) documented the persistent social inequality in French higher education despite years of educational expansion. That study of French student culture also pointed up the difficulty of mobilizing French university students because of the internally differentiated class character of student culture.[44] More recently, *La misère du monde* (1993) provides interview material of experiences of social exclusion and suffering caused by economic transformation in contemporary France.[45] This, and the early work on student culture, have been his most successful attempts to reach a broader audience with a political message.

Not all of his research projects, however, have had significant political impact. His critical study of the *grandes écoles* (*La noblesse d'etat* [1989c]) has had little effect on reforming the socially exclusive character of these elite institutions. And his report for the Collège de France on educational reform did not lead to a broad-based debate and reform of French primary and secondary education, as he had hoped.

But in general, Bourdieu's political engagements have been efforts to

42. Examination of *Le Monde* shows a noticeable increase from 1987 through 1992 in the number of times that Bourdieu was featured in this prominent French daily. Nevertheless, his visibility in *Le Monde* does not equal that of Alain Touraine. Touraine more closely resembles the Sartrean model of the intellectual who maintains a high media profile by taking public stances on a wide variety of issues.

43. He admits that his choice of theoretical problems are prompted by personal confrontations with pressing political issues of the day (Bourdieu 1987b:29).

44. It is ironic that though the book was widely acknowledged by French student leaders (e.g., Lindenberg 1975) as contributing to their critical understanding of the French university, this fundamental thesis of *The Inheritors* was contradicted by the mass student mobilization in 1968.

45. In the case of *La misère du monde*, Bourdieu (1992:201–2) reports being motivated to study "social suffering" as a way of fighting against a technocratic representation of social reality.

enhance the autonomy of intellectual fields from outside economic and political interests. He has directed the bulk of his efforts against the "hidden
vices of the intellectual world" (Bourdieu and Wacquant 1992:56). He
thinks of his practice of sociology as a mode of intervention to correct
distortions in the social-scientific field. Most of this takes the form of sharp
criticism of practices in the social sciences that Bourdieu sees as compro-
mising their scientific integrity. We may discern something of Bourdieu's
preferred type of political engagement in *Homo Academicus* (1988b). In
showing how the French university profession is internally differentiated
by opposing forms of power that mirror to some extent the structure of
the dominant social class in France, this analysis aims to increase awareness
of these sources of distortion in current scientific practices and to enhance
the autonomy of the scientific field from outside distortion (Wacquant
1990:681).

Other modes of intervention in the scientific community are noteworthy. In addition to his own research center and professional journal, *Actes
de la recherche en sciences sociales*, the creation of *Liber* as a kind of European
book review forum follows from his effort to enhance the autonomy of the
scientific field by struggling against obstacles to scientific communication
created by language and national tradition. He has also actively participated
in several social-scientific conferences, where he sees an opportunity to
establish lines of communication across disciplinary specialities, methodological schools, theoretical frameworks, and national cultural traditions.[46]
In general, then, Bourdieu's preferred form of political practice follows
closely his vision for how intellectuals should approach political involvements in modern societies. He holds that by doing good social science, one
can also do progressive politics. This is the basis for his ideal of being a
scientific intellectual.

46. One example is the 1988 Chicago conference, organized with the late James S. Coleman, with whom Bourdieu differed strikingly with respect to both sociological theory and
method and political alliances (see Bourdieu and Coleman 1991). Bourdieu is a sharp critic
of the rational-actor model advocated by Coleman. He is also clearly identified with the
French political left, whereas Coleman identified with the neoconservative National Association of Scholars in the United States. Nevertheless, Bourdieu (1989b:374) saw this conference
as consistent with his "scientific *politique*—that is, policy and politics—whose goal would be to
foster scientific communication and debate across the many divisions associated with national
traditions and with the fragmentation of social science into empirical subspecialities, theoretical paradigms, and methodological schools."

On the other hand, Bourdieu (1989b:373–74) does not participate in what he labels the
"anarchical exchanges" of the regularly organized national or international professional meetings in sociology, such as the French Association of Sociology or the International Congress
of Sociology.

11 | THE STRUGGLE FOR OBJECTIVITY: BOURDIEU'S CALL FOR REFLEXIVE SOCIOLOGY

Since Bourdieu argues that his theory of symbolic power and violence applies to *all* forms of symbolic representations, he faces a critical dilemma in developing a sociological practice designed to expose the hidden forms of symbolic power: how can one practice a social science—itself a symbolic enterprise—and yet not reproduce the effects of social distinction Bourdieu so vigorously denounces? If, as he argues, all symbolic systems—including science itself—embody power relations, and all practices—including intellectual practices—are interested, how is it possible to construct a social science that will not be yet another form of symbolic violence? If one accepts Bourdieu's claim that intellectual work is inescapably bound by viewpoint and functions as strategy within fields of struggle for recognition and legitimation, what form of objective practice is possible? Given his sharp indictment of the intellectual role, how can Bourdieu justify his own existence as an intellectual?

Bourdieu's answer to this dilemma is to call for a *reflexive practice* of sociology (1990f; Bourdieu and Wacquant 1992). He argues that every sociological inquiry requires a simultaneous critical reflection on the intellectual and social conditions that make the inquiry possible. If sociology is the science of social conditions determining human practices, it must also be the science of social conditions determining intellectual practices, including sociology. Bourdieu's analysis of intellectual fields shows that social scientists unwittingly translate into their "explanations" of social phenomena particular epistemological assumptions and intellectual field interests. Only by doing a sociology of sociology, applying sociological methods to the practice of sociology itself, can one hope to gain a measure of freedom from the social determinants of intellectual practice. For Bourdieu, this "reflexive return" responds to a particular urgency, for, "the sociology of the social determinants of sociological practice is the only possible ground for a possible freedom from these determinations" (Wacquant 1989).

Two objectives stand out in Bourdieu's reasoning for why sociology requires a reflexive orientation. First, *reflexivity is necessary for doing good science*. In contrast to radical constructionism (e.g., Ashmore 1989, Woolgar 1988), Bourdieu does not see reflexivity as an attack upon science but as a genuine scientific means to improve the practice of science itself. He sees the sociology of sociology as indispensable because

[it] can help us move toward a unified scientific field of world sociology by increasing our awareness of the socially based effects of domination that are exerted in that field and by promoting struggles aimed at controlling these effects and the mechanisms that produce them. (Bourdieu 1989b:385)

The second objective points to a *moral obligation to extend the chances for unfettered critical examination and communication to others*. A critical reflexivity would "associate the pursuit of the universal with a constant struggle for the universalization of the privileged conditions of existence which render the pursuit of the universal possible" (Bourdieu 1989a:110). Though Bourdieu distinguishes his ideal of science from that of Habermas, here we see a dimension that nonetheless resembles Habermas's ideal speech community.

The focus of this chapter is on what Bourdieu actually means by a reflexive practice of sociology. I begin by examining the three principal steps Bourdieu outlines for a reflexive sociology. Then I consider how Bourdieu has actually employed reflexivity in his own work. Special attention will be given to what is perhaps his most interesting example of reflexive work, namely, his analysis in *Homo Academicus* of the French university teaching profession.

Reflexive Steps toward Objectivity

While Bourdieu provides no single methodological recipe for achieving a properly reflexive posture, in key statements he identifies the essential dimensions for doing the kind of reflexive sociology he has in mind (Bourdieu 1987b:112–16, 1988b:1–35; Wacquant 1989:18–19, 33–34). The principal concern—and longstanding preoccupation of Bourdieu—is the need to control the relationship of the researcher to the object of inquiry so that the position of the researcher is not unwittingly projected into the object of study. This, I noted in chapter 3, is what Bourdieu calls "participant objectivation" (Bourdieu and Wacquant 1992:68, Wacquant 1989:33).

The problem of the relationship between the researcher and the research object emerges already as a central concern in his work on Algeria (Bourdieu 1972, 1977c. 1990h). Bourdieu argues that lack of a reflexive perspective "results in the projection of this relation onto the object" of research (Wacquant 1989:33). Three principal sources of such projection need controlling in order to render sociological investigation more objective and scientific.

First, one needs to control for the values, dispositions, attitudes, and perceptions (i.e., the habitus) that the researcher brings from his or her social background to the object of inquiry. This means cultivating a critical awareness of the social location of the researcher (e.g., class origins, race, or gender) in a particular historical context and of how this background may shape and influence the inquiry. The researcher, Bourdieu (1988b:15) suggests, will be more successful in gaining objectivity on the research topic to the extent that he or she is able to identify those personal dispositions and interests that infiltrate his or her own concepts, choice of research topics, and methods.

The influence of social background is probably the most widely recognized type of bias distorting social-scientific work. Indeed, the classic sociology of knowledge tradition from Durkheim, Marx, and Weber to Mannheim is rooted in the fundamental claim that all ideas—including sociological ideas—are located socially. Nevertheless, Bourdieu contends that researchers too often neglect this important sociological insight and simply project unexamined dispositions of "animosity" or "enchantment" onto the object of their investigation. He singles out for criticism researchers—particularly popular-culture theorists—who simultaneously study and uncritically advocate the cause of politically subordinate groups. For Bourdieu, reflexivity first of all means developing critical awareness of the class lens through which one views the social world.

But Bourdieu sees his work as going beyond the conventional claim of class bias. Indeed, as I discussed in chapter 9, he contends that the influence of the social-class origins and position of the researcher on scientific work is never direct; it is always mediated by the position the researcher holds in his field of cultural production. *Field location* is the second source of bias that the sociologist must confront. Reflexivity, therefore, also means for Bourdieu applying the field analytical perspective to the practice of social science itself.

Sociology is itself a field of specialized symbolic production wedged between the field of science and the political field (Bourdieu 1989b:376). It is traversed by radically different strategies—ranging from purely scientific to purely political—that compete with different resources for the power to define sociology. Reflexivity for Bourdieu means cultivating an awareness that one's intellectual position and work also represent strategies in this struggle for scholarly recognition. It means recognizing that sociologists are motivated in their research by the "practical interests" of struggle for scholarly recognition as well as for intellectual ideals. Reflexivity, therefore, requires constructing the intellectual field of all the competing interests and positions of struggle, including those of the sociologist, in order to decrease the likelihood of the sociologist's projecting a position of intellectual struggle onto objects of inquiry (Bourdieu 1987b:109–10).

Here we see a shift in focus from the individual to the institutional context, which, according to Bourdieu, provides the dominant categories of thought as well as the career opportunities and constraints that shape individual strategies. For Bourdieu, reflexivity means, not intellectual introspection, but ongoing analysis and control of the categories used in the practice of social science. It focuses not on the individual sociologist as subject, but on the organizational and cognitive structures that shape the sociologists's work. This orientation leads Bourdieu to do field analyses of science (Bourdieu 1975b), of French higher education (Bourdieu 1988b, 1989c), and of the contemporary French intellectual field.

But reflexivity for Bourdieu goes beyond field analysis of the intellectual world. It must also address what Bourdieu sees as the "most essential bias," namely, the "intellectualist" or "theoreticist" bias inherent in the scholarly gaze, and in the intellectual posture itself. The third—and most difficult—step in Bourdieu's reflexive program involves examining the epistemological and social conditions that make possible social-scientific claims of objectivity.

Bourdieu (1990i:382) contends, "I believe that there is a sort of incompatibility between our scholarly mode of thinking and this strange thing that practice is."[1] The "outsider," or "scholastic" point of view, requires both a social and a epistemological break with the realm of practices. A necessary condition for constructing a theoretical view means extracting oneself from practice in order to observe practice. Bourdieu understands this "outsider" point of view on the social world as one that requires "an institutionalized situation of studious leisure" (381). The outsider view presupposes a withdrawal from social engagement in order to study it, and such

---

1. This brings us full circle to his critical reflection on how to conceptualize practices, a key issue he began to raise already in the analyses of his Algerian fieldwork.

withdrawal requires leisure time—a fundamental freedom from economic necessity. Thus, Bourdieu (1990h:53) associates the possibility of taking an objectivist view on the social world with privileged economic status.

The scholastic view also presupposes an epistemological break with practical knowledge. The scientific view of the social world offered by formal models, diagrams, and statistical tables is not that of engaged actors who have imperfect information, do not clearly articulate their goals, and do not foresee clearly outcomes. This scholastic mode of apprehending the social world transforms practical knowledge into theoretical knowledge, which is conscious, systematic, and timeless. Failure to employ a reflexive perspective on the epistemological difference between practical and theoretical knowledge leads social scientists to conflate theoretical practice and practical action and to commit what Bourdieu calls the "intellectualist fallacy." They thereby misrepresent the practical and dispositional character of practices by projecting onto ordinary activities the epistemological assumptions of theoretical practices. Bourdieu (1990i:382) writes that

scientists or scholars who have not analyzed what it is to be a scientist or a scholar, who have not analyzed what it means to have a scholastic view and to find it natural, put into the minds of agents *their* scholastic view.

Bourdieu locates in the scholarly gaze the most essential source of bias that a researcher can bring to an understanding of practices. It is "the most serious epistemological mistake in the social sciences," and much of Bourdieu's writing is devoted to this error (see in particular Bourdieu 1990h: 14). He cites Chomsky's linguistics, Lévi-Strauss's structuralist analysis of kinship and myth, and rational action theory as prime examples of nonreflexive perspectives, each in its own way lacking a practical understanding of agency.[2] Each reduces agency to a mirror image of intellectual practice by depicting human action as either a reflection of structures or an innate rational capacity of individuals. For Bourdieu, however, agency is practical and dispositional, and a fully reflexive sociology of practices must simultaneously provide a theory of theoretical practices as well as a theory of ordinary practices.

Why, according to Bourdieu, are intellectuals inclined to conflate model and reality even though they derive from radically different cognitive and social postures toward the social world? Bourdieu's answer is that intellectuals are blinded by their own professional ideology, which emphasizes

2. Chomsky, Bourdieu (1990i:382) writes, "operates as if ordinary speakers were grammarians."

universality, neutrality, and objectivity. These ideals in fact represent interests and weapons in the struggle for intellectual recognition. Among social scientists, claims of objectivity, or for the "best explanation" of the social world, represent attempts to relativize all other viewpoints. Social scientists, like other intellectuals, struggle to hold the "absolute viewpoint," to attain primacy over all other views (Bourdieu 1987b:44–45). They therefore misrecognize the interested character of their own practices by failing to realize the extent to which their intellectual practices are shaped by the competitive logic of their own cultural fields.

This reflexive process leads Bourdieu to conclude that the scholarly view embraces epistemological sovereignty. The scholastic view is fundamentally *political,* for it involves a search for power. This "will to know," Bourdieu (1988b:xiii) writes, is motivated by a "special kind of will to power." The claim of objectivity consists in "taking up the absolute point of view upon the object of study . . . to assume a sort of intellectual power over the intellectual world" (Bourdieu and Wacquant 1992:11; Wacquant 1989:32). Bourdieu contends that this temptation is "inherent in the posture of the sociologist." He also asserts that it is the "deep truth" of the university world and, in a moment of rare self-disclosure, admits that this motivation has governed his own behavior (Wacquant 1989:3). A fully reflexive practice, Bourdieu argues, requires the researcher "to objectify the very intention of objectifying," to submit to critical examination the very intellectual ambition to achieve a totally objective, unbiased view, especially as it represents a weapon for domination of other viewpoints. He therefore wants to relativize the claim for epistemological sovereignty that has emerged today as the dominant expression of truth, but which instead invariably embodies specific interests (Bourdieu 1987b:43–44).

In sum, Bourdieu's reflexive focus on the scholarly mode of reasoning suggests that "the social foundations of the propensity to theorize or to intellectualize" are twofold: first, the separation from practice in order to obtain an "external and superior point of view" on practice; and second, the "false consciousness," or "bad faith," of intellectuals who refuse to recognize their drive to achieve an objective view for what it is, namely, accumulating symbolic capital by discrediting other views. Reflexivity provides the sociologist with critical distance from these two factors shaping his or her sociological practice.

Taken together, these three reflexive steps outline an ambitious program for self-critical examination in order to produce more objective social science. But Bourdieu (1990f) does not believe that a fully reflexive view can ever be achieved, that critical theorists can ever reach a full self-understanding of the "interested" character of their scientific practice and the effects it is likely to produce. No "absolute" standpoint outside of fields of struggle is conceivable. Bourdieu (1988b:6) writes that "there is no object that does not imply a viewpoint, even if it is an object produced with the intention of abolishing one's viewpoint." Reflexivity can only be carried out by degrees.[3] The escape from social determination is always partial for Bourdieu, since reflexive practice itself takes place within socially determined conditions. Since all of our practices, including intellectual practices, are socially determined, the promise of Bourdieu's sociology of sociology is that by exposing the underlying social conditions of intellectual practice one can hope to achieve a partial escape from ideology into a more objective grasp of practical social life.

For Bourdieu, then, the problem addressed by reflexivity is one of how to achieve objectivity without objectivism. What are the social and intellectual conditions that make possible the position of the detached observer, and what effect does that "outsider" posture have upon the effort to objectify human practices? A general science of all human practices—including intellectual practices—obtains only with a reflexive return upon the practice of science itself. If intellectual practice is to be transformed from professional ideology into science, this can occur only by reflexive examination of our efforts to objectify the social world.

Bourdieu's reflexivity is, therefore, first and foremost a field analysis of the practice of science. It does not focus on the person of the individual researcher.[4] Bourdieu's emphasis, rather, is on the *position* of the sociologist in the field of struggle for scholarly recognition. For Bourdieu, reflexivity means subjecting the position of the observer to the same critical analysis applied to the object of sociological investigation. Bourdieu does not conceptualize his reflexivity as one of exposing personal bias that can be expressed through the language of the first person.[5]

3. This leads Bourdieu to criticize attempts to handle the problem by simply offering an introductory statement designed to identify the foundation of one's own thinking. The problem with this technique, he asserts, is that it gives the impression that the problem of bias has been addressed and that subsequent analysis can proceed without further question of its integrity. But, Bourdieu maintains, reflexivity cannot be declared once and for all; it is a matter of degree. The tendency to impose one's view as the objective one is ever present, and therefore continual guard must be taken not to allow the logic of competitive professional interest in the scientific field to color the analysis of struggle in another field.

4. In this respect Bourdieu's perspective differs from that of Gouldner (1970). Gouldner's reflexivity tries to situate the viewpoint of the scientist as a person, warts and all. Bourdieu exempts the personal idiosyncratic dimension from his analysis.

5. In this respect Bourdieu mirrors his French intellectual tradition. Perhaps because of the stronger presence of social psychology and psychoanalysis in the American social-scientific tradition than in the French, "personal" expressions in intellectual style are given more weight on this side of the Atlantic. If in the United States the expression "the personal is political"

Nevertheless, Bourdieu believes that reflexivity in sociology can have a therapeutic function insofar as increasing awareness of the social determinants of behavior increases the possibility for freedom from the unknown.[6] In his search for a reflexive sociology, we find that Bourdieu's metatheoretical and epistemological concerns intersect in a crucial way with his own choice of substantive areas of investigation. Indeed, it is significant that much of Bourdieu's empirical work is devoted to the study of the French educational system and intellectual world where Bourdieu himself has made his career. He contends that these substantive areas, better than others, permit one to probe the *doxa* of intellectual culture, those fundamental, taken-for-granted conceptual categories that shape intellectual practices.

> If the sociology of the education system and the intellectual world are for me primordial, this is because they also contribute to the understanding of the subject of knowledge by introducing, even more directly than all the reflexive analyses, the categories of non-reflected thought that delimit and predetermine what is knowable and what is known. (Bourdieu 1982:10)

At a deeper level, then, one finds that Bourdieu's search for a self-critical objective social science intersects with his own personal and positional interests of making a career in the French intellectual world.[7] Reflexivity is for Bourdieu an intellectual field strategy.

Reflexivity in Bourdieu's Own Work

Bourdieu argues that a reflexive practice of social science must extend to *all* areas of investigation. In his own work, we see signs of it—both in method and choice of substantive area—in his earliest as well as in his more recent studies. Though he has always maintained a critical posture toward the practice of social science, his understanding of what a reflexive return entails has developed over time. Substantively, Bourdieu changed his re-

---

resonates with a certain critical tradition of social thought, we could contrast Bourdieu (oversimplifying somewhat) by saying that "the personal is positional."

6. This aspect of Bourdieu's work has not gone unnoticed by certain critics. Hoffman (1986) sees *Distinction* as much an act of personal catharsis for Bourdieu as a work of science.

7. This raises the interesting issue of how tied Bourdieu's reflexive practice of sociology is to particular substantive areas of investigation, particularly those that are, to him, of considerable professional and political interest. Might this perspective have been less germane had his work focused on substantive areas that were of less political import in France than decolonizing Algeria and expanding educational opportunity? One suspects that the need for a reflexive perspective is less intense in substantive areas where the sociologist has considerable remove and where professional interest and political debate are not particularly intense.

search focus in the early 1960s from Algeria to the French university and intellectual world where he has made his career. Conceptually, we see the perspective crystalize in the concept of field in the early 1970s and more recently in increased attention to the sociological gaze. In the 1980s and '90s a number of texts appeared wherein the reflexive dimension becomes more explicitly stated as the defining feature of Bourdieu's sociology (see in particular Bourdieu 1982, and Bourdieu and Wacquant 1992).

Already in his early work on Algerian peasants, we see a reflexive perspective emerging in his criticism of Lévi-Strauss's structuralism. Bourdieu's (1986b) call for a shift from "rule" to "strategy" clearly emphasized the limited ability of formal structuralist models to account for practices. While patterned and regulated, peasant behavior was not rule- or norm-conforming, as structuralist models implied. Considerable slippage occurred between structuralist models and the reality of peasant practices. This critical observation led Bourdieu to develop the idea of behavior as strategy and to theorize the difference between conceptual models of practices and actual practices. It set the stage for his sharp polemic against the "scholastic fallacy." Thus, Bourdieu's understanding of reflexivity is rooted in his early formulation of a theory of practice. The concept of habitus already builds on the sharp distinction between practical knowledge and formal knowledge, which Bourdieu draws upon in his reflexive criticism of academic knowledge. Much later he would recapitulate his position, and indicate its consequences for research in the following statement:

The change in the theory of practice provoked by theoretical reflection on the theoretical point of view, on the practical point of view and on their profound differences, is not purely speculative: it is accompanied by a drastic change in the practical operations of research and by quite tangible scientific profits. For instance, one is led to pay attention to properties of ritual practice that structuralist logicism would incline to push aside or to treat as meaningless misfirings of the mythical algebra, and particularly to polysemic realities, underdetermined or indeterminate, not to speak of partial contradictions and of the fuzziness which pervade the whole system and account for its flexibility, its openness, in short everything that makes it "practical" and thus geared to respond at the least cost (in particular in terms of logical search) to the emergencies of ordinary existence and practice. (Bourdieu 1990i:384)

This skepticism toward structuralist models of practices was heightened when Bourdieu (1977b) turned his attention to peasant marriage strategies in his home region in Southwestern France. Bourdieu indicates retrospectively that he self-consciously began this study of French peasant marriage practices as a sort of "epistemological experiment" in which he applied the same methods he used to investigate kinship relations among

Algerian peasants to the social world of his youth (Bourdieu and Wacquant 1992:67). He wanted to "observe the effects that objectivation of my native world would produce in me" (163). This research experience, which found French peasant marriage patterns to be complex strategies of material and symbolic exchange, enhanced his skepticism of applying formal structural models to account for social practices.

But it is in the mid-1960s, when Bourdieu shifted his attention to the French university, that we gain a fuller appreciation of the substantive focus of Bourdieu's reflexive concern. What the reflexivity comes to underscore for Bourdieu in his work on French education and intellectuals is that the dichotomy of the interested and the disinterested (which he criticizes and discards in his early anthropological work) now becomes even more central to his analysis of intellectual practices. Reflexivity means viewing intellectual practices as being interest-oriented rather than motivated exclusively by objective ideas or values. The concept of the intellectual field stresses this interest dimension of his analysis.

French academe represents for Bourdieu (1988b:xii–xiii) another epistemological experiment, since it is the institutional locus for the practice of science as well as for Bourdieu's own professional career. Bourdieu clearly believes he can research the structure and dynamics of the academic field without taking up a partisan position within it and without assuming an intellectualist posture toward it. But how successful is he in extracting himself from the competitive struggle within the field of science and intellectual renown in order to describe the French academic world objectively? Consider his most reflexive study of the French university field, which appears in *Homo Academicus* (1988b).

Reflecting his unrelenting critical spirit, Bourdieu poses the problem in the first chapter of *Homo Academicus* by warning that a scientifically constructed account of a familiar social world is likely to be read nonreflexively and interpreted as insider practices of gossip, insult and slander, anecdote, intuition, and ad hominem (2). Bourdieu's particular formulation of the issue has the unfortunate effect of blaming the reader for such interpretative distortions without acknowledging any possible responsibility of the author. This does Bourdieu a disservice, for it invites reader suspicion and defensiveness when an introduction explaining how he proposes to avoid the obstacle would be more likely to invite reader confidence.

Nevertheless, Bourdieu raises a worthwhile issue by asking for a *reflexive reading* as well as a reflexive production of social science. Sociologists live and work in fields of cultural consumption as well as cultural production. How we read a work is shaped by our intellectual field positions. Bourdieu wants a scientific reading of his work: one that does not reduce his analytical constructs to particular individuals, polemical labels, or political positions.

Homo Academicus is strikingly free of academic gossip, ad hominem attacks, anecdotes, personal impressions, or autobiographical excursions. Bourdieu is largely successful in reminding the reader that this is a systematically constructed analysis rather than an impressionistic portrait of French academe. The study offers a structural mapping of a familiar professional world where individual social identities are "submerged" in a relational analysis of field positions. Bourdieu is cautious even in using names of French academics as illustrations in an effort to keep reader attention focused on the structural argument.[8] Nevertheless, readers intimately familiar with French academe can identify particular individuals in the kinds of intellectual profiles Bourdieu constructs. For example, to illustrate the ideal-type professor with considerable academic capital but little intellectual capital, Bourdieu (1988b:84–85) accompanies an interview excerpt with sufficient biographical detail to permit a well-known classics professor characterized as "useless," his work as "pathetic," and as someone who "has absolutely nothing to say" to be fairly easily identified by his peers. Occasionally, he cannot resist a pointed attack against one of his competitors and sharp critics, such as Raymond Boudon, though this is quite exceptional (see ibid., 16–17).

We are told that efforts to objectify the intellectual world without reflexivity amount to strategies of symbolic power and violence, where in the name of science the researcher attempts to "set himself up as a judge of the judges" (15). Yet, just a few pages earlier he dismisses as "semi-scholarly taxonomies" ideal-typical constructions by Gouldner (1957), Clark (1963a, 1963b), and Gustad (1966) as "semi-scientific" forms of symbolic violence. According to Bourdieu (1988b:12), such ideal-types operate as "concept-as-insult" by directing attention toward practical activities of particular individuals rather than toward the field of relations where they obtain true sociological significance. They do not break sufficiently with received wisdom of everyday practices.

Now, it is possible to grant Bourdieu's point that certain ideal-typical constructions, such as "jet sociologist" (one who spends more time at conferences than in the classroom), can function as euphemized forms of insults that had better be left in a David Lodge novel rather than appear in sociological analysis. Yet it is also possible to see that by discrediting competitors as being less "scientific," which most certainly amounts to a form of sym-

8. The English translation displays full names in one field diagram whereas the original French text used only initials.

bolic violence, Bourdieu himself remains locked in the competition to enhance his own position in the scientific field.[9] Moreover, Bourdieu's own *homo academicus* is not a value-free label, but clearly represents in his eyes a less legitimate form of intellectual activity than that of the researcher who produces new knowledge. Thus, Bourdieu himself only partially escapes from the competitive logic of scholarly distinction.

Bourdieu's claim that reflexivity should be first of all used against oneself as a technique to increase self-awareness of the social forces shaping one's intellectual work stands in uneasy juxtaposition with his sharply critical posture toward most other sociological work.[10] He seldom identifies his own position within the intellectual field or those factors that likely shape or even limit his own outlook.[11] Rather, his critical sights are trained on the intellectual field as a whole or on certain positions within it. Seldom does he preface his analysis with a statement of the limits of his particular position and perspective. It is as if in attacking the views of others by showing how they stem from interested positions within competitive fields, Bourdieu believes he is able to achieve a measure of freedom from the field determinations that shape his own work. I believe this to be only partially true. His sharply critical style against opposing positions and his compulsion to separate and distinguish features of his work from others leaves in the final analysis a body of work that is fundamentally shaped—if negatively—by key French intellectuals and intellectual traditions as outlined in chapter 2.

Does this not suggest that Bourdieu's reflexive analysis contradicts his own methodological prescriptions? Is Bourdieu in the final analysis unable to step outside of the values and traditions of the French academic system that he tries to analyze (Jenkins 1989:643)? In my view this criticism points up the limits but does not disqualify the enterprise he is proposing. It points to a fundamental tension in his work that needs clarification.

From a strictly logical standpoint, Bourdieu's claim for the possibility of finding some degree of escape from the interested character of *all* intel-

---

9. Besides, there is affinity, as well as difference, between Bourdieu's analysis of the French academy and Gouldner's classic topology of academic "locals" and "cosmopolitans," which Bourdieu does not acknowledge.

10. Bourdieu (28–29) justifies his criticism of other sociologists as stemming from the "very intention" of "the sociology of scientific knowledge" which is "justified" only if such criticism is carried out "in the name of a more rigorous scientific knowledge of the limits associated with the conditions of its production." Here Bourdieu conflates his own work and critical style with his ideal-knowledge interests, which are to be the exclusive motivating factor in scientific work.

11. Indeed, he is dismissive of such efforts, arguing that they restrict the reflexive moment to the introductory part of a work and tend to be no more than exercises in narcissism.

lectual practices appears contradictory. Since the interested character of all action is premised from the outset, it is strange that Bourdieu would even attempt an escape. Yet in some passages he writes as if the ideal of objectivity means just that: escaping from all interests. In other passages, however, he stresses that this is not possible; indeed, that such a view represents the objectivist illusion he so sharply criticizes. Rather than try to escape all intellectual interests, he seems to believe that a reflexive practice can help free the researcher from the particular economic, cultural, and social interests that distort the singular pursuit of ideal interests of scientific knowledge. In this respect Bourdieu's reflexive analysis is more successful.

Bourdieu's sociology of sociology also provides insight into the institutional base for some of the leading critical French thinkers in the last forty years. Bourdieu's field analysis of French academe helps readers outside of France understand that many of the French intellectuals with recent international renown, such as Althusser, Barthes, Deleuze, Derrida, and Foucault, are not in fact at the pinnacle of French academic power. While they may exercise considerable symbolic and intellectual clout at home and abroad, in terms of national institutional resources they are really quite marginal (Bourdieu 1988b:xviii). Moreover, Bourdieu suggests that his field analysis indicates that the "anti-institutional disposition" manifested in the work of these leading contemporary French thinkers undoubtedly finds its roots in their marginal status with regard to the institutional power of the French academy (Bourdieu and Wacquant 1989:13–14). The same is likely true for Bourdieu, who shares a similar location on the academic field map.

Bourdieu's reflexive analysis of French academe also deepens our understanding of Bourdieu's own intellectual strategy. His reflexive emphasis stems in part from his geographical, social, and cultural origins as an "outsider" to the Parisian intellectual establishment. Bourdieu entered the Parisian intellectual world, not as a cultural inheritor, but as an upwardly mobile cultural accumulator. Consequently, he has been obliged to examine self-consciously the assumptions of the new world he entered but did not inherit. The emphasis he places on the need to break with everyday assumptions and to carefully construct scientific discourse by rigorously controlling its semantic content resonates better with the experience of the cultural outsider than with the cultural inheritor.

Bourdieu's reflexivity also stems from his sharply negative reaction, as a scientific intellectual, to forms of intellectual arrogance he finds pervasive in French academic philosophy. The arrogance he identifies with the Parisian intellectual style of making universal claims and holding in scorn mundane tasks of data collection and analysis.[12] Yet, Bourdieu himself internalized that distinctly critical style transmitted by the Ecole Normale. And he employs it with force against both the French high-brow cultural tradition and positivist social science. Reflexivity can be seen as Bourdieu's strategic effort to mark out a distinct position in the French intellectual field and to advocate a distinct mode of intellectual inquiry. It becomes for him a tool of struggle in the very field it seeks to transcend. Thus, Bourdieu's reflexivity intersects intimately with his own career trajectory.

12. Describing his own experience in the French university world Bourdieu (1988b:xxvi) writes: "And the special place held in my work by a somewhat singular sociology of the university institution is no doubt explained by the peculiar force with which I felt the need to gain rational control over the disappointment felt by an 'oblate' faced with the annihilation of the truths and values to which he was destined and dedicated, rather than take refuge in feelings of self-destructive resentment."

12   CONCLUSION

At the heart of Bourdieu's sociological inquiry is the question of why forms of social inequality persist without powerful resistance. The answer, Bourdieu argues, lies in how cultural resources, practices, and institutions function to maintain unequal social relations. The relationship of culture to power stands at the center of Bourdieu's intellectual project. Bourdieu's analysis of how culture obscures class power and provides the tools for social distinctions represents a key contribution to contemporary sociology of culture. Indeed, Bourdieu's reformulation of the problem of ideology and false consciousness stands as one of his central contributions to the study of class and power in modern societies.

The tremendous growth of education and cultural markets in the advanced societies has fostered the increased use of more subtle and elusive cultural mechanisms of domination than was the case during the period of nascent capitalism. In formulating his political economy of symbolic power, Bourdieu insightfully addresses this change in modes of domination. Bourdieu's work demonstrates that a general shift from physical coercion to softer forms of social control nonetheless fosters the reproduction and legitimation of inegalitarian social relations. His political economy of symbolic power is perhaps the most ambitious and consequential project for the study of the symbolic realm since that of Talcott Parsons (1951). Indeed, Bourdieu tries to do for the cultural realm what Marx attempted for the economic realm: to understand the fundamental structures and dynamics of power in cultural life. Key elements of his conceptual language, such as social and cultural reproduction, cultural capital, habitus, field, and symbolic violence have already become part of the working vocabulary of many social scientists.

Bourdieu's Sociology of Culture in Comparative Perspective

In many respects, Bourdieu's ambitious program spans the four principal traditions and their key theorists that Wuthnow et al. (1984) identify as decisively shaping contemporary approaches to the study of culture. Bourdieu draws upon phenomenology as does Peter Berger (1967; Berger and Luckmann 1966); cultural anthropology—particularly the Durkheimian influence—as does Mary Douglas (1966, 1970, 1982); French neostructuralism, as does Michel Foucault (1972, 1978a, 1980); and critical theory, as does Jürgen Habermas (1970, 1971, 1973). While it would be presumptuous to suggest that he provides a synthesis, the complexity and richness of his approach does incorporate key elements of each of these separate traditions. Like Foucault, Bourdieu searches for deep structures of cultural and social life that are linked to power. The dynamics of power intersect with all aspects of cultural life. Like Douglas, Bourdieu sees culture in terms of categories of social classification; cultural distinctions euphemize underlying social distinctions. Like Habermas, Bourdieu examines critically received cultural categories, and shares with Habermas a concern for the epistemological status of a science of culture. And like Berger, Bourdieu shows that macro structures are also objects of social construction by actors.

More generally, Bourdieu contributes to the current shift in orientation toward the study of culture at the institutional level (Wuthnow 1987). Though he rejects the bifurcation of human behavior into distinct realms— one subjective, having to do with thoughts, beliefs, and ideas, and the other objective, entailing concrete observable behaviors—his overall effort can be seen as part of a broader swing from subjective to more institutional approaches to the study of culture. He focuses on categories of classifications and practices rather than emphasizing rich description of behavior or empathic understanding of actor sentiments and intentions as does the phenomenological tradition. His institutional emphasis can be seen particularly in his concept of field which calls attention to the positions of actors, organizations, resources, and their struggle in the production, transmission, and consumption of culture.

Compared with other leading contemporary cultural theorists, Bourdieu alone manages to combine abstract theory reflecting his Continental philosophical heritage with empirical research and an explicit reflection upon method. He reaches out in both directions—toward the abstract and the concrete—in ways no other contemporary social scientist does. This is all the more remarkable in a sociologist at a time when the social sciences—sociology in particular—are becoming more and more fragmented and internally differentiated by competing specializations in method, theory, and substantive areas of inquiry (Swartz, 1988).

Bourdieu is a source of inspiration to those who labor in social sciences, for he demonstrates that doing social theory is not incompatible with carrying out empirical research. Immersion in data need not mean loss of theoretical grounding; on the contrary, it may solidify it. His ethnographic research on peasant households in colonial Algeria, which is reported in *Outline of a Theory of Practice* (1977c) and *The Logic of Practice* (1990h); his study of consumer and lifestyle patterns in contemporary France, which is present in *Distinction* (1984a); his study in *Les règles de l'art* (1992) of French literature; and his research into the various mechanisms of inter- and intra-institutional stratification in French higher education, reported in *Reproduction* (Bourdieu and Passeron, 1977), *Homo Academicus* (1988b) and *La Noblesse d'Etat* (1989c)—to mention only some of the most comprehensive and notable bodies of work—are all empirical exercises in rigorous social theorizing. Each of these publications will undoubtedly serve as a benchmark for future work in its respective field.

Culture as Power

Of all his concepts, *cultural capital*, which calls attention to the power dimension of cultural resources in market societies, undoubtedly has thus far found the widest reception. This concept is a powerful one, and has stimulated considerable research in the sociology of education, culture, and stratification. By calling attention to the subtle and pervasive ways in which language, knowledge, and cultural style shape interactions, it improves our understanding of the processes through which social-background effects are translated into unequal school performance and subsequent career chances. In the sociology of education, the concept has fostered detailed examination of kinds of cultural resources children bring from families to classrooms that affect academic performance (DiMaggio 1982; Lareau 1989). In the sociology of the arts, the concept has also been employed usefully to show how cultural socialization in families and schools shapes attitudes and behavior toward the arts (DiMaggio 1977; DiMaggio and Useem 1978, 1982; Zolberg 1989).

The concept of cultural capital stands at the midpoint of two radically opposing intellectual traditions in Western thought. On the one hand, in identifying culture as a form of capital, Bourdieu breaks with the Marxist tradition by holding that culture is a power resource standing in its own right; it cannot be reduced to some superstructural derivative of underlying economic factors. On the other hand, Bourdieu also breaks with the humanist tradition that lauds the universal value of the classical canon; he argues that ideas and aesthetic values embody the practical interests of those who produce and appropriate them. Bourdieu thus bridges two radically different intellectual traditions by means of his theory of culture as a form of power.

Bourdieu makes a convincing case that the opposition between cultural capital and economic capital operates as a fundamental differentiating principle of power in modern societies. It distinguishes among elites who base their claim to power on cultural resources and those who rely more on economic resources. Particularly in *Distinction* do we see Bourdieu's effort to conceptualize and empirically display class and intraclass groups in terms of their respective configurations of different types of capital and their corresponding lifestyles as a bold and original approach to the study of stratification. Conceptualizing social classes in terms of their volume and composition of capital and social trajectory through fields gives a multidimensional and dynamic perspective on class hierarchies not captured in mainstream status-attainment research.

At a time when Marxism as a theory of advanced industrial societies appears less compelling, Bourdieu provides an attractive alternative, for he focuses attention on those knowledge and service occupations that are gaining in number and importance in late capitalism. But unlike postindustrial society theorists, such as Daniel Bell (1973, 1988), Bourdieu shows how these new cultural practices embody new forms of domination and social interests. Moreover, Bourdieu's theory and empirical research on the unequal distribution of cultural capital and its intergenerational transmission through schooling have produced an important insight into the internal differentiation of elites in modern societies: the primary beneficiaries of the expanded educational meritocracy are not members of the capitalist class but the children of professional families with cultural capital.

Bourdieu's meticulous efforts to demonstrate how cultural resources mediate class differences, particularly in the realm of tastes and lifestyles, stands in critical opposition to postmodern theories of consumer culture that posit a waning of class differences in consumer patterns in postindustrial societies (Baudrillard 1981). Despite growth in mass consumer markets, Bourdieu contends that cultural practices continue to be markers of underlying class distinctions in the case of France. His analysis invites comparisons with other national contexts, such as the United States, where differences in consumer choices may be perceived more as the result of differences in income than as disguised status distinctions of social honor, as Bourdieu claims. Moreover, the kind of class-culture distinctions Bourdieu stresses may be more characteristic of upper- and lower-class groups than of middle-class groups where consumer choices may be more directly influenced by mass-market product standardization.

Culture as a form of capital is a useful conceptualization for analyzing stratification processes in advanced societies, where market mechanisms penetrate virtually all realms of modern life. The concept seems less useful for societies where market mechanisms are less developed. Its currency appears less promising in societies with a less imposing high-culture tradition and with more cultural diversity than France. In addition, the concept suggests a view of agency that reduces actors to strategizing investors driven to maximize their investment opportunities regardless of where they are located in the stratification order. The culture-as-capital metaphor works best for certain professions in the media, the arts, and academe, where individuals seek to convert their valued cultural resources into economic rewards, and for those families who seek out valued types of education for their children. The concept is less useful for analyzing groups with few power resources.

Bourdieu is able to extend and reformulate with particular insight both Weber's idea of legitimation and the Marxian concept of ideology when he analyses how cultural practices assume symbolic value and obscure their role in justifying social inequality. However, Bourdieu's emphasis on the legitimating aspects of power, particularly their indirect and hidden effects, leave him with relatively little to say about the continued importance of sheer economic power or physical coercion in modern societies. The stress he places on misrecognition probably overstates the role that false consciousness has in maintaining groups in subordinate positions. Individuals and groups often see clearly the arbitrary character of power relations but lack the requisite resources to change them. And his insightful analyses of the important role that intellectuals play in providing cognitive classifications for ordering society probably overstates the importance of intellectuals to governing elites in some modern societies.

Social Change

Bourdieu was an early and key architect of the widely influential theory of social reproduction. His focus on the role of culture in social reproduction, however, leaves the important question of social change undeveloped. While Bourdieu is not rigidly deterministic, as some critics charge, his conceptual framework is clearly more attentive to patterns of continuity than to change. The concepts of habitus, cultural capital, and field stress the tendency to perpetuate structures inherited from the past. The propensity of habitus is clearly to address new situations in habituated ways, it takes capital to accumulate more capital, and field permits an impressive mapping of social positions and their continuity over time. His framework does not encourage researchers to seek out forms of change. Sources of change, as I point out in chapter 8, are suggested here and there in his work but never mobilized into a convincing demonstration of their dynamics. One conceptual possibility for resistance and change rests on the mismatch between the expectations of habitus and the opportunities offered by fields. Yet the conditions under which disappointed expectations might turn into effective motors of change remain to be specified.

Habitus

One of Bourdieu's main contributions is to propose a framework that addresses the agency/structure problem in contemporary social theory. He in fact was one of the first poststructuralist sociologists to bring actors back into structural models of stratification by showing that the idea that structures reproduce and function as constraints is not incompatible with the idea that actors create structures. Bourdieu's actors are strategists, though he does not think of strategy primarily as conscious choice but as a tacit calculation of interest and pursuit of distinction. His concept of habitus both offers a programmatic research agenda for addressing the agency/structure issue and points to an ideal-typical pattern of action. The research agenda derives from his theory that action is generated by the encounter between opportunities or constraints presented by situations and the durable dispositions that reflect the socialization of past experiences, traditions, and habits that individuals bring to situations. An adequate account of human behavior needs to combine the observed regularities of human behavior and the representations of individuals and groups. His programmatic agenda mounts a challenge to academic sociology by claiming that micro and macro, and objective and subjective levels of analysis are not to be separated by forms of theoretical or methodological specialization. He argues that theory and empirical research must proceed simultaneously on both levels rather than, as is the frequent practice today, confining attention to just one type of data or level of analysis.

Though difficult to specify empirically, habitus also points to an ideal-type of action that is habituated, practical, tacit, dispositional, and at the same time structured. Culture is conceptualized as practices following common master patterns that range over cognitive, corporeal, as well as attitudinal dimensions of action. Some of Bourdieu's most suggestive analyses point to such common dispositions, as in the case of the aristocratic asceticism among French university teachers who display cultivated restraint in sports, diet, entertainment, and bodily care. While I criticized Bourdieu in chapter 5 for being reluctant to specify conditions in which one dimension prevails over the other, I nonetheless believe that his understanding of individual action comes much closer to conceptualizing the complexity of human conduct than simplified rational-actor or structural models that attribute action to either calculated choice or to external constraints. Yet he also criticizes interpretative and phenomenological approaches for not situating action with respect to broader structural constraints. Bourdieu's idea that action is generated by the *interaction* of the opportunities and constraints of situations with actor dispositions—the repository of past experience, tradition, and habit—seems to constitute a considerable advance over these alternative views.

While habitus calls attention to the dynamics of self-selection in competitive social processes, the internalization of objective chances into expectations and the adaptation of aspirations to actual opportunities are often more complex and contradictory processes than the concept suggests. Moreover, both adaptation to external constraints and distinction from competing actors are two distinct types of agency juxtaposed in Bourdieu's concept without their exact relationship being clarified. Bourdieu calls upon one or the other dynamic depending on the issue he is addressing and without specifying the conditions in which one assumes the more prominent role.

Field

If habitus provides a valuable orientation for conceptualizing and researching relations between agency and structures, the concept of field is useful for studying the operation of culture at a more institutional level. His field-analytic framework contributes to our understanding of ways that culture mediates class relations at an institutional level. It offers a political economy of culture by identifying areas of production, transmission, and consumption of various forms of cultural capital. Of all his concepts, field is currently the least well understood and yet the most promising for future sociological work.

Bourdieu's concept of field draws on his insight that social units develop their identity in opposition to others and that an adequate grasp of their sociological character requires that they be situated within this broader arena of opposing forces. The concept points to arenas of conflict and struggle that develop with the emergence of particular kinds of valued resources, and shows how forms of social closure result from structures and processes that engage individuals and groups in competition for valued cultural resources as fields gain in autonomy. Bourdieu's field concept encourages the researcher to seek out sources of conflict in a given domain, relate that conflict to the broader arenas of class and power, and show what opposing parties actually share, but rarely acknowledge.

Bourdieu's effort to define some of the structural properties of fields gives this concept more analytical promise than the concept of markets for the analysis of culture. Fields indicate much more than the "invisible hand" of the market. They specify power relations and hierarchy. The ideas of structural polarities, hierarchial positions, competition for scarce resources, struggle between heterodoxy and orthodoxy, and a shared *doxa* among competitors indicate mechanisms of internal structuring that generate fields and contribute to their autonomy and functioning. They offer a much richer analysis of producer-consumer relations than does the image of a market.

The idea of the relative autonomy of cultural fields goes beyond both instrumentalist and structuralist views of how social classes, markets, and government shape cultural life, particularly education, in modern societies. By calling attention to the internal structuring mechanisms as groups of specialists develop, transmit, and control their own particular status culture, the idea of relative autonomy usefully stresses how particular organizational and professional interests can emerge and come into conflict with outside demands. Here Bourdieu's thinking intersects with issues raised in the debate over the relative autonomy of the state (see Block 1977; Skocpol 1979: 24–32). Bourdieu's contribution to the debate is to call attention to the cultural and professional as well as structural interests that give to central institutions, such as education or the state, some autonomy from capitalist class interests.

The idea of relative autonomy leads Bourdieu to give priority to the internal analysis of cultural fields. In so doing Bourdieu leaves undeveloped the important question of interfield contradictions as a possible source of crisis and change. To suggest that works of art or curriculum in schools reflect as much patterns of hierarchy and conflict among artists and educators as they do broader social, economic, or political interests is a useful rejection of class reductionism. Yet, by concentrating on the internal structuring mechanisms of fields, Bourdieu's concept gives short shrift to potential sources of conflict between cultural fields and their external demands.

Bourdieu's field analysis of intellectuals substantiates his framework by showing how intellectuals are situated in competitive arenas that have their own structures and dynamics that shape both their intellectual and political behavior. Field analysis is useful, for it suggests dimensions of influence on intellectual behavior that are not fully tapped by social-class background or position, *Zeitgeist*, or location in an organization. Rather, field analysis requires the researcher to move through all of these levels in search of the mechanisms of struggle for scarce resources and symbolic recognition that are important to the intellectual milieu. This important shift in focus for the study of intellectual and cultural life can be seen in Fritz Ringer's (1992) comparative analysis of German and French intellectual history.

The idea of cultural field sidesteps the old debate between idealism and materialism by offering a mediation concept that anchors intellectual life socially but avoids class reductionism. The contribution of field analysis of intellectuals suggests that New Class theories mistakenly try to assess the political significance of the highly educated largely in terms of their class position. Field analysis suggests that we can better understand the political behavior of intellectuals by situating them within their professional milieu. Yet the problem of reductionism does not go away, but reemerges in a kind of field reductionism as individual ideas and artistic styles reduce to their field positions. Indeed, there seems to be little chance for Bourdieu's cultural producers to transcend their field interests.

Field analysis provides an attractive structural mapping of arenas of struggle over different types of capital for power and privilege. It offers an insightful way of charting cultural as well as economic resources that can be mobilized in the politics of modern life. Bourdieu uses it to make many perceptive observations on political relations between culturally rich intellectuals and economically subordinate groups. He shows that both intellectuals and workers occupy subordinate positions relative to capitalists (though in different fields of struggle) and argues that this creates a basis for political alliance, albeit a precarious one. Yet, this powerful analytic technique leaves unexamined the social processes through which such an alliance might be formed. The difficulty is that many groups occupy homologous positions in their respective fields, but not all of them form alliances with one another. To conflate an observation of the homologous relations with an explanation of the formation of an alliance runs the risk of what I observed in chapter 6 as a form of "structuralist mystification." Bourdieu's field analysis needs a sociology of politics that would examine the actual processes of political action and mobilization.

Reflexivity, Science, and Politics

We have seen that Bourdieu rejects scientific positivism in favor of a thoroughly reflexive practice of sociology. For Bourdieu, the organization and analysis of empirical data, the use of both commonsense and scientific categories, professional interests, and the attitude of the social scientist toward the subject of inquiry all embody fundamental value orientations that prohibit a fully objective grasp of that world. Indeed, Bourdieu maintains that it is only by subjecting the full range of research procedures and professional interests to critical examination that the sociologist can gain a measure of freedom from their distorting influence.

Bourdieu believes that by doing a sociology of sociology he, as a researcher, can achieve a significant measure of freedom from the distorting effects of competition within the academic field rather than simply reproduce them. Nevertheless, a tension emerges between this vision for a reflexive practice of sociology and his analysis of possible sources of resistance to the cycle of reproduction. In Bourdieu's framework, the conceptual possibility for resistance and change rests on the mismatch between habitus and the opportunity structures of fields rather than on the power of reflexive thought. Yet Bourdieu articulates a vision of sociology as a source of human emancipation that seems to emphasize the power of theory as well as the structural underpinnings for resisting the status quo. If the source of change indeed derives from a structural dislocation between habitus and field, then what critical role can Bourdieu claim for the social sciences, or for himself? If, on the other hand, scientific reason, in spite of its interested quality, holds a measure of hope for gaining some greater control over the social forces that shape our behavior, then the view of culture as a form of capital seems too limiting. Bourdieu affirms both the power of reason and the necessary material conditions under which it finds expression as science. But these affirmations reside in uneasy tension and as of yet remain unreconciled in his work.

Bourdieu believes that the critical thrust of social science can help subordinate groups in their struggle against elites and he sees his sociology as a form of political intervention against all forms of domination. Yet he has very little to say on the central questions of when subordinate groups will have the inclination and capacity to act upon the critical findings of social science to actively resist domination. This suggests an idealized political role that Bourdieu envisages for the sociologist but one that remains to be grounded in a genuine political sociology.

If Bourdieu himself does not fully free himself from the competitive struggle for recognition in the scientific field, his efforts nonetheless give him an exceptional degree of critical distance from and insight into the French academic world. *Homo Academicus* identifies the institutional basis of the sharply critical posture of many contemporary French intellectual superstars, including Barthes, Derrida, Foucault, and Bourdieu himself;

they are all marginalized from the center of organizational power within the French university system and teaching profession. Not since Gould-ner's *The Coming Crisis in Western Sociology* appeared more than two decades ago have sociologists been so challenged to submit their own practices to the same critical examination they apply to others. While certainly not free of either analytical or moral dilemmas, Bourdieu's call for reflexivity speaks to one of the most pressing tasks for social scientists today: the need to gain a more objective, albeit not objectivist, grasp on the social world—including our own.

REFERENCES

Accardo, Alain. 1983. *Initiation à la sociologie de l'illusionnisme social.* Bordeaux: Editions le Mascaret.

Accardo, Alain, and Philippe Corcuff. 1986. *La sociologie de Bourdieu: Textes choisis et commentés.* Bordeaux: Editions le Mascaret.

Alexander, Jeffrey C., Bernhard Giesen, Richard Munch, and Neil J. Smelser, eds. 1987. *The Micro-Macro Link.* Berkeley and Los Angeles: University of California Press.

Althusser, Louis. 1970. *For Marx.* New York: Vintage Books.

Amiot, Michel. 1984. L'enseignement de la sociologie en France: Résumé et conclusions d'une enquête conduite à l'initiative de la Société française de sociologie. *Revue Française de Sociologie* 25: 281–91.

Ansart, Pierre. 1990. *Les sociologies contemporaines.* Paris: Editions du Seuil.

Apple, Michael, ed. 1982. *Cultural and Economic Reproduction in Education: Essays on Class, Ideology and the State.* London: Routledge and Kegan Paul.

Apple, Michael W., and Lois Weis. 1985. Ideology and schooling: The relationship between class and culture. *Education and Society* 3: 45–63.

Aron, Raymond. 1965. *Main Currents in Sociological Thought.* New York: Basic Books.

———. 1968. *La révolution introuvable.* Paris: Julliard.

———. 1983a. *The Committed Observer.* Chicago: Regnery Gateway.

———. 1983b. *Mémoires: Cinquante ans de réflexion politique.* Paris: Julliard.

Ashmore, Malcom. 1989. *The Reflexive Thesis: Wrighting Sociology of Scientific Knowledge.* Chicago: University of Chicago Press.

Bachelard, Gaston. 1980. *La formation de l'esprit scientifique: Contribution à une psychanalyse de la connaissance objective.* 11th ed. Paris: J. Vrin.

Baudelot, Christian, and Roger Establet. 1973. *L'école capitaliste en France.* Paris: François Maspéro.

Baudelot, Christian, Roger Establet, and Jacques Malemort. 1973. *La petite bourgeoisie en France.* Paris: François Maspero.

Baudrillard, Jean. 1981. *For a Critique of the Political Economy of the Sign,* trans. Charles Levin. St Louis: Telos Press.

———. 1988a. Fatal strategies. In *Jean Baudrillard: Selected Writings,* ed. M. Poster, 185–206. Stanford: Stanford University Press.

———. 1988b. The masses: The implosion of the social in the media. In *Jean Baudrillard: Selected Writings,* ed. M. Poster, 207–19. Stanford: Stanford University Press.

Baverez, Nicolas. 1993. *Raymond Aron: Un moraliste au temps des idéologies.* Paris: Flammarion.

Becker, Gary. 1964. *Human Capital.* New York: National Bureau of Economic Research.

———. 1976. *The Economic Approach to Human Behavior.* Chicago: University of Chicago Press.

Bell, Daniel. 1973. *The Coming of Post-Industrial Society.* New York: Basic Books.

———. 1976. *The Cultural Contradictions of Capitalism.* New York: Basic Books.

———. 1988. *The End of Ideology.* Cambridge, Mass.: Harvard University Press.

Benda, Julien. 1927. *La trahison des clercs.* Paris: Grasset.

Bénéton, Philippe. 1975. Discours sur la genèse des inégalités dans les sociétés occidentales contemporaines. *Revue française de science politique* 25 (1): 107–22.

Benzécri, J.-P. 1973. *L'analyse des Données: Leçons sur l'analyse factorielle . . . du Laboratoire de statistique de l'Université de Paris VI.* Rediges et publies sur la direction du professeur J.-P. Benzécri. Vol. 1: L. Bellier et al., *La taxinomie;* vol. 2: J.-P. Benzécri et al., *L'analyse des correspondances.* Paris: Dunod.

Berger, Bennett. 1986. Taste and domination. *American Journal of Sociology* 91 (6 May): 1445–53.

Berger, Peter. 1967. *The Sacred Canopy.* Garden City, N.Y.: Doubleday.

Berger, Peter, and Thomas Luckmann. 1966. *The Social Construction of Reality.* Garden City, N.Y.: Doubleday.

Bernstein, Basil. 1971–75. *Class, Codes and Control: Theoretical Studies towards a Sociology of Language.* 3 vols. London: Routledge and Kegan Paul.

Besnard, Philippe. 1987. *L'anomie: Ses usages et ses fonctions dans la discipline sociologique.* Paris: Presses Universitaires de France.

Block, Fred. 1977. The ruling class does not rule: Notes on the Marxist theory of state. *Socialist Revolution* 33: 6–28.

Bloom, Allan David. 1987. *The Closing of the American Mind: How Higher Educa-*

tion has Failed Democracy and Improvished the Souls of Today's Students. New York: Simon and Schuster.

Bloor, David. 1976. *Knowledge and Social Imagery.* London: Routledge and Kegan Paul.

Blumer, Herbert. 1969. *Symbolic Interactionism.* Englewood Cliffs, N.J.: Prentice-Hall.

Boltanski, Luc. 1987. *The Making of a Class: Cadres in French Society.* Cambridge: Cambridge University Press.

Boschetti, Anna. 1988. *The Intellectual Enterprise: Sartre and 'Les temps modernes.'* Evanston: Northwestern University Press.

Boudon, Raymond. 1969. La crise universitaire française: Essai de diagnostic. *Annales* 24 (May–June): 738–64.

———. 1970. Mai 68: Crise ou conflit, aliénation ou anomie? *L'année sociologique* 19: 222–42.

———. 1971. Sources of student protest in France. *The Annals of the American Academy of Political Science* 395 (May): 139–49.

———. 1974. *Education, Opportunity, and Social Inequality.* New York: John Wiley and Sons.

———. 1979. *La logique du social.* Paris: Hachette.

———. 1980. *The Crisis in Sociology: Problems of Sociological Epistemology.* New York: Columbia University Press.

———. 1986. *L'idéologie: Ou l'origine des idées reçues.* Paris: Fayard.

Bourdieu, Pierre. 1962a. *The Algerians.* Boston: Beacon Press.

———. 1962b. Célibat et condition paysanne. *Etudes rurales* 5/6 (April): 32–136.

———. 1963. Sociologues des mythologies et mythologies de sociologues. *Les temps modernes* 211 (December): 998–1021.

———. 1965. The sentiment of honour in Kabyle society. In *Honour and Shame: The Values of Mediterranean Society*, ed. J. G. Peristinay, 191–241. London: Weidenfeld and Nicholson.

———. 1966. Condition de classe et position de classe. *European Journal of Sociology* 7 (2): 201–23.

———. 1967a. Postface. In *Architecture gothique et pensée scolastique*, ed. E. Panofsky, 136–67. Paris: Editions de Minuit.

———. 1967b. Systems of education and systems of thought. *Social Science Information* 14 (3): 338–58.

———. 1968. Structuralism and theory of sociological knowledge. *Social Research* 35 (4): 681–706.

———. 1970. The Berber house, or the world reversed. *Social Science Information* 9 (2): 151–70.

———. 1971a. Champ du pouvoir, champ intellectuel et habitus de classe. *Scolies* 1: 7–26.

———. 1971b. Genèse et structure du champ religieux. *Revue Française de Sociologie* 12 (3): 295–334.

Bourdieu, Pierre. 1971c. Intellectual field and creative project. In *Knowledge and Control: New Directions for the Sociology of Education*, ed. M. F. D. Young, 161–88. London: Collier-Macmillan.

———. 1971d. Le marché des biens symboliques. *L'Année Sociologique* 22: 49–126.

———. 1972. *Esquisse d'une théorie de la pratique. Précedée de trois études d'ethnologie kabyle.* Geneva: Droz.

———. 1973a. Cultural reproduction and social reproduction. In *Knowledge, Education, and Cultural Change*, ed. R. Brown, 71–112. London: Tavistock.

———. 1973b. The three forms of theoretical knowledge. *Social Science Information* 12 (1): 53–80.

———. 1974a. Avenir de classe et causalité du probable. *Revue Française de Sociologie* 15 (1): 3–42.

———. 1974b. Is a sociology of action possible? In *Positivism and Sociology*, ed. A. Giddens, 101–13. London: Heinemann Educational Books.

———. 1974c. The school as a conservative force: Scholastic and cultural inequalities. In *Contemporary Research in the Sociology of Education*, ed. J. Eggleston, 32–46. London: Methuen.

———. 1975a. La lecture de Marx: Quelques remarques critiques à propos de *Quelques remarques critiques à propos de "Lire le Capital."* *Actes de la recherche en sciences sociales* 5/6: 65–79.

———. 1975b. The specificity of the scientific field and the social conditions of the progress of reason. *Social Science Information* 14 (6): 19–47.

———. 1977a. The economy of linguistic exchanges. *Social Science Information* 16 (6): 645–68.

———. 1977b. Marriage strategies as strategies of social reproduction. In *Family and Society: Selections from the Annales*, ed. R. Foster and O. Ranum, 117–44. Baltimore: Johns Hopkins University Press.

———. 1977c. *Outline of a Theory of Practice.* Cambridge: Cambridge University Press.

———. 1977d. Symbolic power. In *Identity and Structure*, ed. D. Gleeson, 112–19. Driffield: Nafferton Books.

———. 1979. *Algeria 1960.* Cambridge: Cambridge University Press.

———. 1980a. *Le sens pratique.* Paris: Editions de Minuit.

———. 1980b. The production of belief: Contribution to an economy of symbolic goods. *Media, Culture and Society* 2 (July): 261–93.

———. 1980c. *Questions de sociologie.* Paris: Editions de Minuit.

———. 1980d. Sartre. *London Review of Books* 2, no. 20 (October 20): 11–12.

———. 1981. La représentation politique. Eléments pour une théorie du champ politique. *Actes de la recherche en sciences sociales* 37 (February–March): 3–24.

———. 1982. *Leçon sur la leçon.* Paris: Editions de Minuit.

———. 1983a. The field of cultural production, or the economic world reversed. *Poetics* 12 (November): 311–56.

——. 1983b. The philosophical establishment. In *Philosophy in France Today*, ed. A. Montefiore, 1–8. Cambridge: Cambridge University Press.

——. 1984a. *Distinction: A Social Critique of the Judgement of Taste*. Cambridge, Mass.: Harvard University Press.

——. 1984b. La délégation et le fétichisme politique. *Actes de la recherche en sciences sociales* 52–53 (June): 49–55.

——. 1984c. Le champ littéraire: Préalables critiques et principes de méthode. *Lendemains* 36: 5–20.

——. 1985a. Delegation and political fetishism. *Thesis Eleven* 10/11: 56–70.

——. 1985b. The genesis of the concepts of "habitus" and "field." *Sociocriticism* 2 (2): 11–24.

——. 1985c. Les intellectuels et les pouvoirs. In *Michel Foucault, une histoire de la vérité*, 93–94. Paris: Syros.

——. 1985d. The market of symbolic goods. *Poetics* 14 (April): 13–44.

——. 1985e. Social space and the genesis of groups. *Theory and Society* 14 (6): 723–44.

——. 1986a. The forms of capital. In *Handbook of Theory and Research for the Sociology of Education*, ed. J. G. Richardson, 241–58. New York: Greenwood Press.

——. 1986b. From rules to strategies. *Cultural Anthropology* 1 (February): 110–20.

——. 1986c. La science et l'actualité. *Actes de la recherche en sciences sociales* 61 (March): 2–3.

——. 1987a. The biographical illusion. *Working Papers and Proceedings of the Center for Psychosocial Studies*, no. 14. Chicago: Center for Psychosocial Studies.

——. 1987b. *Choses Dites*. Paris: Editions de Minuit.

——. 1987c. The force of law: Toward a sociology of the juridical field. *Hastings Journal of Law* 38: 209–48.

——. 1987d. Legitimation and structured interests in Weber's sociology of religion. In *Max Weber, Rationality and Irrationality*, ed. S. Lash and S. Whimster, 119–36. Boston: Allen and Unwin.

——. 1987e. Revolt of the spirit. *New Socialist* 46 (February): 9–11.

——. 1987f. What makes a social class? On the theoretical and practical existence of groups. *Berkeley Journal of Sociology* 32: 1–18.

——. 1988a. Flaubert's point of view. *Critical Inquiry* 14 (Spring): 539–62.

——. 1988b. *Homo Academicus*. Stanford: Stanford University Press.

——. 1988c. La vertu civile. *Le Monde* (November 16): 1–2.

——. 1988d. *L'ontologie politique de Martin Heidegger*. Paris: Editions de Minuit.

——. 1988e. Penser la politique. *Actes de la recherche en sciences sociales* 71/72: 2–3.

——. 1988f. Program for a sociology of sport. *The Sociology of Sport Journal* 5 (2): 153–61.

——. 1988g. Vive la crise! For heterodoxy in social science. *Theory and Society* 17, no. 5 (September): 773–88.

Bourdieu, Pierre. 1989a. The corporatism of the universal: The role of intellectuals in the modern world. *Telos* 81 (Fall): 99–110.

———. 1989b. On the possibility of a field of world sociology. Keynote address to the Russell Sage Conference on "Social Theory in a Changing Society," the University of Chicago, April. Reprinted in Bourdieu and Coleman 1991.

———. 1989c. *La noblesse d'Etat: Grands corps et grandes écoles*. Paris: Editions de Minuit.

———. 1989d. Social space and symbolic power. *Sociological Theory* 7 (1): 14–25.

———. 1990a. Animadversiones in Mertonem. In *Robert K. Merton: Consensus and Controversy*, ed. J. Clark, C. Modgil, and S. Modgil, 297–301. London: The Falmer Press.

———. 1990b. Droit et passe-droit. Le champ des pouvoirs territoriaux et la mise en oeuvre des règlements. *Actes de la recherche en sciences sociales* 81/82: 86–96.

———. 1990c. *In Other Words: Essays toward a Reflexive Sociology*. Stanford: Stanford University Press.

———. 1990d. The intellectual field: A world apart. In *In Other Words: Essays toward a Reflexive Sociology*, 140–49. Stanford: Stanford University Press.

———. 1990e. La domination masculine. *Actes de la recherche en sciences sociales* 84: 2–31.

———. 1990f. A lecture on the lecture. In *In Other Words: Essays toward a Reflexive Sociology*, 177–98. Stanford: Stanford University Press.

———. 1990g. Les conditions sociales de la circulation des idées. *Romanistische Zeitschrift für Literaturgeschichte* 14 (1/2): 1–10.

———. 1990h. *The Logic of Practice*. Stanford: Stanford University Press.

———. 1990i. The scholastic point of view. *Cultural Anthropology* 5 (4): 380–91.

———. 1991a. Aspirant philosophe. Un point de vue sur le champ universitaire dans les années 50. In *Les enjeux philosophiques des années 50*, 15–24. Paris: Centre Georges Pompidou.

———. 1991b. Genesis and structure of the religious field. *Comparative Social Research* 13: 1–43.

———. 1991c. *Language and Symbolic Power*, trans. Gino Raymond and Matthew Adamson. Cambridge, Mass.: Harvard University Press.

———. 1991d. Le champ littéraire. *Actes de la recherche en sciences sociales* 89 (September): 4–46.

———. 1991e. The peculiar history of scientific reason. *Sociological Forum* 5 (2): 3–26.

———. 1991f. *The Political Ontology of Martin Heidegger*. Stanford: Stanford University Press.

———. 1992. *Les règles de L'art: Gènese et structure du champ littéraire*. Paris: Editions du Seuil.

———. 1993a. Esprits d'État: Genèse et structure du champ bureaucratique. *Actes de la recherche en sciences sociales* 96/97: 49–62.

———. 1993b. *The Field of Cultural Production: Essays on Art and Literature.* New York: Columbia University Press.

———. 1993c. Haute couture and haute culture. In *Sociology in Question,* 132–38. Thousand Oaks, Calif.: Sage Publications.

———. 1993d. *Sociology in Question,* trans. Richard Nice. Thousand Oaks, Calif.: Sage Publications.

———. 1994. *Raisons pratiques: Sur la théorie de l'action.* Paris: Editions du Seuil.

———. 1995. La Cause de la Science: Comment l'histoire sociale des sciences sociales peut servir le progrès de ces sciences. *Actes de la recherche en sciences sociales* 106–7 (March): 3–10.

———. 1996. *Sur la télévision.* Paris: Liber.

Bourdieu, Pierre, and Luc Boltanski. 1975. Le titre et le poste: Rapports entre le système de production et le système de reproduction. *Actes de la recherche en sciences sociales* 2: 95–107.

———. 1977. Changes in social structure and changes in the demand for education. In *Contemporary Europe: Social Structures and Cultural Patterns,* ed. S. Giner and M. Scotford-Archer, 197–227. London: Routledge and Kegan Paul.

———. 1981. The educational system and the economy: Titles and jobs. In *French Sociology: Rupture and Renewal Since 1968,* ed. C. C. Lemert, 141–51. New York: Columbia University Press.

Bourdieu, Pierre, Luc Boltanski, Robert Castel, Jean-Claude Chamboredon, and Dominique Schnapper. 1965. *Un art moyen: Essai sur les usages de la photographie.* Paris: Editions de Minuit.

———. 1990. *Photography: A Middle-Brow Art,* trans. Shaun Whiteside. Stanford: Stanford University Press.

Bourdieu, Pierre, Luc Boltanski, and Pascal Maldidier. 1971. La Défense du Corps. *Social Science Information* 10 (4): 45–86.

Bourdieu, Pierre, Salah Bouhedja, Rosine Christin, and Claire Givry. 1990. Un placement de père de famille. La maison individuelle: Spécificité du produit et logique du champ de production. *Actes de la recherche en sciences sociales* 81/82: 6–35.

Bourdieu, Pierre, Salah Bouhedja, and Claire Givry. 1990. Un contrat sous contrainte. *Actes de la recherche en sciences sociales* 81/82: 34–51.

Bourdieu, Pierre, A. Casanova, and M. Simon. 1975. Les intellectuels dans le champ de la lutte des classes. *La nouvelle critique* 87 (October): 20–26.

Bourdieu, Pierre, Jean-Claude Chamboredon, and Jean-Claude Passeron. 1991. *The Craft of Sociology: Epistemological Preliminaries.* 2d ed. New York: Walter de Gruyter.

Bourdieu, Pierre, and James S. Coleman, ed. 1991. *Social Theory for a Changing Society.* Boulder, Colo.: Westview Press.

Bourdieu, Pierre, Alain Darbel, Jean-Pierre Rivet, and Claude Seibel. 1963. *Travail et travailleurs en Algérie.* The Hague: Mouton.

Bourdieu, Pierre, and Monique de Saint Martin. 1974. Scholastic excellence and the values of the educational system. In *Contemporary Research in the Sociology of Education*, ed. J. Eggleston, 338–71. London: Methuen.

———. 1978. Le patronat. *Actes de la recherche en sciences sociales* 20/21: 3–82.

———. 1982. La sainte famille. L'épiscopat français dans le champ du pouvoir. *Actes de la recherche en sciences sociales* 44/45: 2–53.

Bourdieu, Pierre, and Hans Haacke. 1994. *Libre-Echange*. Paris: Seuil/les presses du réel.

Bourdieu, Pierre, and Otto Hahn. 1970. La théorie. *VH 101* 2 (Summer): 12–21.

Bourdieu, Pierre, and Jean-Claude Passeron. 1967. Sociology and philosophy in France since 1945: Death and resurrection of a philosophy without subject. *Social Research* 34 (1): 162–212.

———. 1968. L'examin d'une illusion. *Revue Française de Sociologie* 9 (special issue): 227–53.

———. 1977. *Reproduction in Education, Society and Culture*. London: Sage.

———. 1979. *The Inheritors: French Students and their Relation to Culture*. Chicago: University of Chicago Press.

Bourdieu, Pierre, Jean-Claude Passeron, and Monique de Saint Martin. 1965. *Rapport pédagogique et communication*. The Hague: Mouton.

———. 1992. *Academic Discourse: Linguistic Misunderstanding and Professorial Power*. Cambridge: Polity Press.

Bourdieu, Pierre, and Abdelmalek Sayad. 1964. *Le déracinement. La crise de l'agriculture traditionnelle en Algérie*. Paris: Editions de Minuit.

Bourdieu, Pierre, and Loïc J. D. Wacquant. 1989. For a socioanalysis of intellectuals: On *Homo Academicus*. *Berkeley Journal of Sociology* 34: 1–29.

Bourdieu, Pierre, and Loïc J. D. Wacquant. 1992. *An Invitation to Reflexive Sociology*. Chicago: University of Chicago Press.

Bowles, Samuel, and Herbert Gintis. 1976. *Schooling in Capitalist America: Educational Reform and the Contradictions of Economic Life*. New York: Basic Books.

Brint, Steven. 1984. 'New Class' and cumulative trend explanations of the liberal political attitudes of professionals. *American Journal of Sociology* 90 (1): 30–71.

———. 1991. The powers of the intellectuals. In *Sociology and the Public Agenda*, ed. W. J. Wilson, 51–70. Newbury Park, Calif.: Sage Publications.

———. 1994. *In an Age of Experts: The Changing Role of Professionals in Politics and Public Life*. Princeton: Princeton University Press.

Brint, Steven, and Jerome Karabel. 1989. *The Diverted Dream: Community Colleges and the Promise of Educational Opportunity in America, 1900–1980*. New York: Oxford University Press.

Brubaker, Rogers. 1985. Rethinking classical sociology: The sociological vision of Pierre Bourdieu. *Theory and Society* 14 (6): 745–75.

———. 1993. Social theory as habitus. In *Bourdieu: Critical Perspectives*, ed. C. Calhoun, E. LiPuma, and M. Postone, 212–34. Chicago: University of Chicago Press.

Brym, Robert J. 1987. The political sociology of intellectuals: A critique and a proposal. In *Intellectuals in Liberal Democracies: Political Influence and Social Involvement*, ed. A. G. Gagnon, 199–209. New York: Praeger.

Caillé, Alain. 1981. La sociologie de l'intérêt est-elle intéressante? *Sociologie du Travail* 23 (3): 257–74.

———. 1992. Esquisse d'une critique de l'économie générale de la pratique. *Cahiers du LASA* 12/13: 109–219.

———. 1993. *La démission des clercs: La crise des sciences sociales et l'oubli du politique.* Paris: Editions la Découverte.

Calhoun, Craig. 1993. Habitus, field, and capital: The question of historical specificity. In *Bourdieu: Critical Perspectives*, 61–88. Chicago: University of Chicago Press.

Calhoun, Craig, Edward LiPuma, and Moishe Postone, eds. 1993. *Bourdieu: Critical Perspectives.* Chicago: University of Chicago Press.

Camic, Charles. 1986. The matter of habit. *American Journal of Sociology* 91 (5): 1039–87.

Caute, David. 1964. *Communism and the French Intellectuals, 1914–1960.* London: André Deutsch.

Centers, Richard. 1949. *The Psychology of Social Classes: A Study of Class Consciousness.* Princeton: Princeton University Press.

Charle, Christophe. 1987. *Les élites de la République, 1880–1900.* Le sens commun. Paris: Editions de Minuit.

———. 1990. *Naissance des "intellectuels," 1880–1900.* Le sens commun. Paris: Editions de Minuit.

Cherkaoui, Mohamed. 1981. Changement social et anomie: Essai de formalisation de la théorie durkheimienne. *European Journal of Sociology* 22 (1): 3–39.

Chiari, Joseph. 1975. *Twentieth-Century French Thought: From Bergson to Lévi-Strauss.* New York: Gordian Press.

Chomsky, Noam. 1965. *Aspects of the Theory of Syntax.* Cambridge, Mass.: MIT Press.

Cicourel, Aaron V. 1973. *Cognitive Sociology.* New York: Free Press.

Clark, Burton R. 1962. *Educating the Expert Society.* San Francisco: Chandler.

———. 1963a. Faculty culture. In *The Study of Campus Culture*, 39–54. Boulder, Colorado: Western Interstate Commission for Higher Education.

———. 1963b. Faculty organization and authority. In *The Study of Academic Administration*, ed. T. F. Lunsford, 37–51. Boulder, Colo.: Western Interstate Commission for Higher Education.

———. 1973. The Wesleyan story: The importance of moral capital. In *Academic Transformation: Seventeen Institutions under Pressure*, ed. D. Riesman and V. A. Stadtman, 367–81. New York: McGraw-Hill.

Coleman, James S. 1990. *Foundations of Social Theory.* Cambridge, Mass.: Harvard University Press.

Collectif "Révoltes logiques." 1984. *L'empire du sociologue.* Paris: Editions La Découverte.

Collins, James. 1993. Determination and contradiction: An appreciation and critique of the work of Pierre Bourdieu on language and education. In *Bourdieu: Critical Perspectives*, ed. C. Calhoun, E. LiPuma, and M. Postone, 116–38. Chicago: University of Chicago Press.

Collins, Randall. 1971. Functional and conflict theories of educational stratification. *American Sociological Review* 36: 1002–19.

———. 1975. *Conflict Sociology: Toward an Explanatory Science.* New York: Academic Press.

———. 1979. *The Credential Society: An Historical Sociology of Education and Stratification.* New York: Academic Press.

———. 1981a. Cultural capitalism and symbolic violence. In *Sociology Since Mid-Century: Essays in Theory Cumulation*, 173–82. New York: Academic Press.

———. 1981b. On the micro-foundations of macro-sociology. *American Journal of Sociology* 86: 984–1014.

———. 1989. Review of *Homo Academicus. American Journal of Sociology* 95 (2): 460–63.

Colquhoun, Robert. 1986. *Raymond Aron: The Sociologist in Society 1955–1983.* 2 vols. Beverly Hills, Calif.: Sage Publications.

Connell, R. W. 1983. The black box of habit on the wings of history: Reflections on the theory of reproduction. In *Which Way is Up? Essays on Sex, Class, and Culture*, 140–61. London: George Allen and Unwin.

Cookson, Peter W., Jr., and Caroline Hodges Persell. 1985. *Preparing for Power: America's Elite Boarding Schools.* New York: Basic Books.

Coser, Lewis A. 1965. *Men of Ideas: a Sociologist's View.* New York: The Free Press.

Crozier, Michel. 1969. *La société bloquée.* Paris: Editions du Seuil.

Crozier, Michel, and Edouard Friedberg. 1977. *L'acteur et le système.* Paris: Editions du Seuil.

Current Research. 1972. Paris: Ecole Pratique des Hautes Etudes, Maison des Sciences de L'Homme.

Dalton, George, ed. 1968. *Primitive, Archaic and Modern Economies: Essays of Karl Polanyi.* Boston: Beacon Press.

Debray, Regis. 1981. *Teachers, Writers, Celebrities: The Intellectuals of Modern France.* London: Verso.

DiMaggio, Paul. 1979. Review essay on Pierre Bourdieu. *American Journal of Sociology* 84 (6): 1460–74.

———. 1982. Cultural capital and school success: The impact of status culture participation on the grades of U.S. high school students. *American Sociological Review* 47 (2): 189–201.

DiMaggio, Paul, and John Mohr. 1984. Cultural capital, educational attainment, and marital selection. *American Journal of Sociology* 90 (6): 1231–61.

DiMaggio, Paul, and Walter Powell. 1983. The iron cage revisited: Institutional isomorphism and collective rationality in organizational fields. *American Sociological Review* 48: 147–60.

Domhoff, G. Willliam. 1983. *Who Rules America Now?* Englewood Cliffs, N.J.: Prentice-Hall.

Dougherty, Kevin J. 1994. *The Contradictory College: The Conflicting Origins, Impacts, and Futures of the Community College*. Albany: State University of New York Press.

Douglas, Mary. 1966. *Purity and Danger: An Analysis of the Concepts of Pollution and Taboo*. New York: Pantheon Books.

———. 1970. *Natural Symbols: Explorations in Cosmology*. New York: Pantheon Books.

———. 1982. *In the Active Voice*. London: Routledge and Kegan Paul.

Drouard, Alain. 1982. Réflexions sur une chronologie: Le développement des sciences sociales en France de 1945 à la fin des années soixante. *Revue Française de Sociologie* 23: 55–85.

Dufay, François, and Pierre-Bertrand Dufort. 1993. *Les normaliens: De Charles Péguy à Bernard-Henri Lévy: un siècle d'histoire*. Paris: Editions Jean-Claude Lattès.

Durkheim, Emile. 1951. *Suicide*, trans. John A. Spaulding and George Simpson. Glencoe, Ill.: The Free Press.

———. 1966. *The Rules of Sociological Method*, trans. Sarah A. Solovay and John H. Mueller. New York: The Free Press.

———. 1977. *The Evolution of Educational Thought*. London: Routledge and Kegan Paul.

———. 1995. *The Elementary Forms of Religious Life*, trans. Karen E. Fields. New York: The Free Press.

Durkheim, Emile, and Marcel Mauss. 1963. *Primitive Classification*, trans. and ed. Rodney Needham. Chicago: University of Chicago Press.

Eisenstadt, S. N. 1973. *Tradition, Change and Modernity*. New York: John Wiley.

———. 1987. Intellectuals and political elites. In *Intellectuals in Liberal Democracies: Political Influence and Social Involvement*, ed. A. G. Gagnon, 157–65. New York: Praeger.

Elias, Norbert. 1978. *What is Sociology?* New York: Columbia University Press.

Elster, Jon. 1979. *Ulysees and the Sirens: Studies in Rationality and Irrationality*. New York: Cambridge University Press.

———. 1985. *Making Sense of Marx*. New York: Cambridge University Press.

Eribon, Didier. 1991. *Michel Foucault*, trans. Betsy Wing. Cambridge, Mass.: Harvard University Press.

Eyerman, Ron, Lennart G. Svensson, and Thomas Soderqvist, eds. 1987. *Intellectuals, Universities, and the State in Western Modern Societies*. Berkeley and Los Angeles: University of California Press.

Featherstone, Mike. 1987. Consumer culture, symbolic power and universalism.

In *Mass Culture, Popular Culture and Social Life in the Middle East*, ed. G. Stauth and S. Zubaida, 17–46. Boulder, Colo.: Westview Press.

Ferry, Luc, and Alain Renault. 1990. French Marxism (Pierre Bourdieu). In *French Philosophy of the Sixties: An Essay on Anti-Humanism*, 153–84. Amherst: Universitty of Massachusetts Press.

Feyerabend, Paul. 1978. *Science in a Free Society*. London: New Left Books.

Foucault, Michel. 1972. *The Archeology of Knowledge*. New York: Random House.

———. 1978a. *The History of Sexuality*. Vol. 1: *An Introduction*. New York: Random House.

———. 1978b. Introduction to Georges Canguilhem. In *On the Normal and the Pathological*, ed. R. S. Cohen, ix–xx. Dordrecht: Reidel.

———. 1980. *Power/Knowledge: Selected Interviews and Other Writings, 1972–1977*, ed. C. Gordon. New York: Pantheon Books.

Gagnon, Alain G. 1987. The role of intellectuals in liberal democracies: Political influence and social involvement. In *Intellectuals in Liberal Democracies: Political Influence and Social Involvement*, ed. A. G. Gagnon, 3–16. New York: Praeger.

Galbraith, John Kenneth. 1971. *The New Industrial State*. Boston: Houghton Mifflin.

Garfinkel, Harold. 1967. *Studies in Ethnomethodology*. Englewood Cliffs, N.J.: Prentice-Hall.

Garnham, Nicholas. 1986. Extended review: Bourdieu's *Distinction*. *The Sociological Review* 34 (2): 423–33.

———. 1993. Bourdieu, the cultural arbitrary, and television. In *Bourdieu: Critical Perspectives*, ed. G. Calhoun, E. LiPuma, and M. Postone, 178–92. Chicago: University of Chicago Press.

Garnham, Nicholas, and Raymond Williams. 1980. Pierre Bourdieu and the sociology of culture. *Media, Culture, and Society* 2 (3): 297–313.

Gartman, David. 1991. Culture as class symbolization or mass reification: A critique of Bourdieu's *Distinction*. *American Journal of Sociology* 97 (2): 421–47.

Geertz, Clifford. 1974. *The Interpretation of Cultures*. New York: Basic Books.

Gerth, H. H., and C. Wright Mills. 1964. *Character and Social Structure*. New York: Harcourt Brace Jovanovich.

———. 1970. *From Max Weber: Essays in Sociology*. London: Routledge and Kegan Paul.

Giddens, Anthony. 1973. *The Class Structure of the Advanced Societies*. New York: Harper and Row.

———. 1979. *Central Problems in Social Theory*. Berkeley and Los Angeles: University of California Press.

———. 1982. Durkheim, Socialism and Marxism. In *Profiles and Critiques in Social Theory*, 117–32. Berkeley and Los Angeles: University of California Press.

Giroux, Henry A. 1983. Theories of reproduction and resistance in the new sociology of education. *Harvard Educational Review* 53 (August): 257–93.

Goffman, Erving. 1950–51. Symbols of class status. *The British Journal of Sociology*: 294–304.

———. 1961. *Asylums*. Garden City, N.Y.: Doubleday.

———. 1967. *Interaction Ritual*. New York: Doubleday.

———. 1969. *Strategic Interaction*. Philadelphia: University of Pennsylvania Press.

———. 1971. *Relations in Public*. New York: Harper and Row.

———. 1974. *Frame Analysis*. New York: Harper and Row.

———. 1981. *Forms of Talk*. Philadelphia: University of Pennsylvania Press.

Goldthorpe, John H. 1980. *Social Mobility and Class Structure in Modern Britain*. Oxford: Clarendon Press.

Gouldner, Alvin W. 1954. *Patterns of Industrial Bureaucracy*. Glencoe, Ill.: The Free Press.

———. 1957. Cosmopolitans and locals: Toward an analysis of latent social roles—I. *Administrative Science Quarterly* 2 (3): 281–307.

———. 1970. *The Coming Crisis of Western Sociology*. New York: Basic Books.

———. 1973a. Anti-minataur: The myth of a value-free sociology. In *For Sociology: Renewal and Critique in Sociology Today*, 3–26. New York: Basic Books.

———. 1973b. The norm of reciprocity: A preliminary statement. In *For Sociology*, 226–59. New York: Basic Books.

———. 1973c. The politics of the mind. In *For Sociology: Renewal and Critique in Sociology Today*, 82–127. New York: Basic Books.

———. 1979. *The Future of Intellectuals and the Rise of the New Class*. New York: Oxford.

———. 1980. *The Two Marxisms*. New York: Seabury.

———. 1985. *Against Fragmentation: The Origins of Marxism and the Sociology of Intellectuals*. New York: Oxford University Press.

Gramsci, Antonio. 1971. *Prison Notebooks*, trans. and ed. Quintin Hoare and Geoffry Smith. New York: International Publishers.

Greenacre, Michael J. 1984. *Theory and Applications of Correspondence Analysis*. New York: Academic Press.

Grignon, Claude, and Christiane Grignon. 1980. Style d'alimentation et goûts populaires. *Revue Française de Sociologie* 21: 531–69.

Grignon, Claude, and Jean-Claude Passeron. 1984. *Sociologie de la culture et sociologie des cultures populaires*. Vol. 4. Paris: Documents du GIDES.

———. 1985. A propos des cultures populaires. *Cahiers du CERCOM* 1 (April).

Gurr, Ted Robert. 1970. *Why Men Rebel*. Princeton: Princeton University Press.

Gustad, J. W. 1966. Community, consensus, and conflict. *The Educational Record* (Fall): 439–51.

Habermas, Jürgen. 1970. Toward a theory of communicative competence. In *Recent Sociology*, ed. H. P. Dreitzel, 114–48. New York: Macmillan.

———. 1971. *Knowledge and Human Interests*. Boston: Beacon Press.

———. 1973. *Theory and Practice*. Boston: Beacon Press.

———. 1979. What is universal pragmatics? In *Communication and the Evolution of Society*, 1–68. Cambridge: Polity Press.

Halbwachs, Maurice. 1959. *The Psychology of Social Class*. Glencoe, Ill.: The Free Press.

Halle, David. 1991. Bringing materialism back in; Art in the houses of the working and middle classes. In *Bringing Class Back In: Contemporary and Historical Perspectives*, ed. S. G. McNall, R. F. Levine, and R. Fantasia, 241–59. Boulder, Colo.: Westview Press.

Hanks, William F. 1993. Notes on semantics in linguistic practice. In *Bourdieu: Critical Perspectives*, ed. C. Calhoun, E. LiPuma, and M. Postone, 139–55. Chicago: University of Chicago Press.

Harker, Richard. 1990. Bourdieu: Education and reproduction. In *An Introduction to the Work of Pierre Bourdieu*, ed. R. Harker, C. Mahar, and C. Wilkes, 86–108. New York: St. Martin's Press.

Harker, Richard, Cheleen Mahar, and Chris Wilkes, eds. 1990. *An Introduction to the Work of Pierre Bourdieu: The Practice of Theory*. New York: St. Martin's Press.

Harker, Richard K. 1984. On reproduction, habitus and education. *British Journal of Sociology and Education* 5 (2): 117–27.

Héran, François. 1987. La seconde nature de l'habitus. Tradition philosophique et sens commun dans le language sociologique. *Revue Française de Sociologie* 28 (3): 385–416.

Hoffman, Stanley. 1986. Monsieur Taste. *New York Review of Books* 33 (6): 45–48.

Hofstadter, Richard. 1963. *Anti-Intellectualism in American Life*. New York: Alfred A. Knopf.

Hollander, Paul. 1981. *Political Pilgrims*. New York: Oxford University Press.

———. 1987. American intellectuals: Producers and consumers of social criticism. In *Intellectuals in Liberal Democracies: Political Influence and Social Involvement*, ed. A. G. Gagnon, 67–86. New York: Praeger.

Honneth, Axel. 1986. The fragmented world of symbolic forms: Reflections on Pierre Bourdieu's sociology of culture. *Theory, Culture, and Society* 3 (3): 55–66.

Honneth, Axel, Hermann Kocyba, and Bernd Schwibs. 1986. The struggle for symbolic order: An interview with Pierre Bourdieu. *Theory, Culture, and Society* 3 (3): 35–51.

Hout, Michael, and Maurice Garnier. 1979. Curriculum placement and educational stratification in France. *Sociology of Education* 52: 146–56.

Hout, Michael, and William R. Morgan. 1975. Race and sex variation in the causes of the expected attainments of high school seniors. *American Journal of Sociology* 81: 364–91.

Huszar, George B. de, ed. 1960. *The Intellectuals: A Controversial Portrait*. Glencoe, Ill.: The Free Press.

Inglis, Roy. 1979. Good and bad habitus: Bourdieu, Habermas and the condition of England. *The Sociological Review* 27 (2): 353–69.

Isamberg-Jamati, Vivane, and Monique Segré. 1971. Systèmes scolaires et systèmes socio-économiques. *L'Année sociologique* 22: 527–51.

Jacoby, Russell. 1987. *The Last Intellectuals: American Culture in the Age of Academe.* New York: Basic Books.

Jakobson, Roman, and Morris Halle. 1956. *Fundamentals of Language.* The Hague: Mouton.

Jenkins, Richard. 1982. Pierre Bourdieu and the reproduction of determinism. *Sociology* 16 (2): 270–81.

Jenkins, Richard. 1989. Language, symbolic power and communication: Bourdieu's *Homo Academicus. Sociology* 23 (4): 639–45.

———. 1992. *Pierre Bourdieu.* London: Routledge.

Johnson, Paul. 1988. *Intellectuals.* New York: Harper and Row.

Joppke, Christian. 1986. The cultural dimension of class formation and class struggle: On the social theory of Pierre Bourdieu. *Berkeley Journal of Sociology* 31: 53–78.

Judt, Tony. 1992. *Past Imperfect: French Intellectuals,* 1944–1956. Berkeley and Los Angeles: University of California Press.

Kahl, Joseph. 1953. Educational and occupational aspirations of "common man" boys. *Harvard Educational Review* 42: 521–62.

Karabel, Jerome. 1972. Community colleges and social stratification. *Harvard Educational Review* 42 (November): 521–62.

———. 1994. Marx and the question of intellectuals. Princeton: School of Social Science, Institute for Advanced Study. Manuscript.

Karabel, Jerome, and A. H. Halsey, eds. 1977. *Power and Ideology in Education.* New York: Oxford University Press.

Karady, Victor. 1981. The prehistory of present-day French sociology 1917–1957. In *French Sociology: Rupture and Renewal since 1968,* ed. C. C. Lemert, 33–47. New York: Columbia University Press.

Karen, David. 1990. Access to higher education in the United States, 1900 to the present. In *Education and Society: A Reader,* ed. K. J. Dougherty and F. M. Hammack, 264–79. New York: Harcourt Brace Jovanovich.

Kuhn, Thomas S. 1962. *The Structure of Scientific Revolutions.* Chicago: University of Chicago Press.

Lamont, Michèle. 1989. Slipping the world back in: Bourdieu on Heidegger. *Contemporary Sociology* 18 (5): 781–83.

Lamont, Michèle, and Annette Lareau. 1988. Cultural capital: allusions, gaps and glissandos in recent theoretical developments. *Sociological Theory* 6 (2): 153–68.

Lareau, Annette. 1989. *Home Advantage: Social Class and Parental Intervention in Elementary Education.* New York: The Falmer Press.

Latour, Bruno. 1987. *Science in Action.* Milton Keynes: Open University Press.

Latour, Bruno, and Steve Woolgar. 1979. *Laboratory Life: The Social Construction of Scientific Facts.* London: Sage.

Lebard, L., A. Morineau, and K. Warwick. 1984. *Multivariate Descriptive Statistical Analysis: Correspondence Analysis and Related Techniques for Large Matrices.* New York: Wiley.

Lenski, Gerhard E. 1952. American social classes: Statistical strata or social groups? *American Journal of Sociology* 58 (2): 139–44.

———. 1954. Status crystallization: A non-vertical dimension of social status. *American Sociological Review* 19 (4): 405–13.

Le Roy Ladurie, Emmanuel. 1982. *Paris-Montpellier: P.C.-P.S.U. 1945–1963.* Paris: Gallimard.

Lévi-Strauss, Claude. 1966. *The Savage Mind.* Chicago: University of Chicago Press.

———. 1969. *The Elementary Structures of Kinship.* Boston: Beacon Press.

———. 1973. Introduction à l'oeuvre de Marcel Mauss. In *Sociologie et anthropologie,* ed. M. Mauss, ix–lii. Paris: Presses Universitaires de France.

Lewin, Kurt. 1951. *Field Theory in Social Science.* New York: Harper.

Lindenberg, Daniel. 1975. *Le Marxism introuvable.* Paris: Calmann-Lévy.

Lipset, Seymour Martin. 1991. No third way: A comparative perspective on the Left. In *The Crisis of Leninism and the Decline of the Left: the Revolutions of 1989,* ed. D. Chirot, 183–232. Seattle: University of Washington Press.

MacLeod, Jay. 1987. *Ain't No Makin' It: Leveled Aspirations in a Low-Income Neighborhood.* Boulder, Colo.: Westview Press.

———. 1995. *Ain't No Makin' It: Aspirations and Attainment in a Low-Income Neighborhood.* Rev. ed. Boulder, Colo.: Westview Press.

Mann, Michael. 1970. The social cohesion of liberal democracy. *American Sociological Review* 35 (June): 423–39.

Mann, Michael. 1973. *Consciousness and Action Among the Western Working Class.* London: Macmillan.

Mannheim, Karl. 1955. *Ideology and Utopia: An introduction to the sociology of knowledge,* trans. Louis Wirth and Edward Shils. New York: Harcourt, Brace and World.

———. 1956. The problem of the intelligentsia: An enquiry into its past and present role. In *Essays on the Sociology of Culture,* 91–170. London: Routledge and Kegan Paul.

Martin, Bill, and Ivan Szelenyi. 1987. Beyond cultural capital: Toward a theory of symbolic domination. In *Intellectuals, Universities and the State,* ed. R. Eyerman, T. Svensson, and T. Soderqvist, 16–49. Berkeley and Los Angeles: University of California Press.

Marx, Karl, and Friedrich Engels. 1978. Manifesto of the Communist Party. In *The Marx–Engels Reader,* ed. R. C. Tucker, 469–500. New York: W. W. Norton.

Mauss, Marcel. 1967. *The Gift.* New York: Norton.

McCall, Leslie. 1992. Does gender fit? Bourdieu, feminism, and conceptions of social order. *Theory and Society* 21 (6): 837–67.

Merleau-Ponty, Maurice. 1962. *Phenomenology of Perception.* Atlantic Highlands, N.J.: Humanities Press.

Merton, Robert K. 1968. *Social Theory and Social Structure.* Enlarged ed. New York: The Free Press.

———. 1973. *The Sociology of Science: Theoretical and Empirical Investigations,* ed. N. W. Storer. Chicago: University of Chicago Press.

Meyer, John W. 1970. The charter: Conditions of diffuse socialization in schools. In *Social Processes and Social Structures,* ed. W. R. Scott, 564–78. New York: Holt, Rinehart and Winston.

———. 1977. The effects of education as an institution. *American Journal of Sociology* 83 (1): 55–77.

Michelson, Roslyn Arlin. 1990. The attitude-achievement paradox among black adolescents. *Sociology of Education* 63 (1): 44–61.

Miller, Don, and Jan Branson. 1987. Pierre Bourdieu: Culture and praxis. In *Creating Culture: Profiles in the Study of Culture,* ed. D. J. Austin-Broos, 210–69. Boston: Allen and Unwin.

Miller, S. M. 1976. *Breaking the Credentials Barrier.* New York: Ford Foundation.

Mills, C. Wright. 1959. *The Sociological Imagination.* New York: Oxford University Press.

La misère du monde. 1993. A. Accardo et al., under the direction of Pierre Bourdieu. Editions du Seuil.

Mouriaux, R. 1980. Review of *La distinction. Sociologie du Travail* 22(4): 475–77.

Murphy, Raymond. 1988. *Social Closure: The Theory of Monopolization and Exclusion.* New York: Oxford University Press.

Nettl, J. P. 1969. Ideas, intellectuals and structures of dissent. In *On Intellectuals: Theoretical Studies, Case Studies,* ed. P. Rieff, 53–122. New York: Doubleday.

Nisbet, Robert A. 1966. *The Sociological Tradition.* New York: Basic Books.

Oakes, Jeannie. 1985. *Keeping Track: How Schools Structure Inequality.* New Haven: Yale University Press.

Ogbu, John U. 1978. *Minority Education and Caste: The American System in Cross-Cultural Perspective.* New York: Academic Press.

———. 1990. Social stratification and the socialization of competence. In *Education and Society: A Reader,* ed. K. J. Dougherty and F. M. Hammack, 390–401. New York: Harcourt Brace Jovanovich.

Ogburn, William Fielding. 1922. *Social Change.* New York: Viking Press.

O'Gorman, Hubert. 1986. The discovery of pluralistic ignorance. *Journal of the History of Behavioral Science* 22 (October): 333–47.

Ory, Pascal, and Sirinelli, Jean-François. 1986. *Les intellectuels en France, de l'Affaire Dreyfus à nos jours.* Paris: Armand Colin.

Parkin, Frank. 1971. *Class Inequality and Political Order: Social Stratification in Capitalist and Communist Societies.* New York: Holt, Rinehart and Winston.

———. 1979. *Marxism and Class Theory: A Bourgeois Critique.* New York: Columbia University Press.

Parsons, Talcott. 1947. Introduction. In *The Theory of Social and Economic Organization*, 3–86. Glencoe, Ill.: The Free Press.

———. 1951. *The Social System.* London: Routledge and Kegan Paul.

———. 1968. *The Structure of Social Action.* 2 vols. New York: The Free Press.

Pels, Dick. 1995. Knowledge politics and anti-politics: Toward a critical appraisal of Bourdieu's concept of intellectual autonomy. *Theory and Society* 24: 79–104.

Peterson, Richard A. 1985. Six constraints on the production of literary works. *Poetics* 14: 45–67.

Polanyi, Karl. 1944. *The Great Transformation.* Boston: Beacon Press.

Poster, Mark. 1975. *Existential Marxism in Postwar France.* Princeton: Princeton University Press.

Poulantzas, Nicos. 1975. *Classes in Contemporary Capitalism.* London.

———. 1977. The new petty bourgeoisie. In *Class and Class Structure*, ed. A. Hunt, 113–24. London: Lawrence and Wishart.

Powell, Walter W., and Paul DiMaggio, eds. 1991. *The New Institutionalism in Organizational Analysis.* Chicago: University of Chicago Press.

Prost, Antoine. 1970. Une sociologie stérile: *La reproduction. Esprit* 12: 851–60.

Przeworski, Adam. 1977. Proletariat into a class: The process of class formation from Karl Kautsky's *The Class Struggle* to recent controversies. *Politics and Society* 7: 343–401.

Ringer, Fritz. 1992. *Fields of Knowledge: French Academic Culture in Comparative Perspective*, 1890–1920. New York: Cambridge University Press.

Rist, Gilbert. 1984. La notion médiévale d'"habitus' dans la sociologie de Pierre Bourdieu. *Revue européenne des sciences sociales* 22(67): 201–12.

Ritzer, George. 1988. Sociological metatheory: A defense of a subfield by a delineation of its parameters. *Sociological Theory* 6 (Fall): 187–200.

Robbins, Derek. 1991. *The Work of Pierre Bourdieu: Recognizing Society.* Boulder, Colo.: Westview Press.

Robinson, Robert V., and Maurice A. Garnier. 1985. Class reproduction among men and women in France: Reproduction theory on its home ground. *American Journal of Sociology* 91: 250–80.

Rosenbaum, James E. 1976. *Making Inequality: The Hidden Curriculum of High School Tracking.* New York: Wiley.

Ross, George. 1987. The decline of the Left intellectual in modern France. In *Intellectuals in Liberal Democracies: Political Influence and Social Involvement*, ed. A. G. Gagnon, 43–65. New York: Praeger.

———. 1991. French intellectuals from Sartre to soft ideology. In *Intellectuals and Politics: Social Theory in a Changing World*, ed. C. C. Lemert, 47–73. Newbury Park, Calif.: Sage.

Sahlins, Marshall. 1981. *Historical Methaphors and Mythical Realities.* Ann Arbor: University of Michigan Press.

Sartre, Jean-Paul. 1960. *Critique de la raison dialectique.* Paris: Gallimard.

Saussure, Ferdinand de. 1974. *Course in General Linguistics.* London: Fontana.

Schiltz, M. 1982. Habitus and peasantisation in Nigeria: A Yoruba case study. *Man* 17 (4): 728–46.

Schücking, L. L. 1966. *The Sociology of Literary Taste,* trans. B. Battershaw. London: Routledge.

Schumpeter, Joseph A. 1975. *Capitalism, Socialism and Democracy.* 3d ed. New York: Harper and Row.

Schwartz, Barry. 1981. *Vertical Classification: A Study in Structuralism and the Sociology of Knowledge.* Chicago: University of Chicago Press.

Sewell, William, Robert Hauser, and Alexander Portes. 1969. The education and early occupational attainment process. *American Sociological Review* 34: 82–92.

Sewell, William H., Jr. 1992. A theory of structure: Duality, agency, and transformation. *American Journal of Sociology* 98 (1): 1–29.

Shils, Edward. 1972. *The Intellectuals and the Powers and Other Essays.* Chicago: University of Chicago Press.

Sirinelli, Jean-François. 1988. *Génération intellectuelle.* Paris: Fayard.

Skocpol, Theda. 1979. *States and Social Revolutions.* New York: Cambridge University Press.

———. 1986. The dead end of metatheory. *Contemporary Sociology* 16: 10–12.

Smith, David N. 1974. *Who Rules the Universities? An Essay in Class Analysis.* New York: Monthly Review Press.

Sulkunen, Pekka. 1982. Society made visible: On the cultural sociology of Pierre Bourdieu. *Acta Sociologica* 25 (2): 103–15.

Swartz, David. 1977. Pierre Bourdieu: The cultural transmission of social inequality. *Harvard Educational Review* 47 (November): 545–54.

———. 1981. Classes, educational systems and labor markets. *European Journal of Sociology* 22 (2): 325–53.

———. 1988. Introduction. *Theory and Society* 17: 615–25.

Swidler, Ann. 1986. Culture in action: Symbols and strategies. *American Sociological Review* 51: 273–86.

Szelenyi, Ivan, and Bill Martin. 1988/89. The three waves of New Class theories. *Theory and Society* 17 (5): 645–67.

Thapan, Meenakshi. 1988. Some aspects of cultural reproduction and pedagogic communication. *Economic and Political Weekly* (March 19): 592–96.

Thompson, E. P. 1963. *The Making of the English Working Class.* London: V. Gollancz.

Thompson, John B. 1991. Editor's Introduction. In *Language and Symbolic Power,* 1–31. Cambridge, Mass.: Harvard University Press.

Tiles, Mary. 1984. *Bachelard: Science and Objectivity*. London: Cambridge University Press.

———. 1987. Epistemological history: The legacy of Bachelard and Canguilhem. In *Contemporary French Philosophy*, ed. A. P. Griffiths, 141–56. Cambridge: Cambridge University Press.

Tilly, Charles. 1978. *From Mobalization to Revolution*. Reading, Mass.: Addison-Wesley.

Touraine, Alain. 1968. *Le Mouvement de Mai ou le communisme utopique*. Paris: Editions du Seuil.

———. 1973. *Production de la Société*. Paris: Editions du Seuil.

Tucker, Robert C. 1978. *The Marx–Engels Reader*. 2d ed. New York: W. W. Norton.

Veblen, Thorstein. 1979. *The Theory of the Leisure Class*. Harmondsworth: Penguin Books.

Verdès-Leroux, Jeannine. 1981. Une institution totale auto-perpétuée: Le parti communiste français. *Actes de la recherche en sciences sociales* 36/37: 33–63.

Wacquant, Loïc J. D. 1987. Symbolic violence and the making of the French agriculturalist: An enquiry into Pierre Bourdieu's sociology. *The Australian and New Zealand Journal of Sociology* 23 (1): 65–88.

———. 1989. Toward a reflexive sociology: A workshop with Pierre Bourdieu. *Sociological Theory* 7 (1): 26–63.

———. 1990. Sociology as socio-analysis: Tales of *Homo Academicus*. *Sociological Forum* 5 (4): 677–89.

———. 1992. Toward a social praxeology: The structure and logic of Bourdieu's sociology. In *An Invitation to Reflexive Sociology*, 2–59. Chicago: University of Chicago Press.

———. 1993a. Bourdieu in American: Notes on the transatlantic importation of social theory. In *Bourdieu: Critical Perspectives*, ed. C. Calhoun, E. LiPuma, and M. Postone, 235–62. Chicago: University of Chicago Press.

———. 1993b. From ruling class to field of power: An interview with Pierre Bourdieu on *La noblesse d'Etat*. *Theory, Culture, and Society* 10 (3): 19–44.

———. 1993c. Solidarity, morality and sociology: Durkheim and the crisis of European society. *The Journal of the Society for Social Research* 1 (Autumn): 1–7.

Warner, Loyd W., and Paul S. Lunt. 1941. *The Social Life of a Modern Community*. New Haven: Yale University Press.

Warner, R. Stephen. 1993. Work in progress toward a new paradigm for the sociological study of religion in the United States. *American Journal of Sociology* 98: 1044–93.

Weber, Max. 1978. *Economy and Society*, ed. Guenther Roth and Claus Wittich. 2 vols. Berkeley and Los Angeles: University of California Press.

Williams, Raymond. 1963. *Culture and Society*. 3d ed. Harmondsworth: Penguin Books.

———. 1965. *The Long Revolution*. Harmondsworth: Pelican Books.

Williams, Rhys, and N. J. Demerath. 1991. Religion and political process in an American city. *American Sociological Review* 56: 417–31.

Winch, Peter. 1958. *The Idea of a Social Science and Its Relation to Philosophy.* London: Routledge and Kegan Paul.

Wolpert, Lewis. 1993. *The Unnatural Nature of Science.* Cambridge, Mass.: Harvard University Press.

Wood, Robert Coldwell. 1993. *Whatever Possessed the President? Academic Experts and Presidential Policy,* 1960–1988. Amherst: University of Massachusetts Press.

Woolgar, Steve. 1988. *Science: The Very Idea.* London: Tavistock.

Wright, Erik Olin. 1985. *Classes.* London: Verso.

Wuthnow, Robert. 1981. Two traditions in the study of religion. *Journal for the Scientific Study of Religion* 20 (March): 16–32.

———. 1987. *Meaning and Moral Order.* Berkeley and Los Angeles: University of California Press.

Wuthnow, Robert, James Davison Hunter, Albert Bergesen, and Edith Kurzweil. 1984. *Cultural Analysis.* London: Routledge and Kegan Paul.

Zolberg, Vera L. 1989. Le Musée des Beaux-Arts, entre la culture et le public: Barrière ou facteur de nivellement? *Sociologie et Sociétés.* 21 (2): 75–90.

AUTHOR INDEX

SUBJECT INDEX

Academic power, 241–43
Academic selection, 197–202
Actes de la recherche en sciences sociales, 2,
   20n, 26–28, 190n, 259, 261n, 269
Action, 8, 50, 59, 68, 95
   as conscious calculation, 70–71
   interested, 66–73, 78
   as resulting from habitus, capital, and
      field combined, 141–42
   as strategy, 67, 98–100
   and time, 98–100
   Weber's types of, 42.
   See also Agency; Practices
Agency, two types of, 114. *See also* Action;
   Practices
Agency/structure problem, 8–9. *See also*
   Action
Algeria 1960 (Bourdieu), 100n
Algerian peasants (Kabyles), 2, 7n, 51, 64,
   68–69, 90, 98, 100–101, 112–14, 278
Algerians, The (Bourdieu), 2, 22n, 23n, 24
Althusser, Louis, influence of on Bour-
   dieu, 20–21, 40, 65–66, 128
American Journal of Sociology, The, 2n
An Invitation to Reflexive Sociology (Bour-
   dieu and Wacquant), 3n
Anthropology, 3, 7
Antinomies, 63, 84–88, 107, 202

Aristocratic asceticism, 178–79, 225, 238,
   291
Artistic field, 231
Aron, Raymond, influence of on Bour-
   dieu, 21–25, 46
Aspirations/expectations, 105–14
"Avenir de classe" (Bourdieu), 162n

Bachelard, Gaston, influence of on Bourdieu, 31–35
Behaviorism, 69n
Bias, in sociology, 272–77
Binary oppositions. *See* Antinomies
Bourdieu, Pierre
   career of, 12–13, 15–28
   as conceptual strategist, 5
   fieldwork in Algeria, 22, 23n, 24n, 48–
      51
   education of, 16–17, 22
   election of to Collège de France, 1, 24,
      27
   and existentialism, 30
   and French sociology, 21–25
   intellectual orientation of, 4–6
   intellectual vocation of, 37–38
   as outsider to Parisian intellectual elite,
      13, 18
   and phenomenology, 29–30